$3.50

Conflict & Stability in Southeast Asia

Edited by Mark W. Zacher and R. Stephen Milne

A Doubleday Anchor Original

Conflict and Stability in Southeast Asia

Conflict and Stability in Southeast Asia

Edited by MARK W. ZACHER
and R. STEPHEN MILNE

ANCHOR BOOKS

Anchor Press/Doubleday
Garden City, New York
1974

*Published under the Auspices of
The Institute of International Relations,
The University of British Columbia*

ANCHOR BOOKS EDITION: 1974
ISBN: 0-385-07176-0
LIBRARY OF CONGRESS CATALOG CARD NUMBER 73–81127
COPYRIGHT © 1973, 1974 BY MARK W. ZACHER
ALL RIGHTS RESERVED
PRINTED IN THE UNITED STATES OF AMERICA
FIRST EDITION

ontents

IV. International Security Arrangements

Notes on Contributors

CORAL BELL (Professor, Department of International Relations, Sussex University). Author of *Survey of International Affairs, 1954* (Oxford: Oxford University Press for the Royal Institute of International Affairs, 1956); *Negotiation from Strength: A Study in the Politics of Power* (London: Chatto & Windus, and New York: Alfred A. Knopf, 1961 and 1962); *The Debatable Alliance: An Essay in Anglo-American Relations* (Oxford: Oxford University Press for Royal Institute of International Affairs, 1965); *The Balance of Power in Asia: A Comparison with European Precedents* (London: International Institute for Strategic Studies, Adelphi Paper, 1968); *The Conventions of Crisis: A Study in Diplomatic Management* (Oxford: Oxford University Press for Royal Institute of International Affairs, 1971). Editor of *Europe Without Britain* (Melbourne, Australia: Cheshire, 1963).

PAUL BRIDLE (a member of Canada's Department of External Affairs, which he joined in 1945). He spent three years, 1949–52, in the Canadian High Commission in India; was Head of the Commonwealth Division in Ottawa, 1953–54; led the Canadian Delegation on the International Commission in Laos, 1955–56; attended the Imperial Defence College London in 1960; was Deputy Head of the Canadian Delegation to the Laos conference in Geneva, 1961–62; and returned to Laos as Head of the Canadian Delegation to the International Commission, 1962–64. He is now in Ottawa as a member of the Historical Division.

CHARLES A. FISHER (Professor, School of African and Oriental Studies, University of London). Author of *Southeast Asia, A Social, Economic and Political Geography* (London: Methuen & Co., 1st edition, 1964; 2nd edition, 1966). Editor of *Essays in Political Geography* (London: Methuen & Co., 1968). Co-editor of *Geographical Essays on British Tropical Lands* (London: George Philip & Son, 1956); and *The Changing Map of Asia* (London: Methuen & Co., 5th edition, 1971).

MELVIN GURTOV (Associate Professor, Department of Political Science, University of California, Riverside). Author of *The First Vietnam Crisis: Chinese Communist Strategy and United States Involvement, 1953–54* (New York: Columbia University Press, 1967); *Southeast Asia Tomorrow: Problems and Prospects for U.S. Policy* (Baltimore: Johns Hopkins Press, 1970); and *China and Southeast Asia: The Politics of Survival* (New York: D. C. Heath, 1971). Co-author of *The Cultural Revolution in China* (Berkeley: University of California Press, 1971).

LORNE KAVIC (Visiting Associate Professor, Department of Political Science, University of British Columbia). Author of *India's Quest for Security: Defense Policies, 1947–1965* (Berkeley: University of California Press, 1967)

FRANK LANGDON (Professor, Department of Political Science University of British Columbia). Author of *Politics in Japan* (Boston: Little, Brown & Co., 1966); *Japan' Foreign Policy* (Vancouver, Canada: University of British Columbia Press, 1973). Co-author of *Business Associations and the Financing of Political Parties* (The Hague: Martinus Nijhoff, 1968).

MICHAEL LEIFER (Reader, the London School of Economic and Political Science, University of London). Author o *Cambodia—The Search for Security* (New York: Frederick A. Praeger, 1967); *The Philippine Claim to Saba* (Hull: Monograph on Southeast Asia No. I, 1968) *Dilemmas of Statehood in Southeast Asia* (Singapore Asia Pacific Press; Vancouver, Canada: University of British Columbia Press, 1972). Editor of *Nationalism Revolution and Evolution in Southeast Asia* (Hull: Mon ograph on Southeast Asia No. II, 1970); *Constraints and Adjustments in British Foreign Policy* (London: George Allen & Unwin, 1972).

USHA G. MAHAJANI (Professor of Political Science, Department of Political Science, Central Washington State College). Author of *The Role of Indian Minorities in Burma and Malaya* (Bombay: Vora and Co., 1960); *Soviet and American Aid to Indonesia, 1949–1968* (Ohio University Center for International Studies, Southeast Asia Program, Southeast Asia Series 14, 1970); *Philippine Nationalism: External Challenge and Philippine Response, 1565–1946* (Brisbane, Australia: Queensland University Press, 1971).

T. B. MILLAR (Professorial Fellow, Department of International Relations, The Australian National University). Author of *Australia's Defence* (Melbourne: Melbourne University Press, 1965, 2nd ed., 1969); *The Commonwealth and the United Nations* (Sydney: Sydney University Press, 1967); *Australia's Foreign Policy* (Sydney: Angus and Robertson, 1968); *The Indian and Pacific Oceans: Some Strategic Considerations* (London: Institute of Strategic Studies, Adelphi Papers, No. 57, May 1969); *Foreign Policy: Some Australian Reflections* (Melbourne: Georgia House, 1972). Editor of *Britain's Withdrawal from Asia* (Canberra: Australian National University Press, 1967); *Australian-New Zealand Defence Co-operation* (Canberra: Australian National University Press, 1968).

STEPHEN MILNE (Professor, Department of Political Science, University of British Columbia). Author of *Government and Politics in Malaysia* (Boston: Houghton Mifflin, 1967). Co-author of *Straight Fight* (London: Hansard Society, 1954); *Marginal Seat, 1955* (London: Hansard Society, 1958); *The Malayan Parliamentary Election of 1964* (Kuala Lumpur: University of Malaya Press; London: Oxford University Press, 1967); *East Malaysia: New States in a New Nation* (London: Frank Cass, 1974). Editor of *Planning for Progress, the Administration of Economic Planning in the Philippines* (Manila: Institute of Public Administration, 1960); *Bureaucracy in New Zealand* (Oxford: New Zealand In-

stitute of Public Administration and Oxford University
Press, 1957).

DONALD R. SHERK (Professor and Chairman, Department of
Economics, Simmons College). Author of *The United
States and the Pacific Trade Basin* (San Francisco: Federal Reserve Branch of San Francisco, 1971); and *Private Investment in Asia: Cooperation and Conflict Between the United States and Japan* (Washington, D.C.:
Overseas Development Council, 1972).

JERRY M. SILVERMAN (Professional Staff Member, Institute
of Public Administration, New York and Saigon; previously Assistant Professor, Department of Political
Science, McMaster University).

SHELDON W. SIMON (Associate Professor, Department of Political Science, The University of Kentucky). Author of
The Broken Triangle: Peking, Djarkarta, and the PKI
(Baltimore: Johns Hopkins University Press, 1969); and
*War and Politics in Southeast Asia: Actor Perception
in the Cambodian Conflict* (Durham, N.C.: Duke University Press, 1973).

GARY D. WEKKIN (Graduate Student, Department of Political
Science, University of British Columbia).

MARK W. ZACHER (Director, Institute of International Rela-
tions and Associate Professor, Department of Political
Science, University of British Columbia). Author of *Dag
Hammarskjöld's United Nations* (New York: Columbia
University Press, 1970).

Map of Southeast Asia

Preface

The papers included in this volume were initially presented to a seminar comprised of faculty and graduate students in the Institute of International Relations at the University of British Columbia during the first half of 1972. They were then rewritten and submitted for publication in the fall of 1972 and early 1973. The purpose of the seminar was to explore the sources of conflict and stability in Southeast Asia, and the consideration of these issues fell under four headings: historical and geographic factors, internal factors, the policies and/or interventions of extraregional states, and international security arrangements. The papers in this volume are organized under these four headings. Although not meant to be construed as an exhaustive treatment of the international politics of Southeast Asia, the volume attempts to come to grips with some of the most important issues in interstate relations in that crucial region of the world. These range from examinations of the impact of subnational politics through studies of historical relations between national groups and interventions of extraregional powers.

We would like to note that another publication which was prepared for the seminar by Professor Geoffrey Hainsworth of the Department of Economics at UBC will be published as a separate monograph. The title of this monograph is "Strategy Alternatives for Economic Development in Southeast Asian Countries."

The Institute would like to note its gratitude to the Canadian Institute of International Affairs (Toronto) and the Koerner Foundation (Vancouver) for having provided financial assistance for bringing the writers who are not at the University of British Columbia to the university, and for preparing the manuscripts for publication. Without their generous assistance the seminar and this volume would not have been possible. We would also like to express our gratitude for the enthusiastic participation of the many faculty and graduate students at this university who took part in the seminar, and to the authors from other institutions whose presentations were so insightful and stimulating. Professor Zacher as Director of the Institute would also like to thank Dean Ian McTaggart Cowan and Assistant Dean John Stager of the Faculty of Graduate Studies for their assistance and encouragement in promoting international relations research seminars and projects at this university. Throughout the preparation of these manuscripts for publication, Ms. Carol Goldberg of Doubleday has been a most cooperative and helpful editor, and we are most grateful to her. We have also received a great deal of assistance from Professor Sheldon Simon, who has been a visiting professor in the Institute during the 1972–73 academic year, in preparing the papers for publication, and we would like to thank him for his many helpful and insightful comments. Finally, we would like to express our gratitude to the Director's secretary, Ms. Lou Whitehead, for her help with both the typing and editorial tasks associated with preparation of such a volume for publication, and to Mr. Gary Wekkin for his editorial assistance.

Mark W. Zacher
R. Stephen Milne

Vancouver, B.C.
Canada

Introduction

This book deals with contemporary international politics in Southeast Asia, and its main focus is the effect of external intervention on conflict and stability in the region. According to Michael Leifer, whose article[1] below sets the tone for the volume, stability is what intervention is all about—states outside the region either intervene to maintain regional (or national) stability or they intervene to subvert it, because one or the other is to their political advantage. Therefore, the volume is centrally organized around the topic of extraregional intervention: the articles in Section I seek to establish a historical and geographical background to extraregional intervention; the articles in Section II are essentially "linkage politics" studies which examine internal factors influencing external intervention; the articles in Section III, which is the core section of the volume, concentrate on the extraregional powers and their intervention in Southeast Asian politics; and those in Section IV, which is essentially a subsection of Section III, deal with various international security arrangements which have been formally or informally created to deal with security problems in the region.

In Section I, Charles Fisher's essay on "Geographical Continuity and Political Change in Southeast Asia" examines the geographic factors which have influenced and are still influencing international politics in Southeast Asia. The Southeast Asians have always been susceptible to extraregional intervention because, first, their land mass is draped around the most complex maritime crossroads in the world and,

[1] See p. 181.

second, Southeast Asian societies have never been populous and wealthy enough to dominate these waters. The region is weak and easily accessible from the sea, and has experienced a long history of political and commercial penetration and a great mingling of peoples, ideas, and cultures.

However, as several prominent historians[2] have asserted, Southeast Asia has had a dynamic history all its own, and outside influences have only added enrichment to this history rather than having been its source. This reality is sometimes forgotten by scholars studying the impact of extraregional intervention; perhaps one of the worst forms of imperialism practiced by non-Southeast Asians is their tendency to perceive everything that has happened there recently as the result of foreign intervention, which is tantamount to denying the Southeast Asians their own history. Jerry Silverman's "Historic National Rivalries and Interstate Conflict in Mainland Southeast Asia" reminds us that in order to assess the potential for stability and conflict in that region, it is necessary (1) to identify precolonial patterns of political authority in Southeast Asia and the ways in which they have endured, and (2) to understand how these patterns of rule have affected and are affecting relations between national groups.

Silverman pays particular attention to Southeast Asian "nation-building" efforts and their effect on conflict and stability. He concludes that these efforts, which usually consist of attempts to assimilate and control various minority groups, often result in violent internal conflicts rather than stability. One of the studies in the second section, Gary Wekkin's "Tribal Politics in Indochina: The Role of Highland Tribes in the Internationalization of Internal Wars," addresses itself directly to these minority conflicts and discusses how insurgent political movements and their external allies utilize disaffected minorities for political gain. Wekkin, who ultimately seeks to demonstrate the international implications of minority group

[2] See especially John R. W. Smail, "On the Possibility of an Autonomous History of Modern Southeast Asia," *Journal of Southeast Asian History*, 1961 (Vol. II, No. 2), pp. 72–102; and John F. Cady, *Southeast Asia: Its Historical Development* (New York: McGraw-Hill, 1964), pp. 590–96.

politics (and in so doing contributes to the study of "linkage politics"), asserts that in three different theaters of the Indochina Wars, alienated highland minorities have played key roles in the provision of external military assistance to insurgent military forces. Noting that tribal alienation has thrice proven to be a source of both internal and international instability, Wekkin suggests to Southeast Asian "nation-builders" that a structural recognition of the basic differences between minorities and core populations may result in better integration (and more stability) than attempted assimilation.

Another article in the second section concerned with minorities and their impact on international politics is R. S. Milne's "The Influence on Foreign Policy of Ethnic Minorities with External Ties." Milne seeks to discover the effect that overseas Chinese and Indians in Southeast Asia have on the foreign policies of the countries in which they reside, as well as on the policies of the countries of their origin. He concludes that the Indian minorities in Burma, Malaysia, and Singapore have little or no influence on the foreign policy of any state; however, the Chinese populations of these and other Southeast Asian states definitely affect the foreign policies of the countries in which they live—"not by bringing their influence to bear upon [them] but rather by the mere fact of their conspicuous and disturbing existence."[3] Concerned Southeast Asian policy-makers sometimes find it difficult to distinguish "China" and "Communism" from the overseas Chinese, and their policies toward China usually reflect their reaction to the Chinese in their midst. To the extent that this is true, the overseas Chinese in Southeast Asia are also probably more a liability than an asset to China's foreign policy toward the region.

Unlike the other two articles in the second section, Sheldon Simon's "Cambodia in the Vortex: The Actors' Perceptions, Goals, and Settlement Prospects" does not deal with minority groups and their effect on international politics. However, Simon does seek to discover, among other things, how *other* internal factors, such as the perceptions of rival internal political groups, can affect internal conflict and international

[3] See p. 81.

politics. In the interest of obtaining this information, Simon
conducts a thematic content analysis of the elite statements
and mass media output of both internal and external actors
in the Cambodian War. Much of the paper is devoted to a discussion of the antagonists' attitudes toward the war, toward
each other, and toward future political arrangements in the
region.

Michael Leifer's essay on "Great Power Intervention and
Regional Order," which is the first paper in Section III,
examines (1) the nature of intervention and stability, (2)
the goals of the interventionist powers, and (3) the "means"
of intervention. Though it is primarily meant to be a general
theoretical introduction to the section, it also serves as an excellent transition between the second and third sections because it complements articles in both sections. Consider, fo
example, his wide-ranging discussion of external patron-
internal client relationships as a means to successful intervention.[4] This discussion complements both Wekkin's article,
which revolves around the problem of securing logistical links
between insurgent movements and their external benefactors
and Usha Mahajani's "U.S. Intervention in Laos and It
Impact on Laotian Relations with Thailand and Vietnam,
which describes in great detail how the United States ha
repeatedly set up and maintained Laotian governments ame
nable to American intervention in their affairs. Leifer also re
fers to the United States as "the interventionist power *po
excellence*"—a charge which is subsequently substantiated b
both Mahajani's article and Melvin Gurtov's "Security b
Proxy: The Nixon Doctrine and Southeast Asia." Mahajani
study, which is essentially a reinterpretation of Cold Wa
events in Laos, is similar in many respects to the type of scho
arship found in *America's Asia*,[5] though perhaps better doc
mented, more detailed, and—consequently—more damnin

---

[4] See pp. 191–92.
[5] Edward Friedman and Mark Selden (eds.), *Americ
Asia: Dissenting Essays on Asian-American Relations* (New Yor
Pantheon Books, 1971). See especially the article on U.S. interve
tion in Laos by Jonathan Mirsky and Stephen Stonefield, pp. 25
323.

Mahajani not only explores the nature and depth of American intervention, but also takes pains to point out how this intervention has exacerbated traditional Thai-Vietnamese competition in Laos.

While Mahajani is pessimistic about the possibility of an end to American interventionist practices in Laos, Gurtov's analysis of U.S. policy since the announcement of the Nixon Doctrine raises doubts about the likelihood of an end to its politico-military involvement throughout the region. His study indicates that the United States is not withdrawing from Southeast Asia to the extent which many have expected; it has brought its ground forces home, but U.S. alliance commitments, military assistance, and air and naval power in the region have not been reduced. Gurtov argues that what the Nixon Doctrine really involves is a return to the "massive retaliation" deterrence strategy of the 1950s. The resumption of heavy bombing in North Vietnam in December 1972 and the bombing of Cambodia in the summer of 1973 indicate that Gurtov may be only too correct in this respect.

The purpose of the Nixon Doctrine, according to Gurtov, is to establish a balance-of-power system in Asia. To obtain this end, Nixon has said that America will play a less direct security role in Southeast Asia and has taken significant steps to improve relations with both China and the Soviet Union. Both Gurtov's article on "The Soviet Presence in Southeast Asia: Growth and Implications" and Frank Langdon's "China's Policy in Southeast Asia" indicate that such a balance-of-power system will come to pass, if it has not done so already. Langdon's study of post-Cultural Revolution Chinese foreign policy indicates that China now wishes the United States to remain in Southeast Asia (1) to help balance the Soviet Union's growing influence in the region, (2) to prevent the possibility of Japan's economic domination of the area, and (3) to assist in promoting a "balkanization" of the region and preventing the growth of North Vietnamese influence. (Simon concurs, on the basis of his content analysis of Chinese perceptions, that China would indeed prefer a "balkanization" of Southeast Asia.) Furthermore, the gains and benefits of China's new government-to-government relations with the Southeast Asian states are pushing its interest in revolutionary proselytization into the background for the present (although it is still not above temporarily increasing its vocal and material support for liberation movements in countries whose governments it wishes to influence).

According to Gurtov, the Soviet Union would also be satisfied with a Southeast Asian balance-of-power system. Its increasing interest in Southeast Asia is not directed against the United States as much as it is against China. It only wishes to neutralize, not to replace, American power in Southeast Asia. Its recent naval expansion into that area is designed (1) to indicate the reach of Soviet power in the hope of psychologically checking Chinese influence and lessening Southeast Asian attachments to the United States; (2) to improve Soviet trade with Japan and secure stopover ports for Soviet ships plying between Vladivostok and the Black Sea; and (3) to counter British and U.S. naval superiority in the Indian and Pacific Oceans and protect sea lanes for its trading vessels.

Japanese influence in Southeast Asia takes a much different form than that of the United States, China, and the Soviet Union. Frank Langdon's "Japanese Policy Toward Southeast Asia" indicates that Japan's influence in that region stems almost entirely from its aid programs and initiative in organizing and leading regional economic development projects. Langdon stresses that Japan is presently not strong enough militarily even to consider playing a role in the defense of Southeast Asia; nor does it seem likely to be interested in playing such a role in the foreseeable future, even though it fears Chinese and Soviet intentions in that region. Langdon's article on Japanese foreign policy is complemented by Donald Sherk's "Foreign Investment in Asia: A Reconsideration," which looks at Japanese and American investment in Southeast Asia. Because the nature of foreign investment has changed somewhat in the past two decades, host country attitudes are now improving toward foreign investment. Other countries in the region which have permitted significant amounts of foreign investment to enter have prospered along with the foreign companies, and there are now enough wealthy industrial powers interested in investment in Southeast Asia so that the host states are able to demand certain conditions and to apply the principle of "countervailing power" to protect their sovereignty and independence. The Southeast Asians are especially interested in luring manufacturing concerns, which provide jobs, technical knowhow, and other social advantages, to locate in the region.

The final article in this section deals with Canada, a country which can hardly be said to be an interventionist power in Southeast Asia. Nevertheless, as Lorne Kavic's "Canada and the Security of Southeast Asia" and Paul Bridle's "Canada and the International Control Commissions in Indochina, 1954–72" (in section four) indicate, Canada has played an important peacekeeping role in the region for the past twenty years, and has actively participated in the international diplomacy surrounding the many international crises which have occurred in the region since the Second World War. The Canadian government has often been cross-pressured in such crises by, on the one hand, its general support for Western strategic interests and desire to maintain close relations with its Western allies, and, on the other hand, its desire to further decolonization, nonintervention, and its own diplomatic autonomy. As a result, Canadian policies, which have often reflected this tension, have been criticized both at home and abroad as inconsistent and lacking in direction.

Bridle's article on Canada's experience in the International Control Commissions, which is the first essay of the final section on international security arrangements, goes systematically through the various functions which the commissions were assigned and the factors which both supported and undermined their performance. He notes that the commissions established in 1954 were intended to last only two years, and functioned quite successfully until 1956, when the increasingly conflictual stances taken by the major regional and extraregional actors forced the commissions to extend their stay and assume tasks they were not designed to perform. Bridle also analyzes the political structures and resources of the commissions, and reviews the Canadian government's criticisms of their character. Apart from its general lessons for

international peacekeeping, the article also sheds a great deal
of light on why Canada withdrew from the new peacekeeping
operation in South Vietnam in July 1973.

The other two articles in the final section, T. B. Millar's
"Prospects for Regional Security Cooperation in Southeast
Asia" and Coral Bell's "Security Preoccupations and Power
Balances After Vietnam," are general treatments of past and
emerging security arrangements in Southeast Asia. Millar
devotes considerable attention to an examination of the Five-
Power Treaty, and speculates as to the future direction of
Southeast Asian organizations such as ASPAC and ASEAN
now that *détente* seems to be the prevailing trend in Asian
international politics. Millar also examines several bilateral
defense agreements, such as Thailand's agreement with Laos
and the United States' SEATO commitment to Thailand
(which he views as the only major *raison d'être* for SEATO),
and foresees an eventual American pullback to an offshore
position. This view coincides with Bell's view of future American involvement in Southeast Asia, but is in conflict with
Gurtov's interpretation of U.S. policy under the Nixon Doctrine. Bell talks of both China and the United States as having
come of age, in that both have realized that a constellation of
three to five powers which have both competing and complementary interests may be more conducive to their interests
than a situation of rigid hostility toward one's ideological enemies. Millar agrees with Langdon that Japan will not become
involved in any Southeast Asian security arrangements; however, Bell implies that Southeast Asia is too important to
Japan not to be defended. Nevertheless, she agrees that
Japan's future military role in the region is at best an
ambiguous one.

While this volume is by no means a complete treatment of
extraregional interventions, the editors hope that the essays
will assist in furthering our understanding of the nature of
external interventions in Southeast Asia, their impact on the
international politics and the domestic societies of the region,
and those domestic and international conditions which affect
the character and influence of the interventions. While most
of the essays were finished shortly before the 1973 ceasefires

in Vietnam and Laos, they were written after the beginning of the Sino-American rapprochement and the emergence of what has been termed a balance-of-power or multipolar system in Asia. Many of the writers have thus been able to gauge how these developments might influence future patterns of intervention, conflict, and cooperation among external powers and the regional states—and hence the prospects for greater stability in this area, which has experienced so much hardship and violence in recent years.

I
Geographical and Historical Factors

Geographical Continuity and Political Change in Southeast Asia

CHARLES A. FISHER

It has been said that history repeats itself because geography remains a constant, but neither part of this statement is strictly true. The element of repetition which some claim to recognize in history never applies to more than a limited range of factors in any given situation, and conversely even physical geography is not wholly static, while human interaction with the physical environment proceeds at an accelerating rate of change as technology advances.

Nevertheless certain distinctive geographical characteristics of particular countries or regions are so fundamental that new generations living there may—even after a lapse of many centuries—find themselves faced with remarkably similar problems or opportunities to those which confronted their predecessors at critical periods in the past. Few parts of the world provide more striking evidence of this phenomenon than does Southeast Asia.

THE GEOGRAPHICAL ENVIRONMENT OF SOUTHEAST ASIA

The most fundamental characteristic of Southeast Asia is the extent to which it has always tended to be overshadowed by its larger continental neighbors in South and East Asia. And indeed Southeast Asia is not merely overshadowed, in the sense of being much less populous and less powerful than these neighbors, but is so culturally diverse and politically subdivided as to raise doubts in some minds as to whether it constitutes a meaningful entity in any positive sense at all.

These differences between Southeast Asia and its two great

neighbors are clearly rooted in geography. South and East Asia are easy to define because in each case one great country of subcontinental proportions has, by virtue of its vast population and the related depth and continuity of its civilization, set its own unmistakable stamp on the region of which it forms the central and dominant component. But within Southeast Asia there is no such dominant landmass, focused like India and China on vast riverine lowlands which have provided the ancestral hearths of their respective great cultures. Instead, its central geographical component consists not of land but of sea, as indeed is implicit in the names Nanyang and Nanyo (both meaning the southern seas) by which the region has long been known to the Chinese and Japanese respectively. For it is around what we may call the primary Southeast Asian seas, namely the Andaman Sea, the Malacca Straits, and the South China Sea, that the curiously ill-balanced assemblage of its territories is draped, in the shape of one great elongated and branching peninsula, and a series of elaborately contorted archipelagoes stretching from Sumatra to Luzon, which together include a dozen or so large islands and an immense profusion of smaller ones.

Moreover, when to the primary seas are added the secondary seas lying between the inner and outer islands of both Indonesia and the Philippines, the total area of salt water in Southeast Asia far exceeds that of its entire land surface, and indeed no part of the world of comparable size is so thoroughly interpenetrated by the sea. Finally in this connection, both the primary and the secondary Southeast Asian seas are not merely of local significance, but together provide links between the Indian and Pacific Oceans and hence, from west to east, between India and China and, from north to south, between the Far East and Australasia. In short, the interconnected seas of Southeast Asia combine to form the most complex series of maritime crossroads in the entire world.

The corollary of this situation is that the lands of Southeast Asia possess a uniquely high degree of maritime accessibility, and it is therefore appropriate to consider the following observations of the distinguished West Indian economist, Sir

Arthur Lewis, who comes from an area somewhat similar geographically:

> Accessibility plays a decisive part in stimulating economic growth. It stimulates trade, therefore widening the range of demand, encouraging effort, and furthering specialization. It also results in a mingling of peoples, with different customs and ideas; and this keeps the mind active, stimulates the growth of knowledge, and helps to keep institutions free and flexible. Degree of accessibility must play a large role in explaining the economic vigor of any people.[1]

Clearly many of these observations fit Southeast Asia remarkably well. Beginning far back in prehistory, successive migrations of peoples, having moved down its mainland valleys, dispersed thence by sea from island to island, toward Australia and the Southwest Pacific, and in so doing left a diverse residue of human types within Southeast Asia itself. Then, around the dawn of the Christian era, Hindu-Buddhist civilization, following in the wake of Indian traders seeking gold and other exotica, and subsequently exploring the sea route to China, spread along the shores of both the primary Southeast Asian seas and much of the inner Indonesian seas as well. And, roughly a thousand years later, there followed the diffusion of Islam along both sides of the routes pioneered by Indian Muslim spice traders, via the Straits of Malacca and thence through the secondary Southeast Asian seas, to the Moluccas and the southern Philippines.

This repeated infusion of new peoples and new ideas, meeting and mingling with those that had arrived before, and meanwhile developing new forms in adaptation to local circumstances, has added still further to the human diversity of the lands bordering the Southeast Asian seaways. In fact the only intrinsic cultural ingredient which did not come in by sea was the Sinitic element in the Vietnamese core area in the Songkoi delta which, owing to its exceptional ease of access overland from southern China, was incorporated into

[1] W. Arthur Lewis, *The Theory of Economic Growth* (London: George Allen & Unwin, 1957), p. 53.

the imperial Chinese domains from 181 B.C. to A.D. 939.[2] But by the twelfth century A.D. Chinese and Japanese traders and buccaneers were increasingly frequenting Southeast Asian waters, a process which declined only after the arrival, in greater numbers and with greater persistence, of European seafarers, beginning in the sixteenth century and reaching its peak in the heyday of Western imperialism in the nineteenth and early twentieth centuries. Yet, as these last remarks imply, the main benefits accruing from the accessibility of an area go to those who control the access routes,[3] and it is therefore necessary to consider the extent to which geography has facilitated or hindered the achievement of indigenous control over the region's seaways.

Measured against the great distances over which it extends, the total land area of Southeast Asia, as has already been noted, is small, and the potential strategic weakness which this implies is aggravated by several other factors. First, only 12 per cent or so of this land area is good cultivable lowland, able to support a high density of population by traditional farming methods, and such areas as do come within that category are widely separated from one another. Within historic times these comprised the middle valleys of the Irrawaddy and the Menam Chao Phraya, the Cambodian lake basin, and the Songkoi delta on the mainland, together with the lowlands of east-central Java and the central plains of Luzon, respectively in the Indonesian and Philippine archipelagoes. Significantly all these areas lie well away from the equator and hence experience a good dry season, which is important for the ripening and harvesting of rice. But before the nineteenth century the list did not include the greater part of the Irrawaddy and the Mekong deltas, whose extremely severe floods remained beyond the range of traditional tech-

[2] The introduction of Chinese hydrotechnology enabled the floods of the Songkoi delta, which are less severe than those of the Mekong delta, to be controlled at an early date and this in turn explains the early buildup of population density in this part of Southeast Asia.

[3] Cf. Friedrich List's view that whoever controls a country's railways controls that country.

nology to control,[4] while the even larger areas of swamp fringing the inner coasts of Sumatra, Kalimantan, and Irian, all of which lie within the equatorial zone, still await effective utilization.

Thus none of the main historic centers of rice production —and hence of population—was within 1,000 kilometers of the most critical focus in the whole Southeast Asian seaways system, namely the area immediately to the south of the Malay peninsula, around which the shortest shipping route from India to China has to make a great southerly detour almost to the equator, where it meets the inner seas of the Indonesian archipelago and the alternative approach from the Southern Indian Ocean via the Sunda Straits.

Besides this primary strategic focus of Southeast Asia there is another of secondary importance in the Kra isthmus, a neck of land some 80 to 120 kilometers wide, to the north of the Malay peninsula. Here several overland portage routes, notably that between Phang Nga and Surat Thani, have in the past been used to bypass the Malacca Straits which, owing to their narrowness and the cover provided by their fringing swamps, afforded great opportunities for piratical raids on sailing ships becalmed in this zone of uncertain winds. But while in a local sense the Kra isthmus has repeatedly benefited from this situation, it has hitherto been much less significant than the great maritime crossroads to the south. It is against the background provided by this interlocking pattern of land and sea that the political geography of Southeast Asia, both past and present, needs to be seen.

EARLY POLITICAL GEOGRAPHY OF SOUTHEAST ASIA

Although the earliest Indianized kingdoms of Southeast Asia grew up at key points—mainly near important river

[4] Between the second and sixth centuries A.D. attempts were made under the Funan kingdom to control the floodwaters of the Mekong delta, but this early canal system was eventually destroyed, probably by natural causes. Bernard Groslier, "The Mekong River in History," *Indian Journal of Power and River Valley Development*, 1966 (Vol. 16), p. 68.

mouths—along the sea routes of the western two-thirds of
the region, the first protonational states eventually emerged
not on the coasts but in the relative seclusion of the afore-
mentioned interior lowlands,[5] each of which worked out its
own distinctive accommodation between incoming cultures
and pre-existing indigenous traditions. However, while all of
these kingdoms, namely Burma, Siam, and Cambodia (the
Khmer Empire) on the mainland and Madjapahit in east-
central Java, continued to share a common Indianized tradition, a major difference emerged during the fourteenth-
sixteenth centuries between the three mainland states, which
adopted the Theravada form of Buddhism, and Madjapahit
which, like most of its lesser Malayo-Indonesian neighbors,
was converted to Islam.

Within their original core areas, consisting of a complex of
irrigated rice lands focally situated within their respective
river or lake basins, the mainland states gradually became
sufficiently populous and powerful to expand their influence
outward and so to claim suzerainty over the ethnically different and mostly animist peoples occupying the surrounding
upland regions. Nevertheless these prevailingly rugged and
fever-ridden uplands constituted severe barriers to lateral
communications, so that interaction between the various lowland states was slight, apart from the intermittent wars usually
precipitated by the attempts of one or the other to over-
expand beyond its own drainage basin. Indeed the enduring influence—both positive and negative—of the drainage
system on the state pattern is the most striking feature of the
political geography of mainland Southeast Asia. Thus both
Burma and Siam, with their broad lowlands and navigable
rivers, show a remarkable degree of territorial continuity
however, the basin of the Mekong, which for most of its
length flows through a succession of plateaus and is obstructed by rapids and falls, was only briefly united under the
great Angkor kingdom, which focused not on that river but
on the Cambodian lake basin. Neither the Shans nor the
Karens ever came within sight of establishing a single state

---

[5] Except Luzon, where no comparable development occurred at
this stage.

around the great gorges through which the Salween swirls southward to the sea.

In the Malayo-Indonesian archipelago, on the other hand, the historic political units were mostly much smaller and focused typically not on a river (or lake) basin but on a pair of facing coastal lowlands, linked together by their own ships across a common stretch of sea. Here also the lowlanders often claimed authority over the less advanced peoples of the interior uplands but, in contrast to the riverine peoples of the mainland states, the coastal peoples of the archipelagoes were much more closely interconnected by indigenous shipping routes, so that the linguistic differences between them were far less pronounced than those between the various mainland states. Likewise the political divisions within the archipelagoes were more fluid than those on the mainland, because any state which for a time achieved local maritime supremacy could extend its authority along the interconnected seas until some other state became strong enough to challenge it.

Two outstanding instances of this process occurred in precolonial times. The first was under the maritime trading empire of Sri Vijaya, which developed out of an earlier Indianized kingdom centered near Palembang in the lower reaches of the Air Musi, the largest river of southeastern Sumatra. By extending its influence along the east coast of Sumatra and the facing shores of Malaya, Kalimantan, and western Java, Sri Vijaya commanded the primary maritime focus of Southeast Asia for most of the period between the seventh and the thirteenth centuries. Nevertheless it suffered from a strategic weakness in the low food-producing capacity of its home territories, and it seems that a rapid growth of the insalubrious swamp belt separating Palembang from the coast later compounded this weakness. Thus Sri Vijaya was eclipsed by its rival, Madjapahit, which, with a much richer agricultural base in the Javanese heartland, came to dominate the coastal ports of that island, and through them extended its influence widely over the central and eastern seas of the Indonesian archipelago. But, although Madjapahit defeated Sri Vijaya *c.* 1377, it also began to decline as, with the coming of Islam, the port cities of the north Java coast broke away from its control, leading to its final collapse in the six-teenth century.

Notwithstanding their ultimate disintegration, the maritime imperial achievements of these two Indonesian kingdoms raise the question as to why no indigenous Southeast Asian power ever welded the entire South China Sea basin into a single imperium as Rome had once united the comparably extensive lands surrounding the Mediterranean. For certainly the focality of the Malay peninsula, which in many ways occupies an analogous position in Southeast Asia to that of Italy between the eastern and western halves of the Mediterranean, had been recognized from very early times. This is evidenced, for example, in the rise of the entrepôts of Takola and Sabora, which were mentioned by Ptolemy and were probably situated in the respective vicinities of Singapore and Phuket,[6] or in other words at the key points on the all sea route and on one of the main Kra portage routes between the Andaman Sea and the Gulf of Thailand. Moreover, in later times, Temasek, an outpost of Sri Vijaya on Singapore island, enjoyed brief importance after the collapse of Sri Vijaya, before being itself eliminated by the rival pressure of Madjapahit and of Siam, the latter of which was then in the process of becoming the leading power in peninsular Southeast Asia. Both of these larger states appreciated the significance of Temasek's focal situation and when, after its destruction, a small group of survivors established a new port city at a less exposed position at Malacca, this also was soon threatened by Siam. However, the unexpected intervention of China, which likewise recognized the strategic importance of the Malay peninsula, enabled Malacca to survive. For between 1405 and 1431 the new Ming dynasty sent a series of naval expeditions to the Nanyang in order to demonstrate China's continuing concern that none of the Southeast Asian states should become excessively powerful, and formal Chinese protection was extended over Malacca in 1409.

[6] Cf. Paul Wheatley, "The Golden Khersonese," *Transactions of the Institute of British Geographers*, 1955 (No. 21), pp. 74–7. Note that Phuket is an island near Phang Nga.

Yet, although Malacca revived some of the functions of the former Sri Vijaya and in the following century became the principal entrepôt in the vicinity of the Straits area, it suffered even more than its great predecessor from the agricultural deficiencies of its immediate hinterland. Thus it is most improbable that the entire Malay peninsula supported more than a few hundred thousand people at the time of Malacca's zenith, and as late as 1826 Crawfurd estimated its total population as being a mere 350,000.

This extreme discrepancy between the paucity of its human resources and the immense locational potential of the peninsula overlooking the strategic focus of Southeast Asia has throughout historic times constituted a built-in geopolitical weakness of the entire region. But while this shortage of manpower is most strikingly apparent here at the center, the fact remains that this is merely the extreme case of a weakness which, at least until recently, has been characteristic of all Southeast Asian states. For, partly because of the smallness of their individual core territories, and perhaps more because of their isolation from one another, none of the six or so main historic nuclei within Southeast Asia, except that in northern Vietnam,[7] ever succeeded before the nineteenth century in achieving what may be called the population takeoff, which only occurs when a community has attained sufficient numerical strength to gain the upper hand over its environmental problems.[8] Thus even at the beginning of the nineteenth century the entire population of Southeast Asia was probably under 25 million, or about one-eighth that of India and one-twelfth that of China.

In contrast to these greater Asian neighbors, therefore, Southeast Asia remained weak and divided, and hence incapable of imposing a common control over its central seaways. Conceivably, as the Ming exploits suggest, some form of externally based control might have been imposed over the

[7] See note 2 above.
[8] Charles A. Fisher, "Some Comments on Population Growth in South-East Asia, with special reference to the period since 1830," C. D. Cowan (ed.), *The Economic Development of South-East Asia* (London: George Allen & Unwin, 1964), pp. 48–71.

Southeast Asian seaways by one or other of its neighbors
But in the absence of any such initiative the way was lef
open for the more remote but also more thrusting maritime
powers of Europe, which began early in the sixteenth century
to take advantage of the opportunity.

THE WESTERN TRANSFORMATION
OF SOUTHEAST ASIA

Like the traders from other parts of Asia the first Euro
peans to frequent the seas of Southeast Asia came in search
of exotic produce. Lying halfway round the globe from
Iberia, the Spice Islands (Moluccas) were approached in op
posite directions, the Portuguese arriving first in 1511 vi
the Cape of Good Hope, Goa, and Malacca, to be followed
a decade later by the Spaniards who sailed westward, via th
Atlantic, the Straits of Magellan, and the Pacific, to reach
Tidore in 1521. However, when it became clear that th
Moluccas lay within the Portuguese sphere as defined by th
Treaty of Tordesillas, the Spaniards turned their attention in
stead to the hitherto isolated and backward Philippines int
which the Muslim religion was beginning to spread. By in
corporating these islands into their own imperial domain
as an appendage of New Spain (Mexico) and subjectin
them to intensive Christian missionary activity, the Spaniard
succeeded in pulling the Philippines away from Southea
Asia just as these islands were for the first time becomin
effectively part of it.

Even at this early stage in European relations with Sout
east Asia, the region quickly came to be valued not mere
for its own sake but also as a base from which to develo
links with China, whose tea, silks, and porcelain were high
prized in Europe. In the seventeenth century the Dutch, wh
gradually displaced the Portuguese from all of their Southea
Asian possessions except eastern Timor, also extended the
Oriental trade well beyond Southeast Asia, and in the eigh
eenth century they began to concentrate their attentions i
creasingly upon exploiting the great agricultural expo
potential of Java. Yet, although the Dutch made nomin
claims to virtually the whole of the Indonesian archipelag

heir hold over most of the islands outside Java remained
xtremely tenuous until the nineteenth century. Indeed, it was
ot until the Industrial Revolution had begun simultaneously
o give a new thrust to overseas trade and dramatically to
hrink the effective distance between Europe and Asia that
Vestern imperialism made anything more than a marginal
npression, geographically speaking, upon Southeast Asia as
whole.

Thereafter it was Britain, as the pioneer of the Industrial
evolution, which set the pace and for nearly a century and
half played the leading role in the modern transformation
f Southeast Asia. Significantly, moreover, it did so by turn-
ag the primary seas of the region into what was in effect a
ngle British-controlled lake, with a strategic pattern which in
any respects resembled that of the Mediterranean. Yet, once
gain, what happened in Southeast Asia was initially in large
easure subservient to developments in India and China.
hus, having during the eighteenth century emerged as the
rongest naval power in the world, Britain proceeded to beat
e French for control of India and to make rapid progress
 the commercial exploitation of the new industrial technol-
gy. It was against this background that the East India Com-
any began both to consolidate its position in India and to
ok also to China as yet another great center of population
hich could provide further markets for British textiles.

This dual process began with the acquisition in 1786 of
enang, to serve as a naval station for the defense of
eninsular India and to command the northern approach to
e Straits of Malacca. In 1819 a second island, Singapore,
as annexed on the initiative of Stamford Raffles, who sought
 establish a center of British influence in the Indonesian
chipelago, on account of its commercial prospects and its
otential role as a geopolitical bridge between India and the
cently acquired Australian colonies. But what persuaded
ondon to accept the annexation of Singapore, which
affles appropriately called "the Malta of the East," was its
rategic importance in relation to the sea route to China.
wenty years later, as the first steamships were coming into

use in the eastern seas, the British fought in the Opium W
against China and proceeded to annex Hong Kong.

With the establishment of new port cities on each of the
three small offshore islands, the British were superbly plac
to take the lead in opening up the China trade. But, in add
tion, with the introduction of the revolutionary policy
making all these into free ports, open alike to traders ar
immigrants from wherever they wished to come, the Penan
Singapore-Hong Kong axis came to play a complementa
role, as the primary artery of innovation within Southea
Asia. Indeed that process had in some degree begun
operate before the axis had been extended to Hong Kong, b
its full significance was not apparent until after the openi
in 1869 of the Suez Canal, which owed nothing to Briti
initiative though it was certainly a consequence of oth
Western interests not merely in Southeast Asia but also
India and China.

Ever since Talleyrand had argued that the opening of
sea route to India via Suez would be as disastrous for En
land as the discovery of the Cape route had been for Veni
and Genoa,[9] the French had dreamed of cutting such
canal and, with the rapid advance of technology and the add
tional incentive of the open door into China, De Lesseps b
gan to translate these dreams into reality in 1859. Besid
thus short-circuiting the British Cape route to India, t
French also proposed to bypass Singapore and Hong Ko
respectively by constructing a canal across the Kra isthm
and approaching the deep interior of China via the Mekor
an idea first suggested by Van Wuysthoff in the seventeer
century. However, as exploration successively confirmed tl
both the Mekong and the Songkoi were unnavigable, the K
canal project was also abandoned, though the French, w
had obtained control over Vietnam and Cambodia betwe
1862 and 1884, eventually completed a railway link betwe
Haiphong and Kunming in southwestern China in 19
Meanwhile the British, originally in pursuit of a stable ea
ern frontier for India, annexed the whole of Burma in st

[9] André Siegfried, trans. H. H. and Doris Hemming, *Suez a
Panama* (London: Jonathan Cape, 1940), p. 54.

cessive stages, but despite the pressure of many commercial interests, official policy remained consistently opposed to the construction of a British railway through Burma to China.

With the opening of the Suez Canal these territories, whose economic importance had hitherto been very limited, rapidly acquired a new significance. For a widening range of cheaper bulkier goods henceforth proved capable of withstanding the cost of transport to European markets, and an equally important reduction took place in the cost of bringing into Southeast Asia the heavy equipment needed for opening up vast areas of hitherto neglected forest and swamplands. Moreover, small steamships suitable for local use in the sheltered inner seas of Southeast Asia could now make the initial journey from Europe under their own power both economically and safely.

Thus the great mainland deltas, with their vast expanses of alluvial soil and monsoonal climate, began to be cleared and drained for large-scale cultivation of rice which, though originally destined for Europe, soon found its main outlets in the densely populated neighboring lands of South and East Asia. Likewise the tin mining, already being undertaken by immigrant Chinese who had begun to stream into the Malay peninsula and nearby parts of Burma, Siam, and Indonesia, experienced a major expansion which led indirectly to the extension of British protection over the interior of Malaya. This in turn was followed by an even more rapid growth of plantation agriculture, both in Malaya and also in the outer islands of Indonesia, for while these equatorial areas were not well suited for rice, they gave excellent results in the production of tree crops such as coffee, rubber, and palm oil. Thus the Dutch, having hitherto concentrated obsessively on Java, now began to develop a major new plantation district in northeast Sumatra, where they soon struck oil as well. And even the remote Philippines, which had been linked to Spain via the South China Sea and the Indian Ocean after Mexico became independent in 1821, began to experience some outer ripples of this economic expansion after a British merchant had introduced modern sugar processing machinery into the Visayas around the middle of the century.

Along with Western development and exploitation of Southeast Asian resources came a series of other related changes. First, effective Western administration was successively extended until by the early twentieth century the only area still under indigenous control was a much reduced Siam, substantial parts of which were British or French spheres of influence. Meanwhile the whole of historic Burma became administratively part of India until 1937; the Vietnamese lands were incorporated into the Union of Indochina along with Laos and Cambodia, which were already under Vietnamese pressure when the French took over; and British control under a variety of forms was extended over Malaya and northern Borneo, whose areas approximated those of the old Malacca and Brunei sultanates respectively. Paradoxically the Netherlands, the smallest of the European powers involved (apart from the Portuguese who merely held their ground in eastern Timor), acquired the largest holding of all. For, with the help of modern naval and commercial shipping, the Dutch were able to unite the whole archipelago from Atjeh to Irian in a single Java-centered sea state, which represented a twentieth-century version of the old Sri Vijaya and Madjapahit rolled into one.[10] Finally, with their annexation by the United States after the Spanish-American War of 1898, the Philippines were subjected to a new trans-Pacific alignment just as, for the second time in their history, they had appeared to be drawing closer to the rest of Southeast Asia.

With the introduction of Western rule came a major improvement in the maintenance of law and order and the suppression of internecine warfare which, together with the gradual spread of Western hygiene, sanitation, and medical services, and the effects of the new railways and roads in eliminating local famine, combined to bring about a revolutionary reduction of the death rate. Since these innovations were not accompanied by any appreciable drop in the birth rate, Southeast Asia rapidly achieved the population takeoff, and between 1830 and 1935 population increased over five

10 Cf. A. E. Sokol, "Communications and Production in Indonesian History," *Far Eastern Quarterly* (now *Journal of Asian Studies*), August 1948 (Vol. 7, No. 4), pp. 339–53.

old to approximately 140 million. Although all but 7 per cent of this last total comprised indigenous Southeast Asians, there had also been a massive influx of immigrants from China and a lesser one from India. While the Indians went almost exclusively to the British territories of Burma and Malaya, the Chinese penetrated into every part of Southeast Asia. And although most of the original immigrants had arrived as impecunious laborers and many had no desire to settle permanently, these two communities, particularly the Chinese, had by the 1930s acquired a position of commercial and professional importance out of all proportion to their numbers in their respective countries of domicile.

The British entrepôts, in their dual capacity as meeting points for local and long-distance shipping and as major regional nuclei of commercial and banking expertise, had played a central role in bringing about this many-faceted process of change in Southeast Asia. Each had its own local geographical sphere of activity but all three were closely interlinked, and within the Southeast Asian context Singapore was the primary center. In addition to these entrepôts, each of the main Southeast Asian territories had one or more major ports of its own, and the largest of these in each country formally served as the capital. Eventually, with the gradual waning of nineteenth-century liberal free trade policies, the main ports of the non-British territories tended to assume an ever-increasing share of the total regional trade, and this trend accelerated after the world economic crisis of the early 1930s. Yet notwithstanding the great setback caused by the latter, the overall economic performance on the eve of the second World War was remarkably impressive, with Southeast Asia as a whole producing 93 per cent of the rubber, 90 per cent of the rice, 90 per cent of the cinchona (for quinine), 5 per cent of the copra, 60 per cent of the tin, and 55 per cent of the palm oil entering international trade, as well as smaller percentages but in absolute terms important quantities of petroleum and many other kinds of primary produce. Nevertheless, the greater part of the wealth produced went to outsiders, both Western and nonindigenous Asian, and the

vast majority of the indigenes were participants and benefi
ciaries only at the lowest level.

Nor was this solely a matter of economics. For althoug
the new colonial units bore a superficial territorial resem
blance to the protonational states of the past, this appearanc
was largely misleading. By following the accepted Wester
practice of drawing precise linear boundaries, each of th
main colonial units now included within its borders a variet
of hill or other peripheral peoples, most of whom had fa
more in common with their ethnic kinsfolk on the other sid
of the political boundary than they had with the majori
peoples of the states into which they had been incorporate
And the common Western tendency to regard these sturd
unsophisticated and mostly animist hill peoples as potenti
converts to Christianity and ideal manpower for the coloni
police and military forces intensified the cleavages within tl
colonies concerned.

More fundamentally, the whole colonial process of effe
tively turning these individual countries inside out to face t
sea struck at the very basis of all their traditions. Inste
of being ruled by their own people according to their ov
customs, from their ancestral interior capitals symbolizing t
whole ethos of the countryside in which they were roote
they were now controlled from the brash new Western-sty
port-city capitals by a small top layer of inscrutable Europea
assisted by a much larger but no more congenial layer co
prised mainly of alien Asians or Eurasians.

Thus although the countries of colonial Southeast As
focused as they were around Singapore and the great ma
time trade routes, outwardly seemed to be drawing closer
gether into a single functioning regional whole, this was t
only with respect to commerce. Even most of this comme
was not intraregional, except insofar as it used the m
entrepôts *en route* to and fro between individual Southe
Asian countries and the wider world outside. The clima
homogeneity of Southeast Asia was such that many of
countries produced much the same range of agricultural a
forest products, and the extension of both tin and oil b
over more than half of the region produced a similar situat

with respect to mineral wealth. Moreover, since the whole process of Westernization was carried out through the medium of different European languages, the indigenous Southeast Asians, far from drawing closer together culturally and politically, were in many vital respects becoming more severely isolated from one another than they had ever been before, notwithstanding the manifest improvements in transport.

As the colonial era drew to its close, therefore, the several countries of Southeast Asia certainly possessed many problems in common, but little had been done to provide common solutions, and scarcely anyone within the region, least of all its indigenous peoples, evinced any apparent awareness that Southeast Asia was an entity in its own right. But the Japanese, who in emulating the West aspired to their own stake in the tropics, and in particular to the tropical region which lay closest at hand, could see the wood as well as the individual trees. Their strategists appreciated that the conquest of Southeast Asia, as a preliminary to its incorporation within the Co-prosperity Sphere, called for naval control of the South China Sea, which in turn implied also the military occupation of both the peninsula and the Philippines. Recognizing these same facts, but concluding that the Japanese lacked the resources to undertake so immense a task, the colonial powers neglected their defenses. Admittedly the British had built a great naval base at the strategic linchpin in Singapore, and had also insisted that the Siamese, who by the 1930s were being assiduously wooed by the Japanese, should not permit any foreign power to outflank Singapore by building a canal across the Kra isthmus. The Americans likewise had bases in the Philippines, but neither they nor the British seemed concerned to devise any coordinated strategy for the region as such, which in fact they viewed in different but equally remote terms, the British as the outer fringe of the Indian Ocean and the Americans as the ultimate periphery of their Pacific Ocean defense system.

Meanwhile the Japanese, brandishing their slogan "Asia for the Asiatics"[11] and gaining rather than losing indigenous

[11] The term "Asians" began to be used only after the Second World War, to replace "Asiatics" which was held to be derogatory.

Southeast Asian sympathy from their war against China
seized the opportunity provided by the fall of France to mov
overland from China into northern Vietnam, the "doorway
which Marshal Lyautery had insisted "must be kept bolted.
Too late the remaining powers involved patched up the ABC
front which, however, was a front without a back, as Sing
pore was a base without a fleet. Within a few months c
Japan's simultaneous surprise attacks on Pearl Harbor, Hon
Kong, and Singapore, all Southeast Asia for the only time i
its history came under the control of a single power.

THE SHAPING OF A NEW ASIA AND THE PLACE OF SOUTHEAST ASIA WITHIN IT

Whereas the spread of Western rule over Southeast As
had been a slow and piecemeal process which took near
four hundred years to reach its maximum extent, the proce
of decolonization was swift and well-nigh all-embracing, bei
accomplished, except for the minute vestigial remains of t
old order in Brunei and Portuguese Timor, within a quart
of a century. Yet, despite the many and profound chang
initiated during the colonial and postcolonial periods, ce
tain elements of continuity stand out with remarkable cl
ity. Of these none has been more striking than the way
which, as the West began to withdraw, Southeast Asia car
to experience new forms of overshadowing by its more powe
ful Asian neighbors.

This tendency was already evident from the time whe
with Southeast Asia still under Japanese occupation, t
Allies, led by the United States, began to formulate the polic
which they hoped to pursue in Asia once the war was ov
For while the starting point in all such planning was t
Japan must be prevented from ever again disturbing t
peace, President Roosevelt, apparently in line with the ge
political concepts of Nicholas Spykman,[12] assumed that t

[12] Nicholas John Spykman (Helen R. Nicholl, ed.), *The Ge
raphy of the Peace* (New York: Harcourt, Brace & World, 19
reprint Hamden: Archon Books, 1969), pp. 45–61. Note that t
work, which was published posthumously, was based mainly o
lecture delivered in 1942.

achievement of this goal would require the building up of strong, independent, and friendly regimes in both China and India, which would thus serve as giant stabilizers for the entire region. Within such a framework, it also appeared to be tacitly assumed that the Southeast Asian countries would present few problems, though the United States left its European allies in no doubt that it favored a speedy winding up of colonialism in Southeast Asia as well as in the Indian subcontinent.

However, while the several Southeast Asian countries were thus cast in essentially negative roles in the new postwar Asian order, both India and China, in anticipation of their impending restoration to positions more in accord with their historic importance, were already beginning to consider what their own policies should be toward this neighboring area which American policy seemed likely to turn into a power vacuum.

The first major expression of this new trend appeared in 1943 in the study *The Future of South-East Asia* by the distinguished Indian scholar K. M. Panikkar. Starting from the premise that South and Southeast Asia formed a single interlinked strategic unit, basically dependent upon seapower for its security, Panikkar argued that the continuity of the Indian Ocean defense system built up by the British should be maintained on a modified basis after the War, with India as a free and stable power playing a major role within it. Otherwise Southeast Asia would remain "a prey to the predatory urge of any Power which is strong enough to attack ,"[13] and hence by implication a source of danger to India itself. Moreover, the economics of India and Southeast Asia would become increasingly complementary after the war, with the former exceptionally well placed to supply the latter with manufactured goods in return for a wide range of primary produce. To this end Panikkar recommended that India and Southeast Asia should "work out a 'Co-prosperity Sphere' based on their interdependence."[14]

[13] K. M. Panikkar, *The Future of South-East Asia* (New York: Institute of Pacific Relations, 1943), pp. 11–12.
[14] *Ibid.*, p. 16.

While it was not surprising that a blockaded and embattle
China produced no comparably detailed forecast of its ow
future attitude toward Southeast Asia, certain hints were con
tained in Chiang Kai-shek's book *China's Destiny* which als
appeared in 1943. Meanwhile Panikkar obviously believe
that China had interests in Southeast Asia, and he even sug
gested that it might conceivably bring peninsular Southeas
Asia within its orbit.[15] This suggestion might reasonably hav
been inferred from Chiang's own comments on that are
which he called the "mid-South peninsula,"[16] and furthe
more, when viewed against the wartime background of Kuc
mintang China's enforced withdrawal deeper into the interio
it was wholly understandable. For while the Chinese ha
shown scant interest in earlier Western attempts to open u
backdoor routes into their country, the Haiphong-Kunmin
railway and later, after this was blocked by the Japanese i
1940, the approach via Rangoon and the newly built Burn
Road suddenly became vital life lines between China and th
outside world, and were accordingly expected to remain o
major importance even when China had regained control o
its coastline after the war. Thus Panikkar put the matter o
access routes at the head of his list of China's three interes
in Southeast Asia, the others being "the important proble
of population" and "the growing problem of her econom
interests."[17] And while not everyone believed that Chin
would follow Japan's lead in demanding *lebensraum*
Southeast Asia, few disputed the view that China as well
India would seize the opportunity afforded by the defeat a
related economic setback of Japan to expand its trade wi
that region.

By the time the Second World War ended, however, the
considerations were themselves being overtaken by even mo

[15] *Ibid.*, p. 57.
[16] Chiang Kai-shek, *China's Destiny and Chinese Econom
Theory*, notes and commentary by Philip Jaffe (New York: R
Publishers A.N., 1947), p. 35. Note that *China's Destiny* was fi
published on March 10, 1943, in Chungking by the Chung Che
Publishing House. *Ibid.*, p. 19.
[17] Panikkar, *op. cit.*, p. 102.

ndamental developments in the wider world. Above all, e basic assumption on which Spykman's and Roosevelt's sessments and plans had been based, namely that coopera- n between the United States, the United Kingdom, and the viet Union would continue in the postwar era, was mani- stly becoming untenable. In these circumstances, therefore, e suddenness of the Japanese decision to surrender led e United States swiftly to revise the arrangements for re- iving the Japanese surrender before Soviet forces should ve time to establish themselves more widely over North- st Asia. And in the general rearrangements thus necessi- ed, the British South-East Asia Command (SEAC), which ce its establishment in 1943 had covered Ceylon, Burma, m, Malaya, and Sumatra, was suddenly enlarged on gust 15, 1945, so as to take the Japanese surrender over : whole of Southeast Asia except for the Philippines and lochina north of the sixteenth parallel. For the first time history, therefore, the name Southeast Asia was officially d to cover most of the geographical area to which it is now bitually applied. But significantly the main exception in this pect arose from the decision to allow Chiang Kai-shek's ces—notwithstanding their immense commitments in China take the Japanese surrender in northern Indochina, an a which had been Chinese territory for over a thousand rs prior to A.D. 939.

Nevertheless, any hopes which Chiang Kai-shek may have ertained of profiting from that situation were quickly over- dowed by the resumption of the Chinese Civil War. Thus, il after the Communists had emerged victorious in 1949, na was in no position to play an active role *vis-à-vis* South- Asia, and the initiative here accordingly rested almost lusively with India, where Nehru convened the first Inter- an Conference at New Delhi in 1947.

However, Nehru's views, formerly very close to those of ikkar, had been profoundly affected by the onset of the d War and by the dropping of the atomic bomb, signif- tly as it seemed to many, on an Asian country. Accord- y, while continuing to encourage closer economic links ween India and Southeast Asia, Nehru had now become

obsessively concerned that this Indian Ocean region shou
seek peace and security through nonalignment *vis-à-vis* tl
developing polarization of the world between the Unit
States and the Soviet Union. And in the weak and inexpe
enced Southeast Asian states, understandably preoccupied
their internal problems, and anxious not to have to squand
their limited funds on military expenditures, Nehru's doctri
evoked an overwhelmingly sympathetic response. It w
against this shifting background that independence car
to Southeast Asia.

As expected, the process of decolonization began in t
Philippines, where in 1946 the United States formally ho
ored an undertaking given well before the War. In Burr
likewise the transition had already begun, in association w
the British separation of that country from India in 19:
and full independence followed in 1948. Meanwhile in 19
the British had also initiated a major reorganization of th
administratively fragmented and ethnically diverse Malaysi
territories, in a belated attempt to promote a sense of co
mon nationhood transcending the differences between
indigenous Malaysians and the intrusive Chinese and India
By 1957 this process had advanced sufficiently to justify
granting of independence to the Federation of Mala
though Singapore, which had been excluded from Mala
since 1946, understandably resented being kept in a depe
ent status after 1957. As this resentment, which was exploi
by local Communists, threatened to become explosive, a sc
tion was attempted in 1963 by bringing Malaya, Singapc
Sabah, and Sarawak together in a new federation
Malaysia. But in 1965 Singapore was forced to withdr
and thereafter become an independent republic in its c
right.

Nevertheless, it was in the two largest and most popul
colonial territories, namely the Netherlands Indies and Fre
Indochina, that decolonization encountered the greatest
stacles. To begin with, each of them, respectively in Java
northern Vietnam, possessed areas of exceptionally high po
lation density and consequent land hunger, which had alre
given rise to more radical forms of nationalism than w

typical elsewhere. Secondly, both the metropolitan powers concerned had before the War been slow to prepare their dependencies for independence and, having subsequently experienced the humiliation of German occupation at home, had become even more reluctant to deal with indigenous nationalists whom many tended to regard simply as collaborators with another occupying power. Thus both at first tried by military means to retain control of their former Southeast Asian dependencies, and although the Dutch finally agreed in December 1949 to relinquish sovereignty over all except West Irian, their determination to hang on there, eventually until 1962, tragically embittered their relations with the new Indonesian republic.

Besides the similarities with Indonesia already noted, the situation in Indochina was complicated by two further factors. First, the Japanese, having themselves relied on the administrative cooperation of the local French representatives until early in 1945, had then appealed to indigenous sentiments by splitting the country into its three main national units, Cambodia, Laos, and Vietnam, each of which they placed under the titular rule of an indigenous ruler. Secondly, in temporarily allocating northern Indochina to the Chinese in August 1945,[18] the Allies inadvertently precipitated the chaos of a totally undisciplined Kuomintang occupation, during which the Viet Minh leader, Ho Chi Minh, established a popular front government in Hanoi. Thus when the Communists came to power in China four years later, most Americans and British, who knew little of Vietnam's traditional distrust of China, or of the Cambodians' and Laotians' resentment of the Vietnamese, automatically assumed that Vietnam would henceforth provide an open door for the infiltration of Chinese Communism into the rest of Southeast Asia. In order to prevent this, the United States became increasingly involved in Vietnam, a process which was intensified following the French defeat and withdrawal in 1954.

The Western powers were not alone in fearing a southward expansion of Chinese Communist influence after 1949. Thus,

[18] See above p. 23.

for example, K. M. Panikkar, who was serving as Indian Ambassador to China in 1949, drew up a memorandum which argued that "without immediate and adequate help in the economic field, the political structure of South-East Asia would provide no more than a frail barrier to the expansion of Communism."[19] Knowing that India "could not move in this matter effectively," he asked the British and Australian Ambassadors to forward his document to the Commonwealth governments as a joint proposal which, he was later told, formed the basis of the discussions which led to the Colombo Plan of 1950.[20]

Representing as it did a kind of mutual aid association, heavily buttressed by external financial support, the Colombo Plan for Cooperative Economic Development in South and Southeast Asia may fairly be described as an economic counterpart to Panikkar's strategic ideas of 1943, put forward at a time when economic development had become far more acceptable locally than talk of military preparation. Moreover, although the Plan was launched under Commonwealth auspices, all the South and Southeast Asian countries except North Vietnam soon agreed to participate, and besides the developed Commonwealth countries—Australia, Canada, New Zealand, and the United Kingdom—Japan and the United States also came in as donor members.[21]

However, while the Colombo Plan made a useful contribution in strengthening the economies of its South and Southeast Asian members, the attempt of the United States, following the Geneva settlement of 1954, to provide military support for the same area under SEATO was not generally welcomed in the region, and the only Southeast Asian countries to join were the Philippines and Thailand.

Nevertheless the widely expected Chinese threat did not materialize for, notwithstanding the new Communist regime's

19 K. M. Panikkar, *In Two Chinas* (London: George Allen & Unwin, 1955), p. 55.

20 *Ibid.*, p. 56.

21 The United States became much the largest contributor of aid under the Colombo Plan, far outstripping Britain or any other developed Commonwealth country.

professed sympathy for revolutionary change in the developing countries, its overriding concern was to come to grips with China's own acute economic and demographic problems. Thus, with a fellow Communist regime established in North Vietnam and with Burma carefully following a more nonaligned course than India and an even more introvert policy than China itself, Peking was presumably prepared to forego whatever aspirations the former regime may have entertained regarding access routes to the south, at least for the foreseeable future.

Such an interpretation was consistent with the image, skillfully presented by Chou En-lai at the Afro-Asian Conference at Bandung in 1955, of an essentially reasonable China, not seeking to manipulate its overseas kinsfolk to further its own ends, or to interfere in other ways in the affairs of neighboring countries. But although many of his hearers were at least partially reassured by his words, the foreboding aroused by continuing guerrilla activities in many areas was not easily assuaged. Thus the growing respect which China came to command as a purposeful and vigorous power was tinged with apprehension, while India, though still regarded as a good neighbor, was increasingly felt to be a rather ineffectual one. This change in the relative standing of China and India in Southeast Asian eyes ran parallel to that in the volume of trade which each respectively maintained with Southeast Asia during the period in question, though more recently both have been overshadowed by the spectacular growth of Japanese commercial and economic penetration into virtually every part of the region.

PROBLEMS FACING THE NEWLY INDEPENDENT STATES OF SOUTHEAST ASIA

In the process of decolonization the existing territorial units were for the most part handed over intact, and the outward appearance of the new map of Southeast Asia accordingly shows a high degree of continuity with that existing immediately before the Second World War. Nevertheless the new map differs from its predecessor in three obvious respects, namely the dismemberment, along both national and ideological/geopolitical lines, of the former Indochina; the federation of the component states of the Malay peninsula and the former British Borneo (except Brunei); and the isolation of Singapore to become a free-standing city-state of predominantly ethnic Chinese population at the geographical focus of the region.

Meanwhile, thanks largely to wartime advances in tropical medicine, Southeast Asia has experienced a spectacular increase in its population which has virtually doubled since 1935, though in average density it still remains far below the Indian subcontinent and China proper, let alone Japan. Moreover, in inheriting the boundaries of their colonial predecessors, most of the newly independent states contain a much greater ethnic and cultural diversity of peoples than has usually been included within nation-states in the West, where the concept of the nation-state originated. Thus they have been faced with the extremely difficult task of creating a common sense of nationhood transcending the cleavages between their advanced and more retarded indigenous peoples as well as those of immigrant derivation, and several of them have also inherited awkward frontier problems arising from the presence within their borders of peoples whose traditional allegiance has hitherto been focused on the other side of the line.

More fundamental, however, is the question of whether the proper expression of the national identity calls for a reversion to the predominantly inward-looking traditions of precolonial times or is better served by retaining the new outward orientation imposed on most parts of Southeast Asia under colonial rule. While most if not all the governments concerned appreciate that, if they are to attempt to satisfy their peoples' aspirations for better living standards, it will be necessary to maintain and indeed increase participation in international trade, there are powerful sentiments pulling in the opposite direction, and wherever distrust of the outside world is strong such feelings may prove decisive. Thus for the past decade Burma has been following its own lonely "road to socialism," and Indonesia also experienced a prolonged period of more or less comparable introversion under the Sukarno regime. Yet, while both of these extreme courses tended to produce more evils than they cured, it would be wrong to assume that all-out pursuit of Western-style modernization provides the best way to economic well-being and social harmony.

What is needed above all is for the Southeast Asian countries individually and collectively to work out a balance between the traditional and the modern which is appropriate to their own particular conditions and aspirations. Here, however, the new states have relatively little room for maneuver, though unfortunately this fact has sometimes been dangerously obscured by misleading Western assessments of the supposedly immense scale of their natural resources. Basically the reason why Southeast Asia had achieved such importance as an exporter of tropical produce was its quite exceptionally high degree of accessibility in relation to the major maritime highways. This distinctive characteristic of its geography thus made it an unusually profitable area for outsiders seeking to exploit such products for export, but that is not at all the same thing as saying that the Southeast Asian countries are exceptionally well provided with natural resources relative to the needs of their own population.

Moreover, for reasons already considered, these countries still tend to rival rather than to complement one another in the kind of commodities they produce, a fact which has recently been re-emphasized by the widespread success of IR8 and the other high-yielding varieties of rice in many parts of the region. For although potentially these new rices can greatly benefit such overcrowded rural areas as east-central Java which have become heavily dependent on imported rice, the prospects are naturally viewed quite differently by the established rice-exporting countries of mainland Southeast Asia, which are losing some of their best markets.

Finally, in this connection, the relatively small size of the home markets of most Southeast Asian states, compared with those of India, China, and Japan, makes it difficult for the former to produce more than a comparatively limited range of manufactured goods as cheaply as they can import them from these established neighbors. Thus at present industrialization in Southeast Asia is still largely restricted to the commoner and cheaper forms of consumer goods and the processing of local raw materials prior to export.

On all these grounds, therefore, there is need for closer collaboration between the several Southeast Asian countries. In different ways both the Greater East Asia Co-prosperity Sphere and the Colombo Plan recognized this need, though the former was an attempt to keep the Southeast Asian countries in a state of permanent economic subordination, and even under the Colombo Plan the expectation was that Southeast Asia would long remain the junior partner of South Asia. Meanwhile, although several Southeast Asians had come to see the need for regional collaboration as soon as the era of Co-prosperity was over, no really effective organization for this purpose could be developed until all the main states concerned had achieved their independence and hence, so to speak, had been able to find their own level. For under colonialism the status of any Southeast Asian territory was a function not so much of its own inherent potential as of the strength of the metropolitan powers which controlled it, and the process of adjustment to the new realities has taken some time to effect.

Nevertheless the beginnings of this adjustment may be discerned in the enhanced position which Thailand began to acquire almost immediately after the Second World War. During the colonial era the old Siam—though preserving its independence—had remained the least developed of the main Southeast Asian countries but, largely because of its having offered only token resistance to the Japanese in 1941, it emerged in 1945 with the least devastation and thus became the leading source of rice in the midst of a region of acute shortage. By virtue of its noncolonial past, moreover, it was regarded by the United States as a natural focus for a region about to be decolonized, and since the major air routes, unlike the seaways, did not need to make the southerly detour via Singapore, Bangkok quickly became the primary air crossroads of Southeast Asia.

This new modality led to other things. In 1949 FAO set up its regional headquarters at Bangkok, a practice which was subsequently adopted by several other international and regional bodies, including the Economic Commission for Asia and the Far East and SEATO. Meanwhile, with mounting disorder in both Vietnam and Burma, Thailand, which only partially modified its traditional autocratic monarchical form of government, stood out as a center of stability in the middle of the Southeast Asian mainland, and, in both total population and per capita income, moved steadily ahead of its neighbors to east and west. Perhaps the first hint of Thailand's new postwar role appeared when a "Manifesto of representatives of the countries of Southeast Asia" was issued, on behalf of spokesmen from Indonesia, Malaya, Vietnam, Cambodia, Laos, and Thailand, in Bangkok on July 27, 1947, though in fact this was merely a vague declaration of mutual support against Western colonialism which was already on its way out.

In the early postwar years the Philippines, being the first Southeast Asian state to be decolonized and on cordial terms with the United States, also aspired to some form of regional leadership, first under Carlos Romulo's proposed Pan-Malayan Union, to include Indonesia, Malaya, and the Philippines, and later, in 1950, with President Quirino's suggestion for an organization embracing the whole area from Pakistan to Australia. However, neither of these plans aroused much interest, basically because other Southeast Asian peoples tended to regard the Filipinos as the least Asian of them all. More recently the continuing unwillingness of the Philippines to tackle its increasingly explosive social problems has marred its image in neighboring countries.

During the early 1950s the initiative of ECAFE pointed the way to another and more practical form of regional cooperation between the countries of mainland Southeast Asia, all of which—except North Vietnam—border upon the Mekong, the greatest river in the entire region. However, because of the severe natural obstacles along its course, communications have throughout historical times been obstructed and the basin has remained politically divided. Moreover, related natural difficulties have greatly restricted the use of its waters for irrigation, and the consequently retarded agriculture over most of the area has supported only a low density of population at a low standard of living. The belief that all these interlocking problems could be resolved by a coordinated plan, involving hydroelectric power generation, irrigation, and flood control and the improvement of navigation, agriculture, and fisheries, lay behind the ECAFE decision to investigate these possibilities and, as successive reports proved increasingly encouraging, the Committee for the Coordination of Investigations of the Lower Mekong Basin was set up with its headquarters at Bangkok in 1957. Ironically, however, the hostilities in Vietnam were already casting lengthening shadows over the Mekong basin; although Cambodia, Laos, South Vietnam, and Thailand were all members of the Committee, North Vietnam was never invited, and Burma, although it received an invitation in 1957, was too preoccupied with other problems to accept.[22] Yet despite these difficulties work on tributary projects has gone ahead in many parts of the basin, and much of lasting value has already been accomplished.

Pragmatism of a different kind underlay another attempt to promote regional collaboration by means of the Association of Southeast Asia (ASA). According to Bernard Gordon, ASA had its origins when Tunku Abdul Rahman, the Prime Minister of Malaya, met President Garcia of the Philippines at Manila in 1959. It was formally inaugurated, with Malaya (later Malaysia), the Philippines, and Thailand as members, at a meeting in Bangkok in July 1961.[23] While there were precedents for Thai and Philippine interest in regional association, that of Malaya marked a new departure a mere two years after its achievement of *Merdeka* in 1957. Because he was a Kedah Malay with close and friendly personal links with Thailand, and because he was increasingly anxious over the problem of how to prevent the frustrations of Singapore from also infecting Malaya's large Chinese pop-

[22] Louis A. Cohen, "International Cooperation for Development —The Mekong Project," Alice Taylor (ed.), *Focus on Southeast Asia* (New York and Washington: Praeger, 1972), p. 22.

[23] Bernard K. Gordon, *Toward Disengagement in Asia* (Englewood Cliffs, N.J.: Prentice-Hall, 1969), pp. 98–99.

ulation, the Tunku was understandably drawn toward regional collaboration, and it seems probable that he came to see ASA as an appropriate and stable setting within which the proposed but problematical Malaysian Federation could be effectively established. Essentially ASA represented a regional organization for economic and cultural cooperation between like-minded Southeast Asian states, and its only ideological commitment was to the proposition that improved economic development offered the best defense against Communist subversion. Nevertheless, this was sufficient to arouse the opposition of Indonesia which accordingly refused to join as also did Burma and the former Indochinese states.[24]

Virtually from the beginning of Indonesia's effective independence at the end of 1949, Sukarno had been determined that his country, which under the rule of one of the lesser European powers had been almost unknown to the rest of the world, should now assume a role proportionate to its size as by far the largest country in Southeast Asia and indeed the fifth most populous in the world. In order for Indonesia at that time to achieve the leadership of Southeast Asia, it was first necessary to undermine the position which India had already assumed as the spokesman for both South and Southeast Asia, and as the key state in the nonaligned Indian Ocean region. This Sukarno attempted to do most obviously by convening—at Bandung in 1955—not another Inter-Asian Conference but the first Afro-Asian Conference, in effect calling in Africa, as the newest of the newly emerging regions, to redress the balance of Asia which presumably by this time had fully surfaced. Moreover, in providing Sukarno with the opportunity of hosting Chou En-lai as the representative of the newly re-emerged great Asian power which had already begun to outpace India, the Bandung Conference served still further to advertise Indonesia's claims to be riding the wave of the future.

These aspirations, which had been intensified rather than checked by the abortive PRRI revolution of 1958 and further stimulated by the massive purchase of Soviet equipment for

[24] North Vietnam alone was not invited to do so. *Ibid.*

the armed forces after 1959, underlay both Indonesia's refusal to join ASA and Sukarno's subsequent attempt, by
hostile confrontation beginning in 1963, to prevent the formation of the Federation of Malaysia. In this objective he somewhat surprisingly came to enjoy at least the moral support of
the Philippines, which had revived an almost forgotten claim
to Sabah. This development may have provided the inspira-
tion for Sukarno's proposal of June 1963 to resuscitate and
refurbish Romulo's idea of a Pan-Malayan Union by setting
up a joint consultative body to prepare the way for the confederation of Malaya, the Philippines, and Indonesia, to be
known as Maphilindo.

Whether or not Sukarno really believed that the proposed
Federation of Malaysia, which he regarded as a neocolonialist
plot to encircle Indonesia, had been designed as a means of
extending British power in Southeast Asia, it is impossible to
say, but his actions certainly deflected Indonesia still further
from the urgent tasks of solving its mounting economic problems. The irony of this situation was that, while Sukarno was
entirely right in believing that Indonesia, alone in Southeast
Asia, had the potential to become a major power, his own
distorted ideas of economics and of international affairs combined to set back, probably by several decades, the possibility
of its achieving that status.

Nevertheless, by the time the inevitable nemesis overtook
his regime on September 30, 1965, both the rest of Southeast
Asia and the major outside powers had become alive to the
crucial importance of Indonesia's position within the region
and, once a new and more realistically minded Indonesian
government had emerged under General Suharto, serious attempts were made to repair the economic and political rav-
ages of the previous fifteen years. Thus ten of the world's
leading powers have collaborated in an intergovernmental
effort (IGGI) to enable Indonesia to reschedule the repayment of its immense foreign debts and to carry out an emergency program to bring inflation under control. Meanwhile
Indonesia began to prepare and later to implement a realistic
Five Year Plan for 1969–74; and in 1967, in order to bring
this chastened state back into a cooperative relationship with

its neighbors, the Foreign Ministers of Thailand and Indonesia jointly promoted a new regional grouping, the Association of South East Asian Nations (ASEAN) comprising, besides their own two countries, Malaysia, the Philippines, and Singapore. While in spirit and purpose ASEAN is essentially a successor to ASA, geographically it represents a combination of the ASA and Maphilindo groupings (including Singapore which as part of the original Federation of Malaysia was common to both), and so bridges the divergences of recent years.

As yet ASEAN is little more than a forum for the interchange of ideas on matters of common concern to its five member countries, though useful work is also being done in improving regional communications and disseminating new information and skills. This modesty is understandable at the present early stage, and not least so because the Association has not yet been extended to include Burma, which shows no sign of wishing to join, or to the former Indochinese states, at least some of which would like to do so.

Besides the previously mentioned obstacles to effective economic collaboration caused by cultural differences and the lack of regional complementarity in primary produce, the data provided in the accompanying table help to illustrate the further difficulties which arise from the wide diversity in size and degree of development between the several Southeast Asian states. Thus among these eleven states there is one very large unit, Indonesia, with 121 million people, or 41 per cent of the entire regional total; five medium-sized units, Burma, Thailand, the Philippines, and the two Vietnamese states, each with between 18 and 38 million; and four smaller units, Singapore, Laos, Cambodia, and Malaysia, each with between 2 and 11 million inhabitants. However, if the view is restricted to the ASEAN member countries, which comprise one very large, two medium, and two small units, the predominance of Indonesia with 58 per cent of the total population is even more overwhelming; on the other hand, if the emphasis is placed upon Gross Domestic Product (GDP), Indonesia is not strikingly ahead of Thailand and the Philippines, both of which are in ASEAN, and Malaysia is not far

behind it. For obvious reasons, the much smaller state of
Singapore has the lowest GDP of the ASEAN group, though
it is ahead of Laos, Cambodia, and even Burma outside.

Southeast Asia—Selected Data, 1970

Country	Area km²	Population thousands	Density of Population per km²	% of Ethnic Chinese	GDP per capita £ sterling	GDP £ sterling millions
THAILAND	514,000	35,814	70	11.6	70	2,506
MALAYSIA	332,633	10,798	32	36.0	161	1,739
SINGAPORE	581	2,050	3,528	75.5	404	848
INDONESIA	1,491,564	121,198	81	2.9	26	3,146
PHILIPPINES	300,000	38,493	128	1.1*	64	2,464
Burma	678,033	27,584	41	1.5	31	856
Laos	236,800	2,962	13	1.2	46	138
North Vietnam	158,750	21,154	133	0.7	40	846
South Vietnam	173,809	18,332	105	8.9	59	1,080
Khmer Republic (Cambodia)	181,035	6,700	37	7.5	54	362
Portuguese Timor	14,925	602	40	n.a.	n.a.	
Brunei	5,765	121	21	26.0	393	48
Total/average	4,087,895	285,905	70(ave.)	5.5(ave.)	45(ave.)	13,033

Member states of ASEAN are shown in capitals (as THAILAND).
Other independent Southeast Asian states are shown in lower case (as Burma).
Dependent territories are in lower case underlined (as Brunei).

*If allowance is made for Chinese as mestizos, this figure should be approximately 5.
(See below, note 25.)

However, in the politically far more sensitive matter of per
capita GDP which, though not a direct measure of living
standards, gives a useful indication of comparative levels,
the ranking is totally different, and is clearly related to other
factors. Thus a significant measure of correlation exists between the respective countries' rankings in per capita GDP
and in the percentage of ethnic Chinese in their populations.
Moreover, if appropriate numerical allowance is made for the
fact that the great majority of the older established Chinese
element in the Philippines became socially absorbed into the
mestizo population and hence no longer regarded as Chinese,
the correspondence becomes even closer and indeed, within
the ASEAN five, is exact.[25]

[25] Since Chinese mestizos alone formed some 5 per cent of the
total population of the Philippines early in the nineteenth century,
and a major increase of Chinese immigration occurred during the
nineteenth century, it seems safe to assume that Chinese plus Chi-

Nevertheless, the reasons for this are more complex than they might at first sight appear. For as immigrants the Chinese initially went in greatest numbers to the areas of greatest opportunity, which in turn depended not only on natural resources but also on the policies of the then mostly colonial governments concerned. Moreover, although in Southeast Asia a relatively high proportion of Chinese in the population is invariably accompanied by a relatively high average standard of living, it is equally important to stress that in all the Southeast Asian countries the average living standards of the Chinese communities are much higher than those of the indigenous population. The extreme example of this is of course Singapore which, with 75.5 per cent of its population of Chinese origin, has much the highest per capita GDP of any independent Southeast Asian state. However, Singapore is situated cheek by jowl not only with Malaysia, which has a high per capita GDP (though this does not apply to most of the 50 per cent or so of its people who are Malays), but also with Indonesia, which has the lowest per capita GDP in the whole region and by far the lowest within the ASEAN group. This juxtaposition of extremes at the heart of Southeast Asia is potentially very dangerous politically, but the problem is hardly of Singapore's making.

Created originally as the maritime focus and entrepôt for Southeast Asia, and having served as the primary center of innovation in the modern transformation of that region during the nineteenth century, Singapore was already in the early decades of the present century adjusting itself to the new situation caused by the waning of the liberal free trade system under which it had grown up, and was becoming increasingly dependent upon its role as the primary port and commercial capital of the British Malaysian sphere. But now, having finally been excluded politically from the proposed "Malay-

nese mestizos together comprise at least 5 per cent of the present total population. On this whole subject see Edgar Wickberg, *The Chinese in Philippine Life, 1850–1898* (New Haven, Conn.: Yale University Press, 1965), and also my review of this outstanding work in *Royal Central Asian Journal*, 1968 (Vol. 55), pp. 209–10.

sian Common Market" grouping which was to have been the postcolonial successor of that sphere, Singapore's only way of providing for its two million inhabitants is to exploit to the full its two main assets of geographical focality and the high levels of education, skills, and adaptability which, appropriate to its role as a great regional metropolis, its people have already developed. This course it has in fact followed with immense energy and determination since 1965, so that today it is the world's fourth largest port (after New York, Rotterdam, and Yokohama) in terms of tonnage handled and, with its recent adoption of containerization, by far the most modern port in Southeast Asia. Moreover it is a major banking center and has developed much the widest range of industries —including precision engineering and electronics—of any state in Southeast Asia, and in so doing it is no longer aiming merely at local or regional markets but at those of the entire outside world.

By any standards these achievements are extremely impressive, but to talk, as one expert has recently done, of Singapore's becoming "the brain of Southeast Asia"[26] is not likely to endear it to its neighbors, which presumably are expected to content themselves with remaining as less exalted parts of the region's anatomy. In this respect, at least, the analogy with Israel is both striking and disturbing, for among Singapore's technically less advanced neighbors, remarks of the kind just quoted are bound to intensify both their sense of humiliation and their fear of being exploited by what they see as an unwanted alien element which has intruded itself into their midst. Moreover, since every other Southeast Asian country is already in varying degree resentful and suspicious of the economic position of its own Chinese minority, there is an understandable tendency for them to fear that Singapore —however much it may disclaim any such intention—will serve as a "brain" for coordinating local Chinese attempts to get a still greater degree of control over the economies of all parts of Southeast Asia.

[26] *Singapore Trade and Industry,* Singapore, 1970, p. 43.

CHANGE AND CONTINUITY
IN THE SOUTHEAST ASIAN SEAS

All things considered the isolation of Singapore, through its exclusion from the Federation of Malaysia in 1965, has created as many problems as it has solved. Manifestly, if it continues to be allowed to do so, Singapore can fend very effectively for itself. But the spectacular degree of economic success which it has already achieved in so doing tends to estrange it still further from its neighbors, especially Malaysia and Indonesia, with both of which it shares a focal position relative to the central maritime artery of Southeast Asia. And this unfortunate state of affairs is made the more serious by the fact that these vital seaways are now becoming subjected to new and conflicting pressures of various kinds.

This process may be said to have begun with the Indonesian claim, announced on December 13, 1957, to territorial rights over all the seas surrounding its three thousand or so islands, within an outer limit of twelve nautical miles "measured from straight base lines connecting the outermost points of the island." Taken literally (which fortunately it has not been) this claim could be said to extend in places to the shores of Malaya and perhaps even to Singapore harbor itself, placing it within Indonesian territorial waters. Although it was put forward during the time of Sukarno's conflict with the Dutch and specifically aimed at intercepting Dutch shipping en route to West Irian, it has never since been rescinded. Later, as traffic congestion created growing problems in the Malacca Straits, the new Indonesian government stated in its 1969–74 Five Year Plan that the ports of Tjilatjap and Padang would be developed to take the larger vessels of the future,[27] in anticipation of the diversion of more traffic from the Malacca Straits to the outer route via the Southern Indian Ocean. Moreover, with the increase in the size of oil tankers, these difficulties have become even more acute. Already the Japanese tankers of over 200,000 dwt. are too big to use the Malacca Straits, and the havoc that could be caused to the

[27] *The First Five-Year Development Plan 1969/1970–1973/ 1974* (Djakarta: Department of Information, Republic of Indonesia, 1969, Vol. 1), p. 77.

fisheries of Indonesia, Malaysia, and Singapore by pollution from a tanker damaged by grounding or collision might be immense. Thus in November 1971 Malaysia (which also had meanwhile claimed a limit of 12 nautical miles to its territorial waters) associated itself with Indonesia in a joint statement to the effect that the Malacca Straits were not international waters. Understandably, as the primary shipping focus of the entire region, Singapore was pre-eminently concerned with the freedom of navigation, and accordingly reserved its position by merely taking note of this statement.

Japan was also much concerned by this new development. Ever since the 1950s and particularly since it became deeply involved in the Inter-Governmental Group for Indonesia in the 1960s, Japan has rapidly expanded its commercial and economic activities in virtually all parts of Southeast Asia. Nevertheless, Japan's interest in Southeast Asia is not merely a matter of its trading relationships with these countries, which are far exceeded by those it now maintains with the Middle East–South Asia–Australia group of countries, respectively providing its main sources of oil and major supplies of metals and other essential raw materials. And the fact that all these critical and bulky supplies are transported to Japan via the Southeast Asian seaways has inevitably intensified its interest in free and secure rights of passage in and through that region.

Accordingly Japan has taken an active part in the recent search for practicable alternatives to the Malacca Straits route, and in June 1972 it was reported that a joint Japanese-Indonesian hydrographic survey of the Makasar and Lombok straits would begin shortly.[28] Meanwhile there has been speculation that Japan is interested in the possibility of developing the Indonesian island of Batam,[29] similar in size to, and less

[28] This survey is promoted by the Malacca Strait Council, a Japanese organization of shipping and allied interests for improvement of channels for easier navigation of Japanese oil tankers. *Japan Times Weekly,* June 24, 1972. The use of the Makasar-Lombok straits route would add five days to the voyage between the Middle East and Japan at a cost of £25,000 per tanker. Michael Hornsby, "The Plan to Link Two Oceans," *The Times* (London), August 3, 1972.

[29] S. Iskander, "Japan's Indonesian Inroads," *Far Eastern Economic Review,* May 27, 1972 (Vol. 76, No. 22), p. 33.

than 20 kilometers south of Singapore, as a new oil storage base at which the smaller tankers still using the Malacca Straits could offload their cargoes which giant tankers in turn could take to Japan.

Perhaps even more significant, however, has been the revival of interest in the Kra isthmus, a tendency which invariably seems to recur whenever uncertainty arises regarding the right of passage through the Malacca Straits. This happened, for example, during the late 1950s and early 1960s, when fears that an increasingly disaffected Singapore might come under Communist control led Marshal Sarit of Thailand to suggest building a Kra canal which would enable American naval units, operating in support of SEATO strategy, to bypass Singapore and the Malacca Straits en route between the South China Sea and the Indian Ocean. But with the stabilization of Singapore's internal political situation under Lee Kuan Yew, this idea was abandoned, and in 1964 Thailand officially announced that the canal would not be built. However, during the past few years the question of constructing a canal, or possibly instead an oil pipeline, across the Kra isthmus has been reopened.

After much discussion of the rival merits of these alternatives, the National Executive Council of Thailand announced in July 1972 that a canal would be built, though there seems to be some support for the view that a pipeline is also needed.[30] The proposed canal, 155 kilometers long[31] and 120 meters wide, between Phang Nga and Bandon Bay in Surat Thani province, is expected to take nine to ten years and 9,000 million Baht (£180 million) to build, and would be able to take tankers and freighters of up to 100,000 dwt. Besides providing a major maritime short cut, it has been suggested that the scheme should also include the promotion of new industries within a related free trade zone, an idea which is apparently based on the experience of Singapore and, if adopted, would doubtless involve some competition with the latter.

[30] "Green Light for the Kra Canal," *Far Eastern Economic Review,* July 15, 1972, (Vol. 77, No. 29), p. 29.

[31] This is considerably longer than the width of the isthmus, owing to the fact that the proposed route follows a roughly north/south course, though even so the canal would require five locks.

Nevertheless, in view of the rapid growth of trade and shipping within and through Southeast Asia, it would seem that the time will come, well before the end of the present century, when such a second seaway—some 700 kilometers shorter than the present one—through the middle of the region would be economically justifiable. Moreover, especially if it were accompanied by the creation of the proposed new industrialized zone, it might greatly reduce neighboring countries' fears of Southeast Asia's being excessively centralized in Singapore, without destroying the capacity of the latter to survive and prosper in the era of widening horizons that lies ahead.[32] At present, however, Japan still appears to regard an oil pipeline as all that is needed, but in view of the expectation that Japanese imports of crude oil will increase threefold by the early 1980s, it remains to be seen whether this is merely a short-term appraisal of the situation.[33]

Besides Japan the Soviet Union is also becoming increasingly interested in the Southeast Asian seaways. This development is clearly a facet of the Soviet Union's widening naval policy which is most strikingly evident in the Indian Ocean and is conceived, at least in part, as a means of containing China. Thus the Soviet Union is no less anxious than Japan to maintain established rights of passage through the Southeast Asian seas. China, on the other hand, has been widely assumed to have little or no interest in such matters, and indeed its supposed lack of a naval tradition has often been adduced as evidence that it remains essentially land-minded and has no significant overseas aspirations. However, without seeking in any way to revive the myth of the Yellow Peril, one must surely admit that such an assessment is grossly oversimplified when viewed against the background of the ex-

[32] There is after all a limit to the amount of industrial plant which can be crowded into Singapore island without doing irreparable damage to the quality of life there.

[33] At present 90 per cent of Japan's crude oil is imported from the Middle East. The proposed pipeline would provide the link between a fleet of 500,000-ton tankers plying between the Persian Gulf and the Andaman Sea and another of 200,000-ton tankers operating between the Gulf of Thailand and Japan. Michael Hornsby, *op. cit.*

ploits of Cheng Ho and the wide-ranging Chinese junk trade, which for centuries interlinked the lands bordering the South China Sea before the arrival in strength of the Western maritime powers. Moreover, the rapid rise of the Soviet Union— the least navally renowned of all the great powers prior to the Second World War—to its present status as the second sea power in the world suggests that it would be foolish to rule out the possibility that, if only for defensive purposes, China might at one time aspire to a major naval role at least in the seas adjacent to its own shores.

In this connection it is pertinent to note the differences of views recently expressed following a statement by the Soviet Ambassador to Japan, calling for the "internationalization" of the Malacca Straits. While Japan unequivocally concurred in this view, it was immediately opposed by a Malaysian spokesman on March 6, 1972.[34] But four days later the Chinese representative, speaking in the Seabed Committee of the United Nations, accused Japan of renewed aspirations in the South Pacific, and of claiming that "the area from South Korea, Taiwan, and Indochina to the Straits of Malacca is the lifeline of Japan." Thereupon the Philippine delegate riposted by stating his country's reservations concerning claims recently made by China to rights over the Spratley Islands in the South China Sea.[35]

As is implied by the name of the Committee in which these last exchanges took place, the issues involved here are no longer simply a matter of the rights of maritime passage, but also of rival claims to the underlying continental shelf, which has recently begun to attract attention on account of its oil potential. While consideration of the volatile history of oil exploitation suggests that one should be extremely chary of accepting at face value the enthusiastic forecasts which during 1972 have repeatedly appeared in the Southeast Asian press, the prospects are clearly attracting widespread interest in the outside world.

[34] "Malaysia Rejects Soviet Call on Malacca Straits," *Financial Times,* March 8, 1972.
[35] "Chinese Stake a Big Sea Claim," *The Times* (London), March 11, 1972.

On these grounds alone Southeast Asian statesmen would be well advised to study the recent experience of the Persian Gulf countries and in the light of this to consider how best they can coordinate their policies to avoid being played off one against another by powerful and experienced international concerns. For it cannot be too strongly emphasized that the integrity of Southeast Asia turns upon its seaways; if effective control of these passes into the hands of outsiders interested primarily not in the lands or the peoples of Southeast Asia but merely in exploiting—perhaps only for a few decades—the oil underlying these vital seas, ASEAN's aspirations to draw Southeast Asians closer together in meaningful regional cooperation may be irreparably frustrated.

Throughout the past two millennia the history of Southeast Asia has been profoundly affected by the focal geographical position which its territories occupy astride one of the world's greatest maritime highways. Notwithstanding the immeasurable benefits which successive waves of seaborne migration and acculturation have brought to it, there have been many times when the disadvantages arising from such a situation have seemed to outweigh the advantages. For owing to their relatively small population, the Southeast Asian countries have never yet achieved a really commanding position in relation to their central seaways which, while potentially capable of linking them together, can nevertheless if controlled by outsiders, be used to divide and hence to subordinate them.

It is therefore peculiarly ironic that, at a time when population growth and the achievement of independence from colonial rule have together begun to make possible a solution of this problem, the discovery of new resources, which might serve further to assist this linking process, also threatens to subject these still relatively inexperienced countries to new and powerful extraneous forces operating in the opposite direction. But if this potentially dangerous development should provide the necessary challenge to make the Southeast Asian nations resolve the differences which continue to limit their collaboration, it would indeed mark a turning point in the history of this part of Asia.

Historic National Rivalries and Interstate Conflict in Mainland Southeast Asia

JERRY M. SILVERMAN

INTRODUCTION

In order to make an assessment of the potentialities for stability or instability in mainland Southeast Asia, it is necessary to understand the nature of precolonial patterns of authority there, at both the governing elite and rural community levels, and to see how these patterns have either altered or been perpetuated into the contemporary period. The first section of this paper concerns itself with examining the historic patterns of interaction; the second section focuses on several contemporary sources of conflict which are rooted in these historic patterns; and the third section considers several policy issues facing Southeast Asian governments, the resolution of which will strongly affect future interstate relations in the region. As a preface to Section I, it will be useful to review briefly the nature of the modern sovereign state so that the contrasts posed by the patterns of precolonial authority in Southeast Asia will be apparent.

There are two conditions which must be met if a particular political structure is to be understood as a sovereign state. One condition refers to the pattern of authority, legally defined, within the state. This criterion is that legal authority is structured hierarchically among the people within the state. An ultimate source of legal authority can be identified within the state, and authority is applied uniformly throughout the territory of the state.[1] It is important to emphasize that the

[1] J. L. Brierly, *The Law of Nations* (New York: Oxford University Press, 1963), pp. 7–16, 45–55.

"boundaries" of legal authority are thus defined territorially, not in terms of actual ability to implement decisions or enforce obedience among a particular population.[2]

The other condition refers to the pattern of authority between sovereign states. Among sovereign states, all are legally equal. There is, therefore, no ultimate legal authority which transcends the state itself. Thus, the interstate system is defined by the interactions of legally and territorially identifiable sovereign state actors which are equal in that they all are understood to have within themselves the source of their own ultimate legal authority.

I. HISTORICAL PATTERNS
IN MAINLAND SOUTHEAST ASIA

A. PATTERNS OF INTERACTION BETWEEN
DIFFERENT ETHNIC POPULATIONS

For most of their precolonial history, the kingdoms of mainland Southeast Asia (with the exception of Vietnam) shared an Indianized political culture at the elite level which largely defined and maintained a formal set of authority relationships. However, the continuity of the land mass provided avenues for mass contact among the Chams, Vietnamese, Khmers, and Thais through which the potential for violent conflict between ethnic groups was fully realized. Thus, pressures caused by the expansion of the Chinese within the area originally populated by the Thais in Yunnan and Burmans in eastern Tibet, in addition to increasing population throughout that area and the northern delta of the Vietnamese, induced mass migrations through the river valleys and coastal lowlands of the region. Such pressures were increased by the tendency of dynastic rivals, alienated "intellectuals," convicted criminals, adventurers, and other social "misfits" to move away from the imperial centers of political authority.

It is important for an understanding of contemporary Southeast Asia to realize that these various historical factors resulted in societies which were largely composed of competing frontier populations at the cutting edge of the core civilizations of Southeast Asia. Further, these core civilizations were

[2] *Ibid.*, p. 162.

themselves peripheral to the great and dynamic civilizations of China and India. Thus, in order to comprehend the reality of Southeast Asian politics, it is necessary first to understand the patterns of political authority within and between these expanding and contracting frontier societies as they were influenced by the cultures of China to the north and India to the west.

B. PATTERNS OF AUTHORITY AT THE GOVERNING
ELITE LEVEL

1) *The Indianized Kingdoms*

All of these expanding and contracting frontier societies in Southeast Asia were influenced by the higher cultures of China and India. The political culture of India was introduced to the rulers of Southeast Asian kingdoms at least as early as the first century A.D.,[3] and with the exception of Vietnam, which was primarily influenced by China, all of the traditional civilizations of mainland Southeast Asia adhered to some form of Hindu and Buddhist notions of political authority.[4] This was true throughout the region—from

[3] George Coedes, *The Making of South East Asia,* trans. by H. M. Wright (Berkeley: University of California Press, 1966), p. 10, and Daniel G. E. Hall, *A History of South-East Asia* (London: Macmillan and Co., Ltd., 1964), p. 14. Brian Harrison, *South-East Asia: A Short History* (London: Macmillan and Co., Ltd., 1963), argues that there is no archeological evidence of Indian influence prior to the second century A.D., but acknowledges that Indian influence no doubt predated such evidence by many centuries.

[4] The major differences between Hinduism and the elaborately maintained Buddhism of the Hinayana school had little effect at the mass level. George Coedes (*op. cit.,* pp. 54–56) rightly points out that the extent to which Indian influence penetrated to the "indigenous substratum" of society as a whole is still a matter of controversy. However, within the sphere of formalized political behavior, this controversy matters little. Indian political philosophy was characterized by an operationalized conceptual distinction between the state and society as a whole and Indian kings were advised to allow local people to live according to traditional custom [Arthur L. Basham, *The Wonder That Was India* (New York: The Macmillan Co., 1955)]. Hence, at the palace elite level, the primary differences were subtle, manifesting themselves in alternative ritual forms. It was not until the conversion of large numbers of

the largely extinct civilizations of the Chams (central Vietnam),[5] Pyus (northern Burma), Mons (northern Thailand), and the eclipsed kingdom of Funan (Laos, Cambodia, eastern Thailand, and southern Vietnam) to the more direct historical antecedents of the current states of Burma, Thailand, and Cambodia. In contrast, Vietnam was annexed by China as an integral part of the "Middle Kingdom" from 1407 to 1428 and continued to be a tributary kingdom within the Chinese system until France included Vietnam in its Indochinese colonial system. However, Chinese influence, which became blended with Indian influence, was also felt in many of the other kingdoms in the area. The Funan kingdom, for instance, by far the largest and most important kingdom in the period prior to the sixth century, was a tributary kingdom of China as well as being an Indianized state.

Chinese and Indian patterns of authority and interstate relations differed from each other in some important respects. According to Hindu and Buddhist notions of kingship, a king was a semidivine monarch. But Hindu philosophy was also polytheistic—even if a Hindu ruler was considered to be a god on earth, he was one god among many "equal" gods. As Arthur Basham points out, "divinity was cheap in ancient India,"[6] and by extension in the Indianized kingdoms of Southeast Asia. On the other hand, there existed within In-

---

people within the Angkor kingdom to the Sinhalese Mahavihara Buddhist sect during the thirteenth century that a significant operational difference between Hindu and Buddhist rationales developed. The Sinhalese form of Buddhism was simple and did not require the maintenance of a priesthood responsible for the construction and repair of expensive monuments or the performance of elaborate ceremonials. This apparently contributed to the decline of the Indianized Kingdom of Angkor (Daniel G. E. Hall, *op. cit.*, pp. 116–19). Another major religious influence developed in insular Southeast Asia beginning in the eleventh century: Islam. However, for a variety of reasons beyond the scope of this study, a discussion of Islam in Southeast Asia will be omitted. For a brief survey, refer to Brian Harrison, *op. cit.*, pp. 50–60.

[5] Throughout this study, we will, whenever possible, refer to geographic areas by their contemporary place names, although during the historic period being described such names may not have been in use.

[6] Arthur L. Basham, *op. cit.*, p. 86.

dian thought the ideal notion of a "Universal Emperor" whose function it would be to conquer the mythical continent of *Jambudvipa* and rule prosperously and righteously.[7] Although some emperors apparently claimed such a title during the middle ages in India, the primary result of such a notion was to spur on the ambitious. It was, in essence, on the basis of criteria associated with progress toward such an office that a monarch's status relative to others was established.

The primary method by which a monarch asserted his own authority over another king within the Indianized system was that of suzerainty or vassalage. The Asian system, characterized by emperors with "subordinate" vassals, cannot be equated with modern—or more precisely—Western colonialism. The relationship between a vassal and a superior emperor was largely symbolic. It did not often require obedience by an "inferior" to the substantive decisions of the "superior." Again, in the words of Professor Basham:

> The great vassal was always very powerful, and had his own administration and army. Among the many threats to the security of a king the revolting vassal was one of the most dangerous . . .
>
> In fact the suzerain's hand weighed very lightly on the more powerful and remoter vassals, and many claims to homage and tribute amounted to very little.[8]

War in this system consisted of forays by the professional army of one court upon rival courts for gains that were primarily symbolic. The primary goal of such actions was not material gain, but a largely abstract pattern of authority relationships. So abstract in fact were these relationships that whether submission or tribute had been accomplished was often a matter of interpretation and disagreement. Thus, boundary demarcation between the domestic and international system, both conceptually and territorially, was not clearly maintained.

The characteristic of abstract or symbolic displays of power by governing elites to achieve political prestige was reinforced by Indian political thought on the subject of just and unjust

[7] *Ibid.*, p. 83.
[8] *Ibid.*, pp. 94–95.

wars. Indian theorists differentiated three purposes of aggressive war. *Dharmavijaya* ("righteous conquest") forced a defeated king to render homage and pay tribute to the victor, whereupon the vanquished monarch or a member of his royal family was reconfirmed in his place, but as a vassal. This, as its designation implies, is the only form of conquest considered proper by most precolonial Indian political texts. The two remaining purposes of aggression were *lobhavijaya* ("conquest for greed") and *asuravijaya* ("demonic conquest")—the former waged for enormous booty and the partial annexation of territory, and the latter resulting in the complete annihilation of the vanquished and the incorporation of their whole territory within the kingdom of the victor.[9]

2) *Authority Patterns within the Sinicized "International System" of Southeast Asia*

In contrast to Indian polytheistic thought, on the basis of which each governing elite claimed political authority within its own kingdom, Confucius (Kung Fu-tzu, 551–479 B.C.) and his later interpreters viewed the whole world as a single social and political unit[10] in which all people were more or less the subjects of a single semidivine emperor, the "Son of Heaven." In the sense that this Chinese political philosophy envisioned one hierarchical system which was headed by one central court, it can be termed an international system. But like the Indianized kingdoms, China and the states which paid tribute to it did not constitute a system of political control which can be equated with Western colonialism. The hierarchy of states in the Chinese system was more cultural than political in that status within the system depended primarily on fulfilling cultural criteria of merit. In short, the degree to which a "Barbarian" kingdom became Chinese was the degree to which it exhibited behavior in accord with those codes

[9] *Ibid.*, p. 124.
[10] Edwin O. Reischauer and John K. Fairbank, *East Asia: The Great Tradition* (Boston: Houghton Mifflin Co., 1968), pp. 317–18, and M. Frederick Nelson, *Korea and the Old Orders in Eastern Asia* (Baton Rouge: Louisiana State University Press, 1946).

of conduct in favor at the Chinese court. A people were Chinese to the extent that they behaved as Chinese.[11]

There were more formalized relationships among states in the Sinicized "international system" than existed in interstate relations between Indianized kingdoms, but these diplomatic relationships amounted only to a more or less regular exchange of envoys between the Chinese court and the tributary kingdoms. These intercourt contacts were a means of promoting trade and cultural exchanges rather than means by which the Chinese court compelled its "subordinates" to execute its decisions. Military control was possible over "dependent" nations which directly bordered on China, as was the case with Vietnam to the south, Korea to the northeast, the Mongols to the northwest, and the petty kingdoms to the southwest. The Chinese court did sometimes intervene militarily in these neighboring kingdoms, not only because proximity made it possible, but also because intervention was sometimes necessary in order to destroy opposition movements being mounted in those border areas by rivals who had originally fled or been banished from the Chinese court.[12] But this capability to enforce its will militarily decreased drastically with distance. With the exception of these neighboring kingdoms, the Chinese attitude was generally one of benign involvement.

As was also true of relationships between governing elites in the Indianized kingdoms, vassal or tributary subordination was more symbolic than real. A tributary king accepted his ranking within the Sinicized system in the degree to which he found Chinese culture and the adherence to Chinese etiquette prestigious for himself, and in the degree to which he and his governing elite valued the exchange of information and the exchange of goods and services which were the real "benefits" of participation in the system. Such attitudes of tributary kings were perhaps most explicitly expressed by the Vietnamese King Minh Mang when he wrote the following to the Chinese Emperor in 1840:

Up until this year the Board of Rites of the Ch'ing Coun-

[11] George M. Beckmann, *The Modernization of China and Japan* (New York: Harper & Row, 1962), p. 57.
[12] George Coedes, *op. cit.*, p. 43.

try [China] has been mistaken in its hierarchical arrangements. Surely they should not have a rule that our envoys rank after those from Korea, Luang Prabang, Siam, and the Ryukyus? Korea as a country of literate and worthy men is definitely not worth discussing. As for Luang Prabang, it receives status as a tributary from us, and Siam and the Ryukyus are both Barbarian countries . . . If they rank envoys this way again, I would prefer to abandon their audiences altogether and receive their censure and punishment, rather than stand below those several countries.[13]

As with vassalage among the Indianized kingdoms, the Chinese emperors were determined to perceive a barbarian king and his people as subjects, even if that king refused to pay tribute or to perform the proper rituals of obeisance. Such a barbarian monarch might be viewed as an incorrigible "son" who would deserve and often receive punishment, but generally such punishment would be limited to the withholding of "benefits" or the dispatch of envoys to the barbarian's court with various blandishments. It was one system in that it was composed of a single ranking of states with one constant authority (the Chinese court and emperor) rather than a number of competing and changing suzerain and vassal relationships as typified the Indianized kingdoms. However, relative prestige in both systems was measured in cultural or symbolic terms, and both contrast with the Western colonial system in that ranking was not maintained by statewide bureaucracies or the consistent employment of an army.

Concluding this comparison of Indian and Chinese influence on the precolonial political history of Southeast Asia, the chart below summarizes the major differences between them in terms of their influence on the political cultures of the region.

[13] *Dai Nam Thu's Luc Chinh Bien, De Nhat, Nhi, Tam Ky* [Primary Compilation of the Veritable Records of the First Three Reigns of Imperial Vietnam], quoted in Alexander Barton Woodside, *Vietnam and the Chinese Model: A Comparative Study of Nguyen and Ch'ing Civil Government in the First Half of the Nineteenth Century* (Cambridge, Mass.: Harvard University Press, 1971), p. 243.

Indian	Chinese
1) Acceptance of nonuniversality of ruler.	1) Universal Emperor.
2) Hereditary, noncentralized administration.	2) Nonhereditary, centralized administration.
3) Aggressive interstate behavior resulting from *need to prove superiority* through manifestation of superior power.	3) Relatively benign resulting from belief that superiority was manifest primarily in cultural terms through example and that such superiority was not amenable to proof by force of arms.
4) Vague definition of borders.	4) Relatively clear notion of its own borders but not those of barbarian kingdoms.
5) Conception of distribution of international political power in the form of concentric circles; enemies and friends alternating. Hence, closest neighbor was primary enemy.	5) Conception of concentric circles representing decreasing cultural influence from center implied greater hostility further from center. Immediate neighbors most like younger brothers or close children.

On the other hand, although the normative rationale was somewhat different, both Indian and Chinese political philosophies, concerned with delineating the proper modes of interaction between kingdoms, stressed that the purpose of war was to *punish* unruly regional neighbors rather than to destroy them and annex their territory.

C. AN OUTLINE OF HISTORICAL RELATIONSHIPS

Acquisition of territory in any long-term sense by a governing elite was not fundamentally the result of aggressive war directed by one court against another. There were many military skirmishes between courts, but these did not often result in substantive changes either in the composition of the defeated palace elite or in demographic or sociological changes at the mass level. The changes effected by most of these attacks were simply the changes in prestige of one elite in relation to another, as the defeated court was made to pay verbal and symbolic homage to the superiority of the victor. On the one hand, Southeast Asian history is marked by an almost endless catalogue of duplicate and reciprocal invasions and conquests between rival palace elites. However, the history of lasting change in the area, understood in terms of gradual mass migrations which actually changed the structure and distribution of substantive political authority in precolonial Southeast Asia, is easier to outline. The battle engaged in by the professional army and the destruction of an opponent's palace and retinue which marked the territorial extension of a kingdom rather than just the punishment of a rival was most often the confirmation of prior immigration and settlement by one's own subjects. Prior immigration resulted in subsequent appeals for aid by the pioneers as conflict occurred between settlements of different cultures. These ethnic "pioneers" did not expel the original inhabitants, but rather asserted the authority of their own king over that of the older group. In other words, the migrating ethnic populations were in the long run the real pre-European imperialists, not the rival palace elites.

The distinguishing feature of intergroup conflict in mainland Southeast Asia is that it was often a function of population migration from north to south, followed by the successive displacement of one culture group's central elite by those of the migrant population. The politically dominant ethnic groups of mainland Southeast Asia today represent relatively recent immigration. As recently as the year 500, only three of the five population groups currently dominant in the region inhabited the area we define as Southeast Asia today: the Vietnamese (under Chinese rule) in the Red River Delta, the Khmers in the plateaus of present-day Laos, and the "Malays" of the peninsula and Indonesian islands.

The Khmers themselves were the first Northerners in the recorded history of Southeast Asia to permanently displace a significant southern kingdom. Descending from the northern Chao Phraya River plain into the central delta of present-day Cambodia, these "pilgrims" were followed by the Khmer court which successfully destroyed the capital of Funan in A.D. 539, after which the movement of the Khmer people continued into what is now the southern delta of Vietnam to the east and the Chao Phraya delta to the west. The Khmers, at the peak of their power during the twelfth century, extended their influence over most of Laos, Thailand, the southern Vietnamese delta, and northern Malaya.

The Vietnamese also, though they have been in the region throughout the recorded period, have not been a settled population. In fact, their southward movement, which began prior to the eleventh century and which has continued to the present, has been one of the most dramatic migrations of all. The year 1069 marks the first formal acknowledgment of Vietnamese expansion to the south. In that year the Vietnamese forced the Cham monarch, whom they had just defeated and captured, to cede the two northernmost provinces of Champa to them.[14] This process of the annexation of Champa by the Vietnamese was completed by 1471, with the exception of a small slice of residual territory, within which a Cham kingdom was recognized by China until 1543.[15] From the mid-fifteenth to the end of the seventeenth century there was continued political violence within Vietnam as rival Vietnamese elites turned against each other in a series of palace intrigues and assassinations, local and national uprisings, rebellions of minorities and rural revolts.[16] At the interstate level, Vietnamese governing elites vied with Thai elites, using Cambodia and the kingdoms of Laos as the testing ground of their relative power. The result was a pattern

[14] These two provinces roughly correspond to the present Vietnamese provinces of Quang Binh (the southernmost province of North Vietnam) and Quang Tri (the northernmost province of South Vietnam); Daniel G. E. Hall, *op. cit.*, p. 176.

[15] *Ibid.*, pp. 181–82.

[16] *Ibid.*, pp. 188–89; George Coedes, *op. cit.*, pp. 207–9; and Joseph Buttinger, *Vietnam, A Political History* (New York: Frederick A. Praeger, 1968), pp. 47–49.

of Vietnamese and Thai interventions in Cambodia and Lao
on behalf of various candidates to those thrones and agains
whichever claimants were supported by the other side.

But what was significant throughout the period in "Vie
nam" was not the endless series of skirmishes between riva
Vietnamese emperors or forays against neighboring riva
courts but the overall pattern of continuing southward move
ment by the Vietnamese people, followed eventually by th
annexation of territory by the Vietnamese court. Thus, b
1674 Vietnamese military forces were firmly ensconced i
Saigon, and by 1775 they had annexed all the territory t
the south in which Vietnamese had previously settled. It
perhaps useful to be reminded that 1775 was only ninet
nine years before the first Vietnamese territorial concessic
to the French in 1874. And it should be noted that the mov
ment of Vietnamese beyond the area claimed by any of tl
three current Vietnamese governments has continued to tl
present day.

Migrations of these Vietnamese settlers over the centuri
have been in large part motivated by the impulse to escap
political pressures exerted by palace elites. Such an impul
has always influenced the migrations of peoples in the regio
Thus the settlement by Vietnamese in northeastern and ea
ern Thailand in three successive migrations during the eigl
eenth, nineteenth, and twentieth centuries was primarily m
tivated by the desire to escape the series of wars, religio
persecutions, and anticolonial struggles in Indochina. In t
eighteenth century, a number of Vietnamese migrated acr
the Annamite Cordillera into territory now within the boun
aries of Thailand in order to escape the consequences
the *Tay Son* Rebellion.[17] In the nineteenth century, Vietna
ese who had been converted to Catholicism by the Fren
fled to escape religious persecution by the Vietnamese E

[17] Tamotsu Takahashi, "Thai Ni Okeru Vietnam Jin Mon
No Genjyo To Rekishiteki Haikei" [Present Situation and Histc
cal Background of the Vietnamese Problem in Thailand], *A
Keizai*, August 1971 (Vol. XII), pp. 68–71. For a discussion
the *Tay Son* Rebellion, refer to George Coedes, *op. cit.*, pp. 2
213–14, and Daniel G. E. Hall, *op. cit.*, p. 401.

peror.[18] In the twentieth century yet other Vietnamese fled Vietnam in order to avoid the conflict between the Viet Minh and, in succession, the French, Japanese, French (again), and, most recently in amended form, the Americans and other Vietnamese opponents.[19]

The history of the two major migrations of peoples from the north who were not "indigenous" to the region prior to the seventh century—the Burmans and the Thais—also demonstrates the theme of prior mass migrations of peoples followed only gradually by changes in governing elites and the definition of territories which reflected those migrations.

The first significant population movements into Southeast Asia in modern times were those of the Burmans. The Burmans began their southward movement from the area of eastern Tibet in the seventh century A.D., eventually displacing the indigenous Pyus in what is now central Burma during the ninth century, and the Mons east of Rangoon for the first time in the mid-eleventh century.[20]

The Thais followed the Burmans, leaving southern Yunnan during the ninth century and gradually displacing the remnants of the Pyus and Mons as they moved south through the valleys of the Irrawaddy, Salween, and Chao Phraya river systems until by the middle of the thirteenth century the first significant Thai kingdom was established at Sukhotai. The settlement by the Thais among the Khmers was relatively peaceful and preceded by several centuries the significant presence of their own political organization within Southeast Asia. It was not until 1238 that two Thai kings combined to defeat the Khmer garrison at the northern provincial capital of Sukhotai, after which they united and created a new Thai "state."[21] The thirteenth century witnessed the rapid

[18] Peter A. Poole, *The Vietnamese in Thailand: A Historical Perspective* (Ithaca, N.Y.: Cornell University Press, 1970), pp. 2–34, and Tamotsu Takahashi, *op. cit.*, pp. 71–75.

[19] Peter A. Poole, *op. cit.*, p. 28, and Tamotsu Takahashi, *op. cit.*, pp. 71–75.

[20] George Coedes, *op. cit.*, pp. 112–14; Daniel G. E. Hall, *op. cit.*, pp. 135–39; and Brian Harrison, *op. cit.*, pp. 36–38.

[21] E.g., Donald E. Neuchterlein, *Thailand and the Struggle for Asia* (Ithaca, N.Y.: Cornell University Press, 1965), pp. 1–2.

expansion of the Thai. With the Burmans in disarray as
result of the Mongol invasion and occupation, the Thais wei
able to carve out territories throughout Burma.[22] In additio
the Thai people began to expand south, and in the fifty-tw
years between 1243 and 1295 most of the territory whic
now comprises the modern Thai state was abandoned to the
by the Khmers.[23]

The period from the end of the fourteenth century throug
the sixteenth century was one of constant warfare betwee
the Thai and Khmer courts which resulted in successive r
movals of the Cambodian capital—finally to Phnom Penh
1434. Raids and counterraids between the Thais and Khme
continued through the sixteenth century, although the atte
tion of the Thai court was diverted by the pressures of t
reunited Burmese. With the final withdrawal of Burme
forces from Siam in 1587, the relative positions of the Bu
mese and the Thais became set. The Burmans became t
dominant culture group in the Irrawaddy and Salween Riv
valleys and, with another occupation of the Khmer capital
1594, the Thais established themselves as the dominant pow
in the Chao Phraya River delta.[24] The reduction of Camb
dian authority to their west by the Thais during the sixteer
century was followed by similar losses to the Vietname
in the east during the seventeenth century.

The recorded history of Southeast Asia has consisted p
marily of accounts of such raids and counterraids at t
palace elite level. This attitude toward history as being si
ply the history of palace elites is embedded even in langua
itself. Thus the Thai word traditionally used to refer to h
torical events (*phongsavadan*) identified "activities connec
with the royal families of the past."[25] But the significa
changes in the history of the region—the expansion of Khr
cultural and political influence, followed by the ascendan

[22] For a description of this historical period in Burma, re
to Daniel G. E. Hall, *op. cit.*, pp. 147–57.
[23] *Ibid.*, p. 117.
[24] For a decription of this period, refer to *ibid.*, pp. 129–
[25] Sukich Nimmanheminda, "History and Thailand," *Asp*
and Facets of Thailand (Bangkok: The Public Relations Dep
ment, 1959), p. 31.

of the Thais and Vietnamese at the expense of the Khmers—
which have been briefly outlined above, were a centuries-long
process in which the salient factor was not the outcome of
any battle or series of battles between palace elites, but rather
the movements of peoples and the allegiances they brought
with them. It should also be stressed again that from the
point of view of the governing elites in the precolonial period,
the concern was most often with the relative prestige and
power of rival courts and not substantive administrative control over clearly delineated territory or people who to the
present day have continued to move without regard for territorial boundaries. However, the attitude of governing elites
which viewed "history" simply as court history did not survive the colonial period. The consequences of that change
will be considered in the sections which follow.

II. SOME SOURCES OF CONFLICT
IN HISTORICAL PERSPECTIVE

Historically rooted rivalries in Southeast Asia developed
within a milieu similar to that of prefeudal and feudal Europe,[26] but they did not naturally evolve from those patterns
of authority to the now universally assumed structures of the
sovereign state.[27] At the levels of both the governing elites
and the ethnic populations of the region, the gradual evolution from feudal patterns to the modern concepts of the sovereign state which occurred in the West did not take place.
Such an evolution has not taken place to any significant extent
at the level of the mass, but localized, populations—most of
whom still continue to feel primary allegiances to family and
ethnic group rather than to any country in which they are
"citizens," who have little positive respect for the definite borders that define a sovereign state, and who continue to migrate

[26] Arthur L. Basham, *op. cit.*, pp. 93–96.
[27] Southeast Asian political systems did not evolve naturally
from "quasi-feudalism" to the modern sovereign-state form of organization because, even if they might have eventually done so,
the latter form of organization was imposed on them by external
forces while they were still "quasi-feudal," and the current belief
among many is that intermediate steps in the development process can
be "skipped" by these "latecomers."

in response to economic, political, and social pressures. At th
governing level, those concepts which central governmen
elites have inherited from colonial powers are, first, tha
there should be clear and definite borders (as drawn by th
colonial powers themselves), and, second, that the sovereig
authority of a governing elite must extend from border t
border and encompass those communities which reside eithe
wholly or partially within those borders. With the adoptio
of these concepts the long age was over in which rulers i
their palace centers concentrated on vying with each othe
unconcerned with controlling village populations and largel
indifferent to the movements of peoples at the vague frontier
For the postindependence period the two major sources c
interstate conflict in the region have been, first, the legall
established but often ambiguous state boundaries as drawn b
the colonial powers, and, second, the relationships betwee
central state governments and populations whose movemen
and settlement patterns crosscut these borders. We shall co
sider each in turn and shall, because of space limitation
focus on selected examples.

A. STATE BOUNDARIES
IN THE POSTCOLONIAL PERIOD

The process of establishing clearly defined borders betwee
sovereign states in those previously ambiguous areas whi
separated the core areas of traditional kingdoms h
given rise to a multitude of potentially dangerous confl
situations in mainland Southeast Asia. Since the mi
nineteenth century, the establishment of every legally defin
border in Southeast Asia has been disputed by the involv
parties at one time or another. As an illustration of the pr
ess by which contemporary state borders have been det
mined in the region, let us consider the case of Thailand.

By 1851 the Thai monarch, Rama III, claimed domini
over all present day Thailand, plus various northern pr
inces of what is now Malaysia, much of western Cambo
(including the area around Angkor Wat), most of Laos, a
as far as the banks of the Salween River[28] (north of Chie

28 David A. Wilson, *Politics in Thailand* (Ithaca, N.Y.: Corr
University Press, 1962), pp. 2–3.

mai). The definition of clearly articulated borders for Thailand was the result of a series of treaty concessions to the British and French.[29] Thus, although initially Thailand was able to gain French recognition of Thai sovereignty over the Cambodian provinces of Battambang and Siem-Riep in the treaty of 1867, by 1888 the trend of Thai losses as a consequence of European encroachments on their territory had become set. In that year the French successfully "persuaded" the Thais to relinquish their claims to northern Laos and, in 1893, forced the Thais to accept the French claim—as inheritors of the Vietnamese empire—to all the territory east of the Mekong River.[30]

The final concession to the French came in the treaties of 1904 and 1907, when the Thais yielded the provinces of Battambang and Siem-Riep, as well as the province of Sai Buri west of the Mekong River, opposite Luang Prabang).[31] This was followed by the 1909 treaty with Britain, according to which the Thais relinquished all claims to sovereignty over the four Malayan provinces of Kedah, Perlis, Kelantan, and Trengganu.[32]

It should be further noted that during the Japanese occupation of Southeast Asia in World War II, all the territory ceded to the French in the treaties of 1893, 1904, and 1907 was restored to the Thais (who were during most of World War II allies of Japan).[33] However, this particular modern manifestation of Thai expansionism did not survive the defeat of Japan. It is interesting to note that the name "Thailand," rather than "Siam," has been in use during those periods (1939–45 and since 1950) which correspond to resurgent claims to the territory of neighboring states.[34] The name "Siam," on the other hand, was in use prior to 1939 and between 1946 and 1949. Thus, the term Siamese is generally understood to be limited to those Thai from the Chao Praya valley, while the *Thai* are identified with all those who

[29] Daniel G. E. Hall, *op. cit.,* pp. 643–63.
[30] *Ibid.,* p. 661.
[31] David A. Wilson, *op. cit.,* p. 8.
[32] *Ibid.*
[33] Daniel G. E. Hall, *op. cit.,* p. 768.
[34] David A. Wilson, *op. cit.,* p. 1 (fn. 1).

are descendants of the T'ai (i.e., Lao, Shan, T'ai, as well a Siamese).

The extent to which problems between neighboring state are due to the arbitrary demarcation of borders by forme colonial powers is illustrated by the extent to which thes borders were drawn without regard to the direction of pre viously established commercial and governmental interaction Laos and Thailand is a good case in point. A series of Britisl and French demands on the Thais between 1889 and 190 established all of Thailand's "modern" borders. One of th results of this has been that, because of the European pen chant for viewing rivers as barriers rather than as centra transportation corridors, Thailand's border with Laos cut through the center of an economic and cultural unit whic clusters around *both sides* of the Mekong River. This accoun for the situation wherein the central core of the Laotian pec ple is divided almost evenly between the state of Laos an northeastern Thailand. Given the dictum of the sovereig state that the central government must exert control over a communities within its borders, it is indeed significant th more ethnic Lao live in northeast Thailand than within a the territory of the state of Laos itself.[35]

Not only are borders arbitrary in the sense that they divid groups on paper that comprise single units which are n culturally and economically divisible, but the borders then selves are often demarcated differently for different gover ments. Thus, not only are the borders separating the tw Vietnams from Laos and Cambodia not clearly defined, b the governments of North and South Vietnam each defi them differently.[36]

B. ETHNIC MIGRATIONS
IN THE POSTCOLONIAL PERIOD

The problems created by the arbitrariness of the mode

[35] Richard S. D. Hawking, "Contours, Cultures, and Conflict in Nina S. Adams and Alfred W. McCoy (eds.), *Laos: War a Revolution* (New York: Harper & Row, 1970), pp. 4–5.

[36] Jerry M. Silverman, "South Vietnam and the Elusive Peac *Asian Survey*, January 1973 (Vol. XIII), pp. 19–45, and All Goodman, "Ending the Viet Nam Conflict: Expectations in Har and Saigon," *Orbis*, Fall 1972 (Vol. XVI), pp. 632–45.

borders in Southeast Asia in relation to actual ethnic centers of economic and cultural activity and the requirement that central governments exert authority over the disparate populations within these artificial borders are compounded by the continuing migrations of ethnic groups. Let us first consider what has always been the region's most dramatically mobile population, the Vietnamese—and specifically, the migrations of Vietnamese into Cambodia.

Vietnamese who moved into Cambodia during the nineteenth century performed four economic roles—*fonctionnaires* within the colonial government, commercial middlemen, skilled craftsmen, and rural farmers—all but the last to the almost complete exclusion of the Khmers. The settlement of Vietnamese farmers in eastern Cambodia represented the natural continuation of the four-centuries-long movement south and continued beyond the end of formal cessations of territory by the Khmers during the eighteenth century. Beyond that, the final acquisition of Indochina as a colonial possession by the French added further impetus to Vietnamese settlement in Cambodia and Laos, especially in the urban centers. In the peripheral economic centers of colonial Phnom Penh and Vientiane, Vietnamese assumed the role of middlemen in the commercial activities of both the Europeans and the small (but growing) Khmer urban elite. Vietnamese have also provided since that time the skills necessary in such trades as building and carpentry. In short the Vietnamese role in these peripheral commercial centers has been that performed by overseas Chinese throughout the rest of Southeast Asia.

As well as being commercial middlemen, during the colonial period the Vietnamese assumed the role of political middlemen, at least in Cambodian eyes. The French colonial system provided clerical and lower level civil administrative positions to indigenous people within Indochina, and these positions were most often filled by ethnic Vietnamese. Thus within the colonial bureaucracy the private Khmer would often find an ethnic Vietnamese *fonctionnaire* between himself and the French. It did not relieve Cambodian uneasiness that from the French point of view the Vietnamese was, at best, a clerk.[37]

[37] Discussion with Tamotsu Takahashi at the Institute of Developing Economies, Tokyo, on July 27, 1972. Refer also to Ta-

A Khmer professor of history, Muon Khoeun, has argued
that the French colonial interregnum "saved" Cambodia from
the continued expansion of both the Vietnamese and Thai.
In his words: "It is true that French Colonialism was the
most efficient brake on Siamese and Vietnamese expansionism
which otherwise would have swallowed up Khmer and Laotian territory in the nineteenth century."[38] That conclusion is
accurate, however, only insofar as it is limited to Vietnamese
and Siamese political activity directed from the imperial
courts. Its emphasis is only on the palace elite level of political
interaction. While the French did save Cambodia from the
further assertion of authority by the Siamese and Vietnamese
emperors, there is clearly a sense in which the French increased—at the mass level—both Vietnamese participation in
Cambodian political affairs and Khmer resentment and fear
of the Vietnamese. Ironically, the ultimate assertion by the
French of administrative control over Cambodia and Laos
was based on their prior status as Vietnamese protectorates.

The Khmers' fear has been compounded by their realization that historically the Vietnamese acquisition of territory
was the result not of aggressive war directed from the Vietnamese court, but rather of the court extending its authority
over "pioneers." In a chapter written before the South Vietnamese government intervened in Cambodia (March 1970)
Muon Khoeun warned that the historic pattern of peaceful

motsu Takahashi, "Cambodia Ni Okeru Vietnam Jin Mondai Gen
To Rekishiteki Hai Kei" [Present Situation and Historical Bac
ground of the Vietnamese Problem in Cambodia], *Ajia Keiz*
February 1971 (Vol. XII), pp. 25–37.

[38] Muon Khoeun, *Damnoe Chpoh Tau Teuh Khang Le
Noeung Indochen Khnong Chhnam Peepoan* [The Westwa
March: Indochina in the year 2000] (Phnom Penh: Kromh
Rongpun Khmer, 1970), p. 20. A number of younger Khme
some educated in the West, remarked to me during a visit to Phno
Penh in June 1971 that they disliked the French precisely becau
in their view, the French had brought the Vietnamese into Ca
bodia in "responsible" positions during the colonial period. T
book, written by a professor of history at Phnom Penh Universi
was translated with the help of Ny Bun Heang, to whom I owe
great debt of gratitude.

settlement followed by the "expulsion of the original inhabitants" was being repeated.[39] Actually, the Vietnamese did not expel the "original inhabitants," since most Cambodians remained in what is now South Vietnam's delta. What the Vietnamese did do was deny the Cambodian King's authority in that area, and extend the authority of their own Emperor in its place.

During the period between December 1970 and August 1971, when the Cambodian and South Vietnamese governments were engaging in extreme charges and countercharges regarding the behavior of South Vietnamese military forces in Cambodia,[40] a series of political cartoons appeared in Khmer language newspapers in Phnom Penh which accused the South Vietnamese of killing Khmers instead of North Vietnamese, stealing everything from cigarettes to cattle, and allowing Vietnamese civilians to migrate into Cambodian territory in order to settle under the protection of Vietnamese military forces. It is important to note that there is no acceptable evidence that such movement by Vietnamese civilians into Cambodia has actually occurred, and it is extremely unlikely that such has been the case. However, it is a reflection of Khmer fears that many Khmer intellectuals in Phnom Penh assume that the Vietnamese have done so.

The question as to whether or not Vietnamese population movements into Cambodia might take place in the future, especially following an end to the intra-Vietnamese conflict, is impossible to answer with any degree of confidence. Professor Muon Khoeun's expectation is that large numbers of Vietnamese will indeed begin, once again, to immigrate into Cambodia. His argument rests on two points: Vietnam's *manifest destiny* and a need for *Lebensraum*. It is important to note that there is no distinction made between North and South Vietnam in this regard.

With reference to the Cambodian perception that Vietnam

[39] *Ibid.*, pp. 31–32. Refer also to Charles Meyer, "L'implantation Pacifique des Émigrés Vietnamiens en Territoire Khmer," *Études Cambodgiennes,* Avril–Juin 1969 (Vol. XVIII), p. 2.
[40] Associated Press, December 31, 1970.

has some sort of *manifest destiny*, three quotations from Muon Khoeun ought to suffice:

> The destiny of Vietnam is the destiny of a nation which expands its territory by wars and which needs to continue wars in the future.[41]

> The Westward Movement [of Vietnam], in all of it characteristics, is comparable to water flowing downhill. The plain is Cambodia. *No natural obstacle can prevent this Vietnamese flow*.[42] [Emphasis is added.]

> Even though [South] Vietnamese leaders now sympathize with us—they cannot prevent the danger [of Vietnamese expansion] from falling upon our nation because it is only the natural consequence of the evolution of two civilizations of unequal development.[43]

Muon Khoeun's argument that the Vietnamese will necessarily expand because of a need for *Lebensraum* is somewhat more complex. Specific reference is made to the German theory of vital space propounded during the 1930s and the question is asked—"Will there be another Germany in this Region?"[44] The answer which is provided rests on two fundamental assumptions. The first assumption is that population growth in Vietnam will increase at an exponential rate and that by A.D. 2000 the Cambodian delta to their west will once again represent an opportunity because of its fertility and extremely low population density.[45]

The second assumption might be more questionable, but it is instructive because it serves as a useful reminder that American perceptions of Vietnamese as "weak" are not necessarily shared by others whose positions are even weaker. Thus, this second assumption is itself a perception of North Vietnam as a country with *"mighty industries"* and South Vietnam as a country which has "all of the agricultural resources necessary to fulfill the needs of the North."[46]

41 Muon Khoeun, *op. cit.*, p. 31.
42 *Ibid.*, p. 35.
43 *Ibid.*, p. 49.
44 *Ibid.*, pp. 38–39, 42.
45 *Ibid.*, *passim;* especially pp. 117–22.
46 *Ibid.*, p. 34.

united Vietnam is thus seen as an "Economic Power" which would be compelled to once again initiate its Westward movement in order to maintain the dynamism required by a modern and expanding economy.[47]

It is interesting to note that, although Muon Khoeun does refer to historical losses by the Cambodians at the hands of the Thais,[48] he dismisses any modern Thai threat by arguing that the Thais are diverted because of their own problems with ethnic minorities residing within the Thai state.[49]

As intriguing as Muon Khoeun's projection is, alternative reasons for the settlement of Vietnamese immigrants in eastern Cambodia, without government sanction, might be more immediate. At least two groups of Vietnamese are easily identifiable as potential settlers in Cambodia following an end to the war in Vietnam. As in the past, Vietnamese military personnel, on whichever side, who have spent considerable time in Cambodia, might be attracted by "available" land that they have found there and perhaps even cultivated as part of their military duties. A number of such Vietnamese might accept their discharges *in place* and simply stay.

Further, those Vietnamese within South Vietnam itself, who are not willing to accept the consequences of whatever political settlement is finally reached there, may be attracted by the possibilities of moving to the "new frontier." In this regard, Cambodia may be seen by these Vietnamese in much the same way as the South Vietnamese delta was previously seen by their ancestors, i.e., as a frontier just beyond the effective reach of central government authority and with the capability of providing adventurous immigrants with a new start.

The Vietnamese have not been the only peoples on the move in the modern period. Leaving aside consideration of the perennial movement of highland tribal peoples who do not comprise a dominant culture group within any of the for-

[47] *Ibid.*, pp. 34–35.

[48] In Chapter Three of the book entitled *Ananekumnyum Cheang Bey Pan Tonkeek Khnea Nau Indochen* [Confronting the Three Colonialisms in Indochina], he lists the Thai, Vietnamese, and French as the three imperialist powers in Cambodian history.

[49] *Ibid.*, p. 119.

mally constituted sovereign states of Southeast Asia, the Thais,
Khmers, and Laotians have also migrated. Thus, in recent
times, but prior to 1954, Khmers have migrated into Thailand
to avoid the Indochina War.[50] In addition, reports were cir
culating in mid-1972 that some Cambodian families were emi
grating to Malaysia, arriving unannounced and without pa
pers at Malayan-Thai border posts.

The presence of the Cambodian minority in South Vietnam
makes an interesting parallel to the presence of Vietnamese
in Cambodia; in both countries the relationship between the
central government and the ethnic minority has direct conse
quences on the relationship between the two governments.
Within South Vietnam the *Khmer Krom* (i.e., those ethni
Cambodians residing in South Vietnam) are legally recog
nized, for purposes of representation in the National Assem
bly, as one of three distinct minority ethnic groups.[51] Thus
in addition to a special directorate for Development of Viet
namese of Cambodian Origin within the office of the Prime
Minister of the Saigon government, the Khmer Krom have
a designated allocation of seats in the Lower House of the
National Assembly reserved for them.[52] Provisions such as
these simply confirm the lack of integration in the Vietnames

[50] As early as 1885, there were mass immigrations by Khmer
into Thailand as the result of the 1885–86 revolt by Cambodian
against the French; Milton Osborne, *Region of Revolt: Focus o
Southeast Asia* (Sydney: Penguin Books Australia Ltd., 1971
pp. 45–50.

[51] The other two "ethnic minorities" officially recognized t
the government in Saigon are the Chams (the remnants of th
population of Champa) and Montagnards (the highland tribal peo
ples who, although lumped together administratively, are a hetero
geneous group of approximately 650,000 to 950,000 people). The
can be roughly divided along ethnolinguistic lines between Mo
Khmer and Malayo-Polynesian. Gerald C. Hickey, *The Highla
People of South Vietnam: Social and Economic Developme.
*(Santa Monica, Calif.: The Rand Corporation, 1967), lists thirt
five different ethnic groups which can be identified among the
(pp. 16–22).

[52] The Cambodians have reserved for them a total of six sea
out of a total of 159, distributed as follows: one each from Vi
Binh, Chau Doc, Ba Xuyen, Kien Giang, Chuong Thien, and B
Lieu.

delta, wherein attempts at integrating different ethnic and religious groups within a common political community are of very recent origin.

Thus, given the political experience of the delta, the impact of the Vietnamese has been layered; at the village level one finds a Vietnamese society only in Vietnamese villages, while in others Khmer society remains intact.[53] Above this basic societal level, the Vietnamese superstructure is still to a considerable extent "French" influenced.[54] There are essentially two reasons for this. First, the Vietnamese, as the French after them, emphasized the need for maintaining a clear separation between themselves and other ethnic groups.[55] Second, as pointed out above, the political authority of the Vietnamese did not extend over the delta until only a few years prior to the implementation of the French colonial administration. Vietnamese rule, in short, did not last long enough for them to become established as an effective government. Thus, the normal Cambodian reference to the southern delta as *Kampuchea Krom* (i.e., Lower Cambodia) is still somewhat appropriate.

It has been traditional for these Cambodians born in the Vietnamese delta to move back and forth between Vietnam and Phnom Penh for purposes of education and professional advancement.[56] Khmers born in Vietnam have attended high school and university in Phnom Penh, and, in the past, often entered government service there. However, because they sensed that they were discriminated against under Sihanouk

[53] Discussion with Tamotsu Takahashi at the Institute of Developing Economics, Tokyo, on July 28, 1972.

[54] For a description of the French impact on the central bureaucracy of the South Vietnamese government, refer to Nghiem Dang, *South Vietnam: The Politics of Administration* (Honolulu: The East-West Center Press, 1966).

[55] The reasons why the Vietnamese did so, however, were much different than those of the French. For the French, it was a matter of "divide and rule." For the Vietnamese, it was a matter of separating themselves from *barbarian* peoples.

[56] Milton Osborne, "Effacing the 'God-King'—Internal Developments in Cambodia Since March 1970," in Joseph J. Zasloff and Allan Goodman (eds.), *Indochina in Conflict: A Political Assessment* (Lexington, Mass.: D. C. Heath & Co., 1972), p. 66.

because of their place of birth,[57] many of them maintained a sense of their distinctive identity.[58]

One consequence of this trans-border identity has been a dramatic infusion of Khmer Krom participation in and influence on the Phnom Penh government's attempt to survive the current Indochina War. Although it is impossible to obtain exact statistics on anything of significance in Phnom Penh, estimates were circulating there in July 1972 that as much as 12 per cent of the Cambodian Army's field officers were, prior to 1970, Khmer sergeants in South Vietnam's Civilian Irregular Defense Groups (CIDG).[59] Further, many Khmers and informed foreign residents of Phnom Penh claimed that "all" of Cambodia's front-line maneuver battalions were composed of Khmer veterans of such units or, more recently, Khmer mercenaries from the delta provinces of Vietnam who were recruited directly for the express purpose of serving in Cambodia. In these terms, the political loyalties of the Khmer Krom are not easily determined. Most of them are believed by Phnom Penh intellectuals to be serving in Cambodia largely for the money it provides, and it is expected that they will return to *Kampuchea Krom*. Yet, when asked if these mercenaries are thus seen as foreigners, i.e., as *Viet-*

[57] *Ibid.* Osborne points out that not all Khmer Krom felt the impact of discrimination and, as an example, cites the case of Son Sann, who served as Sihanouk's most important economic advisor for many years (*ibid.*, p. 78 [fn 23]).

[58] *Ibid.*, p. 66.

[59] That written above should not necessarily be understood a a reflection on the leadership qualities of such officers. The rank of sergeant was the highest available to members of the CIDG, the officer ranks of which were held, after 1965, by Vietnamese Special Forces officers who were in turn "advised" by officers of the United States Army's Special Forces. CIDG units were composed of ethnic minority groups who were not subject to the Vietnamese "selective service" laws, such as Highlanders. These groups were not mixed within units, however, and many CIDG camps were organized as hamlets, with family groups remaining relatively intact. As American Special Forces personnel were withdrawn from Vietnam as part of the reduction of ground troops there, CIDG was disbanded and Khmer CIDG personnel who did not eventually serve in Cambodia were integrated into ARVN or Vietnamese Regional Force (ARVN—Army of Vietnam).

namese Khmer, the response in Phnom Penh is most often some variant of "No, they are Khmer—we are all Khmer."

On the other hand, the Khmer Krom themselves are unlikely to see any contradiction, for they are all Khmer within a trans-border society where primary loyalties are to the family, not to the state. However, the continued ambiguity of such questions at the governmental levels in Saigon and Phnom Penh is not guaranteed to last.

III. SOME POLICY QUESTIONS AND THEIR RELEVANCE TO INTERSTATE CONFLICT

Because of the superimposition of a "modern" concept of central government authority and sovereign state boundaries on peoples whose allegiances and mobility often continue to follow historic patterns, the present governments of mainland Southeast Asia are confronted with some serious domestic and international problems. While it is impossible to predict how these new concepts of political authority combined with historic patterns of ethnic behavior will in themselves affect international relations in Southeast Asia, it is possible to point to some of the policy questions facing governments in respect to these sources of conduct which will have a strong impact on regional stability. These major policy questions concern, first, the integration of minority ethnic groups, second, a government's protection of the members of its own ethnic group who are living in other countries, and third, the invoking of the past to promote nation-building.

A. THE INTEGRATION OF MINORITY ETHNIC GROUPS

Notions of the sovereign state—such as legal equality between states and citizenship based on secular loyalties—have affected the national political priorities of many of the new elites. It is no longer thought better to achieve recognition through nominal authority over others in lieu of establishing direct political relationships with one's own citizens. Because of this change in values, contemporary conflicts in Southeast Asia are to a significant extent a function of dominant culture groups attempting to extend their authority over weaker culture groups within "their own" borders through the agency of centralizing sovereign state governments.

This development, resulting from the adherence of some elites to the modern notions of the nation-state, can be seen as one which might moderate interstate tensions in the region in the future because the problems of achieving *intra*state political control may so engage the energies and resources of governing elites that they will have little interest in entering into *inter*state conflicts. On the other hand, a policy decision to enter interstate conflicts rather than to refrain from them can also be seen as a likely outcome of such attempts by governments to achieve substantive hegemony within their state borders. Violent conflicts are likely to develop within these states as a result of efforts to integrate minority groups, and they may then involve regional or minority populations of neighboring states as well. Contemporary sovereign state governments are not normally content with the exercise of only nominal authority over those groups residing in peripheral areas. These governments have assumed a mission derived from Europe: *modernization* (establishing a diversified and integrated political and economic infrastructure), and *nation-building* (integrating the whole population of the state into a political community based on common identification through their roles as citizens of a secular state). Modern centralizing elites do not admit the importance of the fact, for instance, that the Thai government is primarily Siamese in a country wherein not everyone is Siamese (the fact that everyone is Thai obscures; it does not clarify), or that the government of South Vietnam is Vietnamese in a country wherein not everyone is Vietnamese.

This problem becomes an international problem when minority groups within one state have cultural affiliations with the core culture groups of another state, or when the normal patterns of communication and interaction of such groups are within territory which transcends particular sovereign-state boundaries. Perhaps the best example of the former is represented by the Vietnamese in Thailand; and the best examples of the latter probably are the Shans along the Thai-Burmese border and the lowland Lao along the Thai-Laotian border.

Traditional activities engaged in by such minorities are easily perceived, according to modern criteria, as involving smuggling, cooperation with *citizens* of a traditionally hostile neighboring state, or innumerable other negative acts. If, as a result of a central government's attempts to enforce its writ throughout its own territory, such minority groups attack government representatives while continuing their traditional cross-border activities, the government of the neighboring state may erroneously be seen as supporting aggression because of the assumption that it is providing sanctuaries and base areas for the "rebels."

This potentiality for interstate violence as a result of attempts by elites to integrate all minority ethnic groups within rigid state borders could be lessened. Such a moderating effect, however, could result only if the governing elites themselves were willing to qualify their basic policy assumptions about the integration of minority groups within their borders and the strict maintenance of sharply drawn geographical borders. Instead of a policy of control of ethnic minority groups in peripheral areas, it would require a recognition of the political interpermeability of such borders, while guaranteeing the integrity of the core center of the culture group around which these new sovereign states will be built. This would, of course, also require less hard and fast notions of geographically defined boundaries on the part of central government elites. Such modifications of policy assumptions would comprise a truly *modern*, but fundamentally *Southeast Asian*, pattern of cooperative political relationships. However, if these assumptions are not so moderated, the desire to integrate minorities within borders might lead to policy decisions to wholly integrate such groups, even those members residing beyond the state's borders. It might be determined that the most efficient method of integrating the Khmer Krom into modern secular Vietnam, for instance, would require the elimination of any autonomous Khmer government in Phnom Penh (or anywhere else) which could compete for Khmer loyalties. A Vietnamese national leadership might conclude that it is easier to politically integrate *all* Khmers than it would be to integrate only *some* Khmers.

B. GOVERNMENT PROTECTION OF MEMBERS
OF "ITS" ETHNIC GROUP WHO ARE LIVING
IN OTHER COUNTRIES

A second policy problem results from the marriage of central governments, which represent major core ethnic groups, to the political activities of those members of its own ethnic group who reside in other countries. The issue at stake is whether the members of this ethnic group are to be recognized as legitimate subjects of the state in which they are living or as members of a larger ethnic group which seems to require protection by that group's representatives in another state government.

As described above, much of the internecine warfare in precolonial times was the result of one king attacking another for symbolic purposes—without lasting substantive effect. The result was that although conflict event followed conflict event in a chain of actions and reactions, the purpose was most often to confirm a set of prior relationships or reinforce a broader system of conflict behaviors and authority relationships. The consequence of the adoption of modern concepts of the sovereign state by the national centralizing leaderships has been the linkage of the governmental apparatus of the state with the political activities of major cultural groups more broadly defined.

Thus, although historically there were conflicts both at the palace elite level and between culture groups at the level of local communities, seldom were these two levels of intergroup conflict joined. We sometimes see elements of the latter type of conflict without the direct participation of sovereign state governments (e.g., Khmer anti-Vietnamese riots) and at times against the express wishes of such governments (e.g., Malaya anti-Chinese riots). Yet, we also have examples of these governments, which represent—at least in some respects —what used to be the palace elite, assuming the role of advocates in what would have previously remained conflicts between ethnic groups at the local community level. Examples of such behavior are plentiful, but reference to the Vietnamese governments' (the North, the South, and Provisional) protestations over the Khmer population's treatment of Vietnamese residing in Cambodia, the People's Republic of China's role in verbally defending overseas Chinese residents in Southeast Asia, and the attempts by the governments of Thailand and North Vietnam to reach a solution, through negotiations, to the problems caused by the ethnic Vietnamese population in Thailand, ought to suffice as examples. The point is, of course, that the volatility of conflicts between different ethnic groups at the local community level escalates dramatically when sovereign state governments join as advocates for one side or the other.

C. THE INVOKING OF THE PAST
TO PROMOTE NATION-BUILDING

We have seen in the earlier sections of this paper how the precolonial palace elites attempted to win the acquiescence of the peoples in their core regions through lavish displays of pomp and wealth. The modern centralizing governments face the problem of winning the allegiance of their subjects to the *state,* rather than to those symbols associated with the person of the King. In order to accomplish this, they have felt the need to convince their citizens of the glories of the state, just as the precolonial elites felt the need to convince the village level communities around them of the glories of the court and the King. Thus, modern centralizing governments may choose to play on those ancient prejudices of the ethnic communities directed against others which were kept from erupting into violence during the colonial period. John Badgley alluded to this prospect when he wrote:

> The European colonial presence, extending in Southern Asia for periods of 60 to 250 years, stifled popular warfare against enemy neighbor states. This impact may result in less influence by the "traditional enemy factor," since three to ten generations have lived without the violence that was normal prior to the colonial period. It is conceivable, therefore, that suspicion of neighbors may not have significance in this region for another generation, until governments are formed with a wide popular base, which will reintroduce popular traditional

prejudices harbored within the villages throughout the colonial period.[60]

The policy problems posed for a government elite by minority ethnic groups within its borders and by members of its own ethnic group who are living in other countries are compounded by the penchant of the indigenous elites, in their passion for *modernization*, to project their future hopes and aspirations onto their political histories. Thus, a method available to centralizing governments in the region to evoke ethnic prejudices and thus create nationalistic fervor is the creation of nationalistic histories. An anonymous anthropologist has phrased the problem facing the nationalist political leaderships of the previously Indianized kingdoms of Asia in the form of the question: "What past for a glorious future?"[61] That question was echoed by those Indonesian historians who attended a conference in the mid-1950s on the proper role of historiography in a postcolonial "developing" coun-

[60] John Badgley, *Asian Development: Problems and Prognosis* (New York: The Free Press, 1971), p. 159.

[61] An example of a search for a "glorious past" not tainted by the experiences of recent history was emerging in Phnom Penh during 1971–73, where President Lon Nol began to refer to his countrymen as members of the *Khmer-Mon* race (Boris Baczynski, "Lon Nol's Private War," *The Far Eastern Economic Review*, July 1, 1972, Vol. 77, p. 23). This was accompanied by the establishment of an Institute of Khmer-Mon Studies in Phnom Penh. Although it is true that the Mons of Lower Burma and the Khmer are physically related and share certain cultural traits, it is a distortion of Southeast Asian history to imply that the Cambodians and the Mons are "one people." It is not at all clear what prompted the Phnom Penh leadership to articulate this newly discovered definition of their soul. When queried during a visit to Phnom Penh in July 1972, more than one Khmer responded with a variant of "I don't know. If you can figure it out, let us know." Thus, although one can only speculate, it may have been due to a desire by the "republican" government to detach Cambodia's future from the symbolic power of Angkor–both because the Angkor kingdom represented the solidification of Hindu concepts of *kingship* and because of the government's inability to occupy Angkor against their opponents. It is extremely doubtful that it represented a dream of eventual expansion, since–given Khmer fears of their own weakness *vis-à-vis* its immediate neighbors–such a dream would be beyond any conceivable *raison*.

try.[62] However, such a need is not limited to incumbent political leaders; it is also a need of the leaders of opposition elites whose desire it is to replace the incumbents, not to destroy the inherent structures of sovereign state government. Even those leadership elites are not prone to interpret their own histories in a manner which would destroy the rationale for centralized authority within such structures. It is necessary for both these types of "modernizing" elites to ensure that their history is understood in terms which support the projected future of the integrated "nation-state" for which they have assumed the leadership. Thus, the need to project the future into the past is understandable. Sukarno, perhaps, most clearly articulated this need for a nationalist historiography when he wrote:

> First we point out to the people that they have a glorious past, secondly we intensify the notion among the people that the present time is dark, and the third way is to show them the promising, pure, and luminous future and how to get there.[63]

However much one might sympathize with the need for such histories for the new political societies of many of the postcolonial "developing" states in Asia and Africa, such a stress on traditional conflicts can have grievous consequences for the future stability and development of Southeast Asia. In their attempts to create a state-centered nationalism among their citizens, it is easy to project modern nationalist assumptions onto the precolonial conflicts engaged in by the Indianized monarchs of the region. The result of this is often the interpretation of these precolonial conflicts as nation-*state* conflicts rather than the highly stylized interactions of small elites.

The replacement of an international system based on *suzerainty* by one based on *sovereignty* has resulted in a situation wherein modern national elites are cross-pressured—either to expand their actual authority within tertiary areas or to with-

---

[62] Bambang Detom, "Some Remarks on Modern Indonesian Historiography" in Daniel G. E. Hall (ed.), *Historians of Southeast Asia* (London: Oxford University Press, 1961).

[63] Sukarno, as quoted in *ibid.*, p. 75.

draw completely from the exercise of legitimate authority in those areas. Traditionally the rulers of the major kingdoms in Southeast Asia exercised *less control* over the population of *more territory* than that of contemporary sovereign state political leaders. That is, monarchs often claimed authority over vast territory, including that claimed by competitors and occupied by subordinate kings. The traditional pattern of authority, based as it was on the progressive reduction of a monarch's authority as distance increased between the palace and the "border area," resulted in minimal control over extended territory. With only minor exceptions, all the territory in mainland Southeast Asia has at one time or another been claimed by the political ancestors of more than one of the contemporary sovereign states of the region.

Thus, although Siam did exercise some authority over most of modern-day Laos (as did the Vietnamese—sometimes concurrently), it did not exercise the type of authority that a modern sovereign state or derivative colonial government is expected to exercise. In short, the heritage of the past in this regard has been to create an "attraction of opposites" for the centralizing political elites of the region: on the one hand they are drawn to an abandonment of any claims to those peripheral territories which history impressionistically "justifies" as their own, or they feel compelled to assert forms of authority and control which clearly exceed those of the past.

To the extent that the development of modern nationalisms has often been a consequence of a perception of a past characterized by a grandeur which had been destroyed by an externalized enemy, an emphasis upon the "glorious victories" or "treacherous defeats" of the past appear to have some utility. Rupert Emerson has perceptively written: "Reduced to its bare bones, nationalism is no more than the assertion of a particular *we* arrayed against the *they* of the rest of mankind."[64] Nothing could be more disastrous for the peoples of Southeast Asia than if the problems resulting from the attempt to accomplish political integration within these countries were "solved" at the cost of increasing political hostility between them.

[64] Rupert Emerson, *From Empire to Nation* (Cambridge, Mass.: Harvard University Press, 1960), p. 213.

II
Domestic Societies

The Influence on Foreign Policy of Ethnic Minorities with External Ties[1]

R. STEPHEN MILNE

The ethnic minorities considered in this paper are the Chinese and to a lesser extent the Indians. The phrase "with external ties" is taken to mean "with ties outside Southeast Asia," not "with ties external to a particular Southeast Asian country to another inside Southeast Asia." Consequently, minorities such as Cambodians in Vietnam, Vietnamese in Cambodia, Malays in Thailand, Shans in Burma, Vietnamese in Thailand, and so on, will not be considered here. Such minorities are the relics of wars, cessions of territory, and unregulated movements over boundaries having only legalistic significance. Hunter[2] draws some distinctions between Chinese and Indian minorities, on the one hand, and local Southeast Asian minorities, on the other. The former are more likely to be regarded as intruders, who *could* in the final instance be legitimately expelled. They are obviously culturally different, having brought with them the patina of a different major civilization, of which they are openly proud. Sometimes they have a different religion. Often they are felt to be economically threatening.[3] Apart from the "major civilization" point, these distinctions are not completely watertight. Vietnamese in Cambodia have often been regarded as intruders, and sometimes have been actually expelled; they

[1] This paper deals almost entirely with countries whose foreign policies were not being affected by large-scale open warfare in 1972; that is, it excludes Cambodia, both the Vietnams, and all the Laoses.

[2] Guy Hunter, *Southeast Asia–Race, Culture, and Nation* (New York: Oxford University Press, 1966), p. 10.

[3] *Ibid.*

have also been viewed as an economic threat by the Cambodians. Indeed, Vietnamese in Cambodia are decidedly less popular than the "external" Chinese. Also, Malays in Thailand have a different religion from Thais, while most Chinese in Thailand do not. However, by and large, there is a broad distinction between the two types of minorities. An important point not made by Hunter is that Chinese and Indian minorities for the most part have more visibility and hence are likely to produce more marked reactions; they tend to cluster in urban centers or at least in the country's core area, while the other minorities are in remote and amorphous hill or border areas. Certainly, when foreign policy is considered, the status of China, and to a lesser extent India, as an international power is sufficient reason for treating these two types of minorities separately, and for giving prominence to those with external ties. Greater attention will be paid to Chinese than to Indian ethnic minorities for four reasons: the Chinese minorities are the more numerous; they play a role in more of the Southeast countries; China is closer to Super Power status than is India, and it has a greater interest in Southeast Asia.

Before considering Indian and then Chinese ethnic minorities, some basic determinants of foreign policy will be mentioned in order to show the possible complicating effects of ethnic minorities. Some obvious factors may contribute to good relations between Asian Great Powers, in this instance India and China, and particular states in Southeast Asia, such as the wish to promote trade and the desire for stability, and to ensure that other Great Powers are not able to use the existence of conflict in the area in order to penetrate it further. Less tangibly, similar systems of government and common membership of institutions, such as the British Commonwealth, may contribute in a general way toward goodwill. There are, equally obviously, other factors which may lead to conflict; desire for expansion, not necessarily to adjacent territories but possibly through the assertion of hegemony; heterogeneity of political systems, which in an extreme form might lead to ideological proselytizing or subversion by the Great Power. Within these parameters the personalities of politicians may play a considerable part. When minorities with ethnic ties to Asian Great Powers are added to the picture, extra dimensions are introduced. A good deal depends on the characteristics of the minorities. What percentage of the population do they constitute? What is the degree of their assimilation in their country of residence? To what extent do they identify with the cultural tradition, with the form of government, and with the economic policies of the Great Power from whose territory their ancestors derived? Are there memories of past clashes with the government of their country of residence, in which the ethnic group was aided, materially or morally, by the Great Power concerned? How does the existence in Southeast Asian countries of "related" ethnic minorities affect the foreign policy of the Asian Great Power, India or China? Does it give priority to the wish to enjoy friendly relations with the Southeast Asian country concerned, or is it bent upon preserving close ties with the ethnic minority and acting as its protector? On the other hand, what are the effects on the foreign policy of the Southeast Asian state? Does anxiety over the loyalty of its ethnic minority increase its search for security and lead to the conclusion of alliances with external Great Powers, rivals of the Great Power linked to the ethnic minority, which might not otherwise have been made? Does such an anxiety lead it to conclude alliances with other Southeast Asian countries with similar minorities and sharing similar fears? This paper will not go through these questions systematically; the answers are not sufficiently tidy or complete to justify such a procedure. The questions are intended, rather, to indicate how the existence of such minorities may be one element in shaping the foreign policies of Southeast Asian countries.

Indian immigration into Burma on a significant scale began in the second half of the nineteenth century, and was concentrated in the Irrawaddy Delta. Most Indians were in nonagricultural occupations, although Chettiar moneylenders became large landowners in the Delta. In 1931 Indians constituted more than half the population of Rangoon, although only 7 per cent of the whole population of Burma. Since then the proportion of Indians has decreased. About half the Indians who were in Burma when war reached it in December 1941 fled to India. Some came back after the war, although the Chettiars were badly hit financially by postwar legislation. There was a further exodus, probably of at least one hundred and fifty thousand persons, following the Ne Win government's legislation of 1962 and 1963, nationalizing major industries, banks, and wholesale and retail trade, and restricting moneylending licenses to Burmese citizens. There are now probably about three hundred thousand Indians in Burma, slightly over 1 per cent of the population. Each of these reductions in the Indian population led to claims for compensation by those affected and to Indian dissatisfaction with Burma.[4] It is surprising that relations between the two countries were not worse. However, Indian policy toward Southeast Asia in general was one of restraint, except verbally and psychologically. "India's main objective in Southeast Asia was to assist the creation and support the maintenance of independent states in the region. In pursuing that objective India had to face the dilemma that doing anything concrete to that end would also tend to defeat it, because India could be regarded as a powerful alien influence in the area."[5] Perhaps policy toward Burma was especially restrained because India was concerned not to revive memories of the subordinate position to India which Burma had once occcupied under the British. Moreover, U Nu and Nehru had similar social philosophies and foreign policies,[6] and good personal relationships were symbolized in a Treaty of Friendship (1951). India was concerned to have a stable Burma, and to that end was instrumental in giving and co-

---

[4] On Indians in Burma, Malaysia, and Singapore, see: Usha Mahajani, *The Role of Indian Minorities in Burma and Malaya* (Bombay: Vora & Co., 1960); Kernial Singh Sandhu, *Indians in Malaya: Immigration and Settlement, 1786–1957* (Cambridge, England: Cambridge University Press, 1969); N. R. Chakravarti, *The Indian Minority in Burma* (London: Oxford University Press, 1971); R. Hatley, "The Overseas Indians in Southeast Asia: Burma, Malaysia and Singapore," in Robert O. Tilman, ed., *Man, State, and Society in Contemporary Southeast Asia* (New York: Frederick A. Praeger, 1969), pp. 450–66.

[5] Charles H. Heimsath and Surjit Mansingh, *A Diplomatic History of Modern India* (Calcutta: Allied Publishers, 1971), p. 225.

[6] But this did not mean that Burma "followed" India's foreign policy (cf. Chakravarti, *op. cit.,* p. 184).

ordinating economic and military aid to Burma, 1948–50, to help her overcome the threat of Communist and ethnic rebel groups.[7] Even though the nationalization measures of 1962–63 were carried out by Ne Win and not U Nu, they were undeniably "socialist," and therefore not vulnerable to Indian government attack on principle. In point of fact the Indian government's reaction was relatively restrained.[8] Under Ne Win, Burma has not had a very prominent foreign policy, and there is not much evidence that it has been influenced by the Indian minority, now numerically weaker than ever before. In Indo Burma relations contiguity of territory was a more important factor than the existence of the minority. And even India's close geographical presence was overshadowed when India and China came into conflict. Burma was aware that India could not defend it against Chinese intervention.[9]

Before World War Two almost two-fifths of the Indian population of Burma was Muslim, located mainly in Rangoon and Arakan. Despite this, and the fact that Burma has a "short" border with what used to be East Pakistan, Burma has not had very active relations with Pakistan. There have been frictions arising from border disputes and from the exodus of Muslims of Indian origin, but no really serious tensions.[10]

The influx of Indians into Malaya and Singapore occurred mainly between the 1830s and the 1930s. They came overwhelmingly from the south of India, and were predominantly Tamil. Only a very small proportion was Muslim. Indians now constitute almost 10 per cent of the population in West Malaysia (Malaya), a slightly smaller proportion in Singapore. Occupationally, Indians are fairly evenly distributed, but

[7] Sisir Gupta, *India and Regional Integration in Asia* (London: Asia Publishing House, 1964), pp. 14, 75–76.

[8] High Tinker, *The Union of Burma* (London: Oxford University Press, 1961), p. 357.

[9] Heimsath and Mansingh, *op. cit.*, p. 243.

[10] Mujtaba Razvi, *The Frontiers of Pakistan* (Karachi: National Publishing House, 1971), Chapter 5; K. B. Sayeed, "Southeast Asia in Pakistan's Foreign Policy," *Pacific Affairs*, 1968 (Vol. XLI, No. 2), p. 238.

there is a concentration in clerical occupations and among estate workers. Malaya's (and Malaysia's) relations with India have been consistently friendly, as have Singapore's since 1965.[11] However, it is doubtful to what extent the existence of an Indian minority has been responsible for this. To be sure, there is ". . . in Malaysia a sizeable enough minority from the Indian subcontinent to keep Kuala Lumpur keenly sensitive to the currents of Indian foreign policy . . ."[12] Tengku Abdul Rahman gave three reasons why Malaya supported India during the Indian-Chinese war. One was India's peaceful emergence from British rule, faith in democracy and membership of the Commonwealth, through which friendly relations with Malaya had been established. A second was Malaya's sympathy because she herself had suffered from a Communist rebellion (1948–60). A third was that, if China was successful, she might later attack Malaya.[13] These reasons might have been sufficient to account for Malaya's relations with India, even if she had had no Indian minority at all. India was important to Malaya because she was regarded as an obstacle to Chinese expansion.

> India is the world's largest democracy. India is the sentinel of Asia. She stands guard along the Himalayas for the defence of Asia against the most dangerous implacable totalitarian force the world has ever known. If India's power or status is eroded, however slightly, the repercussions would flow like earth tremors throughout non-Communist Asia. And freedom, democracy and all the civilized values we cherish would be dealt a severe blow.[14]

The external ties of the Indian minority in both Malaysia and Singapore are viewed as neither dangerous nor significant, unless there were to be a direct conflict between the attach-

11 Heimsath and Mansingh, *op. cit.,* pp. 249–52.

12 Peter Boyce, *Malaysia and Singapore in International Diplomacy* (Sydney, Australia: Sydney University Press, 1968), p. 188.

13 R. S. Milne, *Government and Politics of Malaysia* (Boston: Houghton Mifflin, 1967), p. 182.

14 Dato M. Ghazali Shafie, October 28, 1965, quoted in Boyce, *op. cit.,* p. 193.

ments of overseas Indians. Indian governmental assurances that Indians who have become nationals of Southeast Asian states should be loyal to their new countries are accepted as genuine. The Indian minorities in Malaysia, Singapore, and present-day Burma do not have much effect on these countries' foreign policies.

Relations between Malaya/Malaysia and Pakistan were not good in the early 1960s, especially during "Confrontation" between Malaya and Indonesia. The former was supported by India and the latter by Pakistan. However, there was no great reaction on the part of Indians of Muslim origin in Malaya. Their numbers were relatively small, and a high proportion of them had become assimilated as Malays.

The overseas Chinese, however, have had a profound effect on foreign policy. While the Indians in aggregate constitute less than 1 per cent of the population of Southeast Asia, the Chinese total[15] amounts to over 5 per cent. The distribution between countries is very uneven, as is shown in Table 1.

The countries in the table may be placed in three distinct groups. In most, the percentage of Chinese is quite low, at most about 10 per cent (Thailand). In the countries which formed Malaysia in 1963, Malaya, Sarawak, and North Borneo (and also Brunei), the percentage was from about one-fifth to about one-third of the total. In Singapore it was three-quarters of the total. Obviously, these great differences are likely to affect both domestic and foreign policy. For this reason Malaysia and Singapore are each analyzed separately in later sections of this paper.

The immigrant Chinese came mostly from the south of China, the main dialect groups represented being Teochiu, Hokkien, Cantonese, Hakka, and Hainanese. The state of peace or war in south China determined the supply, and led to increases in emigration in the middle of the seventeenth

[15] On overseas Chinese generally, see: Hunter, *op. cit.;* Victor Purcell, *The Chinese in Southeast Asia* (London: Oxford University Press, 1965); Maurice Freedman, *The Chinese in Southeast Asia: A Longer View* (London: China Society, 1964); G. William Skinner, *Report on the Chinese in Southeast Asia* (Ithaca, N.Y.: Cornell University Press, 1951).

TABLE 1
Proportion of Ethnic Chinese
in Southeast Asia by Country*

Country	Percentage of Chinese
Burma	1.5
Thailand	10.0
North Vietnam	0.5
South Vietnam	5.5
Cambodia	6.5
Laos	2.0
Malaya	35.5
Singapore	75.0
Sarawak	30.0
North Borneo [Sabah]	21.5
Brunei	26.0
Indonesia	2.5
Portuguese Timor	1.0
Philippines	1.5

* Based on 1960 figures estimated by Purcell, *op. cit.*, p. 3, with some amendments. Figures have been rounded off to the nearest half per cent. Many are unreliable because of lack of accurate censuses, varying definitions of who is "Chinese," or the presence of Chinese who entered the country extralegally.

century and again in the second half of the nineteenth century. The demand for them was great in Thailand, especially during the reign of King Taksin (1767–82); in Java and the Philippines from time to time a drop in demand was signaled by massacres. Demand was increased by the opening up of the British territories during the nineteenth century. Immigration slowed down in the second quarter of the twentieth century. The balance shifted toward the Chinese becoming permanent rather than temporary, and the proportion of locally born Chinese rose. The stereotype of the overseas Chinese was that they were preponderantly traders, financiers, and retailers, people who "knew how to handle money and organize men in relation to money."[16] This was substantially accurate, but it obviously could not apply in countries where the Chinese formed a high proportion of the population. In Malaya, for example, after World War Two agriculture was the most important occupation of the Chinese in every state except Penang.[17] Chinese farmers are also prominent in Sabah and Sarawak. Even in Indonesia the great majority of the Chinese in the Outer Islands were concentrated in three small areas (East Sumatra, the tin-producing islands of Bangka and Belitung, the Singkawang and Pontianak districts of western Borneo), where they were employed largely in agricultural production.

The potential influence of overseas Chinese on the policies of the various Southeast Asian states is obviously related to the extent to which they are assimilated. As an extreme case, thoroughly assimilated Chinese would, by definition, not need to be considered as a factor in foreign policy. The actual picture is not as simple as might be suggested by this hypothetical example. Nevertheless, the question may be approached from two angles: what are the customs, practices, and attitudes of the overseas Chinese?; what have been the policies of the Southeast Asian governments toward them?

Overseas Chinese may be separated from the local population by reason of their skin color or their religion, or by virtue of peculiarly Chinese institutions or organizations, language, schools, clan associations, secret societies, etc. They stand out by reason of their transactions with China, irrespective of who controls China at any given moment, such as returning to China for study, or sending remittances for the support of relatives. Beyond this the prospect is less clear. A statement by Elegant may need some modification, namely that the "loyalty given to China by the overseas Chinese is the more profound because it is largely irrational";[18] per-

---

[16] Maurice Freedman, "The Handling of Money: A Note on the Background to the Economic Sophistication of Overseas Chinese," *Man,* April 1959 (Vol. LIX, No. 89), p. 65.

[17] Skinner, *op. cit.,* p. 41.

[18] Robert S. Elegant, *The Dragon's Seed* (New York: St. Martin's Press, 1959), p. 4.

haps "irrational" should be replaced by "intangible." Many overseas Chinese are said to have an affinity for "Chinese culture," although they may be rather vague about its nature. In effect it may amount to little more than an attachment to what is believed to be traditionally Chinese. A Dutch-educated Chinese in Indonesia put it not very clearly and therefore quite accurately:

> If you ask me what Chinese culture is, I cannot say. We cannot define it exactly, but we know that we like it and want to keep it. Partly it is the language. We believe that our children in this country should go to national [Indonesian] schools, but we also want them to learn Chinese. We want them to be loyal to Indonesia as their country, but we hope that they will not forget Chinese culture.[19]

There is a distinction between "cultural nationalism" and "racial nationalism," on the one hand, and "political nationalism" on the other.[20] Overseas Chinese may be a long way from complete assimilation, yet politically they may identify with the Southeast Asian country in which they live, as did the Indonesian Chinese quoted above.

The degree of assimilation of different groups of Chinese at different times in different Southeast Asian countries may vary considerably. At one end of the time-scale, the early Chinese immigrants, with no fully established Chinese institutions in existence when they arrived and without an adequate supply of Chinese women, probably assimilated fairly easily. More recently, because Chinese immigration to Southeast Asia virtually stopped over thirty years ago, a decreasing proportion of the overseas Chinese have any personal memory of China, which may result in a lessening of emotional attachments to China.[21] In any case, it is possible to see some differences between the "Babas" of the Straits Settlements

[19] Donald E. Willmott, *The Chinese of Semarang* (Ithaca, N.Y.: Cornell University Press, 1960), pp. 228–29.

[20] Donald E. Willmott, *The National Status of the Chinese in Indonesia, 1900–1958* (Ithaca, N.Y.: Cornell University Press, 1961), pp. 68–70.

[21] Although it might have the reverse effect because of "starved curiosity" about China [Lea E. Williams, *The Future of the Overseas Chinese in Southeast Asia* (New York: McGraw-Hill, 1966), p. 75].

in Malaya, who acquired many Malay characteristics, and later Chinese immigrants.[22] A similar contrast is found in Indonesia between the "Peranakans" (native born) and "Totoks" (immigrants, although also including some Indonesian-born with less deep local roots).[23] No complete dividing lines can be drawn between these groups, but some of the more visible signs of "Chineseness" are disappearing. "It is generally recognized that the Totoks are more industrious and enterprising than the local-born Chinese. The latter are simply not willing to work twelve and fourteen hours a day in the struggle for economic success."[24]

Southeast Asian governments have not been very consistent in their treatment of the overseas Chinese. They have been aware of them as a "problem," although its exact nature and the broad lines of the solution have seldom been openly defined. The Chinese are not only highly visible, being concentrated in urban centers, but some are also highly successful financially. In the absence of corresponding financial success by the indigenous people, governmental power is exercised so as to extract tribute from them in their role as "pariah entrepreneurs."[25] They are thus seen as an obvious impediment to postindependence "nationalism," to the doctrine that each Southeast Asian country should have a national language of its own, see itself as a descendant of a precolonial power or empire, search for its own *ethos* or ideology. Faced with the actual presence of overseas Chinese, some governments tried to curtail or eliminate obvious signs of Chineseness which clashed with nationalism. Restrictions were placed on Chinese schools,[26] and only in Singapore was Chinese made an official language. In some countries restric-

---

[22] Compare the more sophisticated categories of overseas Chinese in Malaya used in Wang Gungwu, "Chinese Politics in Malaya," *The China Quarterly*, July–September 1970 (No. 43), pp. 1–30.

[23] Maurice Freedman, *The Chinese in Southeast Asia: A Longer View, op. cit.*

[24] G. William Skinner, *op. cit.,* p. 64.

[25] Fred W. Riggs, *Administrative Behavior in Developing Countries* (Boston: Houghton Mifflin, 1964), pp. 188–93.

[26] D. P. Murray, "Chinese Education in Southeast Asia," *China Quarterly*, 1964 (No. 20), pp. 67–95.

tions were placed on Chinese trading activities in order to make room for expected indigenous enterprises.[27] On citizenship there was considerable confusion, added to in Indonesia by the long negotiations between Djakarta and Peking referred to below. A simple, not to say simplistic, approach, adopted in South Vietnam in 1956, was to impose citizenship on all local-born Chinese in the hope that *ipso facto* this would achieve assimilation by creating new loyalties. In other countries it was made more difficult to acquire citizenship because it was felt that loyalties could not be created by the stroke of the pen, and because there was no desire to defend Chinese against indigenous claims by giving them apparent legal protection. There does not seem to be any evidence to support Simoniya's claim that discrimination against overseas Chinese was intensified after the formation of the Chinese People's Republic in 1949.[28] It is more plausible to see the spread of discrimination as coinciding with the end of colonialism. The colonialists were not nationalists, indeed by definition they were rather the reverse, and the Chinese did not constitute an obstacle to colonial rule. It is significant that the single country in Southeast Asia where discrimination existed before World War Two was independent Thailand. Indeed, one authority says that ". . . Thai nationalism originated as an attitude towards the Chinese minority."[29]

[27] See: Remigio E. Agpalo, *The Political Process and the Nationalization of the Retail Trade in the Philippines* (Quezon City: University of the Philippines, Office of Coordinator of Research, 1962); Edgar Wickberg, "Economic Nationalism and the Chinese in the Philippines" in Charles O. Houston, ed., *Proceedings of the First National Colloquium on the Philippines; Research and Development in the Social Sciences* (Kalamazoo: Institute of International Area Studies, Western Michigan University, 1969). The Indonesian restrictions in the 1950s are summarized in Purcell, *op. cit.,* pp. 487–89.

[28] N. A. Simoniya, *Overseas Chinese in Southeast Asia—A Russian Study* (Ithaca, N.Y.: Cornell University Press, 1961), p. 83.

[29] David A. Wilson, "Thailand and Marxism" in Frank N. Trager (ed.), *Marxism in Southeast Asia* (Stanford, Calif.: Stanford University Press, 1959), p. 75. On the Chinese in Thailand generally, see: Richard J. Coughlin, *Double Identity, The Chinese in Modern Thailand* (Hong Kong: Hong Kong University Press, 1960); G. William Skinner, *Chinese Society in Thailand: An An-*

The extent of the (at least verbal) concern of some Southeast Asian governments about Chinese minorities is shown by their fear of a strengthening of overseas Chinese influence, not in their own countries, but in adjacent territories. Both Indonesia[30] and the Philippines[31] expressed apprehension that the creation of Malaysia would lead to just such a spread of Chinese influence, with a consequent spill over to their own territories. Control of Chinese minorities was probably a tacit aim of the short-lived association of Indonesia, the Philippines, and Malaya in the form of Maphilindo (1963).

There is a wide range of opinion on the degree of assimilation of the overseas Chinese, from those who are basically optimistic[32] to others who are on the whole skeptical.[33] Two points seem to be firmly established. Assimilation is not a one-way affair. It depends not only on the overseas Chinese themselves, but also on the attitude and policies of the Southeast Asian governments concerned, which may be contradictory, measures compelling assimilation being accompanied by others which perpetuate discrimination. Also, it is undeniable that on some occasions the Chinese *have* been assimilated in large numbers, and that even where they have not been assimilated, under some conditions their culture has undergone erosion.[34]

To what extent are the loyalties of the overseas Chinese loyalties to a *Communist* China? It has been remarked that loyalty is not a simple concept. In answering questions about whether the overseas Chinese are "pro-this" or "anti-that," a basis might be that many overseas Chinese are now suffi-

alytical History (Ithaca, N.Y.: Cornell University Press, 1957). Note also that opposition to Chinese economic competition led to the foundation of the Indonesian nationalist organization, *Sarekat Islam,* in 1911.

[30] G. McT. Kahin, "Malaysia and Indonesia," *Pacific Affairs,* Fall 1964 (Vol. XXXVII, No. 3), p. 264.

[31] "London Talks: Statement by Philippines Vice-President, 28 January 1963," quoted in Boyce, *op. cit.,* p. 118–19.

[32] Williams, *op. cit.*

[33] Justus M. van der Kroef, *Communism in Malaysia and Singapore* (The Hague: Martinus Nijhoff, 1967), p. 259.

[34] Maurice Freedman, *The Chinese in Southeast Asia: a Longer View, op. cit.*

ciently detached from China to be primarily "pro-overseas
Chinese." This might be a useful corrective to the view that
the overseas Chinese "are woven into a giant subversive net
ready to paralyze and conquer Southeast Asia on command
from Peking . . ."[35] Yet, on several levels, the appeal of
China to the overseas Chinese is strong. Communism has
the attraction of transcending the narrower bounds of nationalism which they find oppressive in Southeast Asia. At the
same time, especially for the Chinese-educated, the identification of China itself with the major center of Communism in
the region must inevitably, by a rub-off effect, give the impression that Communism is "Chinese." These attractions are
intensified by the enhanced status of China as a world power.
If the overseas Chinese felt devotion to her when she was
relatively weak, it would be only natural for this devotion to
grow when she was strong.[36] The attraction of Communist
China is not limited to youthful idealists; it is felt even by
those who might be expected to oppose Communism on economic grounds. By one estimate, ninety per cent of the Chinese "capitalists" in Pontianak, Indonesian Borneo, were pro-
Communist in the mid-1950s.[37]

It used to be fashionable to make estimates of the relative
numbers of overseas Chinese who supported Peking or Taipei. These have become less and less necessary, because the
influence of Peking is now preponderant. Since Peking's admission to the United Nations and her increasing government-
to-government contacts with Southeast Asian countries, it
is now unmistakable.

Chinese foreign policy toward Southeast Asia is treated
elsewhere. It is necessary here only to state certain basic assumptions, citable from Hinton, Zagoria, and North, which
may still be valid although they date from before the China-
U.S. rapprochement of 1972. Hinton shares a general opinion that China regards Southeast Asia basically as a Chinese
sphere of influence, from which other major external powers

[35] Williams, *op. cit.*, pp. 3 and 21.
[36] C. P. Fitzgerald, *The Third China: the Chinese Communities
in Southeast Asia* (Vancouver, Canada: Publications Centre, University of British Columbia, 1965), pp. 63, 73, 79.
[37] Elegant, *op. cit.*, p. 239.

are to be excluded sooner or later to make way for Chinese hegemony.[38] Zagoria contends that, although China is a dissatisfied power, she probably does not see direct military expansion as a major instrument of foreign policy.[39] North believes that in Asia the Chinese have been anxious to extend the influence of their regime in several directions, but only at a relatively low level of risk and cost.[40] Taken together, these three views form a recognizable stereoscopic picture. They explain why it is possible for Chinese foreign policy to operate on two completely different levels. One is a government-to-government level, although there are variations in which the organizations concerned are of different degrees of officialdom. The other operates by providing help to Communist, and other, insurrectionary movements through propaganda, financial help, or military training (for instance, for minority groups from Burma). There have been fluctuations in the conduct, although not necessarily in the objectives, of Chinese foreign policy toward Southeast Asia. After an aggressive start, following the Communist victory in China in 1949, a high point of "benevolence" was reached at the Bandung Conference of April 1955. Subsequently, a number of treaties were concluded in the late 1950s and early 1960s, for example with Burma, Cambodia, and Indonesia. Emphasis on revolutionary change grew during the period of the Cultural Revolution, but declined toward the end of the 1960s.[41] The present trend, accompanying the admission of China to the United Nations and the increasing popularity of neutrality in the area, is to emphasize relations at the gov-

[38] Harold Hinton, *Communist China in World Politics* (Boston: Houghton Mifflin, 1966), p. 396.

[39] Donald S. Zagoria, *Vietnam Triangle: Moscow, Peking, Hanoi* (New York: Pegasus, 1967), p. 79.

[40] Robert C. North, *The Foreign Relations of China* (Belmont, Calif.: Dickenson Publication Co., 1969), p. 99. On traditional China's perception of the world order and its possible persistence in Communist China, see John King Fairbank (ed.), *The Chinese World Order: Traditional China's Foreign Relations* (Cambridge, Mass.: Harvard University Press, 1968), especially pp. 85–88.

[41] Daniel Tretiak, "Changes in Chinese Attention to Southeast Asia, 1967–1969: Their Relevance for the Future of the Area," *Current Scene*, Nov. 1, 1969 (Vol. VII, No. 21), pp. 1–17.

ernmental level in comparison with subterranean-subversive relations. The latter, however, are not likely to disappear completely; this, as will be shown apparent later, constitutes a major headache for the Southeast Asian would-be-neutral countries.

How does the existence of overseas Chinese affect Chinese foreign policy? Even if the degree of "loyalty" of overseas Chinese toward China were greater and less ambiguous than it is, the Chinese government would still not find it entirely easy to make effective use of it, except in countries with a high proportion of Chinese, such as Malaysia or Singapore. Indeed, the likelihood of Chinese minorities being used to subvert a government has seemed greater to some United States observers than to the Southeast Asian governments themselves.[42] The overseas Chinese may encourage and expedite trade with China, make remittances to China, thus helping China's foreign exchange situation, or even help Communist parties, as they did by rehabilitating the PKI after the Madiun disaster (1948) and financing it at the 1955 elections.[43] These activities are obviously easier if China has diplomatic missions in a Southeast Asian country or other agencies, such as the Bank of China, which can carry out similar functions. Nevertheless, such activities can have only limited effects. Many of them produce only intangible, if important, results such as strengthening "friendship" and "goodwill" for China. Others, such as aid to Communist parties, are more clearly identified as interference or subversion and yet (apart from Singapore, Malaysia, and, to a lesser extent, Thailand), because of the physical appearance of the Chinese, and their concentration in urban centers, are highly visible to an alert Southeast Asian government and thus can be easily countered.

Just as many overseas Chinese have an emotional "loyalty" to China, so the government of China might be expected to

42 Werner Levi, *The Challenge of World Politics in South and Southeast Asia* (Englewood Cliffs, N.J.: Prentice-Hall, 1968), 176.

43 See: Elegant, *op. cit.*, chs. 2 and 11; Hinton, *op. cit.*, 40 413–14, 428; Russell H. Fifield, *Southeast Asia in United States Policy* (New York: Frederick A. Praeger, 1963), pp. 44–45, 6

ave an emotional attachment to the overseas Chinese, without whose help the revolution of 1911 would probably not ave been achieved so quickly.[44] In 1949 the new Communist government's objectives in foreign affairs included the intention "to protect the rights and interests of the Overseas Chinese."[45] Before 1911 Chinese governments had taken the line that all overseas Chinese, even those not born in China, retained and always would retain Chinese citizenship. The constitution of 1954 (article 98) promised protection to the rights and interests of overseas Chinese, without stating whether or not they were regarded as retaining Chinese citizenship; however, one authority believes that there was an assumption of retention.[46] But by late 1954 it was clear that emphasis on the rights of overseas Chinese stood in the way of wooing the governments of Southeast Asia with a policy of peaceful coexistence. China's policy toward the overseas Chinese changed accordingly, although, according to Stephen Fitzgerald, the change did not take the form of a "decision" until 1956.[47] Overseas Chinese were encouraged to observe the laws and customs of the countries in which they lived. China was even prepared to make concessions on citizenship, that all overseas Chinese who were eligible under local laws would be free to acquire nationality in their country of residence. The only country with which an agreement was actually made was Indonesia, and it took over five and a half years of acrimonious discussion to move from a Treaty on Dual Nationality (April 22, 1955) to a Sino-Indonesian Arrangement for Implementation of Dual Nationality Treaty (December 15, 1960).[48] In spite of China's willingness to include a similar agreement with any other Southeast Asian

[44] Williams, op. cit., p. 45.

[45] Quoted in R. G. Boyd, Communist China's Foreign Policy (New York: Frederick A. Praeger, 1962), p. 20.

[46] Hinton, op. cit., pp. 398, 400–1.

[47] Stephen Fitzgerald, "China and the Overseas Chinese: Perceptions and Policies," The China Quarterly, 1970 (No. 44), p. 3. He argues that the policy change was neither a propaganda ploy or a temporary expedient.

[48] Reproduced in G. V. Ambekar and V. C. Divekar (eds.), Documents on China's Relations with South and Southeast Asia (Bombay: Allied Publishers, 1964), pp. 231–37 and 270–74.

country which recognized it, neither Burma[49] nor Thailand
to which Peking apparently made the most serious approaches, showed any great interest at that time.

Cynics might point out that in the short run formal adoption of local citizenship does not remove overseas Chinese
from China's influence entirely. But China's announced
change in policy in 1955–56 did symbolize a shift toward
realism. The Chinese minorities ". . . instead of being an
asset to China's foreign policy, are probably a liability. They
create deep resentments and suspicions and therefore increase
resistance to Chinese influence."[50] In Indonesia in the late
1950s and early 1960s China was prepared to sacrifice overseas Chinese to Indonesian governmental measures designed
to curtail their economic dominance, and pin its hopes on the
future of the largely indigenous PKI.

China's political relations with Southeast Asia are not only
governmental but also take the form of links between the
Chinese Communist Party and local Communist parties.
What is the role of the overseas Chinese in this context? It
appears that in Southeast Asian countries, other than Malaysia
and Singapore, Chinese have been somewhat overrepresented
in Communist parties, compared with their percentage in the
population, but not conspicuously so. At one time they had
some standing in the PKI, especially through Tan Ling Djie
before his expulsion from the party's central committee in
October 1953.[51] In the Philippines some years ago they
seem to have constituted about a fifth of Communist party

[49] However, in September 1971, General Ne Win announced
that he had acceded to a request made to him during his recent
trip to China, to allow second generation descendants of Chinese
settlers, either of pure or mixed Chinese stock, to adopt Burmese
nationality if they wished (Leo Goodstadt, "When in Rome," *Far
Eastern Economic Review,* October 9, 1971, p. 8).

[50] Edwin O. Reischauer, "Fateful Triangle," *The New York
Times Magazine,* September 19, 1971, p. 48.

[51] Arnold Brackman, *Southeast Asia's Second Front* (New York:
Frederick A. Praeger, 1966), p. 200. Cf. the comment that, about
1920, too close an association of the party with the Chinese minority might have endangered its mass support [Ruth T. McVey,
The Rise of Indonesian Communism (Ithaca, N.Y.: Cornell University Press, 1965), p. 225].

members.[52] In Burma they have not had an important role.
The main exception is Thailand, where Chinese Communists
have been separately organized. One 1963 estimate placed
the membership of the Chinese Communist Party in Thailand
at 5,000, while the Thai Communist Party had only 200.[53]
More recently, reports suggest that in Northeast Thailand
the Communist Party branches are dominated by Chinese or
Sino-Thais. The fact is that it would not be expedient for
Chinese to be *too* conspicuous in local Communist Parties.
Maybe their prominence in Thailand is a testimony to their
relatively high degree of assimilation in that country, and even
then it may be significant that the Chinese were segregated
in a separate Communist Party. In commenting on Tan Ling
Djie's role in Indonesia one commentator observed that he
had ". . . the added disadvantage of being of Chinese de-
cent, and was thereby unable to occupy publicly the top
position of PKI in a country where anti-Chinese feeling was
strong."[54] A similar explanation was given for the purging of
other Chinese from office in the PKI at about the same time.[55]
Chinese-dominated Communist parties, like Chinese-dominated businesses, have the problem of finding indigenous
"front men"; if the façade is too thin, the device becomes
transparent.

How are the foreign policies of Southeast Asian countries
(apart from Malaysia and Singapore) affected by the existence of the overseas Chinese? An obvious point is that, as
opposed to hypotheses which might be derived from the operation of western democracies, the overseas Chinese do not
directly exercise an influence on foreign policy by their votes.
There has been only one important "Chinese" party in any

[52] Frank N. Trager, "The Communist Challenge in Southeast
Asia," in W. Henderson (ed.), *Southeast Asia: Problems of United
States Foreign Policy* (Cambridge, Mass.: M.I.T. Press, 1963),
155. This proportion may have altered during the shifts and
splits which have occurred since among Philippine Communists.
[53] Fifield, *op. cit.*, p. 54.
[54] Donald Hindley, *The Communist Party of Indonesia, 1951–
63* (Berkeley and Los Angeles: University of California Press,
1963), p. 26.
[55] Brackman, *op. cit.*, p. 202.

of these countries, BAPERKI[56] in Indonesia, which worked closely with the PKI, and did not long survive the events of September 30, 1965. Nor have the Chinese, through the judicious distribution of their vote as between parties, had the influence on foreign policies toward China that, say, the Jewish vote in New York has had on United States foreign policy toward Israel. Elections are not important enough, and the Chinese vote not sufficiently large, for this to occur. *The Chinese in Southeast Asia affect foreign policy, not by bringing their influence to bear on it, but rather by the mere fact of their conspicuous and disturbing existence.* It should be added that, although the Chinese in Southeast Asia, outside Malaysia and Singapore, do not have much appreciable electoral effect on foreign policy, they do have some defense against extreme ill-treatment. They are not completely at the mercy of the governments of Southeast Asian countries. Their ultimate defense consists not so much in the possibility that they may strike or riot, as they did in opposition to anti-Chinese measures in Thailand in 1910 or 1945, or in South Vietnam in 1956. It lies rather in the dependence of the economy on their skills, which may be withdrawn or exercised not too energetically. One reason why the movement of overseas Chinese to China was halted after the massacres which followed the affair of September 30, 1965, in Indonesia was simply that the economy could not afford to lose them. The present Indonesian government seems to have recognized that any prohibition of Chinese, who are not Indonesian nationals, from engaging in trade must be implemented gradually.

It has been argued that the influence of Chinese minorities in Southeast Asian countries as instruments of Chinese foreign policy is limited, apart from Malaysia and Singapore. But foreign policy makers in these countries have found it ha

---

[56] *Badan Permusjawaratan Kawarganegaraan Indonesia* (Consultative Body for Indonesian Citizenship). See: Hindley, *op. cit.*, p. 216; Mary F. Somers, *Peranakan Chinese Politics in Indonesia* (Ithaca, N.Y.: Cornell University Press, 1964), especially chapter 1. A previous Chinese political organization, derived from a Japanese-occupation-period predecessor, is mentioned in Skinner, *op. cit.*, p. 71. Note that in Thailand the Chinese Communist Party was able to operate legally for only a very short proportion of its existence.

to consider the Chinese minorities apart from China itself. There are ". . . 'two Chinas' in the minds of many Southeast Asians: 'China' the great and perhaps fearsome nation, and 'China' the source of the despised and dominating alien group at home. The two mental images are probably reinforcing . . ."[57] Indeed, there are really three images which overlap: China itself[58]; the overseas Chinese in the Southeast Asian country; and Communism. This is obviously a source of confusion. Few Southeast Asian political leaders are very knowledgeable about China or Communism as such, but many do come into contact with local Chinese; such contacts provide a concrete starting point for conceptualizations, sometimes rather crude ones, focused on the other two related, and often intermingled, images. Foreign policies toward China have been at least partly a reflection of reactions to the Chinese minority in the country and also to Communist activities in it.

The country in which these three elements are least intermingled is probably Burma. China is seen as a powerful neighbor, even though proximity is tempered by poor communications across the borders: great relief was felt in Burma when, after protracted negotiations, a relatively favorable settlement was reached, which satisfied China's border claims. The overseas Chinese in Burma were numerically small and manifestly far less salient than in most Southeast Asian countries. Yet even in Burma the close interrelations among overseas Chinese, China, and Communism led to a dangerous escalation. In 1965 and 1966 the Burmese government had been taking over Chinese schools and closing down Chinese newspapers without too much reaction from Peking. But the Cultural Revolution reached Chinese students in Rangoon, and in June 1967 led to the wearing of Mao badges and the chanting of Maoist slogans. When wearing badges was forbidden, the students demonstrated and seized two schools, resulting in a city-wide riot in which many Chinese were killed and much Chinese property destroyed. Peking then launched

[57] Bernard K. Gordon, *Toward Disengagement in Asia: a Strategy for American Foreign Policy* (Englewood Cliffs, N.J.: Prentice-Hall, 1969), p. 82.

[58] Which may, in turn, be divided into "Peking" and "Taipei," though this subdivision is decreasingly necessary.

an all-out propaganda attack on the Burmese government, and Rangoon was without a Chinese ambassador for some two and a half years.[59] To a degree, this clash was a manifestation of a change to a tougher Chinese policy, just as improved relations later arose from China's switch to a softer line. Yet it was a series of incidents involving local Chinese which actually triggered off the rupture in relations with China, which was especially perilous for Burma because of China's geographical closeness.

It is impossible to speculate on the extent to which government leaders in Southeast Asia are themselves confused by the three, sometimes superimposed, images of overseas Chinese/China/Communism. Under some circumstances they might find such confusion to be inconvenient. Sukarno did not want the economic restrictions being placed on Chinese in Indonesia in the late 1950s to be seen as evidence of hostility to China or to Communism. Nor did successive Philippine governments relish their dealings with the Nationalist Chinese government being harmed by their wrangles with "internal" Chinese traders or illegal, "overstaying" Chinese immigrants. In other situations, however, governments may find the confusion useful. One reason why it may be possible to treat the Chinese minority as a scapegoat, as Skinner says has sometimes been done in the Philippines and Thailand,[60] is because of its easy identification with China and Communism.

The complexity of the relationship between the foreign policies of Southeast Asian states on the one hand, and Chinese minorities and local Communist movements on the other, is apparent from the events which followed the recent ASEAN policy of neutrality. There are great divergences in the interpretations being placed on this policy by the five countries concerned, and these are partly dependent on the Chinese minority situation in each individual country. Although ASEAN, like its predecessor ASA, started with modest aims in the early 1970s it was led into taking a political stance by

[59] "From Coexistence to Condemnation: the New Chinese View of Burma," *Current Scene*, October 17, 1967 (Vol. V, No. 17) pp. 1–11.

[60] Skinner, *op. cit.*, pp. 85–86, 376–77.

evelopments vitally affecting the region. "Britain's acceler-
ted withdrawal, President Nixon's Guam Doctrine, the U.S.
ithdrawal from Vietnam, Japan's increasing economic dom-
ance, China's post-Cultural Revolution emergence and Rus-
a's South Asian assertiveness have together had the effect of
aking ASEAN more and more central to Southeast Asian
alculations."[61] This process culminated in an ASEAN decla-
ation on November 27, 1971, calling for a neutral Southeast
sia, "free from any form or manner of interference by out-
de powers." In effect, although the declaration itself did not
ctually say so, this could be achieved only by the agreement,
it necessarily explicit, of the United States, the Soviet Union,
id China.[62] The ASEAN countries are not without their
vn internal disputes. Some are currently, in varying degrees,
iked to outside powers by alliances and through the exist-
ice of military bases. The bases would have to be phased
it before China and the U.S.S.R. could guarantee neutrality
the ASEAN area.[63] Hence the speed with which they de-
e to have further contacts with China, for example by ex-
anging trade missions or finding a neutral status for all or
rt of Southeast Asia, differs considerably. The lack of
animity is illustrated by the absence of any common time-
ple for establishing relations with Peking; there is only an
reement that if any ASEAN state does plan to establish re-
ions, it will consult the others. Nor has the ASEAN declara-
n of neutrality been accompanied by any defense pact
long the five members. Malaysia, it will be seen, was a
der in the move toward neutrality. The Philippines, because
her ties to the United States and to Taiwan, might have
en expected to be markedly less enthusiastic. But the détente
tween China and the United States and the absence of any
vious direct threat, or memory of a threat, from China has
couraged trade and other contacts between the two coun-

[61] Harvey Stockwin, "ASEAN: Thinking as One," *Far Eastern
nomic Review* 29 April, 1972, p. 15.

[62] For background and prospects, including possible reactions
China, see T. J. S. George, "The Neutralisation Stakes," *ibid.*,
cember 11, 1971, pp. 18–20.

[63] Tun Abdul Razak, interview published in *New Nation*, June
1972, quoted in *Asia Research Bulletin*, July 1972 (Vol. 2,
. 2), p. 987.

tries, and one writer believes that the Philippines is likely to be the first non-Communist Southeast Asian nation to ex change diplomatic representatives with Peking.[64] Indonesia relations with China had not recovered from the dramati break which followed the failure of the China-supported at tempted coup in 1965 and the subsequent rioting in which th Chinese Embassy in Djakarta had been a prominent battle field. Adam Malik, the Foreign Minister, was much more dis posed to establishing normal relations with China than wer most of the top generals. Thailand was cautious because o her SEATO role, her involvement in the fighting in Vietnam Laos, and Cambodia, and her military dependence on th United States. After the 1971 coup she became even less en thusiastic. As in Indonesia, the displaced Foreign Ministe Thanat Khoman, had been more in favor of a rapprochemer with China than the generals. In August 1972 General Prapa rejected the notion of a neutral zone, although soon afterwar there were moves toward closer relations with China. Sings pore's special problems are discussed later in this article.

In the new policies of the ASEAN countries on neutralit and toward China, the Chinese minorities constitute an im portant factor. The year 1965 and the years immediate following marked a tough policy toward the local Chinese Indonesia, because they were believed to have been assoc ated with the abortive coup, and there were pressures o the surviving Chinese to emigrate or assimilate. Therefor measures such as those described below, which were adopte in Thailand and the Philippines in the early 1970s to mate a new foreign policy stance, had in part already been take in Indonesia. Thai government policy toward the overse Chinese has always been too complex to be explained sole in "scapegoat" terms. Of all the Southeast Asian countri considered here (Malaysia and Singapore being excluded it has the highest proportion of Chinese. It is also much mo vulnerable to direct attack or infiltration from China th the Philippines or Indonesia. Thailand has indeed had reas to look for protection on three fronts: against China, Co munism, and overseas Chinese. In point of fact, Thai gover

[64] Richard Butwell, "A Summit Prospect," *Far Eastern E nomic Review,* July 22, 1972, p. 23.

ments have tended to concentrate on the last of these, not exactly as a scapegoat, but rather as the most manageable factor of the three. This was Marshal Phibun's policy after his return to power in 1948, and it was also, less plausibly, the policy behind General Pao's arrests to counter an alleged widespread Communist plot in 1952.[65] It has also been suggested that one of the reasons why Thailand joined SEATO was concern about its Chinese and Vietnamese minorities.[66] The general proposition seems to hold good that to a considerable extent Thai foreign relations "have been seen as a means of balancing the influence of the Chinese community."[67] This interpretation may be useful in analyzing the remarks of Field Marshal Thanom after the coup of November 17, 1971. "We are not certain how many of them [the Chinese in Thailand] sympathise with China, now that Peking is in a position to exert powerful influence all over the world. If a lot of them do, then the possibility that they can assist the Communist terrorists cannot be ruled out."[68] Some weeks before the coup the previous government, and particularly Thanat Khoman, then Foreign Minister, had been working toward closer trade and cultural relations with Peking.[69] After the coup a different kind of "balancing" seems to have been practiced. Foreign relations were no longer seen so much as an instrument for countering the influence of the local Chinese. Policy toward China was now regarded as important in its own right, although immediately after the 1971 coup the move toward closer relations suffered a check. Nevertheless, apparently it was believed that foreign policy and policy toward the Chinese minority had to be "balanced" in the sense that they needed to be coordinated.

In the Philippines the switch in foreign policy and in re-

[65] Donald E. Nuechterlein, *Thailand and the Struggle for Southeast Asia* (Ithaca, N.Y.: Cornell University Press, 1965), pp. 101–3, 110, 127.

[66] Russell H. Fifield, "Another Look at SEATO," in W. Henderson (ed.), *op. cit.*, p. 192.

[67] David Wurfel, "The Pattern of Southeast Asian Response to International Politics," *ibid.*, p. 83.

[68] "Familiar Themes," by a Correspondent, *Far Eastern Economic Review*, November 27, 1971, p. 6.

[69] *Ibid.*, p. 6.

lations with China was accompanied by attempted "Filipiniza-
tion" of the country's Chinese through proposals put forward
both by President Marcos and also by the Constitutional Convention. These differed in detail, but both were concerned with
two main points; the complex processes to acquire citizenship
were to be made easier, and education was to aim at assimilation by provisions on content of curriculum, language of
instruction, and the staffing of key positions in private schools
by Filipinos. Such proposals were not new, but they were
advanced with a fresh sense of urgency early in 1972, simultaneously with the moves being made toward closer relations
with Peking.

China's support for internal subversion constitutes yet another dimension in the new foreign policies of the Southeast
Asian states. In August 1971 Chou En-lai repeated to Ne Win
what he had said to Southeast Asian leaders some fifteen years
earlier, that overseas Chinese should obey the laws of the
countries in which they resided, and that it was the policy of
the Chinese government to see that this principle was observed.[70] But China has given no assurances that she will
cease aiding insurrectionary movements in Southeast Asia,
nor is there any guarantee that, even if assurances are given,
they will be unambiguous.[71] Obviously ASEAN members
would like to receive such assurances, and at one time a
change of policy by China was made a precondition for Thai
recognition of Peking and for normal governmental relations.[72] Similarly, the Indonesian votes on the admission of
China to the UN in 1971, in favor of treating the admission
as an important question and abstention on the Albanian
resolution to admit Peking and expel Taiwan, were based on
China's policy of encouraging subversion in Indonesia. But
it is possible that ASEAN may settle for something less than
watertight assurances, or rather for less than assurances implemented in a watertight way. If the level of insurrectionary

70 Leo Goodstadt, *op. cit.*

71 C. P. Fitzgerald, "China's New Diplomacy: a Symposium
(1)," *Problems of Communism,* November–December 1971 (Vol.
XX), p. 24.

72 See, for instance, "Foreign Minister's Interview on China
Question," *Thai News-Letter* (Ottawa), Dec. 30, 1970 (No. 28/
2513), pp. 7–11.

activity is tolerably low, relations with China on a governmental basis could continue concurrently with low-profile Chinese aid to rebels against Southeast Asian governments.

The recent foreign policies of Malaysia and Singapore require separate treatment because of the proportion of Chinese in their populations—approximately two-fifths and three-quarters respectively, sufficiently high to permit them to participate significantly in the political process. In Malaya, before it became Malaysia, the Chinese component of the government Alliance Party, the MCA, had a difficult role to play.[73] Although the Chinese gained genuine benefits on Independence in 1957, such as liberalized citizenship and freedom to engage in economic activities without discrimination, the MCA and the Indian component in the Alliance (MIC) were clearly subordinate to the dominant United Malays National Organization (UMNO). The MCA found it hard to retain the Chinese vote in the face of the policies of parties which, without a close tie to a Malay party, were able to offer the Chinese more, for example on language and education. The creation of Malaysia in 1963 opened up the non-Malays to the political activities of the Singapore-based People's Action Party. With Singapore's exit from Malaysia in 1965, non-Malay pressures were temporarily checked, but they revived, partly via the PAP's Malaysian successor, the Democratic Action Party. The Alliance Party won the 1969 election, although with a reduced majority, but the election was immediately followed by racial riots.[74] For almost two years parliament did not meet, and even when it did the constitution was altered, so as to place the basic power arrangements between Malays and non-Malays beyond discussion. Thus,

[73] On Malayan (Malaysian) politics until 1967, see R. S. Milne, *op. cit.* On the MCA see: K. J. Ratnam, *Communalism and the Political Process in Malaya* (Kuala Lumpur: University of Malaya Press, 1965); Margaret Roff, "The Malayan Chinese Association, 1948–65," *Journal of Southeast Asian History*, 1965 (Vol. V, No. 2), pp. 40–53.

[74] See Anthony Reid, "The Kuala Lumpur Riots and the Malaysian Political System," *Australian Outlook,* 1969 (Vol. 23, No. 3); Felix V. Gagliano, *Communal Violence in Malaysia, 1969: the Political Aftermath* (Athens, Ohio: Center for International Studies, Ohio University, 1970).

although the Chinese had a share in political power, strict boundaries were laid down beyond which their share could not be extended.[75]

The foreign policy of Malaya was to a large extent a reflection of the views of the Prime Minister, Tengku Abdul Rahman.[76] They were pro-British (except when to be this was obviously also to be anti-Malayan), and determinedly "anti-Communist." The Tengku's hostility to Communism was based largely on his experience of the "Emergency" in 1948–60. A very high proportion of the rebels was Chinese, locally recruited but encouraged from Peking.[77] Fortunately, the overwhelming mass of the overseas Chinese in Malaya did *not* support the rebels, and consequently the resentment of the Malayan government was directed at China rather than focused internally. Surprisingly, in view of the government's anti-Communist policy, Malaya did not join SEATO. Membership in this organization would not only have displeased China, and some overseas Chinese in Malaya, it would also have been unwelcome to India, to some Indians in Malaya, and to the government of Indonesia, with which Malaysia desired to have friendly relations. It was believed that Malaya's defense was being adequately assured by the links with Britain, Australia, and New Zealand, whose troops helped end the "Emergency" and remained, on a smaller scale, after the Emergency was over. Nor did "anti-Communism" drive the government into the embrace of

[75] By constitutional amendments passed after debate in the Malaysian Parliament in late February and early March 1971.

[76] T. H. Silcock, "Development of a Malayan Foreign Policy," *Australian Outlook,* 1962 (Vol. 16, No. 1), p. 42. On foreign policy generally, see Boyce, *op. cit.;* Milne, *op. cit.,* Chapter 11; Robert O. Tilman, "Malaysian Foreign Policy: the Dilemmas of a Committed Neutral," in John D. Montgomery and Albert O. Hirschman (eds.), *Public Policy* (Cambridge, Mass.: Harvard University Press, 1967).

[77] Anthony Short, "Communism, Race and Politics in Malaysia," *Asian Survey,* December 1970 (Vol. 10, No. 12), pp. 1081–89; Frances L. Starner, "Communism in Singapore and Malaysia; a Multifront Struggle," in R. A. Scalapino (ed.), *The Communist Revolution in Asia* (Englewood Cliffs, N.J.: Prentice-Hall, 1969), p. 245.

Taipei; an attempt was made to "insulate" the overseas Chinese from the influence of both rival "Chinas."

With the end of the Emergency in 1960 the Malayan position toward China softened. Although she voted against China's admission to the United Nations, she said she had been favorable in principle, but only if Taiwan were allowed to maintain her own separate political identity. She abstained on an admission vote in 1962, on the ground that the motion was ambiguous. From 1963 onward she voted against; the main reason given for the switch was Chinese "unprovoked armed aggression" on India, which seemed to Malaysia to be the first step toward domination of Asia. Other grounds for friction had come into existence. China strongly supported Indonesia in her Confrontation against Malaysia. And guerrilla activity, believed to be inspired from China, was already endemic in Sarawak (which joined Malaysia in 1963), and was started up again by the relics of the rebel troops who survived the Emergency, near the Malaysian-Thai border. Even after Malaysia's indignation about India had died down and Confrontation had ended, the internal guerrillas remained active.

There were some signs of change in foreign policy before the Tengku formally handed over the Prime Ministership and the direction of foreign affairs to Tun Razak in late September 1970.[78] A trade agreement was reached with the U.S.S.R. which was followed by the establishment of diplomatic relations (1967). ASA was replaced by the broader ASEAN. Provision had to be made to meet the British troop withdrawal from the area, and this took the form of constituting a Five-Power Defence Arrangement (Malaysia, Singapore, Britain, Australia, New Zealand), which was not actually formalized until April 1971. But the five-power arrangement was a temporary expedient from Malaysia's point of view,[79] designed to plug the gap resulting from an ac-

---

[78] Even inside the Alliance Party there had always been a section of opinion hostile to defense treaties with Britain and in favor of closer relations with neutralist Afro-Asian countries (Milne, *op. cit.*, p. 196).

[79] *Malaysia's Foreign Policy: Statement on Foreign Affairs by the Hon. Prime Minister, Tun Abdul Razak bin Hussein, at the*

celerated British withdrawal. The United States' disengagement from Vietnam had been announced. There was increasing talk of the neutralization of Southeast Asia, and a Malaysian policy to achieve this was announced to the Preparatory Conference of Non-Aligned Nations at Dar-es-Salaam in April 1970, and to the Third Summit Conference of Non-Aligned Countries in Lusaka, September 1970. The Malaysian plan called for a guarantee from the United States, U.S.S.R., and China. At the Lusaka meeting the emphasis was on neutrality for the areas in which fighting was then actually taking place, Vietnam, Laos, and Cambodia, but Malaysia made it clear that her objective was neutrality for *all* Southeast Asia. After Tun Razak became Prime Minister there was a further development. On October 3, 1970, the Deputy Prime Minister, Dr. Ismail, who in January 1968, when not a member of the cabinet, had voiced the idea of a neutral Southeast Asia, announced a new Malaysian stand on China's admission to the UN. She would now support admission by simple majority on the ground that, "We cannot ask Communist China to guarantee the neutrality of Southeast Asia and at the same time say we do not approve of her."[80] There were no qualifications about the new stand, but on October 15 Tun Razak said that Malaysia would not enter into a dialogue with Communist China unless Peking changed her policy of hostility toward Malaysia and assured her that she believed in the principle of coexistence and non-interference.[81]

In promoting this policy Malaysia was in advance of her ASEAN partners; among them only Singapore voted for the admission of China to the UN by simple majority in 1970 and 1971. And Malaysia was the only ASEAN member to

Dewan Ra'ayat on July 26, 1971 (Kuala Lumpur, 1971), p. 9. Possibly Thailand now regards its SEATO commitments in a similar way, as designed to fill a gap until a full neutralization policy can be implemented.

The temporary nature of the arrangement was underlined by the election, at the end of 1972, of governments in Australia and New Zealand committed to removing troops from the area.

[80] Dr. Ismail, quoted in *Malaysian Digest,* Oct. 16, 1970 (Vol. 2, No. 19).

[81] *Ibid.,* Oct. 31, 1970 (Vol. 2, No. 20).

exchange official or semiofficial trade delegations with China in 1971.[82] Tun Razak himself referred to the time lag inside ASEAN:

> I remember that when I first made this proposal there was a general attitude of scepticism. It was regarded as unrealistic, idealistic, or even worse. But we have persevered with explaining this concept . . . I think the House will be aware that there has been increasing understanding of this concept and a more favourable response to it in recent months. Indeed as a result of the latest exchanges between China and the United States, there has been growing appreciation that this policy far from being idealistic is in fact a very realistic one.[83]

There are various possible explanations why Malaysia should have been prominent in advocating a "neutralization" policy. One is simply that a new leader, taking a fresh look at foreign policy, made certain inferences from the facts and then constructed an appropriate policy to fit them. If, as seemed clear, China was to play a major role in the area rather sooner than some had expected, it was only logical for the Southeast Asian nations, in the form of ASEAN, or an expanded ASEAN, to make some compensatory adjustment. Malaysia may also have been influenced to some extent by the prospects of additional rubber and other exports, made possible by trade agreements with China, although she had already been exporting rubber to China for some years before 1971. She may also have hoped that China would moderate her support for the rebel movements in Sarawak and on the Malayan-Thai border, although, as mentioned previously, no binding or lasting assurances of this kind can be expected.[84]

[82] Care was taken to reassure Malays about the trade delegation to China by putting at its head a highborn Malay, Tengku Razaleigh.

[83] *Malaysia's Foreign Policy, op. cit.*, pp. 7–8.

[84] See p. 21, above. On Malaysia's part, China's role in supporting rebel movements, for instance by radio propaganda, was not mentioned in official documents or by ministers making speeches in Malaysia (James Morgan, "Malaysia: Bracing for a Long Haul," *Far Eastern Economic Review*, October 9, 1971, p. 18). Some importance has been attributed to the fact that Chinese newspapers and radio, when referring to the Malaysian trade delegation which visited China in May 1971 and the Chinese trade delegation

Undoubtedly the position of the overseas Chinese has had some effect in the framing of the new policy. The rapprochement with China must offer some symbolic gratification to the overseas Chinese in Malaysia. Conceivably this may be intended to enable them to contemplate *Malay* demands for more material goods, catered for in the Malaysian Second Five-Year Development Plan, with greater equanimity. There is, of course, a danger that the Malaysian Chinese may be too pleased, and that "Chinese chauvinism" may be encouraged. Exchanges of trade delegations are not much remarked on by the Chinese in Malaysia, but the visit of a "Silver Star" dance troupe, which "could as well have been called Red Star, even though it was Hongkong based,"[85] had great popular impact. One report from Kuala Lumpur said that the Malays had expressed fears about the effects that China's increasing prestige will have on the attitudes of the local Chinese. A delegate to the United Malays National Organization meeting in January said, "They will become too proud."[86] It might be argued that the new Malaysian China

which visited Malaysia in August 1971, used the term "Malaysia" for the first time. But this may have been just because these were the first governmental, or quasi-governmental, contacts between the countries. It has also been pointed out that the term "Malaysia" was used as a constituent of the title of the delegation. In broadcasts from *Suara Revolusi Malaya* (the Voice of Malayan Revolution), believed to originate from China, about the insurrections in Malaysia, the method of reference varied. In two 1971 broadcasts, both made after the Malaysian delegation had visited China, there was a reference to "reactionary Malayan and Thai troops" (near the Thai-Malayan border) but also to "the Malaysian authorities" (in Sarawak) (FBIS-CHI-71-103, May 27, 1971, No. 103, Vol. 1, A 29 and FBIS-CHI-71-146, July 29, 1971, No. 146, Vol. 1, A 15). Tun Razak has said that Malaysia would not take up the question of radio propaganda with the Chinese government until the neutralization question had been first resolved (interview in *New Nation*, quoted in *Asia Research Bulletin, op. cit.*, p. 988). On China's radio propaganda directed toward Southeast Asia see, generally, Deirdre Mead Ryan, "The Decline of the 'Armed Struggle' Tactic in Chinese Foreign Policy," *Current Scene*, 1972 (Vol. X, No. 12), pp. 1–12.

[85] James Morgan, "Mao on Stage," *Far Eastern Economic Review*, April 3, 1971, p. 17.

[86] According to *The Times* (London), quoted in *The Mirror* (Singapore), May 17, 1971 (Vol. 7, No. 20).

policy is a sign of optimism that the Chinese in Malaysia will not "become too proud." The Malaysian government may be more confident about this than the Thai government, hoping that the constitutional amendments and other measures taken after the 1969 incidents, including the new national ideology, the *Rukunegara,* will be sufficient to prevent internal Chinese unrest. Some governmental sources believe that the new contacts between official or semiofficial Chinese and Malaysian organizations will benefit the Malaysian government in two important political respects. The rather weak Chinese component of the ruling Malaysian Alliance Party, the Malaysian Chinese Association (MCA), is expected to benefit from the rapprochement between the two countries; the MCA will no longer have to be on the defensive against charges that the government in which it is a partner is anti-Chinese-"culture" because it refused to have dealings with the government of China. Also, the Communist rebels in Malaysia, although still given moral support from Peking, can hardly help feeling that the friendly diplomatic transactions between the two countries might be paving the way for their betrayal and abandonment.

Before the moves toward neutralization which started in 1970, Singapore had been "in advance of Malaysia" in its relations with China.[87] There were no formal diplomatic relations with Peking (or with Taipei), but unofficial trade missions had gone to China, the Bank of China[88] did business in Singapore, and from the time of its Independence in 1965, the Singapore pattern of voting on the admission of China to the United Nations had not been completely opposed. Singapore had maintained that admission should be on the basis of a simple majority vote, not treated as an "important question." In principle, the Singapore government favored neutralization, but it stressed the conditions which were necessary to make it work. "If the Chinese, Russians, Americans agree that neutralisation is in their joint

---

[87] Ironically, among all the other reasons for Singapore's caution in encouraging contacts with China, one very important reason was the fear of adverse Malaysian and Indonesian reactions.

[88] It had also operated in Malaysia and Indonesia, but in each the government had forced it to leave. In Singapore it survived one threat of closure in 1969.

interests, there could be a neutral Southeast Asia. Then that, I think, is the best answer."[89] To some degree the stress on conditions rather than on aspirations accounted for the fact that Singapore has not made any move to institute government-to-government relations with China, and that she is now less "effusive" than Malaysia.

However, there is another reason why Singapore wishes to go rather more slowly along this road than Malaysia, namely her extreme vulnerability to Chinese influence because of the Chinese majority in her population. As long ago as 1962 the point was made by Mr. Lee Kuan Yew:

> . . . with China a successful world Communist power, the MCP [Malayan Communist Party] can manipulate and exploit Chinese sentiments and feelings with more advantage than any other person or group in Malaya . . . The pervading influence of a strong Communist China is so deterring a psychological factor with the Chinese-educated mind that there are almost no Chinese-educated political leaders in Malaya who have had the inclination to take a stand against Communism, particularly of the Chinese variety.[90]

Since 1962 in Singapore the Communist Party has been brought under control, and progress has been made toward nation-building. But, although the number of Chinese children being educated mainly in English is now greater than the number being educated mainly in Chinese, more Chinese adults are Chinese-educated than English-educated. The early history of the People's Action Party, accompanied by agitation in the Chinese middle schools and later in Nanyang University, corresponded to a broad division between moderate-English-educated on the one hand and extremist-Chinese-educated, on the other.[91] This is shown, for exam-

[89] Mr. Lee Kuan Yew, quoted in *The Mirror,* March 29, 1971 (Vol. 7, No. 13).

[90] Alex Josey, *Lee Kuan Yew* (Singapore: Donald Moore, 1968), p. 227.

[91] Thomas J. Bellows, *The People's Action Party of Singapore: Emergence of a Dominant Party System* (New Haven, Conn.: Yale University Press, 1970); Tae Yul Nam, "Singapore's One-Party System: Its Relationship to Democracy and Political Stability," *Pacific Affairs,* Winter 1969–70 (Vol. XLII, No. 4), pp. 465–80.

ple, by comparing the type of education of PAP and Barisan Sosialis candidates at the 1963 elections,[92] and also by the change in the nature of PAP membership during the period following the left-wing defections of members who later formed the Barisan.[93]

The People's Action Party's approach to nation-building in Singapore is multiracial,[94] which is consistent with its policy in seeking merger with Malaya in Malaysia, its policy as a political party inside Malaysia, 1963–65, and the policy of its "successor" party in Malaysia, the Democratic Action Party. The National Language in Singapore is Malay, and Chinese is only one of four official languages. Offices of symbolic importance from the nation-building point of view, such as the Presidency and the post of Foreign Minister, have not yet been occupied by Chinese. The government opposes any attempt to interfere with its multiracial policies, but is especially sensitive to threats to work up communal feelings over Chinese language and culture. To the Chinese-educated it might seem that things Chinese, suppressed in countries where the Chinese are in a minority, should be stressed in Singapore where they are in a majority. However, the Singapore government wishes to keep a balance, not merely in the interests of the one quarter of Singapore's citizens who are not Chinese, but also with a view to Singapore's position as an international port and its proximity to two "Malay" countries, Malaysia and Indonesia. Efforts[95] to emphasize the Chineseness of Singapore, for instance by raising the status of the Chinese language, have been firmly put down. The government reacted promptly to the *Nanyang Siang Pau*'s campaign in May 1971, which included a demand that the

[92] Frances L. Starner, "The Singapore Elections of 1963," in K. J. Ratnam and R. S. Milne (eds.), *The Malayan Parliamentary Election of 1964* (Kuala Lumpur: University of Malaya Press, 1967), p. 328.

[93] Pang Cheng Lian, *Singapore's People's Action Party: Its History, Organization, and Leadership* (Singapore: Oxford University Press, 1971), pp. 61–65.

[94] Chan Heng Chee, *Singapore, The Politics of Survival, 1965–1967* (Singapore: Oxford University Press, 1971), pp. 49–50.

[95] For example, by the Chinese Chamber of Commerce in October 1966 (Josey, *op. cit.*, p. 516).

government should publish the *Government Gazette* in Chinese because it was the language of the majority.[96] Four executives of the paper were detained, although it continued publication.

The internal situation in Singapore is basic in determining foreign policy; unlike other Southeast Asian countries, for her the concept of China (and, increasingly, this has been mainland China rather than Taiwan) is inseparable from that of the overseas Chinese. The Chinese in Singapore are not a minority with external ties, they are a majority with external ties. In such a case the government of China does not have to make the decision to ignore appeals to a Chinese minority and concentrate on appeals to the "indigenous" majority. The majority is not indigenous; it is Chinese. Similarly, internally, it is all too easy for Chinese, uninhibited by a government run by indigenous people, to identify uncritically with "China" via language and culture. The possibility of nurturing and inculcating a tolerant multiracial outlook is subject to a proviso, that ". . . there are no extraneous forces which are let loose which will influence our internal situation and cause a reaction against these policies."[97] Consequently, Singapore does not intend to be rushed into too quick and too close contacts with China. It is hoping to be given enough time for a Singaporean national identity to be more fully established.

> I do not think there is going to be a sizeable Chinese presence anywhere in Southeast Asia for a long while. I do not see a Chinese navy, a Chinese Seventh Fleet complete with missile cruisers and aircraft carriers in the South Pacific or the Indian Ocean in the 1970's . . . Meanwhile, a whole new generation is growing up in our

[96] See Lee Kuan Yew quoted in *The Mirror*, May 31, 1971 (Vol. 7, No. 22). At about the same time action was taken against two English-language papers in Singapore on the ground that they had been financed by foreign capital and were anti-Singapore government either currently or in the long run, and they ceased operations. One commentator said that some local observers saw the government action against these newspapers as possible "concessions to Chinese opinion" (Dick Wilson, "A Long View or Bogey?", *Far Eastern Economic Review*, August 7, 1971, p. 33).

[97] Lee Kuan Yew, *We Want to be Ourselves* (Singapore: Government Printers, 1967), p. 3.

schools. The older generation, the first generation migrants, men born and educated in China, they are in their 40's and 50's. And a whole new generation is growing up which is conscious not only of China but of the whole world.[98]

It is beyond the province of this paper to speculate on the success or failure of the ASEAN neutrality proposals. There are many uncertainties involved. How wide is the area of neutrality to be? Will ASEAN membership increase? What is to be ASEAN's relation to ASPAC (Asian and Pacific Council)?; will there even be an eventual merger of the two, as Philippine Foreign Secretary Carlos Romulo has suggested? What will be the consequences of the détente between China and the United States in Southeast Asia? What are the possible effects of the transfer of Chinese-Soviet tensions to the area? How far will the Soviets press a revived version of their own collective security proposals, applying it to an area wider than Southeast Asia, and how adamantly are they opposed to the ASEAN scheme?[99] Many of these questions are beyond the control of Southeast Asian states. However, it is worth drawing attention to one obvious consideration concerning the major powers and stating a minimum requirement for a viable neutral area. Neutrality, if it is achieved, will not be accompanied by the Great Powers losing interest in Southeast Asia or ceasing to compete in it. "The powers that are presently involved in Southeast Asia are not resigning their interests in the region, they are merely re-examining and trying to relate the effect on their interests of their future commitment and involvement in the area."[100] Second, the ASEAN countries do have some power to ensure the mini-

[98] Lee Kuan Yew, interviewed by Henry Kamm, *The Mirror*, June 14, 1971 (Vol. 7, No. 24). See also his comments on the visit of the Chinese Table Tennis team to Singapore, July 1972, quoted in *Asia Research Bulletin*, August 1972 (Vol. 2, No. 3), p. 1095.

[99] These and some other questions are discussed in Peter Lyon, "Reorientations in Southeast Asia," *The Round Table*, April 1972, pp. 234–37.

[100] Tun (Dr.) Ismail, speech given in Singapore, April 22, 1972, quoted in *Asia Research Bulletin*, May 1972 (Vol. 1, No. 12), p. 907.

mum necessary conditions for neutrality in the area, by limiting the overt expression of their differences with each other and by imposing a self-denying ordinance on appeals for help from outside. ". . . Southeast Asian nations should have the wisdom and fortitude to refrain from inviting the intervention of external forces in cases of intra-regional or internal conflict. It is also important for them to keep intra-regional conflict within bounds so as not to entice external interference."[101]

In summarizing the theme of this paper, i.e., the influence of ethnic minorities on the foreign policy of Southeast Asian countries, it is hard to look far into the future. The complex considerations touched upon in the preceding paragraph would make this too speculative. However, by looking as far as the present, it is possible to see the ASEAN neutrality proposal and subsequent related moves by the Southeast Asian countries concerned as marking a new departure in the relation between foreign policy and policy toward the international Chinese minority. It has been suggested that previously this relation was quite different for the Chinese minorities than for the Indian minorities. Indian minorities existed in substantial numbers only in Malaya and in Burma. In the former country the Indian minority was not implicated in any important internal disputes (indeed attention was concentrated on the more numerous Chinese minority), and the two governments concerned had no substantial differences. After the India-China border conflict, India and Malaya shared the bond of having faced aggressive Communism. Their relations were never soured by ideological campaigns conducted by the Indian government. In Burma, economic policies at various times caused severe hardship to many locally resident Indians and resulted in their departure in large numbers. Yet the Indian government was susceptible to Burma's sensitivities[102] and, especially in the earlier immediately postwar period, was sympathetic to Burma's socialist measures at home and to her pacific foreign policy. Relations between the two governments were therefore surprisingly undamaged. India's increased self-confidence in the early 1970s after her successful encounter with Pakistan has not made her feared in either Burma or Malaya. Clearly, she has no territorial ambitions against either, nor are the Indian minorities in either country regarded as even a potential fifth column.

As far as the Chinese minorities are concerned, this paper has argued that it was often impossible for Southeast Asian governments to disentangle three factors: China, Communism (including Communist subversion being carried on in the country), and the local Chinese minority. In the absence of relations with China it was difficult to conceive of China as an independent entity, rather than one seen remotely through the medium of either Communism or the Chinese minority. The main exception to this generalization among the countries discussed in this paper was Burma. Except for the incidents of June 1967, Burma, with a small Chinese minority but bordering on China, saw China in "state-power" terms rather than in "overseas Chinese" terms. Historically, the "overseas minority" had been the Indians. Malaysia and Singapore were also in a good position to see the local Chinese in a clear light because they formed a higher proportion of the population (in Singapore a majority) than in the other Southeast Asian countries, and realistic policies toward them were therefore imperative.

With the emergence of China as an undisputed Great Power in the area, which has disclaimed close interest in the affairs of overseas Chinese, there is an urgent need for the confusion between the three factors to be dispelled. Foreign policies must no longer be primarily reactions to domestic problems or consist of domestic policies masquerading as foreign policies. Recent changes in the foreign policies of the Southeast Asian states, led by Malaysia, seem to be an attempt to meet this requirement. It could be argued that in putting forward a neutralist solution for Southeast Asia, dependent for its effectiveness on the cooperation of China, for the first time they were committing themselves to considering China and the overseas Chinese as separate entities. China itself, now seated in the United Nations and having treated on equal terms with the United States, was acknowledged as a Great Power, with which official and quasi-official missions could be exchanged, and no longer as an amorphous extension of the overseas Chinese. The ASEAN members were now in a situation approximating Burma's over the two previous decades. The main difference was that, being physically more remote from China than Burma, in spite of some shrinkage of strategic distances, the ASEAN countries could hope for an explicit or implicit Great Power guarantee of neutrality instead of being constrained to exist virtually as a dependent of China.

To say that the Southeast Asian countries have now proved their ability to *perceive* foreign policy toward China separately from the perception of policies toward their Chinese minorities, is not to say that their *conduct* of foreign policy will, or should, be divorced from their policies toward minorities. It is rather to argue that now they are better able to see the interrelations between China, Communism, and the Chinese minorities, because each of the three can be perceived clearly in its own right. The policy of "balancing," as practiced in Thailand, the Philippines, and Malaysia in the last year or so, illustrates this point. Intelligent "balancing" consists in each country's *coordinating* policies toward China and toward Chinese minorities (and additionally on Communism); the balancing can only be intelligent if each factor has first been carefully distinguished and sufficiently weighed so as to indicate what the balance ought to be. Unfortunately the sequence of events has been inconveniently fast for Singapore, where, in the short run, because the Chinese are not a minority but a majority, a satisfactory balance is much more difficult to achieve.

Tribal Politics in Indochina:
The Role of Highland Tribes in the
Internationalization of Internal Wars

GARY D. WEKKIN

This is a study of the international significance of highland minorities in Southeast Asia. Students of Southeast Asian politics have long recognized the existence of traditional tensions between the nomadic tribes which dot the Southeast Asian highlands and the core peoples of the lowland plains and deltas. But while they have recognized that these ethnic hostilities pose difficulties for Southeast Asian governments, they have not appreciated the international implications of these hostilities.

This failure of appreciation is partly symptomatic of the underdevelopment of the study of linkage politics. For some time now political scientists have acknowledged that international political systems are responsive to developments occurring within national political systems, and vice versa. Despite this recognition, however, both national-system and international-system specialists have been so confined by their respective "conceptual jails" that the flow of political interaction between the two systemic levels has yet to be sufficiently studied.[1] But even when we have paid lip service to the international ramifications of national politics in Southeast Asia, we have wrongly seen this significant national political action as originating in the lowlands only.

This paper will attempt to show otherwise. This study seeks

[1] James N. Rosenau, "Introduction: Political Science in a Shrinking World," James N. Rosenau (ed.), *Linkage Politics* (New York: The Free Press, 1969), pp. 1–17.

to establish that disaffected highland tribes have been crucial to the internationalization of the internal wars that have raged over Indochina for the past twenty-five years. In order to illustrate this thesis, we shall examine the roles played by highland tribes in three of the four Indochina states—North Vietnam, Laos, and South Vietnam. The fourth Indochina state, Cambodia, will be excluded because its highland population is too small to be of significance. Because of this exclusion, our usage of the popular terms "First Indochina War" and "Second Indochina War" may be confusing; therefore, we shall refer to the three empirical cases of this study as the "Vietnamese War of Independence," the "Laotian Civil War," and the "Vietnamese Civil War."

One pattern of tribal alienation contributing to the internationalization of each of these three internal wars can be distinguished: a strong desire for autonomy or self-rule on the part of the highland tribes. Lowland governments—whether indigenous or colonial—always oppressed or ignored existing patterns of tribal rule in their dealings with their highland subjects. This tribal disaffection is an important link between all three internal wars and the international politics that have centered around Indochina in the past two decades. To understand this linkage we shall examine tribal roles in all three wars in the context of a simple scenario depicting the internationalization of an internal war.

Our basic argument is that the internal war is "internationalized" when either of the two parties to the war (insurgents and incumbents) actively seeks external assistance. Usually it is the weaker party, the insurgents, which first seeks or is first offered outside assistance so it can compete with the stronger party, generally the incumbents. The stronger party may then seek external assistance to counter the international link between its opponents and their outside ally.[2] But in order for either internal party to succeed in obtaining

[2] See George Modelski's "model" for the internationalization of internal wars in "The International Relations of Internal War," James N. Rosenau (ed.), *International Aspects of Civil Strife* (Princeton, N.J.: Princeton University Press, 1964), pp. 14–44.

outside assistance, two basic conditions must be met: first, the internal party must have a secure territorial base area to which external aid can be sent; and second, there must be a safe, handy supply route between this base and the external assistant through which aid can flow. Meeting these conditions is not such a problem for the incumbents, since they are in charge of the legitimate machinery and territory of the state and control access from the outside. But the insurgents are hard pressed to meet these conditions. Not only do they need a secure base just to be safe from military annihilation, but they also cannot receive external aid in quantity unless they have a safe base for it to be sent to. Moreover, it must be logistically possible to transfer material from the external benefactor to the insurgents' base without being intercepted by the incumbents.

The insurgents' need for a stable territorial base and a safe logistical link if external assistance is to be obtained is where the highland tribes assume significance in the internal warfare. The map on page 125 shows that mountainous tribal homelands have served as both territorial bases and supply routes for the insurgents and their external allies in all three internal wars. In order to obtain bases and supply routes in these areas, the insurgents and their outside helpers capitalized upon the discontent of the tribesmen with their respective lowland governments.[3]

In the Vietnamese War of Independence, the Tho homelands northeast of the Red River Delta and adjacent to the Chinese border were the Viet Minh's first base area. The contiguity of this base to China facilitated logistical traffic, and its mountainous terrain made it impenetrable to French mechanized forces. The Tho people identified themselves overwhelmingly with the Viet Minh movement because of

---

[3] On the other hand, incumbents and their external assistants have also exploited tribal discontent in attempts to disrupt insurgent bases and supply routes in the highlands. Examples are the U.S.-led Meo Army in Laos and the U.S.-sponsored CIDG program amongst the Moi in South Vietnam. The author studies America's use of highland tribes against the Pathet Lao and Viet Cong in a larger, unpublished version of this paper.

Map A
Autonomous Zones and Provinces
in the Indochinese highlands

*Adapted from "Vietnam and Asian Continent Maps," House
Document No. 147, 90th Congress, 1st Session, U. S. Government Printing Office, July 17, 1967.*

PEOPLE'S REPUBLIC OF CHINA

(Tho)
(Lao Theng)   (Hill Tai)   (Tho)
(Hill Tai)   Viet-Bac   (Tho)
                              Base
         Pathet   (Meo)   Area
         Lao Base
         Area   Hanoi
(Lao   (Hill
Theng)   Tai)
                  (Meo)   DEMOCRATIC
                  (Mco)   REPUBLIC OF VIETNAM

                              Ho Chi Minh Trail

Vientiane

LAOS

                  (Lao
                  Theng)   (Moi)
Bolovens   Viet
Plateau   Cong

                                  Base
                                  Area

CAMBODIA   (Moi)   Ho Chi
                                      Minh Trail

                              REPUBLIC
                              OF VIETNAM

                  Saigon *

Map B
Insurgent Base Areas and Supply
Routes in Tribal Areas

*Adapted from "Vietnam and Asian Continent Maps," House
Document No. 147, 90th Congress, 1st Session, U. S. Government Printing Office, July 17, 1967.*

French interference in their tribal politics.[4] Similarly, the long-time Pathet Lao strongholds of Sam Neua and Phong Saly provinces in northeastern Laos are essential to the Pathet Lao movement because they provide close logistical access to North Vietnam and a base isolated from the rest of Laos by the rugged mountain terrain in between. The population of these two provinces is mostly Hill Tai and Lao Theng tribesmen, who have always been badly mistreated by the lowland Lao.[5] Control of the Lao Theng and Moi homelands where the Ho Chi Minh Trail runs through southern Laos and enters the south-central highlands of South Vietnam has been essential to the logistics of the Viet Cong insurgents,[6] and one source credits the Moi-inhabited south-central highlands as the first organized NLF resistance base of the Vietnamese Civil War.[7]

Let us now turn to these three internal wars and examine them in the context of the framework of this paper. Beginning with the Vietnamese War of Independence we shall first look at the tribal alienation which set the stage for establishment of insurgent bases and supply routes necessary for securing external assistance, and then at the internationalization itself of the internal war.

AUTONOMY AND FRENCH ALIENATION OF THE THO

The Tho are one of the major hill-dwelling tribes of Indochina. Approximately 400,000 in population, they are the

[4] Joseph Buttinger, *Vietnam: A Dragon Embattled* (New York: Frederick A. Praeger, 1967), Vol. I, pp. 274–75, and Vol. II, pp. 736–37. See also John T. McAlister, Jr., "Mountain Minorities and the Viet Minh: A Key to the Indochina War," Peter Kunstadter (ed.), *Southeast Asian Tribes, Minorities, and Nations* (Princeton, N.J.: Princeton University Press, 1967), Vol. II, p. 795.

[5] Joel Halpern and Peter Kunstadter, "Laos: Introduction," Peter Kunstadter (ed.), *Southeast Asian Tribes, Minorities, and Nations* (Princeton, N.J.: Princeton University Press, 1967), Vol. I, p. 244.

[6] Interview with Nguyen Huu Chi, former chief of Quang Nam province, March 30, 1972.

[7] Wilfred G. Burchett, *Vietnam: Inside Story of the Guerrilla War* (New York: International Publishers, 1968), p. 144.

largest minority in what is today North Vietnam.[8] According to John McAlister, the Tho supported a powerful Vietnamese family's unsuccessful attempt to usurp the Vietnamese throne in the sixteenth century. Determined not to brook any further political interference from the Tho, the victorious Vietnamese incumbents decided to culturally assimilate the Tho peoples. They sent Vietnamese mandarins into the highlands to intermarry with the Tho and administer them. Through these mandarins and their descendants, who were called *Tho-ti,* "acculturation took form in the adoption of a Vietnamese style in land regulations and religious practices."[9] The *Tho-ti* —the mixed-blood descendants of the mandarins—soon became a hereditary elite because of their "hereditary monopolies over the alien Vietnamese culture and their ritualistic role in the religion of their people." Therefore, the Vietnamese were easily able to rule the Tho people through the *Tho-ti,* to whom the Vietnamese evidently gave "the political prerogatives of a mandarinate" on a hereditary basis even though the Vietnamese mandarinate itself had always been —and continued to be—selected by competitive examination.[10] But when Vietnam became a French colony, things changed for the *Tho-ti.*

French Indochina was an ethnic and cultural amalgam. The French arrived in a period of dynamic Vietnamese expansion which threatened all the highland peoples as well as the other lowland peoples of the area. Because most of the highlanders of Vietnam hated and feared the Vietnamese, the French placed them under separate jurisdiction from the Vietnamese and ruled them directly, choosing their own indigenous civil servants and go-betweens, instead of ruling through the Vietnamese.[11] This policy was very popular with most of the highland tribes. But to the Tho—and to the *Tho-ti* in particular—this policy was disruptive and antagonistic, be-

[8] Frank LeBar, Gerald Hickey, and John Musgrave (eds.), *Ethnic Groups of Mainland Southeast Asia* (New Haven, Conn.: Human Relations Area Files, 1964), p. 232.

[9] McAlister, *loc. cit.,* pp. 780, 787–88.

[10] *Ibid.,* p. 780. See also LeBar, Hickey & Musgrave, *op. cit.,* p. 234.

[11] *Ibid.,* p. 789.

cause in passing over the Vietnamese to choose their own subordinates from among the Tho, the French circumscribed the existing pattern of rule by the *Tho-ti,* who had been the traditional link between the Vietnamese government and the Tho people.[12] This rankled among the Tho people until the entry of Japanese troops into Indochina in 1940 diverted the Colonial government's attention, allowing the "pent-up frustrations" of the Tho to find an outlet in a rebellion around Bac Son, "where the influence of the *Tho-ti,* though stymied by the French, was still strong."[13]

THE ROLE OF THO DISAFFECTION IN THE INTERNATIONALIZATION OF THE VIETNAMESE WAR OF INDEPENDENCE

This Tho disaffection was of crucial importance to the Viet Minh movement at the time. After the virtual annihilation of the Indochinese Communist Party (ICP)[14] when it tried to create a guerrilla base area in the lowlands around Nghe An-Ha Tinh in 1930–31, the ICP realized it needed a base area which the military superiority of the French could not penetrate. When the Tho revolted in 1940, the Communists took advantage of the revolt to set up a guerrilla base in the mountainous homelands of the discontented Tho.[15] They

[12] McAlister elaborates on this point: "At the very same time they were guarding the autonomy of the upland people the French were also attempting to establish direct rule among them. Inevitably, this effort involved circumscribing the established patterns of rule and resulted in considerable tensions between those with traditional influence and those with positions created by the French . . . Not only did the position of the *Tho-ti* decline under French rule, but their misfortune also represented a check on Vietnamese cultural influence since this Vietnamized elite was the principal agent of assimilation among the Tho . . . one of the most important effects of the program of direct rule was to strengthen the barriers to assimilation with the lowlanders which were being erected around all the minority people. Except in the case of the Tho, these barriers coincided with the interests of the minority peoples or at least with the desires of their leaders" (*loc. cit.*, p. 789).

[13] *Ibid.*, pp. 792–93.

[14] *Ibid.*, pp. 792–93.

[15] McAlister, *loc. cit.*, pp. 792–93; Buttinger, *op. cit.* (Vol. I), pp. 274–75; Roy Jumper and Marjorie W. Normand, "Vietnam,"

simply promised autonomy and equality to the Tho, and won their strong support.[16] The Tho and the Viet Minh joined forces because they needed each other. Each saw in the other the solution to their own problems.[17]

This new Communist base in the Tho highlands remained unpenetrated until victory in 1954. McAlister claims that the Viet Minh might have been wiped out before they even got started, were it not for this inaccessible base and their new, "almost exclusively Tho" armed forces.[18] The Viet Minh military forces were not "exclusively" dependent upon the Tho for long, but the Tho remained a crucial factor in the Viet Minh's military success throughout the war. Three of the Viet Minh's top generals were Tho tribesmen: one served as Ho Chi Minh's first Minister of Defense and for most of the war commanded the Viet Minh base area in the Tho homelands, while the other two generals eventually commanded two of the six Viet Minh divisions mobilized during the war. These two divisions, the 312th and 316th of Dien Bien Phu fame, were composed almost entirely of Tho tribesmen totaling approximately 20,000 men. These 20,000 Tho represented about 5 per cent of the total Tho population in the early 1950s (or about 0.6 per cent of the population of all Vietnam), and yet comprised approximately 20 per cent of the Viet Minh's regular army in 1954.[19]

But possession of a base area in the Tho homeland was more important to the Viet Minh for another reason. The Tho homeland provided the all-important supply route to

---

George McT. Kahin (ed.), *Governments and Politics of Southeast Asia* (Ithaca, N.Y.: Cornell University Press, 1964), p. 499.

[16] Jumper and Normand, *loc. cit.,* p. 499. These promises were made good as soon as the Viet Minh won control of the North. In 1955 autonomous zones were set up in the highlands, and a considerable degree of tribal self-rule has been permitted. See the 1960 D.R.V. Constitution, which confirms tribal rights of autonomy and equality (Chapter 1, Article 3), in Bernard B. Fall's *The Two Vietnams* (New York: Frederick A. Praeger, 1963), p. 402.

[17] McAlister, *loc. cit.,* p. 794.

[18] John T. McAlister, Jr., *Vietnam: The Origins of Revolution* (New York: Alfred A. Knopf, 1969), p. 342. See also McAlister, *loc. cit.,* p. 795.

[19] McAlister, *loc. cit.,* pp. 795–96.

China through which the Viet Minh obtained external assistance—thereby internationalizing the Viet Minh War. The Tho homeland lies between south China and the heart of the Red River Delta, which makes it perhaps the most strategic location in all Indochina. The advantage of the Tho homeland over other mountain bases was "its contiguity with the Kwangsi-Kwangtung provinces of southern China, which made convenient a lively contraband trade in arms and ammunition," even before China turned Communist in 1949.[20] The Viet Minh so regularly traded opium to the Chinese for weapons that the following exchange rates developed and stabilized:

> 6 kilograms opium = 1 light machinegun & 500 rounds ammunition
> 4 kilograms opium = 1 automatic rifle & 500 rounds ammunition
> 2.5 kilograms opium = 1 rifle and 500 rounds ammunition[21]

One writer believes the Viet Minh movement "would have foundered" could it not have gotten weapons from China for opium.[22] When more war materials became available to the Viet Minh after the establishment of the People's Republic of China in 1949, the importance of the Tho homeland as a logistical link to China increased profoundly. French attempts to block this crucial link were severely crushed in 1950 when the Viet Minh wiped out a six to ten thousand man French force during the "Battle for R.C. 4" (Route Coloniale 4).[23]

The international consequences of Tho tribal politics are now better understood. Were it not for the French Colonial government's alienation of the Tho and their leaders, the

[20] *Ibid.*, pp. 795–97. See also Buttinger, *op. cit.*, pp. 736–37; and David Feingold, "Opium and Politics in Laos," Nina S. Adams and Alfred W. McCoy (eds.), *Laos: War and Revolution* (New York: Harper & Row, 1970), pp. 335–36.

[21] *Ibid.*, pp. 821–22.

[22] Feingold, *loc. cit.*, pp. 335–36.

[23] Bernard B. Fall, *Street Without Joy* (Harrisburg, Pa.: The Stackpole Co., 1961), pp. 26–28. See also McAlister, *loc. cit.*, pp. 773, 796–99.

Viet Minh might never have secured the safe, handy territorial base and supply route they needed to obtain external assistance. Nor would their young movement have derived such strength and popular support from the Tho people. McAlister's tribute to the importance of the Tho tribesmen in the Vietnamese War of Independence seems the most appropriate conclusion to this section:

> In terms of the utility of their territory and the commitment of their population, the contribution of the Tho to the military success of the Viet Minh was vital, if not absolutely decisive.[24]

AUTONOMY AND ALIENATION AMONG THE LAO THENG AND HILL TAI IN LAOS

As in the Vietnamese War of Independence, the Pathet Lao also obtained a safe territorial base and supply route by exploiting desires for tribal autonomy among the Lao Theng and Hill Tai tribes inhabiting the rugged mountains of eastern Laos. The Lao Theng and Hill Tai were not only alienated by French disregard for existing patterns of tribal rule, but also by injustices perpetrated by the lowland Lao who ruled them before and after the French Colonial Period. We will begin by examining these age-old grievances against the lowland Lao.

The Lao Theng have good reason to desire tribal autonomy from the present lowland government. Approximately 500,000 Lao Theng, divided into some sixty tribes belonging to two main language groups (Mon-Khmer and Malayo-Polynesian), presently live in Laos.[25] These Lao Theng were the original inhabitants of the area called Laos. When the lowland Lao first arrived in this area during the Great Thai Migrations from south China, it was part of the Khmer Empire and was populated by "a people less advanced than [the Lao] living under Khmer overlords who referred to them collectively, regardless of differences, as *Kha* [slaves], a name

24 McAlister, *loc. cit.*, p. 796.
25 Frank M. LeBar and Adrienne Suddard (eds.), *Laos: Its People, Its Society, Its Culture* (New Haven, Conn.: Human Relations Area Files, 1960), p. 42.

their descendants retain to this day."[26] The Lao adopted the word *Kha* and its meaning, enslaving many of the Lao Theng and driving the rest of them out of the lowlands into the mountains and forests.[27] They used the Lao Theng as slaves until the French abolished slavery when they took control of the area in the late nineteenth century. But despite the abolition of slavery, the status of the Lao Theng has changed very little. They are still regarded as second-class citizens, little different from the "savages" the Lao once seized and held as slaves. Even in the 1960s the Lao Theng of northern Laos were still subject to *corvée* draft, and could be forced to work for the Lao without pay.[28]

Because of these injustices, the Lao Theng's attitude toward the lowland Lao is simple hatred. There are a few exceptions: certain tribes are said to have resigned themselves to their inferior status, and the Souei, Sapuan, So, and Sek, four very small tribes which dwell in the lowlands among the Lao, have been largely assimilated by them. Most tribes, however, resent their slave-like status and the pejorative term *Kha* which the Lao use to designate them.[29]

Historical tension between the Hill Tai tribes and the lowlanders is more difficult to document. The Lao have accorded the 300,000–500,000 Hill Tai in Laos much the same disdain and arrogance they have shown the Lao Theng. It is said, however, that because of their common linguistic and ethnic heritage (both are Tai-speaking, paddy-cultivating emigrants from south China), the Lao are less condescending toward the Hill Tai than other tribes. Even the issue from which their present mutual contempt is said to have arisen indicates a

[26] *Ibid.,* p. 8. See also Wilfred G. Burchett, *Mekong North* (Berlin: Seven Seas Publishers, 1959), p. 200. These tribesmen, whom the lowland Lao still refer to as *Kha,* were only recently designated as *Lao Theng* by the Royal Lao government (which also refers to the lowland Lao as *Lao Loum* and the Meo as *Lao Xung*), in a concession to the tribesmen's sensibilities.

[27] T. D. Roberts (ed.), *Area Handbook for Laos* (Washington, D.C.: American University Press, 1967), p. 52. See also LeBar and Suddard, *op. cit.,* p. 8.

[28] LeBar and Suddard, *op. cit.,* pp. 73–74.

[29] Roberts, *op. cit.,* p. 59.

close relationship between the Lao and Hill Tai. The issue is one of cultural traditionalism versus cultural modernity. The two people are sprung from the same roots, but the Lao have progressed away from these roots toward modernity while the conservative Tai have retained their traditional heritage. The Lao look down upon the Tai because they have clung to traditional animist religious beliefs and traditional costumes.[30] LeBar and Suddard write that it is according to their costumes and traditions that the Lao distinguish the Tai tribes in an apparently derisive manner:

> The tribal groupings are . . . Tai Dam (Black Tai), Tai Deng (Red Tai), Tai Khao (White Tai), as well as Tai Neua, Tai Phong, and Phou Tai. These names and others seem to be general designations by the Lao, who distinguish these "inferior" peoples roughly according to the color of their traditional costumes, their location, or some other real or imagined identifying characteristic.[31]

On the other hand, the Hill Tai evidently look askance at the Lao over these same issues. They are contemptuous of the Lao's more modern ways of living. They are said to especially disapprove of the Lao elite because of the latter's relatively advanced stage of Western acculturation.[32]

More important than these differences, however, is the long history of Tai raids on Lao settlements, and Lao attempts to conquer and subdue the Hill Tai. In fact, hostilities between the Lao and the Hill Tai enabled France to add the territory that is now Laos to her Indochina empire. In the late 1880s, Tai "Black Flags" under the White Tai chieftain Deo Van Tri sacked and burned the royal capital of Luang Prabang, and the French won dominion over the area by quelling the Black Flags and restoring the King of Luang Prabang to his

[30] *Ibid.,* p. 59. See also Halpern and Kunstadter, *loc. cit.,* p. 236.

[31] LeBar and Suddard, *op. cit.,* p. 40. See also Wilfred G. Burchett, *North of the Seventeenth Parallel* (Hanoi: Burchett, 1955), p. 212.

[32] Roberts, *op. cit.,* p. 59.

throne.[33] Finally, the Hill Tai, as well as the Lao Theng, are not enfranchised by the Royal Lao government. They are treated as second-class citizens, and neither have ever been represented in the Laotian National Assembly (as of 1967), despite comprising at least 40 per cent of Laos' total population.[34] Indeed, only a handful of Lao Theng have ever held office higher than village chief.[35] Small wonder these tribesmen wish to be autonomous of the Royal Lao government.

Turning to the Colonial Period, French circumscription of existing patterns of highland rule evidently alienated tribesmen in Laos, too. The French did not go out of their way to protect tribesmen from the lowland Lao by setting up separate administrative devices for them as they did for the tribes in Vietnam.[36] Tribesmen and Lao alike were ruled together under the traditional Lao system of rule, with French and Vietnamese civil servants superimposed at the top. This did not, however, prevent the French from interfering with existing tribal patterns of rule at the local level. In establishing the Colonial government's links in highland areas where lowland Lao authority had failed to penetrate or had suffered a rollback, the French frequently bypassed traditional tribal ruling elites when they appointed village chieftains or district officers. Since these appointees were usually the only visible representatives of the Colonial government in their respective localities,[37] tribesmen could be alienated if the French-appointed local officer was the wrong person for the job in their eyes.

One tribe which posed this problem for the French was the Lamet, a large and important Lao Theng tribe. When

[33] Arthur J. Dommen, *Conflict in Laos* (New York: Frederick A. Praeger, 1964), pp. 9–10. See also Halpern and Kunstadter, *loc. cit.,* p. 234.

[34] Halpern and Kunstadter, *loc. cit.,* pp. 241, 243–44.

[35] *Ibid.,* p. 241. Those who have risen beyond village chief have gone no further than the next to lowest level, district chief.

[36] *Ibid.,* p. 241.

[37] See Thomas H. Stanton's observations on the importance of local government representatives in remote highland areas in *Conflict in Laos: The Village Point of View, Paper No. 17* (New York: Southeast Asia Development Advisory Group), June 15, 1967.

the French went among the Lamet, they always appointed one Lamet in each village as chief, and this chief was "never really accepted by his village as a legitimate leader."[38] Most likely this chief was never accepted as a legitimate leader because Lamet villages were traditionally led by a council of the wealthy men of the village, who are called *lem,* rather than by a single leader.[39] If the French picked a single *lem* as leader, they might have alienated the rest of the *lem* of the village. Moreover, the Lamet draw a clear line between the *lem* and commoners (*to*), and if the French picked a *to* as village chieftain, the entire council of *lem* would probably have been alienated. Since the *lem* are greatly admired by the Lamet people,[40] the entire village would probably have shared the *lem*'s wrath. In short, the French probably alienated the traditional Lamet ruling elite, just as they did the *Tho-ti.*

The French may have encountered the same problem in selecting local officials among other Lao Theng tribes, such as the Akha.[41] The French also alienated certain Hill Tai tribes by encroaching on the autonomy of local Tai leaders. Alfred McCoy mentions two incidents between the French

---

[38] Alfred W. McCoy, "French Colonialism in Laos, 1893–1945," Nina S. Adams and Alfred W. McCoy (eds.), *Laos: War and Revolution* (New York: Harper & Row, 1970), p. 80.

[39] LeBar, Hickey, & Musgrave, *op. cit.,* p. 119. See also Roberts, *op. cit.,* p. 72.

[40] Robbins Burling, *Hill Farms and Padi Fields* (Englewood Cliffs, N.J.: Prentice-Hall, 1965), pp. 56–67. See also Roberts, *op. cit.,* p. 72.

[41] Peter Kandre, "Autonomy and Integration of Social Systems: The Iu Mien ('Yao' or 'Man') Mountain Population and Their Neighbors," Peter Kunstadter (ed.), *Southeast Asian Tribes, Minorities and Nations* (Princeton, N.J.: Princeton University Press, 1967), Vol. II, p. 628. Kandre reports there are four important officers in every Akha village: the person responsible for the village's external political relations, the founder or a descendant of the founder of the village, the village smith, and the ritual expert. Government agencies seeking political cooperation from Akha villages have often mistaken the officer in charge of external political relations as the sole leader of the village. On the contrary, this officer is powerless to impose his personal policy on the others. The cooperation of all four officials must be sought before the Akha will cooperate with outsiders (p. 628).

and the Tai-Lu tribe. The first was an ambiguous crisis in the Lu areas of Phong Saly province, resulting from the alienation of a chief named Va Na Poum when the French tried to assume greater authority in his district.[42] In the second incident, the French representative in the Lu canton of Muong Sing "encroached upon the authority" of the local Lu chief, Phra Ong Kham, causing his followers to try to assassinate the French official, and then stir up a rebellion of several years' length after the assassination plot was discovered.[43]

THE ROLE OF LAO THENG AND HILL TAI ALIENATION IN THE INTERNATIONALIZATION OF THE LAOTIAN CIVIL WAR

In the Laotian Civil War, as in the Vietnamese War of Independence, tribal homelands have once again served as insurgent base areas and as supply routes between the insurgents and their outside allies. The key to internationalization of the internal war in Laos by means of external assistance has been the control of the Laotian highlands and the support of the tribesmen who populate them. Two highland areas in Laos serve as direct supply routes between the external assistant, North Vietnam, and the two insurgent recipients of her assistance, the Pathet Lao and the Viet Cong. These two areas are the Bolovens Plateau, through which the all-important Ho Chi Minh Trail passes to the Viet Cong in South Vietnam, and the northeastern provinces of Sam Neua and Phong Saly, through which supplies and perhaps instructions pass from North Vietnam to the Pathet Lao.

The Ho Chi Minh Trail has received so much public exposure we need not dwell on its value as a supply route to the insurgents in South Vietnam. Suffice it to say that no other supply route was available, except straight down through the well-patrolled Demilitarized Zone at the seventeenth parallel. The support of the Lao Theng who lived in the Bolovens area had to be procured so the North Vietnamese could have the safe, reliable supply route their reunification effort would need.

[42] McCoy, *loc. cit.*, p. 90.
[43] *Ibid.*, p. 90.

Though not as well known, the provinces of Sam Neua and Phong Saly are as important a supply route for the Pathet Lao as the Ho Chi Minh Trail is for the Viet Cong. Sam Neua and Phong Saly have been in Pathet Lao control[44] since 1953 when an invasion by four divisions of Viet Minh regulars captured them and parts of other provinces and turned them over to Prince Souphanouvong's 2,000 Pathet Lao troops.[45] Ever since then, these two provinces have served as the Pathet Lao's home base, staging area, and chief logistical link to North Vietnam. Langer and Zasloff argue that Pathet Lao power is concentrated in these mountainous eastern provinces mostly because of their proximity to North Vietnam.[46] The small, weak Pathet Lao movement of the early 1950s was extremely dependent upon the Viet Minh for rice, money, arms, ammunition, and advisors,[47] and the Lao-Vietnamese borders in Sam Neua and Phong Saly "provided ideal conditions for infiltration and exfiltration" because the terrain was rugged and the same tribes lived on both sides of the border.[48] So the Viet Minh installed their Pathet Lao comrades in Sam Neua and Phong Saly in 1953, and took special care at the 1954 Geneva Convention to ensure that these two provinces would remain under Pathet Lao control.[49]

That the Viet Minh gave Sam Neua and Phong Saly to the Pathet Lao on a silver platter did not diminish the importance of procuring the support of the tribesmen who lived here. The Pathet Lao were only 2,000 strong when the Viet Minh turned these territories over to them in 1953, and were only 1,500 to 3,000 strong when the Geneva Convention gave

[44] Some observers, such as Paul Langer, Joseph Zasloff, and Arthur Dommen, would argue with some justification that "Viet Minh control" is more applicable here.

[45] Bernard B. Fall, *Anatomy of a Crisis*, ed. by R. M. Smith (Garden City, N.Y.: Doubleday & Company, 1969), pp. 46–47; Dommen, *op. cit.*, pp. 40–41.

[46] Paul F. Langer and Joseph J. Zasloff, *North Vietnam and the Pathet Lao* (Cambridge, Mass.: Harvard University Press, 1970), p. 13.

[47] *Ibid.*, pp. 37–38, 51.

[48] *Ibid.*, p. 15.

[49] *Ibid.*, p. 57.

them "military and administrative control" of the two provinces in 1954.[50] They were hardly in any shape to control two rugged, sprawling provinces without significant cooperation from the tribal populations. As in the Vietnamese War of Independence, the Pathet Lao (and their Viet Minh advisors) gained much tribal support by capitalizing on the alienation of the tribesmen and promising them autonomy. They promised tribesmen social and political equality with the lowland Lao, and the all-important right to govern their own affairs. Social and political equality is guaranteed in the platform of the Pathet Lao's mass front organization, the Neo Lao Hak Sat.[51] To convince the highlanders of their good intentions the Pathet Lao have given high positions in their movement to several tribal leaders, such as Sithon Kommadam of the Lao Theng in the Bolovens Plateau and Faydang of the Meo in the northeast.[52] Perhaps the most effective enticement to Laotian tribesmen, however, has been the Tai-Meo and Viet Bac Autonomous Zones which the Viet Minh established in the tribal areas of northern Vietnam soon after taking control in 1954.[53] A very real degree of autonomy has been granted the Tai, Meo, and Tho inhabitants of these zones. They are governed by cadre of their own tribe and send a per capita quota of deputies to the D.R.V. national assembly about three times as high as the quota for the lowland areas.[54] The credibility of Pathet Lao promises of autonomy and equality is considerably enhanced by these North Vietnamese autonomous zones, which Communist

[50] *Ibid.*, p. 51.

[51] Roberts, *op. cit.*, p. 208. See also the Action Program of the Second National Congress of the Neo Lao Hak Sat, 1964, in Dommen's appendix, *op. cit.*, 1964.

[52] Bernard B. Fall, "The Pathet Lao: A 'Liberation Party,' " in Robert A. Scalapino (ed.), *The Communist Revolution in Asia* (Englewood Cliffs, N.J.: Prentice-Hall, 1969), pp. 188–89. See also Langer and Zasloff, *op. cit.*, pp. 46–47; Halpern and Kunstadter, *loc. cit.*, pp. 245–46; and Burchett, *op. cit.*, (1959), p. 213.

[53] Peter Kunstadter, "Vietnam: Introduction," Peter Kunstadter (ed.), *Southeast Asian Tribes, Minorities and Nations* (Princeton, N.J.: Princeton University Press, 1967), Vol. II, p. 685.

[54] *Ibid.*, p. 685. See also Fall, *op. cit.*, (1963), pp. 149–51.

working among the Laotian tribes unfailingly point to as evidence of their good intentions.[55]

Thus, the Pathet Lao have taken advantage of the political desires of the Lao Theng, Hill Tai, and other tribes to consolidate the base area and supply route left them by the Viet Minh. They have been very adept in exploiting tribal resentment against the present Royal Lao government as well as against the former French Colonial government.[56]

Like the Tho in northern Vietnam, the tribes of Laos have responded to promises of autonomy with considerable popular support for the Pathet Lao. However, exactly how many tribesmen support the Pathet Lao, and what tribes they belong to, are difficult questions to answer. The size of the Pathet Lao movement or armed forces themselves are very difficult to estimate with any accuracy, and the author has never seen any detailed estimates of their ethnic composition. The most reliable indication of tribal support for the Pathet Lao occurred in May 1959, when 1,500 of the Pathet Lao's best troops reported for induction into the Royal Lao Army under the coalition agreement worked out by Souphanouvong and Souvanna Phouma in 1957. Although no figures on the ethnic composition of these troops could be found, they are described briefly by a prominent Lao official, Sisouk na Champassak:

> Comprised of a strange mixture of Thai [Hill Tai], Meo, Kha, and a minority of Lao, these battalions constituted the elite of the Pathet Lao forces. Experienced soldiers, skilled in the tricks of guerrilla warfare, they compen-

[55] Halpern and Kunstadter, *loc. cit.*, p. 249; Kunstadter, *loc. cit.*, p. 684–85; Gerald Hickey, "Some Aspects of Hill Tribe Life in South Vietnam," Peter Kunstadter (ed.), *Southeast Asian Tribes, Minorities and Nations* (Princeton, N.J.: Princeton University Press, 1967), Vol. II, pp. 764–65.

[56] Peter Dale Scott, "Laos: The Story Nixon Won't Tell," Marvin E. and Susan Gettleman, Lawrence and Carol Kaplan (eds.), *Conflict in Indochina* (New York: Random House, 1970), p. 272. See also Guy Moréchand, "The Many Languages and Cultures of Laos," Nina S. Adams and Alfred W. McCoy (eds.), *Laos: War and Revolution* (New York: Harper & Row, 1971), p. 29.

sated for their disparate dialects and customs with an iron discipline and an absolute faith in their leaders.[57]

The largely tribal composition of the Pathet Lao forces is confirmed by a North Vietnamese Army captain's description of the Pathet Lao battalion he had advised before defecting:

> On our side, there was no substance in our propaganda, only empty words . . . In our unit we had only Lao Theung; no Lao Loum [lowland Lao] were joining the Pathet Lao. How could we say that the people supported us?[58]

Most observers feel that hill tribesmen comprise a majority of the entire Pathet Lao movement. Halpern and Kunstadter write that "it is in the areas where the ethnic Lao are in the minority that the Pathet Lao have been most successful."[59] In 1965 the Pathet Lao controlled nearly half the population and two-thirds of the territory of Laos, a zone of control which showed an "incredibly close concordance with the highland-lowland boundaries."[60] The inhabitants of the two areas linking North Vietnam to the Pathet Lao and the Viet Cong—the northeastern provinces and the Bolovens Plateau —are mostly tribesmen. The populations of Phong Saly and Sam Neua are over one-half Lao Theng and two-thirds Hill Tai, respectively.[61] In the Bolovens Plateau, the inhabitants are mostly members of several Lao Theng tribes.[62] Most of the Loven and a few of the Neahun tribesmen occupying this area are personally led by Sithon Kommadam, the prominent

---

[57] Sisouk na Champassak, *Storm Over Laos* (New York: Frederick A. Praeger, 1961), p. 76.

[58] Captain Mai Dai Hap, NVA, in an interview quoted in Langer and Zasloff, *op. cit.*, p. 143.

[59] Halpern and Kunstadter, *loc. cit.*, p. 244.

[60] Fall, *loc. cit.*, p. 183. Fall's thesis in this article is that the Pathet Lao are largely composed of tribesmen. See also Langer and Zasloff, *op. cit.*, pp. 9–11; and Halpern and Kunstadter, *loc. cit.*, p. 244.

[61] Halpern and Kunstadter, *loc. cit.*, p. 244. Most of the remaining inhabitants of these areas are probably members of other tribes, rather than lowland Lao.

[62] *Ibid.*, p. 234.

Pathet Lao leader.[63] These Bolovens tribes have provided an "impressive number" of insurgent political and military leaders.[64]

It should be realized, however, that not all hill tribes in Laos are pro-Pathet Lao. Most of Laos' Meo tribesmen have resisted rather than supported the Pathet Lao. Many observers agree that the much-persecuted Lao Theng—and to a lesser extent, the Hill Tai—have been the main source of Pathet Lao support.[65] The Meo, on the other hand, were severely alienated by the Pathet Lao and Viet Minh and have tenaciously resisted them.[66]

AUTONOMY AND ALIENATION AMONG THE MOI OF SOUTH VIETNAM

As in Laos, unceasing mistreatment by the lowland majority has fostered strong desires for tribal autonomy among the Moi people of South Vietnam. The 800,000 Moi inhabiting South Vietnam's south-central highlands are in many respects similar to the Lao Theng people of Laos. Like the Lao Theng, the Moi consist of a number of tribes of Malayo-Polynesian and Mon-Khmer stock. In fact, several of these migrant, slash-and-burn cultivating tribes can be found on either side of the border separating South Vietnam's south-central highlands from the Bolovens Plateau of Laos. The Moi have suffered the same problems with the Vietnamese that their Lao Theng cousins have had with the lowland Lao. A history of raiding parties, reprisal expeditions, and enslavement has re-

---

[63] Stanton, *loc. cit.*, pp. 10–11.

[64] Fall, *loc. cit.*, pp. 188–89.

[65] George Moseley, "Voices in the Minority," *Far Eastern Economic Review*, March 3, 1967 (Vol. LV), pp. 463–65. Moseley says that the Pathet Lao have been most successful among the Lao Theng, who were treated the worst by the lowland Lao. Most Pathet Lao soldiers, except for a couple of battalions composed of Hill Tai, are Lao Theng. See also Roberts, who writes that "Pathet Lao troops are generally Mon-Khmer in origin" (*op. cit.*, p. 59).

[66] *Ibid.*, p. 463. McAlister (*loc. cit.*, pp. 783, 820, 836–37) cites conflicts of interest over opium as the main factor behind Meo anti-Communism.

sulted in a mutual hatred between the Moi and Vietnamese which is best summarized by an old Moi saying:

"Ma Kap meo, keo kap lao."
(Dogs and cats: Annamese and Mois.)[67]

Like the pejorative "Kha" (slave) which the Lao use to designate the Lao Theng, "Moi" is a Vietnamese pejorative meaning "savages," and the highlanders are considered such by the Vietnamese, who can be seen pointing and laughing at Moi delegations forced to participate in parades through Saigon on national holidays.[68]

Because of this ethnic clash, the French Colonial government's separate and direct rule of the south-central highlands was very popular with the Moi. The French kept the Vietnamese out of the highlands, and set up tribal schools taught in Moi languages. They let the Moi live under their own laws, and even codified these laws and developed a tribal court system based on traditional Moi courts.[69] After 1954, however, the Diem regime did away with these policies, and tried instead to assimilate or Vietnamize the Moi. The Moi were considered citizens of the Republic of Vietnam, and were expected to abide by Vietnamese rather than Moi laws. Those who broke these laws answered to lowland Vietnamese courts. The Moi were ruled by Vietnamese administrators once again, and attended schools in which only Vietnamese was spoken, if they were allowed to attend school at all.[70] The most oppressive measure, however, was Diem's new land policy in the highlands. He decided to kill two birds with one stone: he would Vietnamize the Moi and resettle the hundreds of thousands of Catholics who had fled North Vietnam by moving the refugees into the highlands among the Moi. He gave land in the south-central highlands, regardless of prior

[67] Gabrielle Bertrand, *The Jungle People* (London: Robert Hale, Ltd., 1959), p. 158.
[68] Don Luce and John Sommer, *Vietnam: The Unheard Voices* (Ithaca, N.Y.: Cornell University Press, 1969), pp. 81–82.
[69] Kunstadter, *loc. cit.*, pp. 678–79.
[70] *Ibid.*, p. 680.

tribal ownership, to over 50,000 Vietnamese by 1960, and to 100,000—200,000 Vietnamese by 1963.[71]

The more Vietnamese refugees Diem resettled in the highlands, the more endangered was the Moi way of life. Resettlement deprived the Moi of large areas of land needed for their shifting, slash-and-burn agriculture. Tribal dislocation had become so serious by 1959, when not even 50,000 Vietnamese had been resettled, that one observer felt compelled to write, "if there is no Communist invasion of Free Vietnam, it would look as if the tribesmen will gradually lose more and more land, and more tribal villages will deteriorate and die out."[72] No one knew this better than the Moi themselves, and anti-Diem sentiment ran rampant among them:

> In the final analysis, the most important aspect of the highland resettlement program was that it confirmed the worst suspicions of the tribesmen concerning the Vietnamese. If the Vietnamese were to settle large areas vital to the shifting ray agriculture of the nomadic tribesmen, eventual tribal extermination was the probable result.[73]

THE ROLE OF MOI ALIENATION
IN THE VIETNAMESE CIVIL WAR

The insurgent Viet Cong had to control the Moi-inhabited south-central highlands to safely obtain external assistance from North Vietnam during the Vietnamese Civil War.[74] The

[71] *Ibid.*, p. 680; Hickey, *loc. cit.*, p. 754; McAlister, *loc. cit.*, p. 38. In addition, some 25,000 Moi were forced to move into these Catholic areas, where they would be Vietnamized and "protected from" (read "denied to") the Viet Cong.

[72] Frederick Wickert, quoted by Charles A. Joiner, "Administration and Political Warfare in the Highlands," Wesley R. Fishel (ed.), *Vietnam: Anatomy of a Conflict* (Itasca, Ill.: Peacock Press, 1968), p. 351.

[73] Joiner, *loc cit.*, p. 351.

[74] The author agrees with those who argue that D.R.V. aid to the Viet Cong is not "external" assistance because Vietnam is one country and should have been reunified as specified in the 1954 Geneva Agreement. However, the eventual unthinking acceptance of South Vietnamese legitimacy by much of the international system (and by most scholars of the period as well) created an inter-

south-central highlands area bordering Laos was the only South Vietnamese region rugged enough to prevent the incumbent forces from easily intercepting material flowing south. Consequently, the highlands became the terminus of all three main routes of the insurgents' main supply route, the Ho Chi Minh Trail. Control of the Moi who live in this area was crucial to the success of this supply operation at the beginning of the war. Nguyen Huu Chi, former chief of Quang Nam province, relates that the Viet Cong and North Vietnamese took great pains to secure the loyalty of the tribes straddling the projected routes of the Ho Chi Minh Trail.[75] However, like the Tho homelands in northern Vietnam, the south-central highlands provided the Viet Cong not only with the best available supply route and base area, but also with many tribal recruits and a staging area with quick access to lowland targets.[76]

The story of the Moi's role in the Viet Cong movement begins in 1956 when Diem undertook a series of anti-Viet Minh mop-up operations. Rather than try to eliminate the bases of popular support the Viet Minh had built up in the south prior to 1954, Diem chose to physically wipe out the ex-Viet Minh cadres.[77] From June 1956 until the end of 1957, troops and police swept the countryside, killing or imprisoning ex-cadres and harassing their families. Wives and children were frequently relocated to "agricultural settlements" or forced to prove their loyalty to the Republic by renouncing their cadre husbands and fathers.[78] Those who managed to survive this repression did so by fleeing to the highlands, where a few Moi tribes which had supported the Viet Minh prior to 1954 protected them:

It is no exaggeration to state that at the peak period of

national status quo of several years' standing which can be used to justify this study's treatment of D.R.V. assistance to the Viet Cong as "external" assistance to an insurgent party in a separate and sovereign state.

[75] Nguyen Huu Chi, Interview, March 30, 1972.
[76] Joiner, *loc. cit.*, pp. 352–53.
[77] Buttinger, *op. cit.*, (Vol. II), p. 74.
[78] Burchett, *op. cit.*, (1968), pp. 126–27.

the repression, virtually all revolutionary forces, all the future activists of the Liberation Front in Central Vietnam, were concentrated in the minority areas, fed, protected, hidden when necessary by the tribespeople.[79]

But Diem's anti-cadre campaign followed the cadre into the highlands, and the tribes hiding them soon became the targets of repression and terror themselves.[80] In January 1959 this repression set off a revolt among the Kor tribesmen in Quang Ngai province, who killed all but one member of a 55-man ARVN garrison stationed among them. Wilfred Burchett calls this revolt the first act of revolutionary violence in all of central Vietnam, and one of the first such acts in South Vietnam as a whole.[81]

Diem immediately sent troops to crush the Kor, but could not corner the elusive tribesmen for a decisive blow. In frustration and anger, he began lashing out at innocent and insurgent tribesmen alike, alienating the innocent in the process.[82] According to Burchett, the surviving ex-cadre in Quang Ngai province met in late 1959 and decided to organize a war of resistance based on the Moi dissidents, who now numbered many tribes because of Diem's indiscriminate brutality. In writing of this decision, Burchett credits the Moi with providing the spark that set off the Vietnamese Civil War:

> An historian could pick on this decision . . . as a starting point of the "two-sided war." As far as I could discover, it was the first such decision taken at that sort of level, and it had widespread repercussions. The example of the Kor tribespeople and the support it finally received from Vietnamese cadres was later used as a decisive argument in changing the "line" at the highest

[79] *Ibid.*, pp. 130–31, 143, 175.

[80] *Ibid.*, pp. 131, 133–34. See also Joiner, *loc. cit.*, p. 352.

[81] *Ibid.*, pp. 131–32.

[82] Joiner writes: "Saigon's military forces . . . sometimes failed to discriminate between Communists and non-Communists in specific [tribal] villages, and their actions not infrequently alienated entire villages. All this was a cause of eventual insecurity in much of the highlands" (*loc. cit.*, p. 352). See also Burchett, *op. cit.* (1968), p. 133.

level and generalizing armed resistance throughout South Vietnam.[83]

As in the Vietnamese War of Independence and the Laotian Civil War, the Viet Cong insurgents successfully capitalized on tribal desires for autonomy. The platform of the National Liberation Front makes the following promises regarding autonomy and equality for minorities:

> To ensure the right to autonomy of the national minorities.
> To set up, within the framework of the great family of the Vietnamese people, autonomous regions in areas inhabited by minority people.
> To ensure equal rights among different nationalities.
> All nationalities have the right to use and develop their own spoken and written languages and to preserve or change their customs and habits . . .[84]

Viet Cong propaganda played effectively on the Moi's fears that Diem would take away all their land, and the two tribal autonomous zones in North Vietnam lent much credibility to the NLF's promises of Moi autonomy.[85] Armed resistance quickly spread from the resistance base set up in the Kor homelands of Quang Ngai province to the Hre and Ngao tribes in the same province, southward to the Hre and Bahnar tribes in Binh Dinh province, northward to tribes in Quang Nam and Thua Thien provinces, and eastward into the coastal plains, where the lowland Vietnamese dwelled.[86] Diem's repression and disregard for tribal rights were ultimately self-defeating.

CONCLUSIONS

We have seen that tribal politics have played a crucial role in the internationalization of three internal wars in Indochina.

[83] Burchett, *op. cit.* (1968), p. 144.

[84] Kunstadter, *loc. cit.,* p. 681.

[85] Hickey, *loc. cit.,* pp. 762, 764–65. See also Kunstadter, *loc. cit.,* pp. 685–86.

[86] Burchett, *op. cit.* (1968), pp. 150–52. See also Joiner, *loc. cit.,* p. 352. It should be noted, however, that the support of the Moi people has not been a significant factor in the Viet Cong's success since these early stages of the Vietnamese Civil War.

Unrest and desire for political autonomy among tribal minorities dwelling in rugged, remote highlands at the periphery of Laos and the two Vietnamese states have facilitated external assistance in three internal wars. Tribal politics can have significant international impact, and should be studied more carefully by students of Southeast Asian and international politics. A proper appreciation of tribal politics in Indochina may enhance our understanding of how internal turmoil facilitates external intervention and international violence.

But let us hope that the governments of Southeast Asia, and not just political scientists, will come to a greater realization of the necessity for just treatment of tribal minorities. It should be apparent by now that any lasting solution of tribal alienation must involve a significant degree of autonomy for the highlanders. A structural recognition of the basic highland-lowland division in these states may lead to a better integration than attempted assimilation or pretended ignorance of the differences between highlanders and lowlanders. So far, however, only North Vietnam and the resistance governments of Laos and South Vietnam have been willing to make such a structural recognition, and the tribesmen of Laos and South Vietnam appear doomed to continued mistreatment so long as the incumbent governments of those two states remain in power.

Cambodia in the Vortex:
The Actors' Perceptions, Goals, and Settlement Prospects*

SHELDON W. SIMON

INTRODUCTION

For the political scientist the Cambodian conflict seems particularly interesting in that it combines almost all the elements which make for ambiguity in modern limited warfare: domestic insurgency, external intervention, a combination of both Great Power and local involvement, and the persistent protestations by the two Cambodian antagonists that they remain nonaligned despite the complete dependence of each on the two major bloc opponents in the Indochina war.

One of the underlying assumptions of this study is that prospects for a negotiated settlement of the Cambodian war increase as shared expectations about the region's future converge. The obverse of this proposition also holds. Thus, widely differing views on the stakes of the war would diminish prospects for a negotiated settlement, as distinct from a military solution.

Events in Cambodia subsequent to Prince Sihanouk's deposition in March 1970 altered the parameters of the Indochina conflict in at least three important respects. First, the number of participants in the new, Cambodian segment of

* This paper is synthesized from the author's booklength manuscript, *War and Politics in Southeast Asia: Actor Perceptions of the Cambodian Conflict* (Durham, N.C.: Duke University Press, 1973). The author wishes to thank the Patterson School of Diplomacy of the University of Kentucky for support for a research trip to the U. S. Department of State in May 1972 to help verify some of the findings.

the war increased to six—the United States, the Democratic Republic of Vietnam (D.R.V.), the Republic of Vietnam (R.V.N.), the Lon Nol government in Phnom Penh or Khmer Republic, Sihanouk's government-in-exile in Peking (R.G.N.U.C.) and its "liberation front" (FUNK), and the Chinese People's Republic (C.P.R.). Sihanouk's choice of Peking for his exile served to involve China directly for the first time in the politics of the second Indochina war. Second, the geographical scope of the war was broadened from a primary location in Vietnam—at least since 1963—to a peninsular-wide conflict with battle sites in Laos and Cambodia integral to the adversaries' Vietnam military strategies. Finally, the direct involvement of Cambodia in the war changed the stakes for several of the actors. Prospects for an Indochina-wide conflict settlement have been complicated by the hostilities in Cambodia as the implications of victory or defeat have varied for the actors involved. Differing tenacities of commitment have resulted, ranging from primarily politico-ideological concerns on the parts of the United States and China, through the desire for long-term regional hegemony for North Vietnam, to the question of political survival for the present governments in Saigon and Phnom Penh.

BACKGROUND

One explanation for the seemingly interminable nature of the Indochina conflict is that, at least in part, it has been a proxy war. That is, the indigenous economic capacities of the belligerents to continue the battle are less important because external support is available. Rather, the political will of the contending leaderships and the extent of national unity behind them are the key variables. The weapons technology of the protracted limited conflict remain well within the capabilities of all belligerents, because shortcomings in either technology or the economic base are alleviated through external aid to the contenders from their backers.

Given the economic and organizational capacities of the belligerents to sustain the conflict, it is necessary next to examine the characteristics of the social milieu in Cambodia for fostering national liberation movements. Most scholarship identifying conditions conducive to successful liberation movements demonstrates a positive relationship between the prevalence of large scale tenancy and support for radical insurgency.[1] This pattern characterized China from the 1860s until 1950, Mexico in the early twentieth century, and the current scene in Vietnam. But it does not characterize Cambodia. The social malaise which aided Viet Cong recruitment in South Vietnam does not seem to prevail in the Cambodian countryside.[2] Some 95 per cent of Khmer peasants own their land in a country 80 per cent of which is cultivable. Overpopulation presents no problem in a country of only seven million; and rural indebtedness does not appear burdensome.

Reflecting this generally prosperous social context, the Khmer Rouge, prior to Sihanouk's overthrow, was estimated at approximately 2,000 primarily urban-based intellectuals.[3] By early 1972, those who identified themselves with this movement may have exceeded 30,000; however, they were concentrated in those areas of eastern Cambodia under virtually permanent occupation by Vietnamese Communist forces.[4]

Despite the relative absence of land hunger, other Cambodian characteristics did seem propitious for a revolutionary movement: the overall economic development level was low, the administration had very little impact beyond the urban centers, and the consequent political vacuum in the countryside permitted an organized external movement to enter the region and engage in political activities with minimal govern-

[1] Donald S. Zagoria, "The Ecology of Peasant Communism in India," *American Political Science Review* (Vol. 55, No. 1), March 1971, pp. 144–60.
[2] Interview with U. S. Department of State officials recently stationed in Cambodia, Washington, D.C., May 1972.
[3] Robert Scalapino, "Communism in Asia: Toward a Comparative Analysis," in Robert Scalapino, ed., *The Communist Revolution in Asia*, Second Edition (Englewood Cliffs, N.J.: Prentice-Hall, 1969), pp. 12, 36.
[4] U. S. Senate Foreign Relations Committee, *Thailand, Laos, and Cambodia: January 1972* (A Staff Report, 92nd Congress, 2nd Session, Washington, D.C.: U. S. Government Printing Office, May 1972), p. 8.

mental harassment. This was precisely the process that occurred in eastern Cambodia beginning in 1967.

The Viet Minh developed eastern Cambodia as a sanctuary for its war in South Vietnam as that effort increasingly became a conventional military confrontation between the North and South Vietnamese militaries after the February 1968 Tet offensive. Heavily canopied jungle in the Cambodian-Laotian-South Vietnamese border region provided an ideal base and supply location for operations into Military Regions Numbers II and III of South Vietnam.

Sihanouk's deposition provided the political pretext for North Vietnam to expand these base areas under the guise of supporting a national liberation movement to restore the Prince to his rightful position. Somewhat paradoxically, the Vietnamese Communists were leading a "restorative revolution" to return a member of Cambodian royalty to office rather than to engage in social revolution. Splits within the FUNK, however, among the Vietnamese Communists, Sihanoukists, and Khmer Rouge, combined with the general absence of popular appeal inherent in an externally directed insurgency, have undercut the credibility of the D.R.V.'s claim to represent Khmer interests.

By the spring of 1972, American intelligence estimates placed 50 per cent of the countryside and some one and one-half million of the population under insurgent control, suggesting that the insurgents were more concerned with controlling territory adjacent to Vietnam than with winning over the majority of the Khmer people.[5]

The absence of a strong Khmer Rouge movement, comparable to the Viet Cong or even the Pathet Lao, meant that the North Vietnamese had to operate the Cambodian Front organization more visibly than either of the other two Indochina fronts. Vietnamese cadres operated as low as the village committees established to administer the "liberated areas" and thus appeared to violate the classical Maoist and Giapist

[5] *Washington Post*, May 8, 1972. R.G.N.U.C. sources, however, claim to control 80 per cent of the country and five million of the population. By early 1973 these figures escalated to 90 per cent of the country and five and one-half million people.

revolutionary paradigms: the leadership core was not well connected to rural society, recruitment lagged, and perhaps more important, the potential for military action remained predominantly North Vietnamese.[6] In sum, the FUNK presented a clear challenge to the Phnom Penh government. However, that challenge was not the challenge of "people's war" but rather the more conventional one of regular North Vietnamese forces.

In Sihanouk's case one can discern an attempt to maintain the balance strategy which had characterized Cambodia's foreign policy prior to March 1970—attenuated in the current instance by the R.G.N.U.C.'s total dependence upon its North Vietnamese and Chinese backers.[7] For the United States and the R.V.N., the war seemed primarily a tactical extension of the military exigencies of the South Vietnamese battle. Cambodia was not viewed as a salient political object *per se* but rather as an extension of the military parameters of the Vietnam conflict.[8] For the D.R.V., involvement in Cambodia was seen as a way of accelerating the attainment of an important pre-1954 national goal: a unified Indochina liberation movement under Viet Minh leadership.[9] For Peking, the

[6] Interviews with the U. S. Department of State officials, May 1972.

[7] The two most thorough assessments of Cambodian foreign policy in the Sihanouk era are Roger M. Smith, *Cambodia's Foreign Policy* (Ithaca, N.Y.: Cornell University Press, 1965), and Michael Leifer, *Cambodia: The Search For Security* (New York: Frederick A. Praeger, 1967). For more current analyses explaining the factors behind Sihanouk's deposition, see Bernard K. Gordon and Kathryn Young, "Cambodia: Following the Leader?" *Asian Survey*, February 1970 (Vol. 10, No. 2); Michael Leifer, "Peace and War in Cambodia," *Southeast Asia*, Winter–Spring 1971 (Vol. I, Nos. 1, 2); J. L. S. Girling, "Crisis and Conflict in Cambodia," *Orbis*, Summer 1970 (Vol. 14, No. 2); and Douglas Pike, "Cambodia's War," *Southeast Asian Perspectives*, March 1971 (Vol. 1).

[8] See President Nixon's April 30, 1970, address to the nation on the limited American ground intervention in eastern Cambodia.

[9] For a definitive analysis of Viet Minh negotiating strategy at the 1954 Geneva Conference and Hanoi's reluctant acquiescence to Chinese pressure to give up its peninsula-wide designs, see Robert F. Randle, *Geneva: 1954* (Princeton, N.J.: Princeton

war sharpened the distinction between China's geopolitical and ideological positions. Based on ideological criteria, China has consistently provided verbal support for an Indochina-wide movement designed to inflict a dramatic defeat on "U.S. imperialism." Geopolitically, however, Peking appears to hold reservations about the prospect of a contiguous border region on its southwest frontier controlled by an independent Asian Communist state which appears quite willing to request Soviet postwar assistance to maintain its independence from Chinese dominance. The C.P.R.'s concern over potential Soviet influence on China's neighbors has been particularly pronounced since the 1969 military confrontation with the U.S.S.R. in the Amur/Ussuri and Sinkiang border regions.[10] From the Chinese viewpoint, a completely victorious North Vietnam in Indochina could lead to a new kind of China encirclement; replacing the United States as the primary adversary might be a combination of Moscow and Hanoi, perhaps linked into the Soviet-Indian security relationship formalized in the August 1971 Security Treaty and tested in the December Bangladesh War. Hanoi's displeasure at Sino-American contacts was quite apparent during the February 1972 Nixon visit to Peking. And, insofar as the Vietnam People's Army has opted for a conventional military confrontation in South Vietnam, its dependence on Soviet armor and petroleum renders it more beholden to Moscow than to Peking. This was shown by the spring 1972 North Vietnamese offensive which relied heavily on Soviet-supplied tanks and petroleum. The subsequent massive U.S. air raids over North Vietnam also reinforced dependence on the U.S.S.R. for more sophisticated SAM emplacements and other antiaircraft devices.

In addition to its external aspects, the Cambodian war con-

University Press, 1969). See also Melvin Gurtov, "Sino-Soviet Relations and Southeast Asia: Recent Developments and Future Possibilities," *Pacific Affairs*, Winter 1970–71 (Vol. XLIII, No. 4).

[10] For a detailed account of the impact of these conflicts on Chinese foreign policy, see Harold C. Hinton, *The Bear at the Gate: Chinese Policy-Making Under Soviet Pressure* (Washington, D.C.: American Enterprise Institute and the Hoover Institution, 1971).

tains an important *internal* dimension. All of the Communist actors as well as Prince Sihanouk claim that the war is an indigenous "national liberation movement." Both Peking (through arms aid, other supplies, and the provision of an exile base for Prince Sihanouk) and the D.R.V. (by supplying organizational cadres and full-scale but unacknowledged military units) have backed the ostensibly Sihanouk-led but Cambodian-based National United Front of Kampuchea (FUNK) and his Peking-based R.G.N.U.C.

Descriptions of the Front's operations emanating from Communist sources suggest it is modeled after Viet Minh and Chinese Communist guerrilla experiences, particularly the "united front from below," in which a relatively small number of Communist—in Cambodia's case, North Vietnamese and Khmer Rouge—cadres attempt to organize revolutionary cells throughout the country both to win the population away from the government and to deny the country's resources to its urban based incumbents. If rural areas can be separated from the cities, then the government is confronted with the dual problem of caring for the flow of refugees (some 400,-000 in Phnom Penh alone by early 1972) into the relatively safe city centers while the foodstuffs and other raw materials necessary to provide for them are diminishing through the enemy's severance of the major transportation arteries.

If, however, the indigenous revolutionary milieu in Cambodia is unpropitious (based on an assessment of land tenure characteristics in which Cambodia, unlike South Vietnam, has a very low rate of tenancy), then Sihanouk's Front becomes little more than a façade for North Vietnamese imperialism.[11] Hence, the Cambodian war may be interpreted

[11] U.S. government sources estimated in early 1972, prior to the buildup for the North Vietnamese spring offensive in South Vietnam, that there were some 60,000 to 75,000 Vietnamese Communist forces in Cambodia and some 18,000 to 20,000 Khmer Rouge. The latter, on the whole, were considered to be anti-Sihanouk and under North Vietnamese direction. In areas under their control, local Communist cells and infrastructure began to appear which were also regarded as anti-Sihanouk. See U. S. Senate, Committee on Foreign Relations, *Thailand, Laos, and Cambodia: January 1972* (A Staff Report, 92nd Congress, 2nd Ses-

as an extension of the Vietnam conflict in which all the Vietnam belligerents extend the scope of their conflict to Cambodian soil. Assuming that neither an indigenous "liberation movement" without outside direction nor an indigenous defence without outside support are viable, then a settlement to the conflict depends on the ability of both contending Cambodian leaderships to convince their backers that the state's continued independence is more useful to them than its incorporation by one side or the other—that is, a Viet Minh-controlled Indochina or separate North and South Vietnam control zones.

THE RESEARCH PROBLEM

Space constraints preclude a setting out of Cambodia's contemporary historical background and its place in the foreign/security policies of the major actors.[12] Rather this study focuses on the evolving conceptions of the war and the actors' reciprocal perceptions of each other's behavior. An examination of these perceptions determines the congruence of orientations toward war for the actors, perceptions of allies and enemies, the author's own assessment of how well these perceptions fit "reality," and derivatively, the prospect for conflict settlement.

These general research considerations can be placed into two sets of questions. First, what are the goals and perceptions of the outside actors or mentor states (the United States/South Vietnam and China/North Vietnam) toward each other and the Cambodian antagonists? And reciprocally, what are the goals and perceptions of the Cambodian actors toward each other and the outside actors?

Second, what are the implications of the goals and perceptions of both the external and Cambodian actors? Can conflicts within states' decisional processes be identified which might lead to compromise decisional strategies? That is, might internally conflicting national goals result in policies designed

---

sion, Washington, D.C.: U. S. Government Printing Office, May 1972), p. 26.
[12] These considerations are covered in the booklength manuscript cited in the first footnote.

to satisfy all policy adversaries partially rather than to advance the nation's position maximally toward a single goal? For example, if China is confronted by a general ideological commitment to wars of national liberation versus considerations of regional balance, might it pursue a policy intended to achieve something less than total victory for its Viet Minh ally? Finally, are the actors' mutual perceptions conducive to moving the conflict from a zero-sum to at least a mixed conflict-cooperation relationship?

The primary data for this study were drawn from the mass media output of the actors in the Cambodian war as monitored and published by the Foreign Broadcast Information Service *Daily Reports*.[13] A daily scanning of the mass media output, as published by FBIS, provided extensive public and official documentation of the cognitions and perceptions of the war on the parts of its actors. These cognitions and perceptions form the basis for a trend analysis of attitudes toward the war, the other actors involved, and the region's future.

More specifically, Cambodia's "rival governments" and their mentors were compared for cognitive congruence to determine the kind of political settlement each preferred for Cambodia and Indochina. The analysis was designed to identify conflicts among national, regional, and global considerations.

Data for the above questions were generated through a thematic content analysis of elite and media statements about the war, its actors, and their preferred outcomes. The salience and meaning of the war to each of its participants were inferred from an analysis of the FBIS *Daily Reports* from April 1970 to June 1972 for non-U.S. actors, and from *The New York Times, Department of State Bulletin,* and various Congressional and Presidential documents for the United States. Thematic frequency tables were developed for each actor and compared for congruence. Additionally, an evaluative assertion form of content analysis was performed on a sam-

[13] The author wishes to acknowledge a grant from the Kentucky Research Foundation which permits him to subscribe to the *Daily Reports* on a regular basis.

pling of Sihanouk's special addresses to the Khmer nation to determine their substance when compared with the cognitions of the Front's major allies—the D.R.V. and China.[14] Thus, one can assess Sihanouk's conception of the power and activity of the targets of his attention as well as his positive or negative evaluation of those targets.

Before proceeding to a discussion of the findings of this study, a *caveat* is in order about the limitations of relying upon public statements as a method of policy analysis. Generally, public statements are a good measure of salience but not necessarily of policy. That is, such statements may mask more than they reveal.

(a) The actual bargaining process cannot be observed through this mode of analysis but only its synthetic product. Thus, diverse individual and organizational viewpoints may be hidden. On the other hand, however, a comparison of messages about the same target from different sources may reveal perceptual and evaluative variations from which policy differences may be inferred as, for example, between Sihanouk and the D.R.V.

(b) Message content may be used to obfuscate real positions in order to deflect the opposition's attention from the sender's real concern.

(c) And finally, verbal behavior alone may be an incomplete event in international politics; it may not necessarily correlate with action behavior. Rather, verbal and action behaviors should be compared to determine their relationship empirically.

RECIPROCAL PERCEPTIONS OF THE MAJOR ACTORS

If the Cambodian conflict is not primarily an indigenous insurgency, then prospects for its settlement must focus on

---

[14] *Evaluative assertion analysis* transforms message content into the psychological categories of Charles Osgood's semantic differential scale (activity, potency, and evaluation) and hence permits a psychological as well as substantive analysis of the message. See Robert C. North, *et al.*, *Content Analysis* (Evanston, Ill.: Northwestern University Press, 1963), Chapter VI, pp. 91–102. Every fourth Sihanouk Special Message was selected for analysis. Few of these have appeared in 1972.

Summary Table of Rank Orderings of Mass Media Targets
Related to the Cambodian War Emanating
From Peking, Hanoi, Sihanouk's R.G.N.U.C.,
and Phnom Penh, April 1970–June 1972*

Target Theme	Actor			
	Peking	Hanoi	R.G.N.U.C./ FUNK	Phnom Penh
Vietnamese Communist Actions	—	3 (16)	3 (26)	1
Attitude Toward the American & South Vietnamese Role in Cambodia	2 (10)	1 (28)	2 (55)†	2
Racial Relations Between Cambodians and Vietnamese	—	—	—	3
The State of the Cambodian Economy	—	—	2 (55)†	4
Attitude Toward Sihanouk and the R.G.N.U.C.	3 (5)	2 (20)	1 (70)	5
Relations with Peking	—		4 (19)	—
Differences Within the FUNK	—	—	5 (4)	—
Attitude Toward Cambodia Within the Indochina Front	1 (27)	—	—	—

* The number in each cell indicates the attention rank each actor gave the Target Theme. Numbers in parentheses represent the N in each category where determinable. In Phnom Penh's case FBIS coverage was incomplete. Therefore, the total N could not be determined.

† These targets are combined into one theme for the R.G.N.U.C.

the conceptions and policies of the external actors as much as, if not more than, the two Cambodian contenders.

The Summary Table provides at a glance a quick profile of the salient themes in the media of the major actors, with the exception of the United States, toward the war.[15] In an examination for congruence, the Cambodian antagonists produce both the most variegated and the most similar thematic patterns. Both Lon Nol's government and the FUNK view the U.S./South Vietnamese role as an important determinant for the outcome of the war. The Khmer Republic also sees Hanoi as salient, while Sihanouk's R.G.N.U.C. assigns it only a middle rank of interest, probably because the Prince and the Front have publicly avoided the issue of North Vietnamese control over the liberation movement, insisting that the war is conducted solely by the FUNK. Symmetrically, the Khmer Republic has downplayed the FUNK's importance in order to foster the impression that the war is primarily an act of D.R.V. aggression. Interestingly, China appears to be excluded as a participant by all of the actors—an observation lending credence to Sihanouk's insistence from his Peking exile that China cannot solve the war bilaterally with the United States. Its settlement must emerge from those actors directly involved. One final general feature of interest in the Table is that neither Peking nor Hanoi take cognizance of the other's role. This mutual circumspection may mask a fundamental disagreement between Peking's preference for a balkanized Indochina, including an independent, neutral Cambodia, versus Hanoi's aim of a postwar Indochina confederation dominated by the Viet Minh.[16]

A cross-national analysis of theme targets reveals the following:

(1) VIET MINH ROLE

For Phnom Penh, the spring 1970 decision to move against the D.R.V. enclaves in eastern Cambodia during Sihanouk's

---

[15] Saigon is excluded from this analysis because FBIS coverage of South Vietnamese governmental statements was very sporadic.

[16] General Giap publicly suggested this outcome in an interview with the West German newspaper *Vorwaerts* (Bonn), April 27, 1972.

absence in Europe led to the demise of the country's long-established posture of nonalignment and plunged it into the vortex of the Indochina war. Phnom Penh leaders appeared aware of the fact that to Hanoi Cambodia was subordinate to the successful prosecution of the war in South Vietnam. Hence, a settlement in Cambodia would await and grow out of a conclusion to the Vietnam hostilities.

For Sihanouk and the Khmer Rouge segment of the liberation front, D.R.V. activities in Cambodia were viewed ambivalently. Successful defeat of Lon Nol's government required North Vietnamese initiative, yet the FUNK's very dependence on North Vietnam for supplies and organizational guidance rendered it likely that its activities would ultimately lead to a Hanoi-directed quisling regime. Both the Prince and his Peking hosts seemed to agree on this assessment, according to American officials.[17] Furthermore, as mentioned above, Khmer Rouge antipathy to both Sihanouk and VPA troops has forced some Vietnamese Communist participation at all levels of FUNK organization in "liberated areas." Generally, the D.R.V. presence is most apparent at the top echelons of territorial control and in the eastern provinces and less visible at village levels and farther west.

Hanoi's self-image with respect to Cambodia is tied to its conception of an Indochina-wide front. The most frequent context in which Cambodia has been discussed in North Vietnamese media through mid-1972 was the Indochina Front established at the C.P.R.-hosted April 1970 Indochinese People's Summit Conference. Interestingly, Communist victories in Cambodia were portrayed more as examples of the weakness of its Saigon adversary than as evidence of Cambodian Peoples Liberation Army (CPLAF) strength—the latter theme being left to the FUNK's own media. Thus, from

[17] Interview with U. S. State Department officers specializing on Indochina, May 1972. References to Sihanouk as the legitimizer of North Vietnam's occupation of Cambodian territory disappeared from Viet Minh propaganda in early 1971. See also, "Au Revoir Sihanouk?" *The Far Eastern Economic Review,* August 5, 1972, p. 10, where the Prince is reported to have gloomily confided that the Khmer Rouge allowed him to retain the "Head of State" title only because he was still useful to them.

Hanoi's perspective, victories on Cambodian soil against Saigon's troops were publicized as an object lesson to all Communist combatants that Vietnamization could be overcome.[18]

(2) ROLE OF THE UNITED STATES AND ARVN

For Lon Nol's government, dependence on American material and ARVN manpower appeared to be the only way to fend off the North Vietnamese adversary. The price for this support has been a heavy one, however—the extension of the Cambodian war from its initial location in the eastern provinces bordering South Vietnam to virtually the entire Cambodian countryside. This development, in turn, has resulted in even greater reliance on U.S./ARVN firepower, thus creating a vicious circle of military escalation over which Phnom Penh has exercised little control.

Just as the American role is viewed by Lon Nol as crucial to his regime's survival, it is similarly viewed by Sihanouk and FUNK, who interpret U.S. intervention as the only obstacle to a Communist victory. Moreover, Phnom Penh's alliance with the United States and South Vietnam is seen by the Prince as justifying his own ties to Peking and Hanoi. FUNK media argue that Lon Nol has chosen the wrong side, for America is inexorably committed to disengage from Indochina while North Vietnam is equally pledged to gain the dominant role in the region.[19] This view of the secular trend renders the FUNK intransigent. It need only wait for the inevitable American exit after which Cambodia will fall into its political grasp.

The D.R.V. also depicts American involvement in Cambodia as hastening a final victory in Indochina since ARVN has been forced to disperse its troops, rendering them more vulnerable wherever the VPA chooses to attack. The persistent defeat of ARVN in Cambodia, according to this reason-

[18] See, for example, the April 25, 1972, editorial in *Nhan Dan* commemorating the second anniversary of the Indochinese People's Summit Conference and the *Quan Doi Nhan Dan* editorial of May 31, 1972.

[19] Sihanouk's thirty-fourth message to the Khmer nation, released by NCNA on April 5, 1972, asserts there is no longer any possibility of Lon Nol winning the war.

ing, will force the United States to recognize that Vietnamization is unworkable and to leave the region. Hanoi's main concern over the American role in Indochina appears to be less a question of battlefield developments than one of Washington's new diplomatic relationship with Peking. Hanoi may fear a repetition of the C.P.R.'s 1954 pressure to settle for less than Indochina-wide control—perhaps even partition. Thus, Hanoi's military press has warned:

> The U.S. imperialists are now intent on maintaining a mild posture in order to block the offensive posture of the revolution and to counter the world revolutionary movement by priority sectors . . . To oppose the Americans is an essential law in the class struggle . . . [and] a requirement of the revolutionary development of all countries . . . Revolution in each country is an organic part of the world's revolution. National interests cannot be detached from the general interests of the world revolution.[20]

(3) THE INTERNAL STATE OF CAMBODIAN SOCIETY

The internal state of Cambodian society was of primary media interest only to the two Cambodian antagonists. Both agreed that the ability of the economy to supply the government with food and revenue was a test of the political strength of the regime. Lon Nol's government has acknowledged Hanoi's success in cutting virtually at will the government's transportation and communication arteries to the seaport of Kampong Som (Sihanoukville) and the rich rice areas of the northwest. Since the end of March 1972 and the major North Vietnamese offensive in South Vietnam, eastern Cambodia has been virtually annexed by the Viet Minh. Sporadic rocket and sapper attacks on Phnom Penh itself have increased through 1972, probably as a warning to the government to keep its forces close to the capital.

As the war has dragged on, Lon Nol's major base of popular support—intellectuals and urban salaried classes—has eroded through the effects of inflation, shortage of goods, and an increasingly corrupt and repressive government. That the

[20] *Quan Doi Nhan Dan Review,* June 18, 1972.

Marshal gained only 55 per cent of the votes cast in the June 1972 Presidential election, despite irregularities in his favor, provided further evidence of the widespread dissatisfaction with the war's course.[21] The defection of substantial numbers of the administrative elites to the FUNK—a major Front media theme during 1972—could go a long way toward destroying the Khmer Republic from within.

(4) SIHANOUK'S ACTIVITIES AND THE FUNK

Sihanouk's activities and the FUNK comprise the last theme on which all actors have taken a position. Phnom Penh depicts the Prince as a traitor and pawn of the North Vietnamese (not the Chinese on whom he has remained, in fact, dependent). He is seen further as a fool, abjuring his own long-term nonalignment policy. Phnom Penh's relative lack of animosity toward China reflects the Khmer Republic's hopes that Peking might be a tacit ally in any long-term settlement, opposing North Vietnamese control of the region. Significantly, C.P.R. media, for example, when referring to Front activities, notably refrain from mentioning such Khmer Rouge leaders as Khieu Samphan, believed to be politically beholden to the North Vietnamese.[22]

Sihanouk has displayed sensitivity to the "figurehead" allegation. He has insisted that his Front is independent and points to the existence of its growing organizational apparatus in the "liberated areas."[23] Moreover, he has asserted that the FUNK and Hanoi have different war priorities which affect the quality and kinds of supplies which filter down to the Front. Other FUNK officials have acknowledged some difficulties with supplies, urging greater self-reliance on their supporters in the wake of the D.R.V.'s spring 1972 Vietnam

[21] See Boris Bacyanskyj, "Lon Nol's Private War," *Far Eastern Economic Review,* July 1, 1972, pp. 23–24.

[22] See the *People's Daily* editorial on the second anniversary of the FUNK, March 23, 1972. By late 1972, however, C.P.R. media acknowledged the Khmer Rouge role in the FUNK, perhaps in recognition of their importance for any final settlement for Cambodia and in hopes of their maintaining a commitment to Sihanouk.

[23] R.G.N.U.C. Politburo communiqué carried by NCNA, March 24, 1972.

offensive—a development suggesting that Hanoi's war requirements are draining supplies away from the CPLAF.[24] Nevertheless, the Prince asserted that just before the Vietnam cease-fire agreement was signed on January 23, 1973, China sent enough new military equipment to the "liberated areas" of Cambodia to continue the war for at least two more years.[25]

More evident than incipient differences between the FUNK and Hanoi are those between Sihanouk and the Front which operates in his name. The latter's political program reveals its dependence on North Vietnam's good will by tying Cambodia's future to a "liberated" Indochina. Sihanouk has tried to loosen this bond by implying that only he can negotiate Cambodia's future in FUNK's name and that both Peking and Hanoi would prefer an independent Cambodia to an overt satellite.[26] Peking has also reminded Hanoi that Sihanouk's Peking-based R.G.N.U.C. "is the only and unique legal and legitimate government of the Cambodian example," a position which "has all along won the resolute support of the Government of the Democratic Republic of Vietnam and the Provisional Revolutionary Government of the Republic of South Vietnam . . ."[27]

The major benefit to Peking from serving as Sihanouk's host probably has lain in the realm of the Sino-Soviet conflict. China's sponsorship of the Indochinese People's Summit Conference permitted it to pre-empt the role of major supporter for the war from the Soviet Union. The spring 1972 D.R.V. offensive, so heavily dependent on Soviet weaponry, however, means that Moscow has more than balanced Peking's influence. It would appear that the longer the Indochina war remains unresolved and the longer Sihanouk and his entourage remain isolated from events in the "liberated areas," the more likely that the Prince's presence in Peking

[24] Statement by R.G.N.U.C. Defense Minister and CPLAF Commander-in-chief, Khieu Samphan, broadcast by the Cambodian Information Agency (AKI) in French, June 23, 1972.

[25] Sihanouk interview with *Al-Ahram* editor Muhammad Haykal as reported by MENA (Cairo) in English, March 1, 1973.

[26] Allesandro Casella interview in the *Bangkok World*, February 7, 1971.

[27] *People's Daily* commentator, February 8, 1973.

will become at best an anachronism and at worst an embarrassment and obstacle to the C.P.R. in establishing relations with the Hanoi-oriented leadership of the FUNK.

American comment on the Cambodian conflict, drawn from official documents and addresses, reveals virtually no attention to Sihanouk or his Front. Rather, as in the cases of Hanoi and Phnom Penh, the war is seen as an extension of the Vietnam hostilities. The American self-image appears based on the Nixon Administration's explanation that U.S. involvement in Cambodia was integral to the Vietnamization strategy by which the United States widened the battlefield into Cambodia in order to protect the withdrawal of American troops from Vietnam, while simultaneously buying time for the development of ARVN proficiency. American support for the Khmer Republic's forces through material assistance and air strikes, according to this reasoning, forced North Vietnam to disperse its forces away from South Vietnam. (Note Hanoi's mirror image of the same process.) Hence American air sorties into Cambodia rose from an acknowledged 9,226 in 1970 to 16,437 in 1971.[28] Cambodia's forced entrance into the maelstrom was the price of Vietnamization.

AN EVALUATIVE ASSERTION ANALYSIS OF SIHANOUK'S PERCEPTIONS OF THE WAR

It is useful at this point to devote some attention to Sihanouk's view of his allies and enemies, the war's evolution, and settlement prospects through an *evaluative assertion* form of content analysis (see fn. 6). As stated above, this form of analysis provides more information than a simple thematic breakdown by assessing the Prince's conception of the potency and activity of his attention targets as well as his positive or negative evaluation of those targets.

Figure 1A displays a typical "black-white" propaganda evaluative dimension in which Sihanouk's enemies (the United States, South Vietnam, and Phnom Penh) score consistently low, while his own movement (the R.G.N.U.C.) is viewed only in the most positive terms. The two observations of the

[28] U. S. Senate Foreign Relations Committee, *op. cit.*, p. 34.

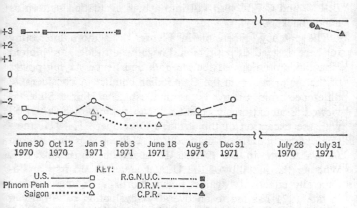

FIGURE 1A: *Graph of Evaluative Assertion Analysis Scores for Selected Attitude Objects in Selected Sihanouk Messages to the Khmer Nation, April 1970–December 1971 (Evaluative Dimension)*

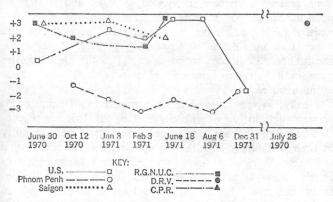

FIGURE 1B: *Graph of Evaluative Assertion Analysis Scores for Selected Attitude Objects in Selected Sihanouk Messages to the Khmer Nation, April 1970–December 1971 (Potency Dimension)*

D.R.V. and C.P.R. also fall into a high evaluation pattern as major backers.

The potency dimension in Figure 1B is more interesting for here, instead of positive and negative attitudes, are plotted Sihanouk's opinions of the *strength* and hence staying power of the major actors in the Cambodian conflict. A considerable difference from Figure 1A is manifest. The United States is viewed as an extremely potent actor through the whole period with the exception of the Prince's December 31, 1971, message, where it falls off markedly as a direct result of Phnom Penh's failure in the Chenla II operation on Highway 6. Whether the inability of the United States to aid its Cambodian ally effectively against heavy North Vietnamese strikes in late 1971 has led to an overall re-evaluation of American strength and commitment to Phnom Penh by Prince Sihanouk cannot be determined from these data, however. The Prince also viewed the Saigon government as strong and very much in command of those sections of Cambodia in which ARVN elements were located through most of this period. The Phnom Penh regime, of course, is viewed as weak and totally dependent on outside support for its survival—an object unworthy of consideration as a legitimate government and hence unacceptable as a negotiating partner. By contrast, the R.G.N.U.C. is seen to be as strong as the United States and South Vietnam—seemingly able to hold its own against all adversaries.

Finally, Figure 1c measures a somewhat more ambiguous concept—activity or persistence, that is, the Prince's perception of whether the actors involved are active and initiatory in their behavior within the Cambodian war or passive and malleable. In general, there appears to be a fairly high correlation between actor scores on this dimension and the potency measures. Those actors considered to be powerful are also viewed as acting independently to influence the course of the war. The United States, South Vietnam, and the R.G.N.U.C. all scale high on this dimension. Interestingly, so does the Phnom Penh government. A substantive interpretation of this finding might be that the Prince has perceived all actors, regardless of their potency or positive or negative

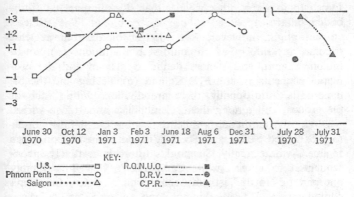

FIGURE 1C: *Graph of Evaluative Assertion Analysis Scores for Selected Attitude Objects in Selected Sihanouk Messages to the Khmer Nation, April 1970–December 1971 (Activity Dimension)*

qualities, as heavily engaged in trying to defeat their adversaries in order to win Cambodia. Such an interpretation could reflect a growing frustration on Sihanouk's part that he is out of the action and unable to affect meaningfully his country's future. He may have come to believe that he has been relegated to the secondary role of propagandist for the "liberation movement" rather than its leader.

IMPLICATIONS OF EXTERNAL AND CAMBODIAN ACTORS' GOALS AND PERCEPTIONS FOR CAMBODIA'S FUTURE

Finally, we come to an assessment of possible actor positions toward conflict settlement to determine (a) whether they emerge logically from the varying conceptions of the war and (b) their degree of compatibility.

Sihanouk has attempted to maintain his traditional balance principle in a position of dependence upon two powers, currently the D.R.V. and China. There has been a flaw, however, in the Prince's assumptions. In the past he had operated successfully in a bipolar context, steering between Cold War antagonists by threatening each with the prospect of being forced to join the other when either side's impact on Cambodian affairs appeared to become dominant. The Prince's current plight, however, is no longer bipolar but at least tripolar, any side of which could veto a solution: (a) Washington, Saigon, and Phnom Penh; (b) Hanoi and the pro-Hanoi elements of the FUNK; and (c) Peking and the Sihanoukists. Additionally, there are divisions within each of the groups; and among them, Cambodia's importance varies.

Obviously, Cambodia's salience is of a much lower order to the United States and South Vietnam than to Lon Nol's regime. Symmetrically, Sihanouk's future is relatively inconsequential to Hanoi, while Cambodia is viewed as merely one part of North Vietnam's conception of a new Indochina confederation. For Washington and Saigon, Cambodia appears to be primarily a tactical appendage to the Vietnam War. When and if that war is terminated, there would be little reason to continue supporting militarily the Phnom Penh government. Hence, the development of potential new conflicts among allies: Phnom Penh hoping to maintain American involvement as long as it is faced with Viet Minh/Khmer Rouge insurgency as against Washington's desire to extricate itself from Indochina once its obligations to South Vietnam have ceased. Sihanouk, similarly, would eventually hope to loosen D.R.V. control over his operations on Cambodian soil with the probable tacit support of China.

In sum, there exists a complex bargaining situation over Cambodia in which there is contention not only between allies and adversaries, but between allies themselves. Moreover, so long as any side's aspiration level remains high (particularly the D.R.V.) it may choose not to bargain. Assuming that successful negotiations occur most frequently when each side can estimate the product of subjective preferences and the probability of preferred outcomes by all actors, then if compromise is to be achieved, all participants should have full knowledge of each others' positions.[29] Even under such opti-

[29] See E. W. Kelly, "Bargaining in Coalition Situations," in E. W. Kelly, Sven Groennings, and Michael Leiserson, *The Study of Coalition Behavior* (New York: Holt, Rinehart & Winston, 1970), pp. 286–92.

mal conditions, however, compromise is not assured if, as appears in the case of North Vietnam, both aspiration level and subjective preference are very high. Thus, Hanoi might reject a compromise solution at a lower preference level, even with a high outcome probability, because it places such a high value on Indochina hegemony. In the author's opinion, this bargaining postulate explains the essential obstacle to a negotiated solution for Cambodia and the remainder of Indochina. That is, D.R.V. aspirations foreclose a compromise solution. Moreover, North Vietnamese intransigence is reinforced by clear signals emanating from Washington that the United States is disengaging and that Hanoi need only wait out an American exit. North Vietnam has attempted to accelerate this American trend by appealing directly to those segments of the U.S. opinion elite who view the prolongation of American involvement in Indochina as morally and politically invalid. Therein lies a major flaw of the Vietnamization policy: it commits the United States to defend Asian territory, hence diminishing American control over *whether* to become involved in a given conflict, but at the same time constrains the kind of involvement permitted, thus increasing the probability that future outcomes will be either defeats or stalemates.[30]

The substitution of South Vietnamese, Cambodian, or even Thai forces for U.S. manpower has been based on a kind of military analogy to the international trade theory of comparative advantage where each side specializes in the commodity it can produce at the lowest comparative cost. However, the analogy breaks down when its underlying assumption is examined: that non-Communist states in Southeast Asia have a *common desire* to share the forward defense of a neighbor's territory. This assumption is another manifestation of the traditional domino theory of Communist expansion in Asia, which initially underlay American involvement in Indochina as far back as the 1954 creation of SEATO. Hence, President Nixon's Vietnamization policy does not signify a basic re-

---

[30] For an expansion of this argument, see Earl C. Ravenal, "The Nixon Doctrine and Our Asian Commitment," *Foreign Affairs*, January 1971 (Vol. 42, No. 2).

evaluation of the U.S. effort to maintain a primarily non-Communist Indochina. Rather it represents an attempt to make the continuation of such a policy politically palatable to the American electorate by substituting Indochinese manpower (Vietnamese, Cambodian, and Laotian) for American ground combat forces.

Under current domestic political conditions in the United States, however, Washington cannot even provide its part of the comparative advantage bargain because of budgetary constraints. With a reduced future American defense role for Asia, one would suppose that some of the slack could be taken up through joint regional defense planning. Yet no such planning has occurred in Asia under ASEAN, ASPAC, SEATO, or any other organizational rubric.[31] Hence, U.S. defense decisions have remained unilateral and imposed upon somewhat reluctant but, in effect, bribable allies. In sum, American security conceptions for Asia in the early 1970s are still being imposed on Asians, some of whom appear to accept them on the basis of derived side benefits (military aid) rather than common threat perceptions.

For Cambodia, then, Lon Nol's decision to align with the United States and Republic of Vietnam increased the former's military capacity without fundamentally adding to his own ability to force Vietnamese Communist forces out of Cambodia. Even limited military victories remained inconclusive as long as Hanoi's infrastructure in eastern Cambodia remained intact.

The most ambivalent actor in the conflict has been the C.P.R. On the one hand, Peking desires an American exit from Southeast Asia for both ideological and strategic reasons. Such a withdrawal would weaken the U.S. capability to intervene militarily on mainland Asia, consequently raising China's own regional stature while simultaneously reducing the probability that it would have to engage in future mili-

---

[31] For an empirical examination of the apparent lack of Asian interest in defense cooperation, see my "A Systems Approach to Security in the Indian Ocean Arc," *Orbis,* Summer 1970 (Vol. 14, No. 2), and "The Nixon Doctrine: An Asian Prognosis," *Asian Forum,* March 1973.

tary operations beyond its borders. This development, in turn, would permit the C.P.R. to direct its energies to domestic affairs or to other frontiers. The only apparent gap in this scenario would be an assessment of Sino-Soviet relations. Insofar as China sees the U.S.S.R. as its primary adversary, a hasty American exit from Asia may not be as desirable as it once was.[32] For similar reasons, Peking is not particularly enthusiastic about the prospects for a North Vietnamese sphere of influence in Indochina, given Hanoi's heavy material dependence on Moscow and the likelihood that Soviet aid for the reconstruction of North Vietnam after the war would far outweigh China's contribution.

NATIONAL POSITIONS
TOWARD CONFLICT SETTLEMENT

As for specific solutions to the war, the United States has proposed both in 1970 and again in 1972 that an international conference be convened to deal with all of Indochina. The proposal has been rejected by the Communist actors and by Sihanouk for differing reasons. Peking is opposed because any full settlement based on the Viet Minh position might confirm the latter's dominance throughout the whole peninsula. The D.R.V. is opposed because of a belief that it can do better on the battlefield in the course of American disengagement than in a peninsular conference which would focus undue attention on its role in Laos and Cambodia. Furthermore, to Hanoi—as evidenced in the Paris talks since 1968—negotiations are not designed primarily to reach a cessation of military hostilities but rather to develop a political settlement only after which hostilities would be terminated. This posture reflects the North Vietnamese belief that it sold out its own interests during both the 1954 and 1962 negotiations by accepting military truces before concluding agreements on the political dispositions of Vietnam and Laos. Nevertheless, it should be pointed out that Hanoi's agreement to the January 1973 Vietnam ceasefire appeared to be something of a compromise in that it was reached *before* a defini-

[32] See Harold C. Hinton, *The Bear at the Gate, passim.*

tive military solution. However, Hanoi may well have calculated a high probability for a satisfactory military outcome given the presence of some 140,000 of its troops south of the seventeenth parallel.

The official North Vietnamese policy toward Cambodia has been stated several times, as in the March 5, 1972, joint communiqué of Prince Sihanouk and the D.R.V. government:

> The U. S. Government must end its aggression and its policy of "Khmerization" of the war, pull out immediately, totally and unconditionally from Cambodia American armed forces, cease the bombing and shelling of Cambodian territory by U.S. air, artillery and naval forces, and by the Saigon and Bangkok puppet regimes, cease all aid, assistance and support to the Lon Nol-Sirik Matak-Son Ngoc Thanh traitor clique, cease all other acts of war and provocation against Cambodia and let the Cambodian people settle their own affairs without any foreign interference, on the basis of the five-point proclamation put forth by Samdech Head of State Norodom Sihanouk on March 23, 1970, and the political program of the FUNK. Samdech Norodom Sihanouk, head of state, is the depository of legality . . . and the continuity of the Cambodian state. The R.G.N.U.C. with Samdech Penn Nouth as Prime Minister and Mr. Khieu Samphan as Vice-Premier is the only and authentic legal and legitimate government in Cambodia.

But D.R.V. Prime Minister Pham Van Dong has admitted publicly that "the struggle in South Vietnam" will have "considerable repercussions in Cambodia and Laos," thus acknowledging both the military and political inseparability of the states of Indochina from Hanoi's viewpoint.[33] Sihanouk himself has stated more directly: "If, one day, a solution acceptable to all is adopted at the Paris conference on the problem of South Vietnam, it is evident that the problem of Cambodia and that of Laos will disappear *ipso facto*."[34]

Nevertheless, by the spring of 1973, although a Laotian ceasefire had been negotiated, the Cambodian imbroglio

---

[33] Pham Van Dong interview in *Le Monde*, May 18, 1972.
[34] Sihanouk speech in Algiers carried by NCNA, June 30, 1972.

showed no signs of diminishing. Hanoi has refused to discuss the future of Cambodia at the Paris Conference on Vietnam which was convened after the ceasefire. Moreover, the FUNK has warned against any attempt to create an international commission to supervise or observe Cambodian developments.[35] These events suggest that Sihanouk, Hanoi, and Peking all wish to sustain the hostilities in Cambodia until some political solution is reached in South Vietnam.

The Prince has tried to remain a viable actor in the contest by insisting that any agreement on Cambodia's future can be concluded only bilaterally between the R.G.N.U.C. and Washington. While he has explicitly excluded Lon Nol's government from any projected negotiations, more significantly, he appears to have implicitly excluded Hanoi as well.[36] The Prince has vigorously rejected the possibility of a Cambodian partition, in effect a formalization of separate North Vietnamese and Cambodian anti-Communist control zones. American appeals for an Indochina-wide ceasefire have been labeled a maneuver designed to "divide" Cambodia both by spokesmen for the R.G.N.U.C. and such high Chinese officials as Chou En-lai.[37] Not only would such a development confer legitimacy on Lon Nol's regime in the major Cambodian cities but it would also confirm North Vietnamese control over eastern Cambodia. Nor would a partition be desirable to Hanoi unless it appeared that the war in South Vietnam was not proceeding satisfactorily. In such an event, partition could be a useful tactical decision which would provide Hanoi with the sanctuary it required to continue a protracted war

[35] The Voice of the FUNK in Cambodian, February 20, 1973.

[36] Sihanouk press conference, NCNA, October 11, 1970. Note, however, that in Algiers in June 1972, the Prince seemed to recognize that a Paris settlement of the Vietnam War would resolve the total Indochina conflict. This suggests that Sihanouk has become less sanguine over time about the maintenance of a separate Cambodian political position in a postwar Indochina. (See footnote 34.)

[37] R.G.N.U.C. Statement released by NCNA, June 28, 1972, and Chou En-lai's banquet address on Sihanouk's second anniversary in Peking, NCNA, March 20, 1972. See also the AFP report on Sihanouk's talks in Hanoi after the Vietnam ceasefire, February 1, 1973.

in South Vietnam at a later time. Partition would probably not be viewed by the D.R.V. as a way of restoring Sihanouk to authority.

THE PROSPECT FOR A RESTORATION OF CAMBODIAN NONALIGNMENT

Perhaps a more appropriate question for this concluding section might be: in a postwar Indochina, how much autonomy will any Cambodian government be likely to exercise? Nonalignment for a small state like Cambodia (or Finland) surrounded by contentious larger states depends on the relationship among those contending states. To determine the degree of Cambodia's political freedom, then, one must project probable attitudes toward the country by the D.R.V. and the R.V.N. or its successor. A content analysis of statements from all participants reveals that only Sihanouk and his Front focused on Cambodian nonalignment as a theme related to the Indochina hostilities. Although the Prince has attempted to commit the D.R.V. to Cambodia's continued independence, by stating on several occasions during his ubiquitous press conferences that Hanoi has assured him of its good intentions toward all small countries, it is noteworthy that Hanoi's own media have remained silent on the issue. Hanoi has endorsed the FUNK's 1970 program under the operational leadership of Khieu Samphan, a man believed by Western analysts to have been trained in and politically committed to North Vietnam.

SUMMARY

The findings of this study—based admittedly only on public documentation—suggest that conceptual congruence on the nature and stakes of the conflict are not sufficient for a negotiated settlement because the preferred outcomes radically differ.

(a) We have found that Hanoi, Washington, Peking, and Phnom Penh agree generally that Cambodia's involvement in the war is closely related to the primary Vietnam theater of operations. The only exception to this view is Sihanouk, who insists that any solution to Cambodia be reached separately through bilateral arrangements with the United States, despite his simultaneous adherence to the Indochinese Peoples' United Front.

(b) There also seems to be general consensus that Peking is not directly involved in the Cambodian hostilities, although once again Sihanouk insists that no solution to the Indochina conflict can be made to work without China's participation and concurrence. The Prince's insistence on a Chinese input into any Cambodian settlement may be interpreted as his attempt to follow a balanced policy even in adversity—in this case to counter any plans by North Vietnam to establish an Indochina federation under its aegis.

(c) Although there is little evidence to suggest that the social and economic milieu in Cambodia is conducive to a locally generated war of insurgency, the military weakness of the central government rendered the country vulnerable to outside intervention. Furthermore, the persistence of North Vietnam's intervention is reinforced by the general belief that the United States is in the process of disengaging from Indochina, while Hanoi's commitment is seen as more salient and hence more long term. Even Phnom Penh authorities have displayed concern that they could be sacrificed for Vietnam in the course of a negotiated settlement.

While points a to c (above) are generally accepted by all of the actors as descriptive of the nature of the war, preferred outcomes do not converge in a similar fashion. For Hanoi, Cambodia provides an indispensable logistical route into South Vietnam and a potential sphere of influence in a postwar Indochina through the D.R.V.'s long-term relationship with the Khmer Rouge and the latter's key position within the FUNK. Any solution to the Cambodian war which would provide political autonomy for the country would appear to be unnecessary to Hanoi. That is, Cambodia is an integral part of its Indochina strategy in which South Vietnam remains the primary but by no means the sole goal for the North.

Peking's main goal in Indochina—one the C.P.R. has sought since the Korean War—has been to see American military power removed from mainland Southeast Asia. China would prefer that this be accomplished in the setting of a balkanized Indochina, thus insuring Peking's dominant role in the region, but appears willing to accept as a "satisficing" solution, North Vietnamese dominance so long as the United States is forced out.

Sihanouk has attempted to buttress Peking's interest in a balkanized peninsula as the only way to restore Cambodian autonomy in a postwar setting. Statements emanating from the "interior" branch of his Front, however, appear to follow the North Vietnamese line on the importance of an Indochina-wide settlement. This disparity suggests that the Prince has become little more than a figurehead in his own liberation movement which in turn is beholden to North Vietnam for its supplies, strategy, and, in all probability, political future.

For the United States the Cambodian war was a tactical afterthought designed to improve the prospects for Vietnamization and hence permit the reduction of American ground forces in Vietnam without too great a loss in international prestige. The American move appears to have had some success in Vietnam. However, its effect on Cambodia has been only slightly short of disastrous. The country is in the midst of a war with which it has neither the financial nor human resources to cope. The Phnom Penh government is dependent for its very existence on air- and water-borne supplies from the U.S. military, just as Sihanouk's Front operates at the behest of North Vietnam. In short, both Cambodian adversaries have become proxies for, or extensions of, the war in Vietnam. And neither side in the Vietnam conflict is likely to permit the restoration of peace in Cambodia before a total peninsular settlement. Indeed, insofar as the long-run trend appears to militate against the United States in Indochina, it is conceivable that elements in the Phnom Penh government may seek clandestine contacts with Hanoi to try to arrange a separate settlement, or even approach Peking as an alternative for its support of Sihanouk. The resolution of the Cambodian conflict, then, will most likely occur as a function of a military decision in Vietnam or a series of diplomatic trade-offs by the outside powers rather than any decision taken by the two Cambodian countergovernments.

III
The Policies of Extraregional States

Great Power Intervention
and Regional Order

MICHAEL LEIFER

The purpose of this paper is to survey the goals and influence of Great Power intervention within Southeast Asia. To this end, the nature of state intervention is discussed, its regional context is described, and the goals of the Great Powers are considered. Various modes of intervention are then examined, of necessity through selective example, and an attempt is made to evaluate this experience in terms of the attainment of Great Power goals and in relation to the prospect of stability.

Intervention is not, in any sense, a unique or remarkable feature of international relations. Its significance does not rest in its occurrence, which is commonplace as between states, but in its purpose, form, and specific context. The possible options on a notional scale of degrees of intervention are considerable, if less than infinite. In consequence, the activity *per se* is best identified without reference to any discrete facet of state conduct. As one author has wisely remarked: "To search for a fine line dividing normal diplomatic behavior, interference, and intervention is not only futile but tends to obscure the important point that there is a continuum from slight to intense interference."[1] Thus, there is little point in trying to identify intervention as a generic activity in even very general terms. There is point, however, in trying to identify intervention in terms of its purpose. To this end, one might suggest as a working, if imperfect, defini-

---

[1] Richard W. Cottam, *Competitive Interference and Twentieth Century Diplomacy* (Pittsburgh, Pa.: University of Pittsburgh Press, 1971), p. 36.

tion: the involvement of one state in the affairs of another for the purpose of assisting, inducing, or compelling it to engage in or forbear from certain policies or to maintain or alter the condition of its domestic order, irrespective of its will.

The expression "irrespective of its will" might suggest for some the validity of a distinction within a definition of intervention in that often what is depicted or denounced as intervention claims legitimacy from an invitation, however contrived. There is, however, no real advantage in drawing any general distinction between so-called solicited and unsolicited intervention except for those whose aim is primarily to justify or condemn state conduct. The only useful distinction that one might draw, albeit of a somewhat different kind, is that between intended and unintended acts of intervention. The latter can occur, for example, if one state releases commodities from a stockpile on to the world market and so affects the economies of countries which depend unduly on the export of such goods. At the beginning of 1971 the Thai Foreign Ministry released a statement which expressed resentment of sales of rice by the United States to traditional markets of Thailand. Such sales were said to "constitute unfair competition and greatly affect the trade and economy of Thailand." Examples of such inadvertence or negligence, whether in economic or other fields, do not, however, fit the terms of our working definition which associates intervention essentially with purpose and which is best evaluated in terms of intention and effect upon a domestic political order and on the policies of its government.

The prospect for successful intervention will depend only in part on the resource capability of an interventionist Power. Such capability will possess additional or reduced effectiveness depending on whether the particular condition of the target state or states serves to facilitate or obstruct its purpose. This will obtain whether the intervention in question is intended either to undermine or to bolster a particular political order. This interrelationship has relevance also for acts designed either to assist or to counter external policies. Obviously, the particular context of intervention is a critical factor and in the case of Southeast Asia it has been fundamental to the experience of both successful and unsuccessful intervention.

The record of external intervention in Southeast Asia has varied with the context, but the region taken as a whole has provided a fertile field for virtually every kind of interventionist activity. This overall "susceptibility" of Southeast Asia is, in great part, a consequence of the febrile political orders of most of the states concerned. These states, and some much more than others, may be described as embryonic in character in that their internal political condition is not reflected accurately by their recognized international status. They tend to be characterized by great social diversity which expresses itself in a variety of striking internal cleavages. One outcome of this somewhat common condition is a lack of substantive congruence between society on the one hand and polity on the other, which promotes attendant problems of political pathology for governments which have succeeded colonial administrations without necessarily establishing a firm foundation of legitimacy. Strains on the fabric of governmental order follow also from deficiencies in material resources, in turn a partial consequence of economies shaped by colonial priorities and from a paucity of administrative and technological skills. In addition, the priorities and related performance of government are not always conducive to the effective mobilization of political support, while negligence and malpractice have served to induce popular alienation despite the populist tone of declaratory postures.

As a consequence of the manner of colonial consolidation and the measure of continuity of territorial form sustained with independence, Southeast Asia is distinguished by the absence of concentrations of effective power. This feature is exemplified by Indonesia, the largest and most populous country of the region, whose geography, social diversity, and political experience has induced acute governmental anxiety concerning the integrity of the state. Individual weakness, and also local antagonisms, have served to limit considerably the degree and content of institutionalized intraregional association, which in turn indicates the subordination of Southeast Asia within the wider international system. This featur has been reflected also in the degree of economic and militar dependence on external patrons which distinguishes the pc litical orientation of many Southeast Asian governments.

Both the fragmented international character of the regio and the febrile quality of internal political order have attracte the competitive interests of external powers, in particular i response to conflicts over political succession arising from colonial decline. The political context for such competitio was created by the dramatic transformation of colonial r gional order under the impact of Japanese military interve tion which marked the onset of the Pacific war. The destru tion of colonial power and its failure, with exceptions, re-establish itself fully following the end of hostilities left a pe litical vacuum both domestically and internationally. Comp tition to determine internal political succession was joined different ways by external powers sponsoring opposed intern clients. Such competition was initially more nominal the actual on the part of the major Communist powers, but b came more substantive with the political schism betwee them.

For the United States, which may be described as the i terventionist power *par excellence,* its goals in Southeast As were a function of its global interests and became defin initially as a product of strategic position and posture in As at the end of the Pacific War. As General MacArthur on explained: "Our strategic frontier then shifted to embra the entire Pacific which became a vast moat to protect us long as we held it . . ." A deep concern with the oppos extremity of a shared ocean was demonstrated, for examp in the establishment of military bases in the Philippines. T concern became an acute anxiety with the successful seizu of power by the Communists in China and the conseque endeavor to apply a policy of containment against what w perceived as the vehicle for the expansion of internatio Communism in Asia and the domination of the oppos extremity of a shared ocean.

The impetus for such a policy was strengthened consid ably with the outbreak of war in Korea which prompted creasing and substantial support for the French position in Indochina. A commitment to that position had been made before the onset of the Korean conflict. Indeed, in February 1950, in the course of recommending to President Truman that he should respond positively to a French request for military assistance in Indochina, Secretary of State Dean Acheson articulated the premise which served to justify an ever entangling process of intervention. Acheson argued: "The choice confronting the United States is to support the legal governments in Indochina or to face the extension of Communism over the remainder of the continental area of Southeast Asia and possibly westward."[2] It was this explicit premise which received public endorsement by President Eisenhower in April 1954 and which served as the philosophical justification for a determination to draw the line against the expansion of Communism in Southeast Asia; a determination given institutional expression with the formation of SEATO in September 1954 and sustained in idea until the enunciation of the more ambiguous Nixon Doctrine from July 1969.

By contrast, the Soviet Union did not entertain any direct security interest in Southeast Asia following the capitulation of the Japanese. Indeed, its Eurocentric priorities led to total neglect of the interests of the Viet Minh and support for a French Communist Party within a governing coalition dedicated to the restoration of colonial position. With the evident breakdown of the Grand Alliance and the onset of the Cold War in Europe, a shift in international orientation found expression in general support for insurrectionary movements in Asia, either against obdurate colonial powers or national-bourgeois successor governments perceived as part of the vulnerable rear of capitalism. Such support, however, during the period of Communist uprisings in Burma, Malaya, Indonesia, and the Philippines, was confined to exhortation and did not incorporate practical measures of assistance. Subsequent to the death of Stalin, Soviet interests in Southeast

[2] *The Pentagon Papers as Published by The New York Times.* Based on investigative reporting by Neil Sheehan, written by Neil Sheehan, Hendrick Smith, E. W. Kenworthy, and Fox Butterfield (New York: Quadrangle Books, 1971), p. 10.

Asia were directed to the expansion of general diplomatic influence through identification with the goals of local nationalism, especially in anti-imperialist sentiment. From the beginning of the 1960s, the exigencies of bitter conflict with China prompted a much more substantive involvement, in particular to secure the political affections of the ruling Lao Dong Party in Hanoi, but also by the end of the decade to secure a general political disposition within Southeast Asia against the Chinese People's Republic, especially among states like Malaysia and the Philippines which are vigorously anti-Communist in internal policy.

If the policies of the Soviet Union have been a product of general global interests expressed in competition with anti-Communist and Communist adversaries, those of the Chinese People's Republic were more directly related to the geopolitical significance of Southeast Asia for China. Such policies have been revisionist as well as revolutionary. They were revisionist in the sense that the extended military presence and influence of the United States in Asia was contemplated as a threatening encirclement which had to be eradicated. They were revolutionary in that to achieve this goal, China was prepared to take action involving limited risk and cost in supporting revolutionary movements within accessible Southeast Asian states which were allied with the United States or perceived as hostile to China.

Insofar as conflict obtained between these three Major Powers at different intensity at different times, it revolved around anticipated international consequences of international political change (most strikingly, of course, in Indochina) and the outcome of interregional disputes which offered scope for external intervention and political advantage. For other external and lesser powers, intervention has related to the attempted preservation of colonial domain and also by Britain to support of a former colonial entity, i.e., Malaya, whose independence was nurtured and whose expanded territorial form as Malaysia was facilitated and defended.

The record of external intervention within Southeast Asia has reflected a concern to protect established interests and to assert new ones. As we have seen, American interests were formed through the experience of the Pacific War and political transformation in China but were undoubtedly extended with the assumption of protecting the French position in Indochina. Chinese activities have represented a determination to assert an interest in the close vicinity of China which preceded in existence the extension of the European state system to Asia, while the Soviet Union has been concerned to assert a closer relationship between an increasing global capacity and global interests. Significantly, the conflict which has followed as a consequence of external intervention has not involved any direct physical confrontation between external states but rather indirect encounters through internal clients. Such a general practice has been, in part, a consequence of disparity between interest and capacity and importantly a reflection of a general concern on the part of Great Powers to avoid any clash between them which could lead to uncontrolled escalation.[3] The prize in this practice of intervention, undoubtedly governed by certain constraints, is a regional order likely to favor the interests of a particular external Power and to deny those of its competitors.

The overt and covert means of intervention are no mystery in the practice of international relations. They range from conventional diplomatic forms through propaganda, the provision of political asylum, subversion and economic instruments to the display and use of naked force. In practice, they are rarely used in complete isolation of each other but are applied in combinations which may or may not be appropriate or judicious. Success in external intervention may be judged in terms of a demonstrable ability to project power and influence at a distance with effect and at tolerable cost in order to achieve political goals. Success in such a varied

[3] The most remarkable example of the avoidance of direct physical confrontation between major Powers occurred in May 1972 when the Soviet Union made no effective response to the American mining of the harbors of North Vietnam. Indeed, it became evident that the two Super Powers were well able to compartmentalize their involvement in a local conflict which was not an obstacle to a critical visit by President Nixon to Moscow.

enterprise, however, has not automatically been guaranteed by conventional criteria of superior power and influence but has been determined by the specific circumstances and context of intervention, the suitability of assistance, inducement, and compulsion brought to bear and, of course, by the nature of any constraints bearing on the intervening Power whether they arise from the international environment or domestic circumstances.

It is not possible in a chapter of limited length to discuss adequately each and every episode of external intervention in Southeast Asia since the transfers of power. Rather, it is hoped to consider certain examples of the activity within loose categories which may highlight the complexities of the undertaking and the constraints operating on it.

The most commonplace act of intervention takes the form of representation by one government to another. Such diplomatic intervention, whether unilateral or collective, takes on a more striking character when it is supplemented by either compulsion or inducement. One of the most useful labels for the former practice is what Alexander George has described as "Coercive Diplomacy."[4] This practice is viewed not simply as a form of flexible and controlled response to a situation of crisis but as an attempt to affect an adversary's will through an incremental and credible use of force sufficient to demonstrate resolution but hopefully not to provoke escalation. Such exercises in communication by pushing up the stakes of conflict through military display have been practiced with mixed success in Southeast Asia. President Kennedy had successful recourse to such a practice to induce acceptance of his demand for a ceasefire in Laos in 1961, prior to the holding of negotiations.[5] However, this example has to be understood in terms of specific context and also in relation to the priorities held by an intervening local adversary, i.e., the Vietnamese Communists, whose political will was the objective of American military display in Laos.

[4] See Alexander L. George, David K. Hall, and William E Simons, *The Limits of Coercive Diplomacy: Laos, Cuba, Vietnam* (Boston: Little, Brown and Co., 1971).

[5] *Ibid.*, p. 212.

President Johnson sought a much more substantive concession from the same local adversary with evident prospect of coercion as a consequence of noncompliance when he dispatched J. Blair Seaborn—a Canadian diplomat in the ICC —to Hanoi in June and again in August 1964. Indeed, Seaborn's second visit followed only days after the Gulf of Tonkin episode and the American acts of alleged retaliation. In the U.S. note delivered at the Canadian Embassy in Washington on August 8, 1964, for transmission to Seaborn, it was indicated that he "should conclude (his secret negotiations) with the following new points." These included: "(a) That the events of the past few days should add credulity to the statement made last time that U.S. public and official patience with North Vietnamese aggression is growing extremely thin," and "(c) That the United States has come to the view that the D.R.V. role in South Vietnam is critical. If the D.R.V. persists in its present course, it can expect to continue to suffer the consequences."[6] Such an indirect representation produced an unsatisfactory response, and the subsequent application of additional coercive measures did not have the desired effect on political will in Hanoi. In this respect, it has been pointed out that the coercive impact of action is not directly related to its magnitude but to measures credible and potent enough for the task in question.[7] Undoubtedly the punitive weight of physical power deployed by the United States under the Administration of President Johnson did not pose that measure of unacceptable damage sufficient to divert the government of North Vietnam from its chosen path. In such circumstances, diplomacy was a feeble instrument for intervention despite the use of coercion to underpin it.

It should be evident that Great Powers have not been automatically in a position to impose their will despite an availability of superior and abundant resources and a facility for intervention. And diplomacy plus an inducement need be no more effective in this respect than representation incorporating a threat of coercive measures. One interesting example of the failure of such an intervention occurred with

6 Sheehan *et al., op. cit.,* p. 299.

7 George, *et. al., op. cit.,* p. 214.

reference to Indonesia during 1959–63 when in the aftermath
of the resolution of the West Irian dispute, the Administration
of President Kennedy sought to persuade President Sukarno
to transform the style of his foreign policy and to tread the
path of economic orthodoxy.[8] The proposed nexus in this
arrangement was a substantial infusion of economic assistance
to be provided through an international consortium. Because
of Malaysia's contentious arrival on the international scene,
however, the prospect of an international aid consortium
could not be entertained by Sukarno. This was not because he
did not appreciate the significance of the offer. Indeed his
rejection can be interpreted as a deep understanding of the
implications of the stabilization scheme. In effect, the American initiative represented a serious challenge to the internal
power structure of the political system of Guided Democracy.
Guided Democracy was an intensely competitive system
within which Sukarno, nevertheless, maintained political preeminence by a practice of almost Byzantine manipulation and
by sustaining what might be described as nonrational romantic
criteria for the exercise of power. The acceptance by Sukarno
(or for that matter any political grouping) of the program
of stabilization in the political climate prevailing in Indonesia
at that time, besides indicating a willingness to place the
country in a dependent relationship with the West, would
have indicated the clear prospect of a fundamental change
in the accepted criteria for the exercise of political power. The
rational criteria demanded by giving priority to economic development were not those which called for the political
talents which distinguished Sukarno and so, if accepted as an
orthodoxy, would have served to undermine his personal
authority.

In the event, Sukarno opted to continue with the mode of
Confrontation against Malaysia. And it was in this context that
the United States government sought without success, early in
1964, to mediate the dispute. One might contrast this experience of diplomatic failure with an earlier diplomatic media-

8 Roger Hilsman, *To Move a Nation: The Politics of Foreign
Policy in the Administration of John F. Kennedy* (Garden City
N.Y.: Doubleday & Company, 1967), pp. 383–84.

tion by the United States in 1962 over West Irian, when the Dutch were persuaded to accept a formula for territorial transfer and the Indonesians agreed to a peaceful settlement which would satisfy their nationalist demands. The initiative of 1964 in which Robert Kennedy, acting for President Johnson, sought to promote a peaceful settlement of the Malaysia dispute did not provide a nexus which could meet Sukarno's priorities at that time. And, although economic assistance from the United States had been cut, it had not been suspended totally so as to apply maximum coercive measures. The general motivation of the United States in intervening was somewhat similar to that which had prompted the initiative over West Irian. Malaysia, however, was not prepared to act like the Dutch over West Irian. Indeed, they welcomed an intervention by external patrons (Britain, Australia, and New Zealand) which provided appropriate military support in the circumstances. In consequence, Robert Kennedy had nothing to offer Indonesia by way of inducement, and as the United States was unwilling to coerce with any effect, Confrontation continued until it was set aside as a consequence of dramatic political change within Indonesia.

The record of collective diplomacy provides examples also of the problems of that form of intervention, especially where an absence of accord exists between external allies as to both ends and means. In institutional form this experience is well exemplified in the noninterventionist record of SEATO, a diplomatic vehicle reflecting differential interest and commitment among its membership from its very inception.

Given a willingness by external adversaries to come to terms, the prospect for their successful noncompetitive diplomatic intervention will depend on the balance between global and local priorities, and also on the nature of external patron –internal client relationships. The Geneva settlement on Indochina of July 1954, especially in relation to Vietnam, pointed up both the relationship between global and local priorities and that between external patrons and internal clients. The Soviet-American accord over Laos between Kennedy and Khrushchev in Vienna in June 1961 also reflected external realities, but they did not match the imperatives of the internal situation. This was not solely a consequence of the irreconcilable nature of internal antagonisms within Laos, but was in great part a product of access to alternative sources of external patron support available to the North Vietnamese who had themselves intervened in Laos. Subsequently, external accord could not manage the competitive internal political order because Laos became inextricably linked to Vietnamese Communist priorities, and also because external Communist patrons competed for the political affections of the government in Hanoi.

The forms of military intervention in Southeast Asia have ranged from the indirect provision of assistance to internal forces through training, advice, and supply of materials to direct physical intrusion from sea, air, and land. The provision of military supplies had been a long-standing feature of external support. For example, the Chinese Communists began to assist the Viet Minh soon after their assumption of power, and made a substantial contribution to military success at Dien Bien Phu through the provision of antiaircraft guns and other artillery. The Soviet Union airlifted military supplies to the disaffected forces of Kong Lé in Laos during 1960–61, while the United States, besides its huge outlay in Indochina beginning in May 1950, airdropped weapons to the regional rebels in Indonesia from 1958. At the level of clandestine activity, the United States through the Central Intelligence Agency has assisted antigovernment groupings in Sihanouk's Cambodia and sponsored the infiltration of South Vietnamese intelligence and sabotage teams into North Vietnam. In Laos, it has used "third-country nationals," i.e., Thais and Filipinos, in its counterinsurgency operations against the Pathet Lao.

On the Communist side, it is the Chinese People's Republic which has sponsored and patronized insurgencies which have arisen essentially out of local circumstances but which have profited from the provision of training facilities for cadres within China. Thailand, in particular, has experienced the effect of such assistance, as greater skill in insurgent techniques and superior equipment facilitate insurgent success in parts of the country where the environment is suitable for the interposition of alternative authority between government and people. If one recognizes the special case of Vietnam—where the nationalist cause was effectively monopolized at the outset by the Communists—it should be evident, however, that successful insurgency is not simply the product of the external supply of arms and propaganda across a porous border. For example, China's support for insurgency in Southeast Asia has never been of great material substance (excluding Vietnam) and is not, in itself, capable of promoting a genuine revolutionary situation; it merely makes a contribution whose significance will depend on those local circumstances which themselves facilitate insurgency. China's support for insurgent movements in Southeast Asia is a consequence, in part, of ideological commitment, but it is also a means of exercising pressure on governments on its southern periphery which appear aligned against its interests or who might be disposed to so align themselves. Thus, China has continued to provide a measure of support for the Burmese Communist Party despite the evident rapprochement with Rangoon indicated by the presence in Peking of Premier Ne Win in August 1971.

It is evident from the experience of direct American military intervention in Indochina that the nature and context of conflict has stood between conventional superior capability and a desirable resolution of conflict. A great variety of problems has arisen at stages in the course of a conflict in Indochina which have both affected and reflected the nature of external intervention. To begin with, in meeting a situation of genuine insurgency, there is the well-known difficulty of the identification of targets and the appropriate deployment of forces. Even superior power, to have effect, has to be applied with a sense of discrimination and control, especially when the engine of the insurgency is fueled by mobilized political support from a sympathetic environment.

In such circumstances, much will depend on the extent to which the government of the day, which has invited or welcomed external intervention, possesses any semblance of legitimacy or, indeed, any inclination to seek it in a way which will make possible the denial of popular support to insurgent forces. Where such forces are able to advance a plausible claim to represent the nationalist cause and where the government of the day may appear to be an instrument of an external power, then the prospect of securing proper title to govern is bleak. This will be especially so if, in addition, there are genuine economic and other grievances ready-made for exploitation, and when the material benevolence of the external power encourages corrupt practice, an evident disregard for popular interests and a general divorce from the social and economic, as opposed to the military, realities of conflict.[9]

Any client assisted by an external power ought to be able to demonstrate some independent capacity for good government plus a willingness to co-operate effectively with the intervening power to utilize its benefactions. This latter quality is essential not only for a government of the day but equally so for insurgent forces operating against such a government. Within Southeast Asia, it has been the Vietnamese Communists who have demonstrated this quality to a remarkable degree, despite a dogged independence of policy and action in the face of allies' advice. The record of other insurgent movements in the region has been much less remarkable in their ability to profit from external support.

Success in external intervention will depend in great part on the nature of the relationship between patron and client. Undoubtedly the experience of the Lao Dong Party with their ideological patrons, beginning with the Soviet Union in 1945, has given rise to sustained suspicion in Hanoi of allies' motives and a determined independence of spirit and policy. Great consternation was displayed at the announcement in July 1971 of President Nixon's impending visit to Peking and the subsequent news that he would also visit Moscow. The prospect of both its political patrons consorting with the principal patron of its antagonist in Saigon gave rise to un-

---

[9] For a discussion of related factors which have served to undermine the more recent phase of American intervention in Indochina, see J. L. S. Girling, "Nixon's 'Algeria'—Doctrine and Disengagement in Indochina," *Pacific Affairs*, Winter 1971–72 (Vol XLIV, No. 4), pp. 527–44.

derstandable fears of Great Power collusion to promote a compromise settlement in Vietnam at the expense of North Vietnamese interests. The subsequent major offensive by North Vietnam across the seventeenth parallel at the end of March 1972, which did not serve the interests of either China or the Soviet Union to any great degree, has to be evaluated, in part, in terms of such prospect of Great Power accommodation, while the Vietnam settlement of January 1973 was facilitated by its evident materialization.

Client recalcitrance, however, has been more acutely a problem for the United States. Indeed, it would seem that the capacity for influence of such a recalcitrant client, or more importantly its ability to resist the influence and advice of an intervening external power, has tended to increase in proportion to the evident stake of the intervening power in the outcome of the internal conflict. In this respect, one author has commented: "Ironically, the actions of the United States in Vietnam have not been consistently frustrated by the enemy but rather by the government of South Vietnam and the members of that government who carry out obstructionism as an act of conscious policy." It is of interest to note that these were not the ill-considered remarks of an armchair philosopher but the opinions of a former colonel in the U. S. Marines who saw extended active service in Vietnam.[10]

External military intervention has been affected also by the nature of external constraints. The prospect of provoking the counterintervention of an external adversary served to set certain limits to military action during the intervention conducted during the Presidency of Lyndon Johnson. Caution was prompted by the fact that both the Soviet Union and the Chinese People's Republic were competing vigorously for the political affections of North Vietnam and, therefore, might have been willing to intervene directly on its behalf. However, recent Soviet and Chinese reevaluations of their relationships with each other and the United States have not evoked a similar self-imposed limitation on the Nixon Administration's military policy, as its responses to the spring 1972

[10] William R. Corson, *The Betrayal* (New York: W. W. Norton & Co., 1968), pp. 14–15.

North Vietnamese military offensive and the December 1972 breakdown in the Paris negotiations indicate.

A further factor of major importance relates to the political will of the intervening power. American intervention in Vietnam has demonstrated that there is an intimate relationship between the conception of tolerable human and material cost of intervention as held by the domestic society of an intervening power and its capacity for persistent military action beyond a certain threshold of cost. In the case of American intervention in Vietnam, attrition of human resources expressed in the flow of coffins to Arlington Cemetery without compensating military gains led to a reappraisal of interventionist policy from March 1968. This followed the psychological defeat at the time of the preceding Tet offensive. One might contrast this reappraisal, enforced by domestic dissent, with the apparent acceptability of a much higher absolute and relative level of cost by the North Vietnamese, which may be explained not only by the disciplined nature of their society, but also by a generally accepted sense of justification of actions and goals, not matched in terms of fundamental national interest within the United States. Undoubtedly, the nature of the domestic society of the intervening power is critical under certain circumstances, and the values associated with the United States, which affected both the approach to war and expectations about the speed of its outcome, served to constrain the exercise of interventionist policy. Subsequently, however, with a shift in the nature of military involvement and a considerable reduction in American casualties, the force of domestic opinion came to play a lesser role in the exercise of interventionist policy, although it has continued to set limits to the nature of intervention.

A contrasting example of military intervention unconstrained by domestic opposition is that of British and Australasian action to counter Indonesian confrontation against Malaysia. This action was marked not only by a very low casualty rate, on both sides, but also by more skillful and appropriate measures of a military and civil kind which, in an environment less hospitable to the insurgent forces than in Vietnam, enabled the external intervening power to overcome a great many of the problems discussed above, admittedly in a different context.[11]

At stages in the preceding discussion, we have considered in passing the nature of the nexus between external patron and internal client. Economic aid has played a key role in this respect, but its allocation is no sure guide to the success of collateral diplomatic intervention designed to change governmental policy. The giving of aid in such circumstances may be construed as the art of political seduction through appropriate benefaction. The problem for the external patron is how much it must bestow on a client before benevolent response becomes political embrace. In the experience of Southeast Asia since the transfers of power, such a prospect has not followed solely from the attraction of the benefaction. Frequently a patron has deployed resources where the political climate is suitable and the client government is already committed to the political orientation valued by the patron power. Other forms of external economic benefaction to countries that have identified themselves as nonaligned have been less rewarding, as in the case of Soviet aid to Burma and Indonesia. They tend to be valued to the extent that they assist the government concerned to maintain an independent position and to reject the prospect of any alignment with another external power.

Aid in itself does not appear to have been a critical factor in bringing about a transformation of political attitudes, although there is no doubt that the internal opponents of Prince Sihanouk before March 1970 were attracted by the prospect of a resumption of American economic assistance. Perhaps a more appropriate question concerning the giving of aid as a political weapon is to inquire whether there may not be a critical point beyond which benefaction makes the donor more vulnerable than the recipient insofar as recurrent donations become necessary to preserve an existing stake. Should such a stake be seriously threatened, as was that of the Soviet Union in Indonesia first under Sukarno by an apparent align-

[11] General Sir Walter Walker, "How Borneo Was Won: The Untold Story of an Asian Victory," *The Round Table,* January 1968 (Vol. LIX, No. 233), pp. 9–20.

ment with China and then under Suharto with an evident
orientation to Western aid-givers, the alternatives of physical
intervention and acquiescence become unrealistic and only
the latter option becomes practicable in the circumstances,
as the Soviet Union demonstrated by its conduct.

Economic aid by itself represents a tenuous association despite the vast quantities of such forms of assistance that have
been allocated within Southeast Asia for political reasons.
Through such benefaction alone, it is impossible to ensure
the prevention of internal political transformation and
changes in external alignment. The actual degree of control
that can be exercised by an external power through economic
benefaction will depend also on the degree of availability
to the beneficiary in question of alternative sources of
economic support in addition to a general sense of need for
such support. In the case of Indonesia, from March 1966
onward, such alternative aid was readily available but only
on condition of firm adherence to externally held notions of
economic and foreign policy orthodoxy. Such priorities, however, were a conscious objective of the succeeding new order
and not dictated solely by external considerations.

The discussion, so far, has ranged loosely over problems
faced by external powers in an activity in which they would
appear to enjoy considerable advantages given their superior
resources and the fragile quality of internal political order
within Southeast Asia. It is evident, however, that apparent
superiority in power, conventionally expressed, does not automatically make for successful intervention. What is decisive
is the particular form of intervention in relation to specific
context and the critical influence of factors such as the
domestic and external constraints on action.

Within Southeast Asia, external intervention has been related in the main to the determination of internal orders
which will match the political priorities of external powers.
It is with reference to such goals that one can talk meaningfully of stability—a condition that is identified more often by
its absence than by its presence. In a very general sense, it
may be said to imply the existence of a tolerable political

order either within a state or between states. It is obvious, however, that what is tolerable is frequently a matter of contention between external powers. Obvious also is the fact that acts of intervention to promote a desirable political order can provoke counterintervention aimed at thwarting such a goal.

The relationship between stability and external perception of desirable order will depend on the fact and extent of external adversary accord, for example, as in the tenuous agreements reached at Geneva in 1954 and in 1962. It was a major factor also in the Vietnam settlement of January 1973. Internal order, however, is not automatically assured through an accord between external powers, as the course of events in Indochina subsequent to the Geneva agreements amply demonstrated by changing the very conditions which made such limited accord possible. Indeed, it is this very problem of securing a sense of congruence between external and internal interests which stands in the way of the scheme for the neutralization of Southeast Asia proposed by Malaysia and accepted, in principle, by ASEAN states in November 1971.

Given the fragile quality of political order within Southeast Asia and the attendant prospect of political change, external powers can be expected to react depending on how they perceive the ensuing balance of advantage. Where competitive intervention is possible, then stability will be in doubt. Intervention will more readily serve the interests of stability (externally perceived) where action, either unilateral or collective, is expeditious in circumstances where adversary response, either local or external, is ineffectual. But such action will prove effective over time only if the internal beneficiaries of an order so sustained are capable of managing the affairs of state in such a way as to render renewed competitive intervention unlikely or insignificant. To this end, they must be able to eradicate those domestic circumstances which facilitate substantive challenge to political order. This would seem a doubtful prospect in many countries in Southeast Asia.[12]

[12] For a discussion of problems of political order, see Michael Leifer, *Dilemmas of Statehood in Southeast Asia* (Vancouver and Singapore: University of British Columbia Press and Asia Pacific Press, 1972).

Southeast Asia has been witness, of late, to a reshaping of external influences which bear on the region. Some form of American disengagement is in train as a direct consequence of an inability to promote the most desirable—as opposed to a tolerable—political order through military intervention. Britain's military commitments have been reappraised and scaled downward substantially in consequence. However, there are other external powers in competitive relationship which seek either to sustain or to increase their influence within the region. The Chinese People's Republic, although increasingly conventional in its diplomatic practice, not only has an evident concern about the political orientation of states on its southern periphery, but has given public notice of its attachment to ideological goals in the joint communiqué released at the conclusion of President Nixon's visit to that country. The Soviet Union, for its part, has sought increasingly to counter any prospect of the extension of Chinese influence within Southeast Asia and to demonstrate its global interests and capacity. Japan, with great military potential and increasingly conscious of its economic stake and of a growing resentment to its presence, is concerned with the future stability of the countries of the region. The changing constellation and emphasis of external interests does not suggest any lessening likelihood of competitive involvement in a region so susceptible to such activity, although the military experience of the United States has been salutary in more capitals than just Washington.

Continuing competitive interest is indicated by external power contention over the status of the Straits of Malacca which provides the principal sea route between the Indian Ocean and the South China Sea. In November 1971, Indonesia and Malaysia, onetime antagonists in confrontation, in their capacity as the littoral states, issued a declaration (of which only Singapore took note) to the effect that the Straits of Malacca (including the Singapore Strait) was not an international waterway although merchant shipping could use it freely in accordance with "the principle of innocent passage." Such an initiative was prompted by Japanese pressure over control and safety of navigation but it fitted also Indonesia's desire to assert sovereign control over waters intersecting and surrounding its archipelago and to oppose any Great Power attempts to fill so-called power vacuums within Southeast Asia. It was no coincidence that in March 1972 the Soviet Ambassador to Japan made public in Tokyo his representation to the Japanese Foreign Ministry that the Straits of Malacca was an international waterway. This statement provoked acrimonious exchanges between the Soviet Union on the one hand, and Indonesia and Malaysia on the other, who subsequently found themselves enjoying the indirect support of the Chinese government on this issue.

This example is one indication of a continuing divergent perception of appropriate regional order by external states who look to Southeast Asia in terms of competitive political advantage. Such competition with its obvious consequences for stability may be expected to continue, if in changed form, as long as Southeast Asia maintains its subordinate character within the wider international system, and as long as its component states retain those features of political life which facilitate that subordination.

Security by Proxy:
The Nixon Doctrine and Southeast Asia

MELVIN GURTOV

INTRODUCTION

Several times in this century, foreign crises have prompted sweeping American pronouncements that have laid the basis for commitments abroad well beyond the area in which the crisis occurred. Such was the case when the United States entered World War I to "make the world safe for democracy"; when Roosevelt and Churchill agreed to implement the Atlantic Charter; when President Truman responded to the alleged Communist threat to Greece and Turkey in 1947 by insisting on the American duty to "support free peoples who are resisting attempted subjugation by armed minorities or by outside pressures"; and when President Eisenhower in 1957 obtained from Congress, after Suez and the growth of Nasser's influence, the authority "to assist any [Middle East] nation or group of nations requesting assistance against armed aggression from any country controlled by international Communism."

Lamenting these universalistic responses, George Kennan has written:

> On many occasions . . . I have been struck by the congenital aversion of Americans to taking specific decisions on specific problems, and by their persistent urge to seek universal formulae or doctrines in which to clothe and justify particular actions. We obviously dislike to discriminate. We like to find some general governing norm to which, in each instance, appeal can be taken, so that individual decisions may be made not on their particular merits but automatically depending on

> whether the circumstances do or do not seem to fit the norm . . .[1]

The Nixon Doctrine—first offered in interview form on Guam in July 1969[2] and formalized in the President's State of the World message of February 1971[3]—in some way does not constitute the type of response to which Kennan objects. The Doctrine is not a substitute for or generalization of a specific crisis decision. Rather, it is supposed to offer the guidelines of future American policy in the period of dissociation from the Indochina crisis. It thus comes closer to fitting the usual understanding of a doctrine than any of its predecessors.

But in the most critical respect, the Nixon Doctrine is vulnerable to the same criticism Kennan has made of other doctrines: it provides a convenient set of generalities that can rationalize U.S. involvement abroad whenever circumstances of the moment so dictate. The relationship of doctrine and action works to broaden the scope of Presidential initiative rather than to define the nature and limits of policy. Nowhere can this conclusion be better illustrated than in the performance of the Nixon Doctrine in Southeast Asia.

THE DOCTRINE AS CONCEPT

Any examination of the Nixon Doctrine must begin with its key concepts, because the definitions commonly given it—"low profile" in Asia, disengagement, self-reliance, multipolar politics—are not consistent with the doctrine's theory, much less with its application.

The overarching principle of the Doctrine is that, in contrast with past American practice, interests will determine commitments. "We are not involved in the world because we

---

[1] *Memoirs, 1925–1950* (Boston: Little, Brown and Co., 1967) p. 322.

[2] Text in *The New York Times*, July 26, 1969, p. 8. The interview is a close paraphrase of Nixon's remarks, not a verbatim transcript.

[3] *U. S. Foreign Policy for the 1970's: Building for Peace* (Washington, D.C.: GPO, February 25, 1971). Cited hereafter as *Nixon Report 1971*.

have commitments; we have commitments because we are involved. Our interests must shape our commitments, rather than the other way around."[4] On Guam, Nixon laid down three policy principles:

> —First, the United States will keep all of its treaty commitments.
> —Second, we shall provide a shield if a nuclear power threatens the freedom of a nation allied with us or of a nation whose survival we consider vital to our security.
> —Third, in cases involving other types of aggression, we shall furnish military and economic assistance when requested in accordance with our treaty commitments. But we shall look to the nation directly threatened to assume the primary responsibility of providing the manpower for its defense.[5]

The first point to note is that the Doctrine excludes any reconsideration of existing commitments, such as those arising from the Vietnam War, the U.S.-Taiwan Mutual Defense Treaty, the SEATO pact, or that portion of the 1962 Rusk-Thanat communiqué which would appear to promise U.S. involvement in Thailand to combat "subversion" as well as "aggression." *Present* commitments clearly do determine U.S. interests.

The Doctrine's relevance hence is narrowed to the question of *future* commitments. But a careful reading of the President's foreign policy reports does not afford a basis for confidence that the critieria governing U.S. interests in Asia have changed much. The United States remains committed to "averting great power dominance over Asia"; U.S. interests are still said to be "important," "basic," "substantial," and "deep" in Asia's security.[6] "Interests," in short, are assumed

[4] *Ibid.*, p. 13.

[5] Speech of November 13, 1969; text in William P. Rogers, *United States Foreign Policy 1969–1970* (Washington, D.C.: GPO, March 1971), p. 324. Cited hereafter as *United States Foreign Policy 1969–1970*.

[6] See the East Asia sections of the *Nixon Report 1971* and the *Nixon Report 1972* (*U. S. Foreign Policy for the 1970's: The Emerging Structure of Peace,* Washington, D.C.: GPO, February 9, 1972).

rather than defined, implying anew that military and/or political commitments to protect those interests will be forthcoming. The spasmodic reactions to Asian crises that in past years have characterized U.S. policy and determined U.S. interests seem destined to continue under Nixon; and the American military response to the overthrow of Prince Sihanouk in March 1970 was in that tradition.

Equally unsettling is the Doctrine's constant reference to Asian stability as a broad U.S. interest separate from those "deep" interests that derive from the U.S. role as a Pacific power. Interestingly, the portrait Nixon presents of increasing economic strength and self-defense capacity within the region does not lead him to conclude that U.S. interests are declining. To the contrary, the greater Asian "stability," the higher the American stake in its maintenance. Nixon evidently attaches more importance to a friendly nation's economic development (in GNP terms) and military proficiency than to its political character and system—which again is no new departure from past practice. So long as a (non-Communist) nation is "developing" economically and militarily, the United States has a continuing and increasing interest in its stability. Whether or not the United States should be associated with and committed to politically unpalatable regimes—such as the military dictatorships and rightist juntas that govern all U.S. allies on the Southeast Asia mainland[7]—is a question not raised in the Nixon Doctrine.

The Doctrine's discussion of internal security problems in Southeast Asia also raises questions.[8] The President cautions against the United States assuming the main responsibility—his third principle—whether the "threat" is entirely domestic or assisted from outside. He sees a growing capacity in Southeast Asia for security self-reliance, as well as a growing interest in collective security (discussed below); but he is aware

[7] Note that two such regimes came to power during the Nixon Administration: the Lon Nol government that overthrew Prince Sihanouk in Cambodia, March 1970, and the Thai military leaders who ended parliamentary government in November 1971.

[8] For the discussion that follows, see the Guam interview and an interview with the President by C. L. Sulzberger in *The New York Times,* March 10, 1971, p. 14.

that U.S. allies are a long way from independence of military support. Faced with a gap between expectations and military realities, Nixon declines to make certain vital distinctions—between an appeal for assistance from a U.S. ally and from a non-Communist non-ally; between civil war and externally assisted, or even externally dominated, rebellion; between revolutions of the left, revolutions of the right, and minority movements for autonomy (some of which the United States might support, some oppose, some neither); between a level of assistance that will promote self-reliance and a level that will induce dependence and a U.S. commitment (Nixon's Doctrine urges only that U.S. aid avoid creating either overdependence or underconfidence).

All these distinctions, obviously, relate to the possibility of new Vietnams. Determined to avoid another such adventure, yet equally determined to preserve U.S. interests, meet commitments, and enforce stability in Southeast Asia, the Nixon Doctrine becomes an equivocation, a substitute for a true redefinition of the American role in Asia. Because, as the sudden and widespread involvement in Cambodia makes plain, when an opportunity appears to gain an anti-Communist ally, when expectations are aroused about U.S. assistance, and when Communist revolution apparently can be combatted at minimal cost to the United States, questions of interest and commitment become academic. And as Richard Nixon has stated, ". . . Cambodia is the Nixon Doctrine in its purest form."[9]

SOURCES OF THE NIXON DOCTRINE FOR ASIA

It should come as no surprise that the Nixon Doctrine is conceptually as loose as previous American statements of foreign policy principles. The basic reason is that the Doctrine rests squarely on past programs and precepts. Four specific sources of the Doctrine seem evident on careful reading: (1)

[9] Speech of November 12, 1971, cited in Melvin R. Laird, *Statement before the Armed Services Committee on the FY1973 Defense Budget and FY1973–1977 Program* (Washington, D.C.: GPO, February 1972), p. 117. Cited hereafter as *Laird Report 1972.*

the Eisenhower New Look defense program of the 1950s; (2) Nixon's interpretation of changes in Asia in the 1960s; (3) Nixon's conviction that the United States has a permanent and vital mission in the Pacific; (4) the impact of U.S. public and Congressional sentiment against "another Vietnam" in Asia.

THE EISENHOWER NEW LOOK
AND THE NIXON NEW LOOK

The New Look program worked out under Eisenhower was designed to reduce Korean War defense spending, take maximum advantage of U.S. air and naval preponderance (thus the phrase, "more bang for a buck"), and rely for deterrence on the credibility of massive retaliation and alliance commitments.[10] With respect to Asia, the Eisenhower Administration made clear that major commitments of manpower to "fringe wars" would not occur. Instead, if the opponent were not deterred by the threat of massive retaliation, he would be dealt with by Asian armies supported by American military aid and, if necessary, by naval power and a highly mobile strategic reserve. These latter features of the program took on new urgency in 1954, when the irrelevancy of massive retaliation was spotlighted in Vietnam. The Administration thereupon turned to collective defense and the SEATO pact. SEATO, which originated in Dulles' abortive attempt to obtain "united action" to save Dien Bien Phu, was supposed to complement existing bilateral treaties and provide an umbrella for U.S. intervention in Indochina after the "disaster" at Geneva.

Nixon's security program for Asia, formulated in an international and domestic climate reminiscent of 1953–54, contains striking parallels to the New Look. With a "1½ war" strategy (i.e., having general purpose forces for one major war in Europe or Asia, and for a less-than-major war), the Administration again seeks to avoid stationing large numbers of U.S. troops in Asia, to deter Chinese aggression with stra-

[10] See the author's *The First Vietnam Crisis: Chinese Communist Strategy and United States Involvement, 1953–1954* (New York: Columbia University Press, 1967), ch. 4.

tegic and tactical nuclear weapons, and to rely for Asia's defense mainly on "strong air, naval and support capabilities."[11] Asian forces, backed by increased U.S. assistance and air power, are expected to be effective substitutes for U.S. ground forces in situations of insurgency. Only in the event of "external aggression or . . . an overt conventional attack" might the United States become directly involved;[12] but even then, "our interests and our commitments" would have to be weighed, and the "emphasis" would be "on our air and naval capabilities."[13] Very much in the Eisenhower tradition, the Nixon Doctrine puts Asian proxy armies on the front line of Asia's defense, and holds aloft the threat of conventional and (where feasible) tactical nuclear bombing should that front line be overrun.[14]

Clearly, U.S. military assistance is intended to be the dominant American contribution to the defense of "free" Asia. As U.S. forces are withdrawn from Asia—during 1969 and 1970, about 265,000 from South Vietnam, 20,000 from Korea, 12,000 from Japan and Okinawa, 16,000 from Thailand, 9,000 from the Philippines, and 1,000 from Taiwan—the forces of U.S. allies in Asia are increasing—to about 2.7 mil-

[11] Melvin R. Laird, *Statement before the House Armed Services Committee on the FY1972–1976 Defense Program and the 1972 Defense Budget* (Washington, D.C.: GPO, March 1971), p. 77. Cited hereafter as *Laird Report 1971.*

[12] President Nixon, as quoted by Earl C. Ravenal, "The Nixon Doctrine and Our Asian Commitments," *Foreign Affairs,* January 1971 (Vol. XLIX, No. 2), p. 203.

[13] *Laird Report 1971,* p. 77.

[14] In keeping with the tradition of "massive retaliation," Nixon says in his 1971 report (p. 179): ". . . having a full range of options does not mean that we will necessarily limit our response to the level or intensity chosen by the enemy. Potential enemies must know that we will respond to whatever degree is required to protect our interests . . ." Earl C. Ravenal (*loc. cit.,* p. 209) has consequently argued that while the Nixon Doctrine does not automatically mean escalation from conventional to tactical nuclear war, "the 1½-war strategy provides the President with fewer alternatives and renders the resort to nuclear weapons a more compelling choice, as well as making nuclear threat a more obvious residual feature of our diplomacy."

lion, according to Secretary of State Rogers.[15] U.S. dollars in grant aid, sales, loans, surplus equipment, and training are required to maintain this trend, and they are being given in increasing amounts.[16] As Secretary Laird has said, the Military Assistance Program is "the key" to keeping U.S. combat units out of Asia; "a MAP dollar is of far greater value than a dollar spent directly on U.S. forces."[17]

But the picture of Asian self-reliance is flawed by several factors. In the first place, the sizable U.S. force reductions in Asia ceased in 1971 except in South Vietnam. To some extent, the continued fighting in Indochina is responsible; it explains, for instance, the fifty thousand men (about 80 per cent Air Force) still in Thailand, and accounts for about two-thirds of the eight thousand men on Taiwan and the off-shore islands. But Laird has pointed out the main reason: the program to improve the performance of Asian allies will

[15] *United States Foreign Policy 1969–1970*, p. 37.

[16] A rough idea of the global increases in military aid, and the predominance of military aid to Asian countries as compared with the rest of the world, can be obtained by reference to the following official U.S. statistics for fiscal years (FY) 1969–1971:

Area	FY	Military grants	Surplus grants	Military credit sales	Military cash sales	Ex-Im Bank military loans
All countries	69	2,634.1	107.5	281.2	1,438.5	225.0
Asia	69	2,332.2	57.8	26.0	132.3	125.0
All countries	70	2,569.2	131.7	184.9	854.6	286.4
Asia	70	2,280.6	81.1	40.0	81.3	128.4
All countries	71	3,025.4	110.2	1,051.6	1,354.6	253.0
Asia	71	2,687.6	52.8	58.2	130.0	133.0

Figures are in millions of dollars. They are drawn from *ibid.*, p. 334 and Rogers, *United States Foreign Policy 1971* (Washington, D.C.: GPO, March 1972), p. 404.

[17] Quoted in John Dower, "Ten Points of Note: Asia and the Nixon Doctrine," *Bulletin of Concerned Asian Scholars*, Fall 1970 (Vol. II, No. 4), p. 51. Note the contrast with Mr. Nixon's expectation, indicated in his Guam interview, that the military assistance program would decline.

take some time, hence "appropriate U.S. strength" will have to be maintained in certain countries.[18] Laird's explanation amounts to an admission that a substantial force presence will accompany a growing military aid program in Asia for the indefinite future.[19]

Secondly, U.S. force reductions have, where requested by anxious partners, been offset with public reaffirmations of commitments. In Southeast Asia, for instance, the Thai government had been reassured several times about the continued validity of the Rusk-Thanat communiqué, for example by Assistant Secretary of State Marshall Green after the President's trip to China. Taiwan's leaders have also been told often that the 1954 Mutual Defense Treaty will remain in force.

Lastly, the United States will continue to have access to a large number of military bases and other facilities throughout Asia despite force reductions and the phasing out of some installations, such as in Japan, Philippines, and Okinawa. Included are the seven major Thai air bases; the massive naval complexes at Sattahip (Thailand), Subic Bay (Philippines), and Cam Ranh Bay (South Vietnam); the air reconnaissance facilities in Laos and Taiwan; the counterinsurgency training centers in Thailand, Laos, Taiwan, and Philippines; and use of air bases in Japan for Korean and Taiwan contingencies, possibly along with transit rights for nuclear arms through Okinawa despite the reversion agreement.[20] These bases are augmented by electronic surveillance and antisubmarine warfare activities that blanket the area from the North China Sea to the Indian Ocean. Additional Polaris submarines are being equipped with Poseidon-MIRV missiles.[21] The

[18] *Laird Report 1971*, p. 84.

[19] *Nixon Report 1972*, p. 87: "We will continue to maintain sufficient U.S. forces in the region to permit us to meet our commitments. Adjustments in our own military deployments in Asia have come only after thoroughgoing reviews with our partners."

[20] Regarding Okinawa, see the report in *The New York Times*, April 25, 1971, p. 8. Concerning the bases in Japan, which were discussed when Prime Minister Tanaka met with President Nixon in Hawaii, see *Los Angeles Times*, September 4, 1972, p. 13.

[21] *Laird Report 1972*, p. 72.

effectiveness and scope of U.S. monitoring, deployment, and retaliatory capability against Asian opponents is not likely to diminish at all under the Nixon Doctrine, and may even increase.

REGIONALISM IN A NEW ASIA

A corollary of the long-standing optimism about Asian military self-reliance is the high expectations for regional collaboration. American expectations have apparently not diminished. Despite the moribund state of SEATO, the necessity of large American financial outlays to induce Asian troop contributions to the Indochina war (as revealed, for instance, in the once-secret U.S.-Thailand agreement of November 1967), the territorial disputes and ill will between Southeast Asian states and peoples, and the opposition of some governments, such as Thailand, to transforming slowly developing regional economic associations into security organizations.

Richard Nixon has long been an outspoken advocate of regional security cooperation "as a counterforce to the designs of China."[22] Again reflecting the thinking in the Eisenhower Administration, Nixon conceives of an all-Asian multilateral appeal for U.S. assistance or intervention as the most desirable future way "to ensure that a U.S. response will be forthcoming if needed . . ."[23] Sensing the evolution in the 1960s of regional no less than national pride, the President looks forward to the day, "five or ten years from now," when collective security can largely replace the U.S. presence and initiative.[24]

Thus far, although regional cooperation is increasing on the economic side, security cooperation has not markedly advanced.[25] Only in insular Southeast Asia—the Five-Power Agreement for the defense of Malaysia and Singapore, which went into effect in November 1971—has the President's hope

[22] Richard M. Nixon, "Asia After Viet Nam," *Foreign Affairs*, October 1967 (Vol. XLVI, No. 1), p. 124.
[23] *Ibid.*, p. 114.
[24] Guam interview.
[25] See Marshall Green, "A Look at Asian Regionalism," *Department of State Bulletin*, November 24, 1969, pp. 445–48.

of shoring up SEATO been realized.[26] Contrary to his suggestion of 1967,[27] the Asian and Pacific Council (ASPAC, formed of nine members in Seoul in June 1966) has not become the "foundation-stone" of a regional security alliance. The hoped-for "solidifying awareness of China's threat" has not materialized, first, because the "China threat" never has been generally perceived in the region (and is a diminishing concern since Nixon's China trip); second, because ASPAC has been split from its inception among far-right (Taiwan, South Vietnam, South Korea), moderate-right (Thailand, Philippines, Malaysia, Australia, New Zealand), and centrist (Japan) factions over involvement in politically charged issues; and third, because Japan has refused to take on the vanguard role Mr. Nixon and others have urged upon her to galvanize what would clearly be another anti-China alliance.[28]

In the absence of further progress in regional security, the Administration's policy seems to be to make Indonesia the focal point of a regional consensus favorable to U.S. policies. As Mr. Nixon has written, "Indonesia constitutes by far the greatest prize in the Southeast Asian area."[29] Her "full participation in the regional groupings of the non-Communist states of Asia invests them with new weight and greater potential."[30] Not surprisingly, therefore, Nixon has given Indonesian economic and especially military assistance requests far higher priority than they were accorded under President Johnson. Economic assistance in grants, loans, and sales was approximately $245 million, $208 million, and $176 million in fiscal years (FY) 1969–1971 respectively. Military aid to Indonesia was $5.4 million, $6.2 million, and $18.1 million

[26] The Five-Power Agreement provides for British, Australian, and New Zealand land and naval forces in Singapore, an Australian air contingent at Butterworth in Malaysia, and joint consultation in the event of armed attack by external forces on Singapore or Malaysia. The new Labour government in Australia, however, is reconsidering its contributions under the agreement.

[27] Nixon, "Asia After Viet Nam," p. 116.

[28] *Ibid.*

[29] *Ibid.*, p. 111.

[30] *Nixon Report 1971*, p. 99.

in the same years; but the last two figures exclude militar cash sales, which are classified.[31]

The figures do not do justice to the American potentia for exerting influence in Indonesia. U.S. economic aid is th largest share (about one-third) in the $640-million progran of the multilateral Inter-Governmental Group on Indonesia and the United States is the leading member of the (non Communist) "Paris Club" of Indonesian creditors (the Indc nesian government has a $215.6 million debt to the Unite States).[32] Moreover, of $1.5 billion in new foreign invest ments approved by the Indonesian government through Sep tember 1970, about one-third ($550 million) was Amer can.[33] Finally, Indonesia relies on the United States as he second largest supplier and as an outlet for 15 per cent of he exports.[34]

The United States has thus become excellently placed t recast the nonalignment policy of the Suharto governmer in ways favorable to Washington. And to some extent, it ha already done so. Djakarta convened an eleven-nation confer ence of foreign ministers in May 1970 that called, in lin with U.S. policy, for the withdrawal of all "foreign" (i.e North Vietnamese)* troops from Cambodia. Thereafte Indonesia accepted Cambodian soldiers for counterinsurgenc training,[35] and, secretly, may be a third-nation conduit fo U.S. military aid that cannot be delivered directly to Can bodia because of Congressional limitations (which may ex

[31] *United States Foreign Policy 1969–1970*, p. 341, and *Unite States Foreign Policy 1971*, p. 410. In April 1972 the Administr tion requested $29.9 million in military assistance for Indonesi

[32] *United States Foreign Policy 1969–1970*, p. 61.

[33] *Ibid.*

[34] *United States Foreign Policy 1971*, p. 85.

[35] At a 1972 House hearing, it was revealed that 360 Camb dians were being trained in Indonesia, assertedly without U. funds paying for the training. Cambodian soldiers, police, ar pilots were also receiving instruction in South Vietnam, Thailan Malaysia, Australia, and Taiwan, but figures were not disclose See U. S. House of Representatives, Committee on Foreign Affai *Hearings on H.R. 13759: Foreign Assistance Act of 1972*, 9: Congress, 2d Session, March 14–23, 1972, GPO, Washingto D.C., p. 83, No. 170.

plain why U.S. military assistance to Indonesia jumped in FY 1971 to over $18 million).

In somewhat similar fashion, U.S. capital may also have foreign policy significance in Singapore, where economic growth was threatened by British force reductions. According to Secretary Rogers' report, American private investment was $203 million (in over 300 firms), and "Another $140 million is already planned by Americans for investment over the next few years."[36] The "fast rate" of investments will help ensure that the valued harbor is always open to the SEATO powers.

ASIAN MISSION

In keeping with the perspective of every American President in this century, Richard Nixon believes that the United States has a destiny to be a Pacific power. From the belief flow certain inescapable responsibilities and basic operating principles. "The United States is a Pacific power . . . , one anchor of a vast Pacific community," Nixon wrote in 1967.[37] Consequently, the United States is obliged "to fashion the sinews of a Pacific community"—one in which military and economic strength are coordinated, China can be counterposed with "a concert of Asian strengths," Japan can play an increasing role," and the United States exercises discreet leadership.[38]

The basic assumption that the United States is a Pacific power is repeated in the President's Guam interview, in his interview with C. L. Sulzberger of *The New York Times,* and in his foreign policy reports. The context is consistent in each case. The President believes that, *historically* and *geographically,* what affects Asia affects the United States, as three wars since 1940 have demonstrated; that, in international political terms, the United States cannot withdraw from Asia without undoing all that long-term involvement, capped by the Vietnam War, has accomplished; and that, in terms of power and peace, Asian Communism led by China

---

[36] *United States Foreign Policy 1969–1970,* p. 60.
[37] "Asia After Viet Nam," p. 112.
[38] *Ibid.,* p. 124.

will continue to pose the major challenge to "Free World interests for years to come.

If these rationales of American involvement in Asia seem closely to resemble those that dictated the prolonged and costly adventure in Indochina, the President has said enough to confirm the resemblance. Even as the Vietnamization program has brought U.S. troop strength in South Vietnam from 549,000 in March 1968 to 16,000 in early 1973, Nixon has often restated the standard themes of his predecessors regarding the regional and global implications of a less-than satisfactory conclusion of that conflict, as shown by these examples.

The domino principle: The success of the Communist effort in South Vietnam would encourage Chinese and Soviet expansionism and would discourage all the non-Communist nations of Asia. "Now, I know there are those who say the domino theory is obsolete. They haven't talked to the dominoes."[39] A U.S. pullout from South Vietnam without victory "would bring peace now, but it would enormously increase the danger of a bigger war later."[40]

The test case: "If we are to move successfully from an era of negotiation, then we have to demonstrate—at the point which confrontation is being tested—that confrontation with the United States is costly and unrewarding."[41]

The costs of humiliation: "Let historians not record that when America was the most powerful nation in the world we passed on the other side of the road and allowed the last hopes for peace and freedom of millions of people to be suffocated by the forces of totalitarianism . . . Because let us understand: North Vietnam cannot defeat or humiliate the United States. Only Americans can do that."[42] And: "... when the chips are down, the world's most powerful nation, the United States of America, acts like a pitiful, helpless

[39] "A Conversation with the President," *Department of State Bulletin,* July 27, 1970, p. 104.
[40] "Peace in Vietnam," *Department of State Bulletin,* June 1969, p. 458.
[41] *Ibid.*
[42] Speech of November 3, 1969, in *United States Foreign Policy, 1969–1970,* p. 376.

giant, the forces of totalitarianism and anarchy will threaten free nations and free institutions throughout the world. It is not our power but our will and character that is being tested . . ."[43]

For Mr. Nixon, then, the Vietnam experience, far from having dictated "no more Vietnams," must mean the retention of the objective to prevent a Communist takeover[44] with a change in the tactical components in order to maximize the overt role of friendly Asian governments. Vietnamization is the Nixon Doctrine in microcosm: "The South Vietnamese have made their country the most dramatic and concrete example of the partnership principle of the Nixon Doctrine."[45] New Vietnams should if at all possible be avoided, he said on Guam; but he would not rule out direct U.S. intervention, saying that each case of externally supported subversion must be separately treated, and that "the role of the United States . . . is to help them [Southeast Asian governments] fight the war but not fight the war for them."[46] President Kennedy, of course, used similar language in September 1963 during the Vietnamese Buddhist crisis.

Nixon's belief in the essential validity of the Vietnam enterprise relates to his view of a Chinese threat, a view also held by Presidents Truman, Eisenhower, Kennedy, and Johnson. Although his, and the State Department's, foreign policy reports contain none of the cold war rhetoric about Chinese bellicosity and quest for hegemony in Asia that have long characterized official declarations, other documents do, for instance Nixon's 1967 article in *Foreign Affairs:* "Vietnam has diverted Peking from such other potential targets as India, Thailand, and Malaysia"; the China "threat is clear, present, and repeatedly and insistently expressed"; China must be persuaded "that it cannot satisfy its imperial ambitions"

[43] Speech of April 30, 1970; *ibid.*, p. 383.
[44] This objective has been stated often but in different forms. Cf., for instance, the *Nixon Report 1971*, p. 63; the interview with Sulzberger cited previously; and Secretary Rogers' comments before the Senate Foreign Relations Committee on April 17, 1972.
[45] *Nixon Report 1971*, p. 61.
[46] Guam interview.

and must accept "the basic rules of international civility."[47] Summing up the policy implications of the China threat, Nixon wrote:

> "Containment without isolation" is a good phrase and a sound concept, as far as it goes. But it covers only half the problem. Along with it, we need a positive policy of pressure and persuasion, of dynamic detoxification, a marshaling of Asian forces both to keep the peace and to help draw off the poison from the Thoughts of Mao.[48]

Nor has Nixon's perception of China fundamentally altered since assuming office—the China trip, Shanghai communiqué, and trade deals notwithstanding. On Guam he characterized China as the one major world power that had adopted "a very aggressive attitude and a belligerent attitude in its foreign policy." More cautiously, his foreign policy report for 1971 admits that China's revolutionary deeds may be less dramatic than her leaders' words, and that China's capacity for making trouble abroad is limited. But nowhere is there recognition that what the United States does in Asia—since 1969, renewal of the air war over North Vietnam, support of increased Thai intervention in Laos, and the ground interventions in Cambodia and Laos—may significantly affect the Chinese leadership's foreign policy and perception of American diplomacy with China. The prevailing assumption in the Administration is that China represents a continuing threat to U.S. friends and allies;[49] that the threat requires nuclear deterrence and military coordination with U.S. partners; and hence, that Sino-American diplomacy should be pursued as an adjunct to containment (as well as for domestic political reasons and for purposes of Soviet-American diplo-

[47] "Asia After Viet Nam," pp. 111, 113, 121, 123.

[48] *Ibid.*, p. 123.

[49] Melvin Laird, for instance, has called attention to China's "ambitions for great power status and regional hegemony," thus making China "a pervading psychological and actual threat to the peace and security of the Asian arena" (quoted by Dower p. 50). In his 1972 defense report, Laird argues that China, along with North Vietnam and North Korea, poses a conventional warfare threat and "foment[s] guerrilla warfare, sabotage, espionage and subversion throughout the area" (*Laird Report 1972*, p. 50).

macy) rather than to rectify the anti-China policies of the last thirty years.

POLITICS AND FOREIGN POLICY

Finally, the Nixon Doctrine is the outgrowth of a political assessment by the President that the American public and the Congress are in no mood soon again to accept a sizable military involvement in Southeast Asia. The Doctrine would appear to be responsive to that mood by vowing, in effect, that "free" Asians will henceforth be fighting Communist Asians, and that U.S. support of Asian friends will stop short of another Vietnam. The Doctrine's timing and appeal clearly parallel the Eisenhower New Look's, which responded similarly to pressures for terminating and not repeating an indecisive war in Korea.

Complicating Mr. Nixon's search for a viable doctrine is his belief that the Vietnam War has significantly contributed to stability in Asia. He has written that the U.S. effort "provided tangible and highly visible proof that Communism is not necessarily the wave of Asia's future"; gave Indonesian generals the confidence to thwart the coup attempt in 1965 and "rescue their country from the Chinese orbit"; and bought time for Asian governments to withstand Peking's pressures for accommodation.[50] This reading of recent history has led him to develop an Asian security program that seeks to remove U.S. involvement from American politics and farther from Congressional scrutiny. The *objectives* of U.S. involvement in Vietnam—to counter Chinese regional ambitions, to sustain non-Communist regimes in Indochina, and to demonstrate that the United States will meet its "responsibilities" to allies and friends—have not changed.

Nixon has said that his Asia policies constitute a midcourse between the two extremes of neo-isolationism (the "superdoves") and Fortress America (the "superhawks").[51] Typically picturing himself as standing on the high middle ground between the extremists, Nixon offers a course that meets U.S. worldwide "responsibilities" without overcommit-

[50] "Asia After Viet Nam," p. 111.
[51] Sulzberger interview, *op. cit.*

ting the nation's resources or credibility. He told Sulzberger:

> The main thing is that I'd like to see us not end the
> Vietnamese war foolishly and find ourselves all alone in
> the world. I could have chosen that course my very first
> day in office. But I want the American people to be able
> to be led by me, or by my successor, along a course that
> allows us to do what is needed to help keep the peace in
> this world. We used to look to other nations to do this
> job once upon a time. But now only the United States
> plays a major role of this sort in the world . . .

Mr. Nixon's doctrine, as will be seen, amounts to tolerable
interventionism in Southeast Asia—"tolerable" in the sense of
sharply diminishing public and Congressional anguish about
the further spilling of *American* blood and treasure. The
Vietnamization and Cambodia aid programs—the proclaimed
models of low-profile U.S. intervention and Asian self-help—
the shift from ground power to air power and covert warfare
in Indochina, and increasing military assistance to allied
and friendly Southeast Asian nations are all in accord with
that goal. To judge from the virtual obliteration of U.S. policy
in Southeast Asia as an issue in the 1972 Presidential campaign, at least until the massive bombing of North Vietnam
began in April, the Nixon Doctrine has, in domestic political
terms, been eminently successful.

THE NIXON DOCTRINE IN ACTION

The troop withdrawals, base reductions, China diplomacy
and self-help rhetoric notwithstanding, the Nixon Doctrine
in action, especially on the Southeast Asia mainland, appears
not to be a great departure from past U.S. policy. Only tactics
and semantics have changed, not overall strategy or objectives. In seeking to demonstrate the point, I shall examine
policy under Nixon in Indochina, Thailand, and Taiwan.

INDOCHINA

As already mentioned, the principal meaning of the Nixon
Doctrine for conflict in Indochina has been a changeover from
massive U.S. ground involvement and accompanying air support to increased bombing and covert warfare amidst troop

withdrawals. The shift is most dramatically revealed in comparative figures for total bombing tonnage dropped on Indochina: more tons of bombs had already, by September 1971, been dropped during the Nixon Administration than were dropped between 1966 and 1968, at the height of the continuous air campaign under Johnson.[52] Johnson's complete suspension of the bombing of North Vietnam in November 1968, in other words, merely led to a shift of locale (mainly, to Laos and Cambodia), not to a reduced role for air power.

The high priority attached by Nixon officials to air power is revealed in these representative comments:

(1) Secretary of State Rogers: "We do not rule out the use of air power to support Asians in any effort they make to fight the common enemy. There is one enemy; it is North Vietnam."[53]

(2) Secretary of Defense Laird: "We will use air power, and as long as I am serving in this job, I will recommend that we use air power to supplement the South Vietnamese forces, as far as the air campaign in South Vietnam, Laos, and Cambodia [is concerned]."[54]

(3) President Nixon: "I am not going to place any limitation upon the use of air power except, of course, to rule out a rather ridiculous suggestion . . . that our air power might include the use of tactical nuclear weapons."[55]

The most careful unclassified study of the air war, the Cornell study,[56] estimates that during 1971, about 270,000 tons of bombs were dropped on South Vietnam (down from about 1 million tons in 1968), over 400,000 tons on Laos (more than double the 1968 level), and about 90,000 tons

[52] *Los Angeles Times,* November 8, 1971, p. 21. The figures are 2,865,808 tons for 1966–68 and 2,916,997 tons for 1969–August 1971. Bombing tonnage declined in 1970 and again in 1971, but when applied to sparsely populated, small countries like Laos and Cambodia, the decline loses significance.

[53] *The New York Times,* January 30, 1971, p. 1.

[54] *Ibid.,* January 21, 1971, p. 13.

[55] *Ibid.,* February 18, 1971, p. 15.

[56] Center for International Studies, Cornell University, *The Air War in Indochina,* November 1971, as summarized by the Indochina Resource Center (Washington, D.C.). (All subsequent references to the Cornell Report are based on the summary.)

on Cambodia (zero in 1968). The amount dropped on North
Vietnam under "protective reaction" cannot be estimated; it
was undoubtedly drastically reduced from over 150,000 tons
in 1968, but the number of U.S. sorties is again increasing.
There were 123 (reported) "protective reaction" strikes
against North Vietnam in 1971, and the figure for 1972 will
be many times that number because of the U.S. air offensive
that began anew in April.[57]

The changed pattern of U.S. air attacks—less in North and
South Vietnam, more in Laos and Cambodia—is also reflected
in the deployment of U.S. air power. U.S. bases in South
Vietnam are being closed or transferred to the Vietnamese,
whose strength in aircraft and personnel is going up. U.S. air
strength is moving almost entirely to Thailand and carriers in
the South China Sea (B-52s will continue operating from
Guam and Okinawa as well as Thailand).[58]

The extensive bombing in Indochina is perfectly compatible with the Nixon Doctrine and Vietnamization. Bombing
is less costly, financially and politically, than continued
ground force involvement, which is now left to the Indochinese allies. Bombing cannot "win" the war—a lesson
learned from Johnson's ROLLING THUNDER—but it can punish
the other side for continuing it (thus, "protective reaction");
it can also prevent the opponent from winning by keeping
him off balance, disrupting new offensives and diminishing
his ability to keep his forces well supplied. The fact that increasing numbers of persons in Indochina are killed or left
homeless because of the bombing,[59] and the high likelihood
that the Vietnamese Communists and their allies in Laos and
Cambodia will not (any more than before) be persuaded by
bombing to accept U.S. peace terms, do not appear to enter
into Nixon's calculations.

In Laos, the Nixon Administration's innovations in the
bombing program have been to increase attacks in the south-

[57] Before the air offensive, reported U.S. sorties were about 100

[58] Cornell Report.

[59] See the Cornell Report and, on Laos, George McT. Kahin
"One-Third of a Nation Uprooted," *New Republic*, August 7–14
1971, pp. 19–21.

eastern (Ho Chi Minh trails) sector, maintain heavy bombing in northern Laos using B-52s for the first time, introduce helicopter gunships in combat, and shift tactical command of air operations to Air Force headquarters in Thailand. Bombing in the trails area (under the BARREL ROLL program) has gone progressively upward since 1966, according to the Cornell study; but after November 1968, when Johnson ordered all bombing in North Vietnam halted, U.S. air power was diverted to Laos.[60] Nixon continued this policy (if, indeed, he is not regarded as its author) with daily, high-tonnage raids against virtually every conceivable target and employing the most "sophisticated" kinds of bombs.[61] Meanwhile, over northern Laos (the STEEL TIGER program), while bomb tonnage has declined under Nixon, the number of sorties flown has increased.[62] Moreover, the Administration began B-52 missions in February 1970—a fact concealed from Senate Foreign Relations Committee inquiries until May 1971.[63] These missions, and at least two raids by Lao T-28 fighter-bombers over the Chinese road network in northern Laos during the same period, may have been responsible for the substantial increase of Chinese antiaircraft defenses to protect the roads.[64]

The intense bombing in the Laotian panhandle, without precedent in modern warfare, was supplemented toward the end of 1970 by the use of helicopter gunships in direct support of Lao ground soldiers[65] (although engaged in combat,

[60] See Fred Branfman, "Presidential War in Laos, 1964–1970," in Nina S. Adams and Alfred W. McCoy (eds.), *Laos: War and Revolution* (New York: Harper & Row, 1971), pp. 221–22.

[61] *Ibid.*, p. 233.

[62] *Ibid.*, p. 234 and note 22. STEEL TIGER was cryptically described (but not named) by President Nixon in his March 6, 1970, report on U.S. involvement in Laos as primarily involving "reconnaissance missions." See *Department of State Bulletin,* March 30, 1970, p. 408.

[63] See the staff report of the Senate Committee on Foreign Relations, Subcommittee on U. S. Security Agreements and Commitments Abroad, *Laos: April 1971* (Washington, D.C.: GPO, 1971), p. 8.

[64] *Ibid.*, pp. 2, 7.

[65] *The New York Times,* January 20, 1971, p. 1.

the U.S. helicopter personnel were officially said not to be combat troops). So much concentrated air power evidently increased pressure on Washington from the Air Force and CIA to take prior approval of Laos air operations out of the hands of the American Embassy in Vientiane. During 1971 it was reported that USAF tactical headquarters in Udorn, Thailand, had assumed that responsibility—a major policy shift that promised increased bombing.[66]

In Cambodia, the air war that began with U.S.-South Vietnamese cross-border operations in March 1970 fits the Laos pattern. Although the President announced at that time a 21-mile limit to U.S. air operations in Cambodia, the limit was soon exceeded. Since the stated objective of the air strikes, and the Cambodian invasion as a whole, was to "save U.S. lives" and "protect the Vietnamization program," bombing *anywhere* could be—and has been[67]—justified. Similarly, after the introduction of U.S. helicopter gunships into Cambodia at the start of 1971, they were officially described as essential to the "interdiction" mission of U.S. air power, and as having the "ancillary benefit of relieving pressure on nearby friendly forces."[68]

The other, less public, half of the Nixon Doctrine for Indochina is covert warfare: the disguised deployment of U.S. personnel and funds to carry on the war without large-scale American ground involvement. Covert operations, of course, have a long history in Indochina, dating back to Colonel Lansdale's Saigon Military Mission, which, at Eisenhower's direction, conducted sabotage raids into North Vietnam within a month of the end of the 1954 Geneva Conference.[69] It would seem worthwhile to enumerate the other kinds of covert activities that previous American leaders have authorized, not only because of their illegality, but also because they set a pattern for Nixon to follow and enlarge upon.

[66] *Los Angeles Times*, September 27, 1971, p. 14.

[67] See, e.g., *The New York Times*, January 19 and 21, 1971, p. 1.

[68] *Los Angeles Times*, January 18, 1971, p. 1. The helicopters operate from Seventh Fleet carriers stationed in the Gulf of Siam.

[69] See Neil Sheehan, *et al.*, eds., *The Pentagon Papers* (New York: Bantam Books, 1971), pp. 53–66.

Eisenhower Administration: Special Forces and CIA activities in Laos with Thai and Meo irregulars;[70] Chinese Nationalist air support in Laos through Civil Air Transport of Taiwan.[71]

Kennedy Administration: Covert South Vietnamese operations in North Vietnam (code-named FARMHAND); psychological warfare and raids against North Vietnam (Plan 34A); "DeSoto" destroyer coastal patrols off North Vietnam; experimental crop defoliation (RANCHHAND).[72]

Johnson Administration: Continuation of the above Kennedy programs; Thai air and ground involvement in Laos;[73] "limited" air and ground strikes in the Laotian panhandle by South Vietnamese forces (with Souvanna Phouma's approval);[74] Operation Leaping Lena—parachuting small U.S. reconnaissance teams into the panhandle.[75]

The Nixon Administration has been relatively more open than its predecessors about covert warfare activities in Indochina. But a comparison of what it has admitted and what remains unpublicized still reveals a considerable gap. For the record, Administration spokesmen have said that in Laos there are a little over a thousand Americans, military and civilian, of whom about one-third are military advisors and trainers; the United States does not have, or intend to have, ground combat forces in Laos; there is a certain number of Thai forces fighting there.[76] In Cambodia the government admits to having Military Equipment Delivery Teams

[70] *Ibid.,* pp. 133–35.
[71] *Ibid.,* p. 137.
[72] All these activities are detailed in Ralph Stavins, Richard J. Barnet, and Marcus G. Raskin, *Washington Plans an Aggressive War* (New York: Vintage Books, 1971), pp. 61–71.
[73] *Pentagon Papers,* p. 305.
[74] *Ibid.,* p. 316.
[75] *Ibid.,* p. 306.
[76] The figures on U.S. personnel are from Nixon's March 6, 1970, statement, cited above.

(MEDT) and an augmented army attaché staff in the embassy; but it denies that there are or will be U.S. advisors or combat troops.[77] Military assistance in FY 1971 is reported to have been $152.4 million for Laos (more than double the FY 1970 figure) and $191.2 million for Cambodia ($9.1 million in FY 1970).[78] For FY 1972, the Senate voted to restrict U.S. aid to $350 million for ground operations in Laos[79] and $341 million for all aid to Cambodia.

Calculating the number and types of Americans involved in Laos and Cambodia in military functions is about as impossible as trying to account for military assistance expenditures. The problems of definition and information are overwhelming. Nevertheless, it is highly probable that the Administration's figures and classifications are significantly misleading. They undoubtedly omit or understate: the American, as well as Thai, Chinese Nationalist, and other third-country pilots in Laos who fly the AID-funded (but CIA-run) troop and supply aircraft;[80] the liaison, logistics, and "delivery team" men in both countries who, though not in uniform and assigned to the embassy (Cambodia) or AID (Laos), are in point of function military advisors;[81] and the

[77] See especially Nixon's report on the Cambodia "operation" in *United States Foreign Policy 1969–1970*, p. 448.

[78] *United States Foreign Policy 1971*, p. 410.

[79] The Senate staff report, *Laos: April 1971*, observes (p. 13): "The cost of military assistance thus doubled every year between fiscal year 1963 and fiscal year 1965, doubled again between fiscal year 1965 and fiscal year 1967, and in fiscal year 1972 it will be more than three times as large as it was in fiscal year 1967 (and 25 times as large as it was when it began 9 years ago)."

[80] See *ibid.*, p. 12. The airlines are Air America, Continental Air, and Lao Air Transport.

[81] On Laos, see *ibid.*, pp. 13–14, where it is noted that there were (in 1971) thirty-four logistics administrators in AID and twenty-four army attachés stationed with Royal Lao Army units all of whom can be considered military advisors. On Cambodia see the reports in *The New York Times,* January 20, p. 5, January 26, p. 1, and January 28, 1971, p. 1; and *Los Angeles Times* January 30, 1971, p. 14. These articles report that 20 of the 95 man U.S. mission in Phnom Penh belonged to the MEDT, and that another 34 were also military personnel. Some U.S. official acknowledged that team members would go into the field with Cambodian combat units to show them how the equipment works.

CIA and Special Forces personnel working in Laos from posts in Laos or Thailand.[82]

CIA activities in supporting and directing Meo tribesmen and Thai "volunteers" are not an innovation of the Nixon Administration, but they fit well the Doctrine's need for *sub rosa* U.S. involvement. The CIA, according to the Senate staff report on Laos,[83] has "trained, equipped, supported, advised, and, to a great extent, organized" the irregular (mostly Meo) *Bataillons Guerriers,* or BGs, a far more effective force than the Royal Lao Army. From the report's context, the BGs appeared to total about 37,000 in 1971; but the exact number, and the CIA budget for the BGs, are classified.[84] CIA operatives also appear to command the Thai army units in Laos, which are ferried into combat by Air America.[85] The Thai soldiers, paid for out of the CIA budget to hide the price, reportedly increased from about 1,000 in 1970 to between 4,000 and 6,000 in 1971.[86]

CIA and Thai involvement in Laos, which has its parallel in Special Forces and South Vietnamese operations in Cambodia, points up the weakness of Congressionally imposed financial restrictions on covert and proxy warfare under the Nixon Doctrine. The Department of Defense Appropriations Act of January 1971 includes an amendment—the so-called Fulbright amendment—that was specifically designed to prohibit U.S. funding of Thai or South Vietnamese intervention in Laos or Cambodia.[87] But the Administration rationalizes

[82] See Branfman's comments, *op. cit.,* p. 249, and Henry Kamm's article in *The New York Times,* March 12, 1971, p. 6. Kamm writes that about 150–175 CIA agents work with Meo soldiers in Laos, while an unknown number commute from Udorn, Thailand, where a station chief coordinates operations.

[83] *Laos: April 1971,* p. 14.

[84] *Ibid.,* p. 15.

[85] *Los Angeles Times,* March 22, 1972, p. 23 (article by Jack Foisie).

[86] See George Ashworth's article in *Christian Science Monitor,* April 19, 1971.

[87] The amendment states that no military funds shall be used to support "Vietnamese or other free world forces in actions designed to provide military support and assistance to the Government of Cambodia or Laos" except as required to ensure U.S. withdrawal from Vietnam or to aid in the release of prisoners of war.

providing such aid on the basis that the Thai units consist of volunteers (when in fact they are regular army units with Thai officers), and that the South Vietnamese forces, which range far and wide over Cambodia, are helping the United States to withdraw from Vietnam (which the amendment allows as a basis for military assistance). Or consider the Special Foreign Assistance Act of January 1971, which rules out funds "to provide U.S. advisors to or for Cambodian military forces in Cambodia," and which declares that no U.S. aid to Cambodia shall "be construed as a commitment by the United States to Cambodia for its defense." The Administration does not consider the MEDT personnel or the army attachés to be "advisors"; nor does it construe the substantial economic and military assistance to or air support of Lon Nol's regime as constituting a "commitment."

The limitations on Administration bilateral aid to Laos and Cambodia are another example. The $350 million ceiling for FY 1972 in Laos does not apply to the STEEL TIGER and BARREL ROLL bombing programs, the costs of which would surely double the allowed amount.[88] CIA support of Meo and Thai forces is covered; but since the CIA budget is secret, overall and for Laos, it is easy enough to provide the BGs and the Thai army with all the money the Administration decides is necessary. The same loopholes would govern the $341 million aid limit enacted for Cambodia. It is no wonder, then, that Administration officials expressed no displeasure when the limitations were passed.

THAILAND

When the Nixon Doctrine was first unveiled, Thai government officials publicly and privately expressed concern that it would mean sharp cutbacks in U.S. military assistance, on which Thailand has relied since the fall of 1950. But, while the total value of U.S. military aid to Thailand has apparently declined since 1969, it remains substantial; and Secretary Laird has reportedly assured Bangkok that it can continue to count on U.S. support for the next decade.[89] In fact, for Thailand the Nixon Doctrine seems only to mean a stream-

[88] See *Los Angeles Times,* October 5, 1971, p. 4.
[89] See *The New York Times,* January 8, 1971, p. 1.

lining of U.S. assistance rather than a reassessment of the program or the commitment that underlies it.

Military assistance for Thailand under the Nixon Administration entails equipment grants and sales to modernize the 125,000-man Thai army, subsidization of Thai involvement in Laos and Cambodia, and support for the Thai counter-insurgency program (in funds and, as indicated below, advisors). Until February 1972, the United States also paid for the 12,000-man Thai contingent in South Vietnam, which was then withdrawn. The costs associated with maintaining the about 50,000 American military personnel in Thailand (at the start of 1973) should also be included, since the base economy has contributed importantly to Thailand's economic growth since 1966. Excluding the latter, U.S. military assistance was $119.4 million in FY 1970 and $93 million in FY 1971.[90]

American military personnel remain active in Thailand outside the air bases.[91] Some 245 advisors and 280 Green Berets (Special Forces) train Thai officers to train their own, Lao, and Cambodian troops. The Americans also are stationed at so-called "ad hoc training areas" within and on the borders of Thailand; some of these camps are reportedly used by U.S. and Thai teams as bases for conducting clandestine operations in Laos, Cambodia, and Burma. Finally, U.S. advisors go along on Thai counterinsurgency missions in the north and northeast regions of the country. Supposedly, they advise only at regimental level, do not enter combat zones, and thus have not suffered any casualties. The Thai government seems determined to keep things that way; it has long been sensitive to the American presence and the convenient propaganda target it presents for the Communist and other rebellious movements.

Nevertheless, the form that the Nixon Doctrine and "self-reliance" have taken in Thailand, because it does not represent a significant change from previous Administrations,

---

[90] *United States Foreign Policy 1971*, p. 411. The FY 1971 figure does not include military cash sales, which are classified. Sales were $21.2 million in FY 1970.

[91] This paragraph is based mainly on the excellent article by Jack Foisie in *Los Angeles Times*, March 22, 1972, p. 23.

leaves ample room for skepticism. Since the bombing of Indochina is the key weapon of the Administration's Indochina policy, the U.S. presence in Thailand is likely to continue for a long time to come, as witness the 1972–73 restoration of U.S. force levels to 50,000 after having been reduced to 32,000 in 1971. This circumstance is bound not only to exacerbate political tensions in Thailand, generated by opponents of the military government as well as by leftist forces. It is also bound to inhibit Thailand's avowed interest in improving relations with China, whose leaders are very unlikely to respond to direct and third-country Thai overtures while U.S. Thai-based aircraft are bombing their Indochina allies and while Thai troops operate in Laos.

The military aid program also needs to be critically examined. Such assistance, and promises of more to come, keeps the United States tied to a military regime which has long relied on U.S. support to maintain its position and, as the events of November 1971 showed, to abolish the structure of meaningful political opposition. U.S. aid, which increasingly will supply the Thai army with Vietnam surplus equipment, may also—as in Vietnam—so conventionalize the Thai forces that their most readily available counterinsurgency weapons will be highly destructive. The Thai command has already availed itself of U.S. helicopters, napalm, and bomb-carrying jets, with results often counterproductive to the objective of winning hearts and minds. And in 1972 the United States added A37B Skyraider jets to the Thai air force's counterinsurgency arsenal. Although the Thai situation is different from Vietnam, and although Thai officials and their U.S. advisors are determined that there shall not be another Vietnam in Thailand, the U.S. assistance program runs the risk of helping a military regime with substantial firepower at its disposal to repeat the "military solution" that failed in Vietnam.

TAIWAN

The President's trip to China culminated in a joint communiqué with Premier Chou En-lai that did much to advance discussion about Taiwan's future. In effect, Washington promised the "ultimate" removal of U.S. forces (about 8,000) and military installations from the island in return for Peking's pledge not to use force to "liberate" Taiwan. Also, Nixon brought the U.S. view of Taiwan's status nearer to where it was in January 1950, when President Truman acknowledged that there is only one China and that Taiwan belongs to China.[92] The "catch" is that even before the U.S. presence finally disappears from Taiwan, which may take a long time,[93] under the Nixon Doctrine substantial military assistance will continue to flow to the Nationalists. Taiwan may no longer be the jump-off point for U.S. reconnaissance and other operations directed at the China mainland and Southeast Asia; but Taiwan's "defense" will be augmented, and other military uses of Taiwan by the United States remain open.

The U.S. military relationship to Taiwan has two parts. The first primarily, but not exclusively, concerns U.S. policy in Indochina. About two-thirds of the U.S. military personnel stationed on Taiwan are associated with tasks such as C-130 airlift of equipment and supplies to the war theater from the Ching Chuan Kang base in central Taiwan.[94] Facilities on Taiwan are also used for antisubmarine warfare patrols and ship repair. And in past years—although current information is not available to the author—Chinese Nationalist aircraft and pilots under CIA contract carried out troop ferrying, airdrop, and reconnaissance missions from Taiwan across Southeast Asia as far as Tibet.[95]

The second part of the U.S.-Taiwan relationship is the mili-

[92] The most recent Nixon and Rogers reports, however, still refer to the Republic of China, making questionable the Administration's "one-China" policy.

[93] On returning from Peking in February 1973, Henry Kissinger declared: "The level of our troops on Taiwan is not the subject of negotiation [with China] . . . There exists no immediate plan for any withdrawal, but there will be a periodic review."

[94] Other activities include intelligence, advisory support, and logistical work through the Taiwan Defense Command and the Military Assistance Advisory Group. A full account is in, *inter alia,* U. S. Congress, Senate Committee on Foreign Relations, *Hearings on United States Security Agreements and Commitments Abroad: Republic of China,* pt. 4, November 24–26, 1969, and May 8, 1970 (Washington, D.C.: GPO, 1970).

[95] *Pentagon Papers,* p. 137.

tary assistance program (grants and sales), which in FY 1970 was $125.1 million and in FY 1971 was $120.4 million.[96] In accordance with the 1954 Mutual Defense Treaty, which was not mentioned in the Nixon-Chou communiqué and which was most recently reaffirmed after the President's trip, the United States continues to modernize the Nationalist army and air force and recently began training eighty-two navymen in submarine warfare, even though the Nationalists do not yet have a submarine.[97] Bypassing regular MAP channels, the Department of Defense has kept the Nationalist air force especially well stocked with surplus equipment, such as the twenty F-104 jets sold to Taiwan for $1 million in 1969.[98] Moreover, according to a Defense official, Taiwan will receive additional (unspecified) aircraft under a two-to-three-year, 600-plane replacement and modernization program for Southeast Asian allies that will cost about $1 billion.[99] It remains to be seen whether or not these latter planes have the offensive capability of the F-104; but in any case, they clearly do not give Peking's leaders confidence about U.S. intentions, since enhanced Nationalist military power only decreases the prospects of a peaceful reunification of Taiwan with the mainland. And frustrating reunification may be the Administration's primary objective. To these aircraft deliveries, past and potential, should be added some potential U.S. military uses of Taiwan. It is to the Nixon Administration's credit that Seventh Fleet patrols in the Taiwan Strait were drastically cut back in December 1970 and that sabotage raids by Nationalist frogmen and U-2 overflights of the

[96] *United States Foreign Policy 1971,* p. 410.

[97] *Los Angeles Times,* March 28, 1972, p. 9. The Defense Department spokesman who announced the training (which takes place in Groton, Connecticut) said the United States might sell or give the Nationalists a submarine once the training is completed.

[98] See *The New York Times,* March 29, 1970, p. 1. The $1 million "package," actually valued at about $157 million, also included four destroyers, medium tanks, over thirty-five F-100 Super Saber jets, and equipment for a missile battery.

[99] See the comments of Deputy Defense Secretary Warren before the Senate Appropriations Committee, as reported *ibid.*, August 19, 1971, p. 1.

mainland from Taiwan ceased in the summer of 1971. But if the Defense Department has its way, Taiwan's military value to the United States—which, obviously, Chiang Kai-shek wishes to keep high—will soon increase. It has already become public knowledge that the Pentagon would like to see U.S. nuclear weapons storage facilities transferred from Okinawa to Taiwan, where a small nuclear stockpile evidently already exists.[100] And the Pentagon probably is attracted to future use of Taiwan air base runways, which the Nationalists have been expanding since the late 1960s to accommodate B-52s.[101] Should the Administration decide in favor of either project, against State Department advice, U.S. diplomacy toward China would suffer a major setback.

FURTHER CONCLUSIONS

Apart from the Nixon Doctrine's concepts, tactics, and strategy in Southeast Asia, some broader implications emerge from the discussion that deserve separate comment. They concern the purposes of American policy and the manner of American policy-making.

I have been arguing that what is new in the Nixon Doctrine is not its objectives but some of its methods. To an extent, even revisions of methods can promote change for the better. The new tentativeness introduced in the international relations of Southeast Asia by U.S.-China diplomacy, the Paris agreements on Indochina, and the promise of a less direct U.S. security role in Asia, enhance the prospects for a widening of political and economic contacts within the region and between Southeast Asian states and the socialist countries. Governments previously tied all too closely to the West, such as Thailand, Malaysia, and the Philippines, today have an incentive to re-examine their foreign alignments and work for more balanced associations with all the major powers.[102]

[100] See *Los Angeles Times,* July 10, 1971, p. 20.

[101] Senate hearings on the Republic of China, *op. cit.,* pp. 1013 ff., and *The New York Times,* July 21, 1970, p. 9.

[102] One expression of an interest in foreign policy realignment occurred in November 1971 when members of the Association of Southeast Asian Nations (ASEAN)—Thailand, Malaysia, Philip-

But while such reorientations would fall within the framework of the Nixon Doctrine, there are limits that the Doctrine itself imposes. The Doctrine's unstated objective is to establish a balance-of-power system in Asia, of a kind that will *secure existing American assets* (commitments, economic and diplomatic influence, military facilities, defense partnerships) and *maintain the status quo* (i.e., prevent "instability" or Communist success through revolution). Like previous big-power hegemonies in Southeast Asia, from the Western colonialisms to the wartime Japanese and postwar containment-through-alliances systems, the Nixon Doctrine seeks to make a changing region amenable to external manipulation, this time through shifts in the deployment and use of American power. So long as these shifts do not amount to a fundamental redirection of policy—including the complete withdrawal of U.S. military personnel, covert operatives, and facilities from the Asia mainland—movement in Southeast Asia toward self-reliance is likely to be painfully slow. That eventuality seems more acceptable to the Administration, even though it means a long-term U.S. military presence and assistance program, than seeing nonalignment or neutralization take hold.

A graver weakness of balance-of-power politics as practiced by the Nixon Administration is that it seems destined further to destabilize the region. By sustaining involvement in Indochina to fit the terms of the Paris agreements; by maintaining a significant presence in Thailand; by funneling increased military aid to Indonesia; by promoting subregional defense; by keeping Taiwan heavily armed; and by trying to promote a larger Japanese regional security role, the United States contributes to the very instability it proclaims requires long-term American involvement in Southeast Asia. Rather than promote or accept the kinds of local accommodations that eventually must be worked out by the contending forces in each area of conflict, the Nixon Doctrine perpetuates great- and small-power confrontations.

---

pines, Singapore, and Indonesia—declared their support of Southeast Asia's eventual neutralization.

In particular, the emphasis on military assistance and local buildups of strength is bound to intensify old rivalries in Southeast Asia and revive both ancient and modern patterns of territorial diplomacy. Thai intervention in Laos has not only created frictions but might someday lead to a *de facto* partition of the country between Thai and Pathet Lao forces. South Vietnamese and Thai involvement in the border provinces of Cambodia may become permanent even if Cambodia survives under Lon Nol. Indonesian leaders may consider the Five-Power Agreement on Malaysia and Singapore directed more at their country than at China or the Soviet Union; and Malaysian leaders may not be pleased to find the United States supplying military assistance to Indonesia.

Within these and other countries of Southeast Asia that are receiving U.S. military aid, there may be serious consequences for minority peoples who refuse to accept integration in the political and cultural framework established by the majority. Heavily armed forces of the central government, dominated by military professionals, are all the more likely to use coercion to assert their authority than to try persuasion and conciliation. Should this happen, local rebellions aiming at autonomy will persist and intensify, increasing the "instability" that frequently is labeled Communist insurgency.

A final disturbing point about the Nixon Doctrine is the policy-making process that is implementing it. Despite the talk about "realistic deterrence" and a "1½ war strategy," policy-making still reflects the crisis management emphasis that characterized the Kennedy and Johnson administrations. The escalation under Nixon of American involvement in Indochina reveals anew how policy doctrine can be overtaken by, or remolded to fit, unforeseen setbacks. It also reveals that American power and political support can be committed without, as well as with, Congressional assent. Through covert operations, the use of proxy forces, the creation of clever euphemisms, and the juggling of defense funds, the United States can stay deeply involved in Southeast Asia's affairs without popular or legislative authorization, and in some cases despite legal restrictions. "Secret wars" may not be kept entirely secret, as in Laos; but access to facts, figures, and projections can be denied.[103] The full meaning of the Nixon Doctrine for Southeast Asia remains to be uncovered; this study may relate only to the tip of the iceberg.

[103] As it has, for example, in the case of U.S. involvement in Laos, the extent and number of U.S. air attacks on North Vietnam, and Defense and State Department projections on military assistance for and policy toward Thailand.

U.S. Intervention in Laos and Its Impact on Laotian Relations with Thailand and Vietnam

USHA MAHAJANI

American intervention has had a far-reaching effect on politics in Laos during the past two decades. This revelation is not at all surprising, given the extreme weakness of the Laotian state and the tremendous capacity and demonstrated will of the United States to exercise its influence in Southeast Asia. The disparity in the capacities of the two states to influence one another is such that interaction between them has taken the form of a one-way flow of preponderant influence. The result is that Laos is subject to an almost intolerable level of American intervention in its affairs.

The purpose of this paper is to examine U.S. intervention in Laos and its impact on Laos' relations with her two most important Southeast Asian neighbors, Thailand and Vietnam.[1] Founded and consolidated in the mid-fourteenth century as *Lan Xang* (Kingdom of a Million Elephants), Laos disintegrated into three royal principalities, Luang Prabang, Vientiane, and Champassak, subject to frequent competitive intervention from Thailand and Vietnam. Significantly, however, Thailand and Vietnam never went to war over Laos, even though their competition lasted until the appearance of French and British imperialism in the latter half of the nineteenth century.

[1] China, though capable of intervening, has generally refrained from doing so, and is not considered by students of Laotian affairs or by the United States as an interventionary power in Laos. Burma has not intervened in Laotian affairs for the past two hundred years, and Cambodia has played no role in Laotian affairs since a Khmer army helped the legendary Fa Ngoum establish the Lao kingdom in the fourteenth century.

Today, Laos is once again the subject of intervention from Vietnam (both North and South) and Thailand. However, the new factor of American intervention in Laos has altered traditional Laotian relations with the two countries so that the present Thai-Vietnamese competition in Laos is fraught with uncharacteristic hostility and danger. This paper will argue that America's intervention in Laos has turned Laos from a buffer zone into a major battleground. What has changed, and how has this change come about? The first section of this paper will begin to answer this question by looking at the nature of traditional Laotian relations with Thailand and Vietnam, and the nature of Thai-Vietnamese competition in Laos before the beginning of American intervention. The remaining sections will try to show: (1) what the nature and depth of American intervention in Laos has been; (2) how the United States has set up and maintained a Lao government amenable to U.S. intervention in its affairs; (3) how this intervention has changed traditional Laotian relations with Thailand and Vietnam; and (4) how this intervention has exacerbated Thai-Vietnamese competition in Laos to include direct conflict where there was none before.

TRADITIONAL LAOTIAN RELATIONS WITH THAILAND AND VIETNAM PRIOR TO AMERICAN INTERVENTION

Laos, or *Lan Xang,* was a sturdy kingdom occupying what is presently northeastern Thailand, and the Mekong Valley region of modern Laos. For 350 years, *Lan Xang* experienced minimal external intervention and enjoyed an equal and stable relationship with Thailand and Vietnam. But after 1700, as noted above, *Lan Xang* disintegrated into three principalities which eventually became subject to competitive intervention from the Thai and Vietnamese. These two competitive forces pulling Laos in opposite directions resulted in Laos becoming the tributary of both, which satisfied Thailand and Vietnam enough so that they never went to war over Laos.

Laotian relations with Thailand predate those with Vietnam by several centuries, and are closer because the Lao and Thai are ethnically related peoples. The Thai and Lao migrated south from the Yunnan Plateau in China, and formed two states, *Siam* and *Lan Xang*. These two states maintained a close, equal relationship based on marriage alliances or common interests against Burma.[2] Relations between Laos and Vietnam began in the fifteenth century when the latter regained independence from China. Apart from a brief encounter in 1427 and a major clash in 1478, they maintained a stable relationship through the highland buffer zones of Xieng Khouang and Sipsong Chau Thai,[3] both of which paid tribute to Laos and Vietnam.

As a unified state Laos preserved these stable relationships with Thailand and Vietnam. Indeed, even after 1700, Vietnam and Thailand were slow to intervene in Laotian affairs. During the eighteenth century, Victnam undertook mediation rather than military intervention in Laos.[4] Twice it prevented a war between Vientiane and Xieng Khouang. Vietnam did not move to counter Siam when the Thais first began to intervene in Laotian affairs, nor in 1771 and 1778 when Siam attacked Vientiane and brought it under Thai military occupation. Nor did Vietnam act when the Thai Chakri dynasty brought Vientiane under its firm vassalage in 1792.[5]

Vietnam began to take an active interest in Laotian affairs after Gia Long unified the country in 1802. After two uneventful decades of Thai-Vietnamese competition in Laos, a war was nearly set off by Chao Anou, ruler of Thai-controlled Vientiane. Earlier, in 1808, he had pledged vas-

[2] M. L. Manich, *History of Laos* (Bangkok: Chalermnit Press, 1967), pp. 2–23, 132–37; D. G. E. Hall, *A History of Southeast Asia* (London: St. Martin's Press, 1968, third edition), pp. 261–62.

[3] Xieng Khouang, today a province of modern Laos, was then a highland principality astride the best invasion route between Vietnam and Laos. Just north of Xieng Khouang, in what are today the provinces of Sam Neua and Phong Saly, lay the Sipsong Chau Thai, a federation of several highland principalities formed by the Hill Tai people.

[4] Hall, *op. cit.*, p. 261; Manich, *op. cit.*, pp. 156–57; Hugh Toye, *Laos: Buffer Zone or Battleground* (London: Oxford University Press, 1968), pp. 12, 15–16.

[5] Manich, *op. cit.*, pp. 156–57; Toye, *op. cit.*, pp. 15–16; Hall, *op. cit.*, pp. 446–49.

salage to Vietnam in order to lessen his exclusive dependence on Thailand. Then, in 1826, he attacked Thailand, was defeated, and fled to Vietnam. Vietnam gave him troops to regain his kingdom, but Anou was again defeated and died in Thai captivity. Thailand then established complete rule over Vientiane and the other Laotian principalities. If this was intended as a defensive move, it only heightened the confrontation with Vietnam, for the buffer zone of Vientiane had been eliminated and a precedent for annexation was set. Vietnam annexed Xieng Khouang in retaliation and stationed its forces there. The situation cooled, however, and as Vietnam itself came under French pressure after 1855, Xieng Khouang gradually became more independent and resumed its dual vassalage to Thailand and Vietnam.[6]

Yet, the arrival of European imperialism in Southeast Asia did not long ease the external pressure directed at Laos from Vietnam and Thailand. Indeed, after France colonized Vietnam and Britain all but colonized Thailand in the 1870s, Laos became the subject of competing Anglo-French pressures superimposed upon, and even going beyond, traditional Vietnamese-Thai pressures. The Thai continued intervention under British prodding. The French took over the mantle of Vietnamese interests in Laos but with an added nineteenth-century European imperialist technique which allowed no rival in one's sphere of influence. The French Commissioner General in Vietnam, Dr. Harmand, wrote in a memorandum of November 1892: "We are now obliged to extend up to the Mekong not merely our influence but *our direct domination*." In the name of fulfilling the "historic Vietnamese ambitions"[7] France expanded its dominion to the mountain principalities of Xieng Khouang and Sipsong Chau Thai, the lowland principalities of Luang Prabang, Vientiane, and Champassak, and molded these two groups of states into the

---

[6] Manich, *op. cit.*, pp. 203–19; Toye, *op. cit.*, p. 21; Hall, *op. cit.*, p. 453.

[7] Quoted in Toye, *op. cit.*, p. 39. In France itself, a former French consular official, François Deloncle, kept up the pressure and, exploiting French distrust of the English, argued that the British were instigating Thailand to commit "aggression" against French Vietnam. Text of Deloncle's report in *ibid.*, Appendix I.

administrative unit of its Indochina empire known as Laos.[8] This new, French-conceived Laos contained two traditionally hostile ethnic groups (the lowland Lao and the highland tribes) of approximately equal strength, each historically backed against each other by close ethnic kindred in Thailand and Vietnam.[9]

When Japan helped Thailand regain some Lao territory from the French during World War II, Thai propaganda for a Pan-Thai movement helped arouse a new Thai-oriented Laotian nationalism among the right-wing, pro-Thailand Lao in southern Laos. However, the French succeeded in co-opting almost all of these right-wing, pro-Thailand nationalists by granting Laos token independence and opening up some governmental offices to them. This led perceptive Laotians, who saw through the French ploy, and pro-Vietnam Laotians, who distrusted the pro-Thailand elements, into a left-wing, pro-Vietnamese Laotian nationalism based on an ideological bond of resistance to a common ruling power.[10]

In summary, Laos' relations with Vietnam and Thailand were generally stable, despite Vietnamese and Thai intervention in Laotian affairs. Laotian dual vassalage lasted until Chao Anou's war with Thailand in 1826, after which relations again stabilized as Thailand occupied the lowland principalities, and the mountain principalities buffered Thailand and Vietnam. All in all, relations between Thailand and Vietnam in Laos were more stable than conflictual. The two fought wars over Cambodia but not over Laos. Neither asserted exclusive suzerainty over Laos until Thailand tightened its rule in the lowland principalities after the Chao Anou attacks of 1826. Even then Vietnam did not undertake counterintervention, except to ensure that Thailand did not

[8] On Anglo-French rivalry in Thailand, see James McCarthy, *Surveying and Exploring in Siam* (London: John Murray, 1900), Ch. XVII; Toye, *op. cit.,* pp. 31–33.

[9] Toye, *op. cit.,* pp. 46–48.

[10] Tran Van Dinh, "The Birth of the Pathet Lao Army," in Nina S. Adams and Alfred W. McCoy (eds.), *Laos: War and Revolution* (New York: Harper & Row, 1971), pp. 424–38; Michael Field, *The Prevailing Wind: Witness in Indochina* (London: Methuen & Co., 1965), p. 42.

also occupy the mountain principalities. The three Lao principalities might have been incorporated into a modern Thai state. The mountain principalities could have been a buffer between Thailand and Vietnam; but history unfolded differently. Thailand itself shrank under British and French expansion, and Laos became a unit of French Indochina. Its preservation as a political entity and the subsequent rise of regional Lao nationalism enabled Laos to regain independence in 1954, but opened it to a new kind of foreign intervention on an unprecedented scale.

THE IMPACT OF U.S. INTERVENTION

American intervention in Laos has been part of an extensive intervention against Communism in Asia, and has consisted of strong support for the pro-Thailand Laotian right-wing against the pro-Vietnam Laotian left. The United States, realizing that Lao collaboration would facilitate its continued intervention in Laotian affairs, has consistently sought to ensure that the pro-Thailand right-wing hold the reins of government in Laos. Consequently, since 1954, Laos, under rightist rule, has maintained much closer relations with Thailand than with either zone of Vietnam. The Democratic Republic of Vietnam (D.R.V.) has responded by backing the pro-Vietnam Laotian left-wing against the rightists. Inevitably, concern for the welfare of their respective Laotian allies has drawn Thailand and the D.R.V. into conflict with each other.

PERIOD I (1945–54):
THE PRE-INDEPENDENCE PERIOD

Laos, Thailand, and Vietnam felt the first impact of indirect American intervention during the period between 1945 and 1954. This intervention immediately concerned itself with Laos' budding nationalist connections with Thailand and Vietnam. The stage was set for U.S. intervention in 1946, when the restoration of French rule in Laos drove all Laotian nationalists, left and right, into exile in Bangkok where they maintained a government-in-exile under the protection of Pridi Phanomyong's civilian, nationalist government until

General Pibun Songgram overthrew Pridi in November 1947. Pibun greatly desired American aid, and to obtain it he had to align Thai policy interests in Southeast Asia with those of the United States. When the United States decided to help the right-wing nationalists at the expense of the left-wing nationalists in the Lao exile government, Pibun followed suit, reversing his earlier policy of support for the Laotian left-wing's activities on Thai soil.[11] Together, he and the United States convinced the Lao right-wing to dissolve its exile government with the left and to return to Laos in late 1949 to accept high offices in a new, French-sponsored Royal Laotian Government (R.L.G.).[12] The following year, the United States and France signed a Mutual Defense Assistance Agreement covering Laos, and the United States established French-administered aid missions in Laos and the rest of Indochina.[13]

Thus, the United States and Thailand jointly helped install a Laotian government of pro-Thai and pro-American politicians. This move was significant, for cooperative native personalities are a more potent instrument of foreign intervention than external financial input, military power, or intelligence agencies. With right-wing Laotians in the saddle, America and Thailand could intervene in Laos almost at will.

Meanwhile, the left-wing Laotian nationalists returned to northeastern Laos, where in August 1950 they formed the Resistance government of *Pathet Lao* (Land of the Lao). Geographical proximity, ideological solidarity, the elimination of choice of other allies, and ethnic ties all helped the Pathet Lao decide to ally itself with the Viet Minh in northern Vietnam. In 1951 the left-wing nationalist movements of Indochina set up the United National Front of the Peoples of

[11] Edwin Stanton, *Brief Authority* (New York: Harper & Row, 1956), pp. 23–35, 238, 275; John Coast, *Recruit to Revolution* (London: Christophers, 1952), pp. 115, 118–19.

[12] Philippe Devilliers, "The Laotian Conflict in Perspective," in Adams and McCoy (eds.), *op. cit.*, p. 40. Although the right-wing dominated this new government, the neutralist Prince Souvanna Phouma became its first Premier.

[13] Statement by Secretary of State Dean Acheson, May 8, 1950, *State Department Bulletin,* May 12, 1950 (Vol. XXII), p. 821.

Vietnam, Pathet Lao, and Cambodia to win genuine independence from their common masters, the French.[14] Under this alliance, Viet Minh troops entered Laos in 1953–54 to help the Pathet Lao win control of more than half of Laos, including Xieng Khouang, Sam Neua, and Phong Saly provinces.

This left-wing success set off a chain of events that clearly illumined the close external relations between Thailand and the R.L.G., and the Lao right-wing's complicity in American intervention. The R.L.G. began the sequence by denouncing "foreign Viet Minh aggression" without any reference to the Pathet Lao, and, reaffirming its loyalty to France, appealed for Western support. Private aircraft flown by U.S. civilians immediately rushed American military aid to the R.L.G.,[15] and the United States claimed that the Pathet Lao offensive would have "serious consequences for Thailand and the whole of Southeast Asia."[16] In the name of combating "Communist subversion," Thailand arrested hundreds of Laotians and Vietnamese in the northeast, crushed domestic opposition,[17] and obtained large-scale U.S. military aid. The two countries held joint naval exercises and called for a "united action" against the Viet Minh.[18] A possible Thai-U.S. intervention on "invitation" from the R.L.G. was also talked about. Since Premier Souvanna Phouma seemed unlikely to issue one, the CIA backed right-wing extremists Katay Don Sasorith and Phoui Sananikone in a spring 1954 attempt to oust him. This

[14] *New Times* (Moscow), July 25, 1951 (No. 30), p. 11.

[15] Souvanna Phouma's statements in Miscellaneous No. 16 (1954), *Documents Relating to the Discussion of Korea and Indochina at the Geneva Conference, April 27–June 15, 1954* (London: HMSO, 1954), cmd., 9186, pp. 166–67. Hereafter cited as *Documents on Indochina, 1954*. Statements by Secretary of State Dulles, April 17.

[16] U.S.-Canadian Communiqué, May 8, 1953, *Documents on American Foreign Relations*, 1953, pp. 402–4.

[17] Russell H. Fifield, *The Diplomacy of Southeast Asia: 1945–1958* (New York: Harper & Row, 1958), p. 252.

[18] This led the U.S.S.R. to charge that the Thai offer was U.S.-inspired and that Thailand was a transit point for raw materials from Indochina to the United States and for U.S. arms into Indochina. See *Izvestia*, December 26, 1953; *Pravda*, April 3, 1954.

move failed, but Phoui Sananikone still became Foreign Minister and led the R.L.G. delegation to the Geneva Conference on Indochina, where he expressed views identical to those of the U.S. delegation: (1) the Pathet Lao was a "phantom"; (2) the D.R.V. was an aggressor, and its presence in Laos was unlawful; (3) the R.L.G., as a legitimate government, was justified in seeking western support, and therefore U.S. intervention was lawful. Both the U.S. and the R.L.G. favored UN intervention, and both eventually declined to affirm adherence to the Geneva Agreements and the Declaration.[19]

Since 1954, both Laos' relations with its neighbors and Thai-Vietnamese interaction have revolved around America's presence in Southeast Asia. As close allies, Thailand and the United States together helped maintain a right-wing Laotian government that forged close integrative relations with Thailand. This intervention impelled the Laotian left to consolidate its alliance with the Viet Minh, i.e., the D.R.V. The historical pattern of Thai-Vietnamese rivalry in Laos was thus revived, but the competition differed from the old in one crucial respect: unlike in the past, Thai intervention was now an offshoot of U.S. policy. Laos as a buffer against Vietnam was no longer accepted by Thailand's anti-Communist, military government.

PERIOD II (1954–56):
PREMIER KATAY DON SASORITH
AND AMERICAN INTERVENTION

Laos emerged from the 1954 Geneva Conference as one country in law under one government (the R.L.G.). In reality, however, it was two territorial units under two governments (the R.L.G. and the Pathet Lao), and contained three operating political forces: (1) Prince Souphanouvong's left-wing Pathet Lao, which demanded a share in government

---

[19] See U.S and Laotian speeches in *Documents on Indochina,* 1954, pp. 112–15, 121–22, 155–57, and *Further Documents Relating to the Discussion of Indochina at the Geneva Conference* (London: HMSO, August 1954), cmd., 9239; hereafter cited as *Further Documents,* 1954.

power; (2) Katay and Phoui's right wing, which dominated the R.L.G. and refused to recognize the legitimacy of the Pathet Lao; and (3) Premier Souvanna Phouma's weak neutralist group, which acknowledged the Pathet Lao's legitimate power in Phong Saly and Sam Neua provinces, and favored a negotiated settlement.[20] However, the United States, which was already busy blocking Vietnamese unification and endowing South Vietnam with an apparent statehood not provided for in the Geneva Agreements, refused to tolerate a left-right bifurcation of Laos. Its containment strategy called for the unification of Laos under the right-wing R.L.G., and the creation of an anti-Communist association between Laos, Thailand, and South Vietnam.

Thailand, South Vietnam, and the Laotian right-wing endorsed this strategy, supported the creation of the Southeast Asian Treaty Organization, and even advocated membership in SEATO for the three Indochina units. Since Souvanna Phouma did not welcome SEATO's protection, the United States acutely distrusted him and was pleased when he resigned in November 1954 after a cabinet crisis resulting from the assassination of his neutralist Defense Minister, Kou Voravong.[21] Katay Don Sasorith, a militant pro-Thai politician and a strong U.S. favorite, became Premier.

In 1953, as a minister in Phouma's government, Katay had sought Thai military aid. As Premier, he immediately forged closer military ties with the United States and declared that Laos was covered by SEATO. U.S. Secretary of State Dulles applauded these moves and called Laos an "outpost of the free world."[22] On January 1, 1955, U.S. aid began to go di-

---

[20] Souvanna Phouma's Declaration of July 21, 1954. Text in *ibid.*, p. 41. International Control Commission, *First Interim Report, 11 August 1954–31 December 1954*, cmd., 9445 (London: HMSO, 1955), p. 21; hereafter cited as ICC, *First Report*.

[21] Kou Voravong had strongly favored negotiating with the Pathet Lao. He had accused the United States of bribing Phoui Sananikone to not affirm adherence to the Geneva Agreements, and he disclosed right-wing military plans to attack the Pathet Lao. See *Survey of International Affairs* (London: Oxford University Press, 1954), p. 95. Also, see footnote 54.

[22] Fifield, *op. cit.*, pp. 255–56; *State Department Bulletin*, February 28, 1955, and March 21, 1955 (Vol. XXXII), pp. 332, 340–61; *Asian Recorder*, 1955, pp. 68, 105–6.

rectly to the R.L.G. That July, a military aid agreement was signed. Soon the right-wing army of General Phoumi Nosavan, a CIA protégé, began to receive $45 million a year. Thai-Laotian military ties were also consolidated. Several Lao army officers and two hundred policemen were trained in Thailand,[23] and Katay and the Thais explored the possibility of using KMT troops from northern Thailand against the Pathet Lao, whom he had opened full-scale military operations against even while Pathet Lao-R.L.G. talks were proceeding.[24]

Katay worked even closer with the Thais in nonmilitary affairs. With U.S. backing he promoted the concept of a Thai-Laotian anti-Communist Buddhist alliance by introducing Thailand's Thammayut sect in Laos, where the Mohanikaya sect is practiced. In 1955 he signed customs and goods-in-transit agreements with Thailand, thus blocking any move to open up old Laotian trade links with Hanoi. A secret protocol granted a Thai transport company, in which Katay had invested heavily, monopoly rights to carry and distribute goods entering Laos from Thailand, including imports. As Laos' main trade and aid pipeline, Thailand possessed a powerful weapon of economic sanction.[25] Katay's other joint enterprises with the Thais included Air Laos, which handled all travel, and the Lao-Thai Bank, which monopolized foreign transactions.

These integrative measures were effected with U.S. help. Almost all U.S. aid supplies to Laos passed through Thailand. The United States built storage facilities, ferry ramps on both banks of the Mekong, and a road and railway link from Bangkok to Vientiane to help strengthen Thai control over northeastern regions. This network was part of the huge U.S.-sponsored communications network in Thailand, Laos, and South Vietnam. American agencies also promoted Thai-Laotian sociocultural and linguistic links, employing Thai nationals to produce information literature on Laos in the Thai-

[23] *State Department Bulletin,* August 22, 1955 (Vol. XXXII), p. 300.

[24] Wilfred Burchett, *Mekong Upstream* (Berlin: Seven Seas, 1959), pp. 246, 249, 254.

[25] *The New York Times,* January 17, 1954; Burchett, *op. cit.,* pp. 275–76, 280–81.

based Laotian language, and arranging for many Laotians to study in Thailand. In 1959, 120 of 198 U.S.-assisted Laotians sent abroad went to Thailand.[26]

In addition to strengthening Lao-Thai relations, Katay also set up a consular mission in South Vietnam. However, neither of these acts resulted in a major exacerbation of relations with the D.R.V. In fact, at the Bandung Conference in 1955, Katay signed an agreement with Pham Van Dong to promote mutual good relations, and considered signing a nonaggression pact with China.[27] Neither China nor the D.R.V. sent protests when he signed the military aid agreement with the United States in July. Nevertheless, a polarization occurred between the Laotian forces themselves. The R.L.G. under Katay was allied with the United States. The Pathet Lao drew closer to the D.R.V. Each adversary viewed its own foreign ally as a friend of Laos whose intervention was needed to counter that by the other party's foreign ally.

Katay's premiership was a landmark in U.S. involvement in Laos because he fully supported its objectives out of convenience and conviction. One of the most pro-Thailand rightists in Laos, Katay had earlier helped forge closer relations with Thailand as a minister in the Souvanna Phouma government; now, as premier, he accelerated this process. He not only consolidated Laotian friendship with Thailand, but opened his country to expanded U.S. intervention. The United States had found its ideal native collaborator.

PERIOD III (MARCH 1956–AUGUST 1956):
SOUVANNA PHOUMA RETURNS TO POWER

The United States was disappointed, therefore, when Katay was unable to command a majority in the Laotian assembly

[26] *United States Operations in Laos, Seventh Report by the Committee on Government Operation*, June 15, 1959, 86th Congress, 1st Session; Union Calendar No. 207, House Report No. 546, pp. 42–43; hereafter cited as *U.S. Aid Operations in Laos, Seventh Report*, 1959; J. D. Montgomery, *The Politics of Aid: American Experience in Southeast Asia* (New York: Frederick A. Praeger, 1966), p. 54; G. F. White, "Vietnam: the Fourth Course," in Marcus Raskin and Bernard Fall (eds.), *The Vietnam Reader* (New York: Random House, 1965), pp. 353–54.

[27] *Asian Recorder*, 1955, p. 80; *New China News Agency*, April 25, 1955.

after the 1955 election, and Souvanna Phouma returned as Premier. Actually, Souvanna Phouma did not deserve the label "soft on Communism." Essentially an anti-Communist, he concluded a significant military agreement with South Vietnam.[28] But he did want peace and neutrality for Laos and opposed U.S. intervention at will. In August 1956 he visited China and the D.R.V. and declared that Laos would neither invoke SEATO protection nor permit U.S. military presence on its soil. Diplomatic and trade relations did not follow, but border clashes with the D.R.V. ceased, and a stable relationship was created.[29] Souvanna Phouma rejected the D.R.V.'s request for a Pathet Lao role in the Lao government commensurate with its military and political strength, but in late 1956 he signed accords with the Pathet Lao to form a coalition government.

At first Souvanna Phouma's rapprochement with the Communists did not annoy Thailand. Pibun Songgram, now tolerant of neutralism, showed understanding for Laos' desire for amicable relations with China and the D.R.V.[30] But Pibun was overthrown in November 1957 by Marshal Sarit Thanarat, a strident anti-Communist, who was very displeased with Souvanna Phouma's coalition government and wanted him removed.[31]

[28] On January 4, 1958, he issued a joint communiqué with South Vietnam agreeing to cooperate to "combat subversive activities" (text in *Asian Recorder*, 1958, p. 1837); later, he invited Diem's brother, Ngo Dinh Nhu, to visit Laos even though no D.R.V. leader had ever been invited. On Souvanna's anti-Communism, see Oden Meeker, *The Little World of Laos* (New York: Charles Scribner's Sons, 1959), p. 96, and Embassy of Laos, *Background Summary: The Political Situation in Laos after the Settlement of the "Pathet Lao" Problem* (Washington, D.C.: January 1958), p. 7.

[29] *New China News Agency*, August 25, 1956; Sisouk na Campassak, *Storm Over Laos* (New York: Frederick A. Praeger, 1960), pp. 47–49; Bernard Fall, *Anatomy of a Crisis*, ed. by R. M. Smith (Garden City, N.Y.: Doubleday & Company, 1969), p. 74.

[30] Interview of a senior Thai official, *The New York Times*, August 15, 1956.

[31] The "scenario" of SEATO exercises Sarit hosted in Thailand in April 1958 stipulated that a neighboring country "X" would bow to a Communist aggressor, but in the end military officials

The United States also strongly disapproved of Souvanna Phouma's neutralism. Ambassador Graham Parsons, helped by Katay, tried to prevent him from forming the coalition government with the Pathet Lao.[32] The United States withheld payment to the Royal Lao Army, but, at India's request, resumed payment at the end of 1956.[33] After the coalition government was formed, Parsons began to appeal to Souvanna Phouma's innate, but repressed, hatred of Communism in an effort to bring him into the U.S. camp. Souvanna Phouma pledged that the coalition government would last only until the election of May 1958, and Parsons, confident that the Pathet Lao would lose the election, advised him to drop his Pathet Lao ministers afterward. When Souvanna Phouma agreed, the United States offered aid on the condition that Souphanouvong, who was then Planning Minister in the coalition government, should not control it. A modest aid program, Operation Booster Shot, was started by the U. S. Embassy to induce villagers to vote for right-wing candidates.[34] In the May 1958 election, however, the Pathet Lao and its electoral ally, Quinim Pholsena's Peace and Neutrality Party, won thirteen of twenty-one contested seats. Souvanna Phouma nevertheless excluded the Pathet Lao from his cabinet, but he was now decidedly unacceptable to the United States. That August, after having forced Souvanna Phouma to expel the ICC from Laos in July, substantial U.S. bribes and the withholding

would assume power. Press Release, Office of Information Services, Headquarters Operation Vayabut, Don Muong Airfield, Thailand, April 21, 1958.

[32] Statements by Assistant Secretary Walter Robertson and Graham Parsons in *U.S. Aid in Laos, Seventh Report,* 1959, p. 47, and *United States Operations in Laos: Hearings before a Subcommittee of the Committee on Government Operations,* House of Representatives, 86th Congress, 1st Session (Washington, D.C.: GPO, 1959), pp. 40–41, 195; hereafter cited as *U.S. Aid in Laos, Hearings,* 1959. Katay's collaboration with the Americans is reported in Sisouk na Champassak, *op. cit.,* pp. 52–57, and Toye, *op. cit.,* p. 112.

[33] *Lao Presse* (Vientiane), January 21, 1957; *Asian Recorder,* 1956, pp. 677, 934, 989–90.

[34] *U.S. Aid in Laos, Hearings,* 1959, pp. 39, 191–92; *U.S. Aid in Laos, Seventh Report,* 1959, pp. 45–46; *State Department Bulletin,* February 3, 1958 (Vol. XXXVIII), p. 168.

of U.S. aid induced the Laotian Assembly to oust Souvanna in favor of Phoui Sananikone.[35] Once again, the United States had maneuvered to install a right-wing premier who could offer full cooperation for its intervention in Laos.

PERIOD IV (AUGUST 1958–JULY 1962): RIGHT-WING SUPREMACY AND CIVIL WAR

This period was similar to that of Katay's premiership in that the government was strongly pro-Thai and pro-U.S. Right-wing Laotians were always in power, except during August–December 1960, when Souvanna Phouma was briefly reinstated by a neutralist coup. However, U.S. intervention in Laos had greatly expanded since the days of Katay's leadership. It had strengthened right-wing business and political interests, and had virtually created a parallel military government. Eighty per cent of the annual $45 million U.S. aid to the R.L.G. went into the 25,000-strong right-wing Royal Lao Army which was controlled by the U. S. Programs Evaluation Office (PEO), a *de facto* military mission staffed by members of the U.S. armed forces whose military ranks were temporarily removed.[36]

The Pathet Lao victory in the May 1958 election heightened U.S. impatience with the Laotian parliamentary system, and strengthened its determination to put the right-wing Lao Army into power. One month after the election, a group of right-wing officers led by General Phoumi Nosavan formed the stridently anti-Communist Committee for the Defense of National Interests (CDNI). When Phoui Sananikone succeeded Souvanna Phouma as Premier two months later, the CDNI—backed by the U. S. Embassy, CIA, and PEO—secured four cabinet posts without having any seats in the Assembly. In January 1959, Phoumi Nosavan and two other

[35] See Sisouk na Champassak, *op. cit.*, pp. 35, 57, 65, and Arthur J. Dommen, *Conflict in Laos* (New York: Praeger Publishers, 1971, revised edition), p. 28.

[36] Since the usual Military Advisory Assistance Group (MAAG) could not be sent to Laos under the Geneva Agreements, the PEO was created at the insistence of the Pentagon, which would not sanction any military aid without its own watchdog being present. *U.S. Aid Operations in Laos, Seventh Report*, 1959, p. 8.

officers belonging to CDNI were added to Phoui's cabinet.[37] This was truly a U.S.-created government.

Phoui's army-dominated government abandoned the concept of political accommodation and sent troops to occupy Pathet Lao strongholds. In February 1959, Phoui repudiated the Geneva Agreements, claiming unilaterally that they had been fulfilled. The United States supported this move, which freed Laos to obtain U.S. military aid openly. New U.S. tanks and trucks were sent to the R.L.G., and two hundred U.S. military officers were added to the PEO for the purpose of expanding the Royal Lao Army from 25,000 to 29,000 men.[38] U.S. influence in the Laotian political process was further strengthened in December 1959 when Phoumi Nosavan deposed Premier Phoui and replaced him with his own man, Kou Abhay. Five months later, Phoumi "legitimatized" Kou's premiership by rigging the Lao general election to ensure a CDNI sweep.[39]

This progressive ascendancy of the right-wing, in conjunction with expanding U.S. intervention, produced conflictual relations with the D.R.V. and military cooperation with Thailand. On the one hand, Phoui, when he was Premier, revived his simplistic Geneva Conference thesis that the D.R.V. was the "aggressor" and ordered troops up to the border in December 1958, precipitating a major armed clash with the D.R.V. in the disputed Huong Lap area.[40] On the other hand, Laos and Thailand took joint measures against Lao

[37] Sisouk na Champassak, *op. cit.*, pp. 63–64; Fall, *op. cit.*, p. 94; Dommen, *op. cit.*, pp. 127–28.

[38] These U.S. officers were to serve only six months in Laos; however, their stay was extended indefinitely in mid-1959 when the R.L.G. precipitated armed hostilities with the Pathet Lao. *The New York Times*, February 11–12, 1959; Dommen, *op. cit.*, p. 116; J. L. S. Girling, "Laos: Falling Dominoe?", *Pacific Affairs*, Fall 1970 (Vol. XLIII, No. 3), p. 374.

[39] Sisouk na Champassak, *op. cit.*, pp. 122–33, 137; *The New York Times*, January 9, 1960.

[40] The border incident involved the Ho Chi Minh Trail that passes through southern Laos. The unauthorized passage of Vietnamese through Laotian territory technically violated Laotian sovereignty, but it did not harm Laotians or destroy Laotian property. Dommen, *op. cit.*, p. 116; Girling, *loc. cit.*, p. 374.

and Thai leftist opposition groups, and, helped by U.S. aid, maintained close military-economic cooperation under the auspices of SEATO. In March 1960, three new U.S. airfields were built in northeastern Thailand, within easy range of Laos.[41]

Thailand, the United States, and the Laotian right-wing had high stakes in preserving right-wing power in the R.L.G. In Thailand, the Sarit government had benefited from the military, ideological, and economic alliance with the United States. The United States had spent over $300 million to bring about Laos' exclusive reliance on American support. This, like the similar U.S. policy in South Vietnam, was undertaken to ensure that the R.L.G. remained firmly in right-wing hands. The three governments had become interlocked in a cooperative relationship.

This cooperation was shaken in August 1960 when a coup staged in Vientiane by Captain Kong Le installed a neutralist government under Souvanna Phouma. Kong Le publicly denounced the United States, which he accused of violating Laotian peace and neutrality.[42] He and the left-wing neutralists in Souvanna Phouma's government favored conciliation with the Pathet Lao and friendly relations with Communist neighbors, while Souvanna Phouma remained at heart an anti-Communist. What ensued, therefore, was not a coherent neutralist foreign policy, but a web of several conflictual and cooperative relationships between different interests within the Laos government and various foreign governments.

At first, the United States warned Communist powers not to intervene on Souvanna Phouma's behalf, and warned him not to try to recapture Luang Prabang from right-wing forces. It affirmed support for Souvanna Phouma's government only in late September after he forced Kong Le's neutralist troops to arrange a ceasefire with those of Phoumi Nosavan, and

[41] *The New York Times,* August 6, 9, and September 9, 1959; *Asian Recorder,* 1959, p. 2876; Fall, *op. cit.,* p. 127.

[42] Kong Le had popular support, and large-scale demonstrations denounced Phoumi for "relying on foreign power." Sisouk na Champassak, *op. cit.,* pp. 157–58; *The New York Times,* August 10, 1960.

agreed to form a neutralist-rightist coalition government by including Phoumi in his cabinet. Unknown to Kong Le and left-wing neutralists, Souvanna Phouma even allowed the United States to redirect some of his government's military aid to the rival government Phoumi had set up at Savannakhet, on condition that it be used only against the Pathet Lao.[43] However, Souvanna Phouma resisted a U.S. demand that he not form a coalition with the Pathet Lao, and U.S. military aid to his government was immediately suspended on the grounds that the neutralist and right-wing forces had split. But Phoumi Nosavan continued to receive U.S. aid, and, backed by the PEO and the limitless resources of the CIA, he bribed a large number of officers, troops, and Assemblymen to join him against Souvanna Phouma.[44]

Thailand's Sarit Thanarat was extremely close to General Phoumi. His bitter hostility toward Souvanna Phouma was motivated by anti-Communism, anti-neutralism, and self-interest. He hoped to prevent any reduction in U.S. military aid to Thailand by stressing that Thai security was threatened by events in Laos. In mid-September 1960 Sarit shelled the neutralist-held Vientiane from across the Mekong, and threw up an economic blockade against the Souvanna government which caused an acute shortage of rice and petroleum in Vientiane. At the same time, he rushed U.S. and Thai military supplies across the border to General Phoumi at Savannakhet.[45]

[43] *State Department Bulletin*, August 29, 1960, and September 26, 1960 (Vol. XLIII), pp. 311 and 498; *The New York Times*, September 22, 1960; Fall, *op. cit.*, pp. 195–96; "The Laos Tangle," *International Journal*, February 16, 1961, p. 149; Toye, *op. cit.*, pp. 148–49; Dommen, *op. cit.*, pp. 150, 154–58.

[44] *Vietnam and Southeast Asia*, Report by Senator Mike Mansfield to the Senate Committee on Foreign Relations (Washington, D.C.: Committee Print, U.S. 88th Congress, first session, 1963), p. 9. On CIA backing for Phoumi, see David Wise and T. B. Ross, *The Invisible Government* (London: Macmillan, 1966), pp. 148–55; Toye, *op. cit.*, pp. 148–49; Dommen, *op. cit.*, pp. 150, 154–58.

[45] *The New York Times*, August 10, 11, 12, 17, 1960; September 18, 19, 20, 22, 25, 26, 1960. Some observers feared these Thai actions would draw the D.R.V. into the Laotian hostilities. On Thai motives regarding U.S. aid, see *Bangkok Post*, August 18 and

The immediate result of this joint Thai-American pressure was just the opposite of what was intended. Souvanna Phouma agreed to form a coalition with the Pathet Lao, established diplomatic relations with the U.S.S.R., and received Soviet economic and military aid in December 1960. He also sent goodwill missions to China and the D.R.V., agreed in principle to accept their aid, and set up post and telegraph communications with the D.R.V.[46] Souvanna Phouma was trying to balance his premiership on two stools. He expected U.S. support for taking Phoumi into his cabinet, but also cooperated with the Pathet Lao under left-wing neutralist pressure. His attempt to remain Premier by any means failed. With heavy Thai-U.S. support, Phoumi's troops marched through Thailand to Vientiane, where, after a fierce battle, he set up and manipulated a right-wing government under Boun Oum. Souvanna Phouma and Kong Le fled to Pathet Lao territory, where they continued their neutralist-Pathet Lao coalition government.

Thailand and the United States promptly recognized the Boun Oum government, and for the first time admitted their joint assistance to Phoumi.[47] However, the Communist powers still recognized Souvanna Phouma's government, and during the ensuing civil war the D.R.V. and the U.S.S.R. countered Thai-American assistance to the rightists by giving military aid to the neutralist and Pathet Lao forces. The Phoumi-Boun Oum government sought UN intervention against what it called "an elaborate D.R.V. invasion" and Soviet aid to the "rebels." However, the UN Secretary-General and the European powers no longer accepted these "cry wolf"

September 19, 1960; *The New York Times*, November 9, 12, 17, 22, 1960; December 15, 1960; and January 4, 1961.

[46] *Current Digest of Soviet Press*, November 2, 1960 (Vol. XII, No. 40), p. 24; *The New York Times*, October 13–14 and November 18, 1960; *Asian Recorder*, 1960, p. 3695. The D.R.V. not only sent aid to Souvanna Phouma, but also sent D.R.V. army elements to serve as "stiffeners" in the Pathet Lao forces (Dommen, *op. cit.*, p. 163).

[47] State Department statement, "Situation in Laos," January 7, 1961, p. 1 (copy supplied to author); statement by State Department spokesman, December 19, 1960, in *Asian Recorder*, 1961, pp. 338–39; *Bangkok Post*, December 14 and 22, 1960.

stories.[48] But the United States did, and in January 1961 it sent six A-6 fighter bombers to Phoumi. American "White Star" teams of advisors were sent to each of Phoumi's battalions, and the United States prepared for unilateral military intervention if necessary.[49]

Hostile confrontations and recriminations occurred between the various foreign interventionist powers. The U.S.S.R. and D.R.V. accused the United States, Thailand, and South Vietnam of interfering with Souvanna Phouma's "legal" government by aiding Phoumi's "rebel forces." The United States claimed it was assisting a "lawful government" against D.R.V. "aggression," whereas the U.S.S.R. was aiding "unlawful," "rebel" elements. The Communists, unable to match U.S. intervention, demanded the reactivation of the ICC and the convening of a fourteen-power conference on Laos. But the United States, content with the success of its intervention, rejected this proposal.[50]

---

[48] Independent sources reported that the U.S., British and French Embassies in Vientiane all said that there was no evidence of a D.R.V. invasion, and western intelligence sources found no D.R.V. troops in Laos. *Keesings Contemporary Archives* (London: Keesings Publications Ltd.), 1961–62 (Vol. XIII), pp. 17977–78; Fall, *op. cit.*, p. 212. *The United States in World Affairs*, 1960, pp. 284–85, viewed the invasion as either a figment of imagination or a feint to help the Pathet Lao seize Xieng Khouang and the Plain of Jars. The United States claimed that 500 Soviet military personnel were at the neutralist headquarters in Khang Khay. *Kingdom of Laos, Hearings before the Subcommittee on United States Security Agreements Abroad of the Committee on Foreign Relations*, United States Senate, 91st Congress, 1st Session, Part 2, October 20, 21, 22, and 28, 1969 (Washington, D.C.: GPO, 1970), p. 419. Hereafter cited as *Laos Hearings*, 1969. *Survey of International Affairs* (London: Oxford University Press, 1959–60), p. 204; *The New York Times*, March 30, 1961.

[49] Statement by State Department spokesman, December 19, 1960, in *Asian Recorder*, 1961, pp. 3738, 3780; *State Department Bulletin*, January 16, 1961, and January 23, 1961 (Vol. XLIV), pp. 76 and 118; *The New York Times*, January 13 and 17, 1961.

[50] D.R.V. statement, December 24, 1960, and letter to India, January 11, 1961 (texts in *Asian Recorder*, 1961, pp. 3738, 3780); Soviet note to the United States and Tass statement, December 13, 1960, and U.S. reply, December 17, 1960 (texts in *Documents on American Foreign Relations*, 1960, pp. 456–59).

In January 1961, President Kennedy inherited this explosive situation. Like Eisenhower, he was prepared to intervene directly if necessary; but, unlike Eisenhower, he did not consider such intervention either necessary or effectual. He warned the Communists the United States would intervene if necessary but announced that he preferred a neutralized Laos with international guarantees and a tripartite coalition government under Souvanna Phouma.[51] This seemed a major departure from Eisenhower's policies; however, Kennedy still intended to install a pro-U.S. government in Laos. During the prolonged deliberations (May 1961–July 1962) of the Geneva Conference on Laos, the United States insisted on obtaining an ICC-supervised ceasefire to prevent further Pathet Lao military gains before proceeding with the negotiations.[52] This gave Averell Harriman time to pry Souvanna Phouma away from a left-wing into a pro-U.S. stance. Harriman extracted Souvanna's promise to cooperate with the Lao right-wing by assuring him of U.S. support only if his government was not "Communist-dominated" and if he permitted the ICC effective power of inspection against the Pathet Lao.[53]

[51] TV news conference, March 23, 1961. Text in U. S. President, *Public Papers of the Presidents of the United States, John F. Kennedy, 1961* (Washington, D.C.: GPO, 1962), pp. 213–18. Hereafter cited as *Public Papers, 1961.* See also Joint Statement with Khrushchev, Vienna, in *Documents on American Foreign Relations, 1961,* p. 136.

[52] Kennedy warned that breakdown of the ceasefire would confront the United States with "the most serious decision," i.e., possible military intervention. News Conference, February 14, 1962, in *Public Papers, 1962,* p. 153. On the U.S. stand at Geneva see Averell Harriman, *Official Report of the United States Delegation to the International Conference on the Settlement of the Laotian Question* (Geneva, Switzerland: May 16, 1961–July 23, 1962), submitted to the Secretary of State, September 21, 1962; mimeographed copy given to author by the Department of State. Also J. J. Czyzak and D. F. Salans, "The International Conference on the Settlement of the Laotian Question and the Geneva Agreements of 1962," *American Journal of International Law,* April 1963 (Vol. 57, No. 2), pp. 300–17.

[53] The United States also had to apply pressure to the right-wing, who were backed by the CIA, to cooperate with Souvanna

While his diplomats at Geneva dragged out negotiations and coaxed Souvanna Phouma to incline the projected tripartite government toward the right, Kennedy increased U.S. military aid to the Lao right-wing and prepared for a possible U.S. invasion of Laos. In April 1961 U.S. PEO personnel, who had been increased to 1,500, openly accompanied and virtually commanded Phoumi's forces. In 1962, U.S. expenditures in Laos reached $73 million a year and were reduced only after the Geneva Accords were signed in July. The United States also dispatched 300 marines to Udorn Air Base in Thailand, where military stockpiles were increased and repair facilities were built for troop-carrying helicopters flown in Laos by civilian pilots.[54] In late 1961 a plan to use South Vietnamese Special Force guerrillas against the Pathet Lao was discussed but not adopted. Instead, Thailand's role in Laos was expanded. U.S. fighter-bombers from Thailand began reconnaissance and strafing missions against the Pathet Lao, and several thousand Thai and KMT troops were reportedly introduced into fighting.[55] When the Pathet Lao defeated Phoumi's forces in May 1962 near the Thai border at Nam Tha, Thailand transferred its military equipment to Phoumi and obtained more U.S. aid. At the same time, the United States began training Thais in counterinsurgency techniques, dispatched a Task Force of the Seventh Fleet to the Gulf of Siam, and sent 5,000 U.S. troops to join the 1,000 already in Thailand for a SEATO exercise.[56]

Phouma. Harriman, *op. cit.*, pp. 6–7; *The New York Times,* September 12, 15, 23, 1961; January 8, 12, 1962.

[54] Testimony by Admiral Harry Felt, in *Hearings on International Development and Security Act,* House of Representatives, 87th Congress, first Session, HR 7372, 1961, p. 33; Statement by Secretary Rusk, March 23, 1961, *State Department Bulletin,* April 17, 1961 (Vol. XXXIV), p. 548; *Asian Recorder,* 1961, p. 4016; *The New York Times,* March 25 and April 12 and 29, 1961.

[55] Kennedy's news conference, October 11, 1961, in *Public Papers,* 1961, p. 660; *The New York Times,* September 23, 1961, and February 22, 1962; *Time,* September 29, 1961, p. 33.

[56] U. S. Marines were withdrawn in July, but Army and Air Force units remained. Kennedy's announcement, *Public Papers,* 1961, p. 396; *The New York Times,* April 26, May 11, 12, 13, 16, and 30, June 1 and 3, and July 3 and 28, 1962. Kennedy's Laotian

Thus, during the years 1958–62, U.S. intervention in Laos continued and actually intensified. Thai and South Vietnamese security were increasingly tied to that of Laos under the domino theory, and Thai-U.S. intervention in Laos rose correspondingly. Joint Thai-U.S. efforts to impose right-wing rule on Laos and bring it into the anti-Communist camp eventually led to a civil war which dangerously aggravated Thailand's conflictual relationship with the D.R.V., as well as the United States' conflictual relationship with the U.S.S.R. This danger, however, did not deter further U.S. intervention, even after the United States had gone to the conference table to "neutralize" Laos in 1961.

PERIOD V (JULY 1962–1972):
U.S. INTERVENTION
AND THE COLLAPSE OF NEUTRALITY

Nevertheless, a step toward peace was taken when a coalition government was formed under Souvanna Phouma on June 24, 1962, and the Geneva Accords were signed the following month. The Geneva Accords were essentially an agreement between the U.S., the U.S.S.R., the D.R.V., and China not to draw Laos into their own camp and risk a major war. Souvanna's coalition government pledged its neutrality, and each foreign signatory agreed to respect this neutrality, refrain from interfering in Laotian affairs, and refrain from using Laotian territory for military purposes. Foreign military personnel were to leave Laos under ICC supervision within seventy-five days of the signing of the Accords. Each party had much to gain by the compromise and much to lose without it. Given the U.S. threat to intervene, a Pathet Lao military victory, though a certainty, could not have produced a Pathet Lao government. Therefore, a coalition government was a reward not to be scoffed at even though it was less than deserved. For the United States, a continued power base for the Laotian right-wing, which had faced total defeat, was a considerable victory.

---

policy is analyzed by Usha Mahajani, "President Kennedy and United States Policy in Laos, 1961–63," *Journal of Southeast Asian Studies,* September 1971, pp. 87–99.

Yet, the fruits of the Geneva Accord were short-lived. Friction between the three Laotian factions increased along with a growing connection between the conflicts in Laos, South Vietnam, and northeast Thailand. U.S. support of Diem and opposition to Vietnamese unification compelled the D.R.V. to send troops and supplies for the liberation of South Vietnam through the Ho Chi Minh Trail in southern Laos. The United States promptly labeled this as D.R.V. "aggression" against Laos and the south, while the D.R.V. countercharged that the United States was plotting to seize Laos, and had stationed troops in northeast Thailand for future armed intervention in Laos and South Vietnam.[57]

The D.R.V. and American troop commitments in Laos and Thailand, respectively, became an intractable issue in Laos, where the right-wing welcomed the growing U.S. military presence in Thailand and the Pathet Lao denounced it as a threat and interference. The Laotian coalition government began to break up in 1962 as Phouma increasingly aligned himself with the right wing. In October he appeared before the rightist-controlled Assembly, which his group and the Pathet Lao had boycotted since January 1961, and secured full powers for one year. In November he visited Thailand and obtained its backing. Meanwhile, the United States warned that the failure to integrate Pathet Lao armed forces into the right-wing Royal Lao Army would imperil the Geneva Accords and the coalition government. To back up this warning, the United States threatened the Pathet Lao with expulsion from the government, adding that it would intervene militarily, the Geneva Accords notwithstanding.[58] Thereafter Souvanna Phouma's break with the Pathet Lao and the left-wing neutralists became public. His last neutralist inclinations were shed in Washington in March 1963, when U.S. officials chastised him for letting the Pathet Lao gain territory and

[57] *State Department Bulletin,* July 30, 1962 (Vol. 47), pp. 172–73; *The New York Times,* June 13, 25, and 27, July 28, and October 6 and 8, 1962; *Peking Review,* August 31, 1962 (No. 35), p. 21, and September 28, 1962 (No. 39), p. 22.

[58] U. S. Embassy statement, January 25, 1963, *State Department Bulletin,* April 15, 1963 (Vol. 47), pp. 567–72; *Asian Recorder,* 1962, p. 4890.

warned that he would be closely watched in the future. Taking the hint, Souvanna began denouncing the Pathet Lao, the left-wing neutralists, and the D.R.V.[59]

The coalition also broke up on the battlefield. Colonel Deuane, together with 4,000 left-wing neutralist troops, joined the Pathet Lao while Kong Le's troops merged with the right-wing army. After several assassinations on both sides, the left-wing neutralists were severely suppressed. Several were arrested by the right-wing police and army in the capitals, and Souphanouvong and his associates had to flee to Pathet Lao territory.[60]

By 1963 the coalition government was destroyed, but the United States preserved Souvanna Phouma as the "neutralist" Premier to give a pretense of continuity to the original coalition. Since then, Souvanna has enjoyed uninterrupted tenure as Premier largely because of his solicitous haste to expedite American intervention in Laos.[61] As the head of a "neutralist" government, he began military action against the Pathet Lao "rebels" in 1963, "invited" the United States to secretly bomb Pathet Lao areas beginning in May 1964, "permitted" U.S. bombing of the Ho Chi Minh Trail beginning in December 1964, and "allowed" overhead flights from

[59] *The New York Times,* March 1, 1963; Roger Hilsman, *To Move a Nation* (Garden City, N.Y.: Doubleday & Company, 1967), p. 153.

[60] This event-packed period is condensed and reconstructed from accounts in *Nation* (Rangoon), February 2, 1963; *Times of Vietnam,* January 31 and March 15, 1963; *Bangkok Post,* February 18–19, 1963; *The New York Times,* March 26, April 2, 5, 6, 7, 8, and 13, 1963; and *Time,* April 13, 1963, pp. 34, 51, and April 26, 1963, p. 30.

[61] In 1969, Averell Harriman admitted that U.S. policy toward Souvanna Phouma was reversed after he was found "trustworthy" in 1961 (*The New York Times,* August 24, 1969). In April 1964 the United States even foiled an attempted coup against Souvanna by General Phoumi. Souvanna, however, had to accept the coup leaders' demands for stronger anti-Pathet Lao measures (*Asian Recorder,* 1964, pp. 5815–16, 5851–52). Today, he has only "symbolic power" and is a prisoner of the right-wing military, which has the only real power in the presently constituted R.L.G. (Girling, *loc. cit.,* p. 376).

Thailand to bomb the D.R.V. He remains an indispensable instrument of U.S. intervention to this day.

As noted above, America's military presence in Laos began to increase even while the Geneva Accords were being signed. This growth corresponded with the growing U.S. military presence in Thailand and South Vietnam under Kennedy.[62] After the Geneva Conference, the United States and Thailand continued to strengthen the Laotian right-wing in an effort to prevent further Pathet Lao-neutralist gains. In July 1962 the Deputy Chief of the U. S. AID mission in Thailand, Leonard Unger, was named Ambassador to Laos. Shortly before the October 7 Geneva deadline for foreign troop withdrawal, the United States, at Souvanna Phouma's "request" (made without Pathet Lao consent—a violation of the tripartite coalition agreement), began to furnish military aid for the defense of Laos under Article VI of the Geneva Protocol. In November 1962 a Military Advisory Aid Group (now known as a Requirements Office) staffed by U.S. officers was set up in Laos to help expand the Royal Lao Army to 70,000, and a special office to handle delivery of U.S. equipment to it was set up under the Joint United States Military Advisory Group in Bangkok.[63]

Secret U.S. bases, including a major radar facility at Phou Pha Thi, were installed to direct reconnaissance and bombing missions over Laos and the D.R.V. The largest U.S. base built in Laos was the CIA's top-secret "Armée Clandestine" headquarters at Long Chen.[64] Here the Requirements Office and the CIA trained, armed, and supported a secret army of 18,000 men from among the Meo, a fierce mountain people

[62] See *supra*, pp. 27–28.

[63] *The New York Times*, July 3, 11, 27, and 31, 1962; *Asian Recorder*, 1962, p. 4764. The text of Premier Souvanna's request for aid, delivered by hand by General Phoumi, was itemized and hinted strongly that U.S. officials helped draft it. *Laos Hearings*, 1969, pp. 368, 423, 441–43.

[64] *Asian Recorder*, 1963, pp. 5006, 5045; *The New York Times*, January 9, 1963; *Washington Post*, January 11–12, 1963. Long Chen was so secret the CIA kept newsmen away from it for years until reporters sneaked into it in early 1970. See T. D. Allman's article in *The New York Times*, March 6, 1970.

who traditionally hated the Vietnamese, Lao, and other mountain tribes. It was easy for the CIA to use the Meo against Pathet Lao and D.R.V. military units whose ranks were filled with their traditional enemies. This guerrilla army, sustained deep in Pathet Lao territory by CIA airdrops, mounted constant offensives against Pathet Lao strongholds and Vietnamese traffic along the Ho Chi Minh Trail.[65] The Pathet Lao warned that U.S. airdrops to the Meo without the sanction of the entire coalition cabinet would violate the tripartite agreement and that U.S. supply planes would be shot down. However, on October 7, 1962, Premier Souvanna signed a secret agreement with Ambassador Unger sanctioning the airdrops.[66]

President Nixon's Guam Doctrine notwithstanding, U.S. military involvement in Laos has continued to deepen and expand. U.S. support for the Meo Armée Clandestine, which now totals 36,000 men, has increased enormously since 1962. According to the General Accounting Office report of April

[65] *Laos Hearings,* 1969, pp. 412, 423–24; Robert Shaplen, "Letter from Laos," *The New Yorker,* October 20, 1962, p. 201; testimony by Leonard Unger, *United States Agreements and Commitments Abroad, Kingdom of Thailand,* Hearings Before the Subcommittee on United States Security Agreements and Commitments Abroad of the Committee on Foreign Relations, U. S. Senate, 91st Congress, first Session, part 3, November 10–17, 1969, Washington, D.C., 1970, pp. 722–23. Hereafter cited as *Thailand Hearings,* 1969. More than 100,000 Meo have died from war-related causes since the United States began exploiting their traditional antagonisms for cold war purposes. U.S. intervention has aggravated the Meos' conflictual relationship with the Vietnamese; if left alone they might have established amicable relations with the D.R.V. and Pathet Lao, as other Meo in Laos have done. See Fred Branfman, "Presidential War in Laos, 1964–1970," in Adams and McCoy (eds.), *op. cit.,* pp. 251–53; and testimony by R. J. Rickenbach, U. S. Refugee Relief Officer in Laos, *Refugees in Laos and Cambodia,* Hearings Before the Subcommittee of the Senate Judiciary Committee, 91st Congress, first Session, May 7, 1970, Washington, D.C., pp. 26–29.

[66] D. G. Porter, "After Geneva: Subverting Laotian Neutrality," in Adams and McCoy (eds.), *op. cit.,* pp. 184, 187; *Washington Post,* September 26, 1962; *The New York Times,* October 1, 1962. For U.S. official justification see *State Department Bulletin,* April 15, 1963 (Vol. 47), pp. 568, 578.

1972, funds from U. S. Refugee Relief Programs, Civilian Health Programs, AID, and the Food for Peace Program have been diverted by the CIA to feed the Meo guerrillas and their 105,000 dependents.[67] In September 1969, Senator Mansfield reported after visiting Southeast Asia that U.S. involvement in Laos had increased to such an extent that it could lead to another "Vietnam War." The United States took part in the Autumn 1969 fighting on the Plain of Jars, ferrying assault troops and military equipment from Thailand. By the end of 1969 over a hundred U.S. pilots had been captured in Laos; today this number is considerably higher, but is kept secret. In January 1971 the United States admitted its combat role in Laos but formally denied that any U.S. combat troops were operating there. However, impartial experts estimate 10,000 U.S. combat troops are now in Laos, and report that in mid-1972 the "Green Berets" even began sending long-range ground missions into Pathet Lao territory and the D.R.V.[68]

The start of U.S. bombing in Laos and the D.R.V. was accompanied by a heavy buildup in Thailand. U.S. troops in Thailand increased from 6,000 in April 1965 to 49,000 in August 1972, including 10,000 engaged in Thai counterinsurgency activities. In 1965, secret contingency plans were drawn up for the use of U.S. troops to help the Thai Army oppose Communist forces in Laos before they attacked Thailand— in short, they planned to invade Laos first. In March 1967, Thailand admitted that Thai bases were being used for bombing missions in Indochina, and stated that the United States could use the base at Uttapo "so long as . . . the threat of

[67] *The New York Times,* February 7, 1971, and February 25 and April 25, 1972.

[68] *The New York Times,* September 22–23, 1969; January 31, 1971; and January 20–22, February 19, 25, and June 9, 15, 17, 1972. See also *Asian Recorder,* 1969, p. 9225. The official cost of U.S. intervention in Laos (excluding secret CIA and Thai mercenary operations) is presently $350 million a year. Testimony of former U.S. ambassador to Laos, G. M. Godley, to Senate Foreign Relations Committee, May 9, 1973, *Facts on File,* May 6–12, 1973, p. 367.

Communist aggression against free nations in Southeast Asia still continues."[69] The number of U.S. bombing missions flown in Laos since Premier Souvanna asked the United States to bomb the Pathet Lao in 1964 has reached astronomical proportions. In 1966 the United States flew two hundred times as many sorties in Laos as it did in 1964. The rate was so high after the United States stopped bombing the D.R.V. that Senator Fulbright spoke of "just 67,000" in 1968. The current number of raids, officially kept secret, is estimated to be a daily average of 400 over Pathet Lao areas and 1,200 over the Trail, at an annual cost of $2 billion and the involvement of 50,000 U.S. personnel.[70]

The United States has also financed, at the rate of $26 million a year, increasing Thai military intervention in Laos, where Thai troop strength has increased from 5,000 in the mid-1960s to 10,000 in 1971 and 20,000 in 1973.[71] These Thai troops are incorporated into the ranks of the Armée Clandestine and the Royal Lao Army, wear Lao army uniforms, and receive wages higher than those of U.S. soldiers from the CIA (contrary to the antimercenary provision in the Defense Procurement Act of 1971). Senate investigators visiting Southeast Asia in January 1972 discovered that the United States is committed to provide up to $100 million a year in support of these Thai irregulars in Laos. Also in January 1972, U. S. Army helicopter gunships with Thai pilots began operating in northern Laos, and the Thai Air Force began using U.S. aircraft on combat missions. Many U.S. troops "withdrawn" from Vietnam in 1972 actually regrouped

[69] *The New York Times,* January 19, March 10 and 24, 1967; and August 16, 1969. *Los Angeles Times,* November 12, 1967; Melvin Gurtov, *China and Southeast Asia: The Politics of Survival* (Lexington, Mass.: D. C. Heath & Co., 1971), pp. 18, 42, and note on p. 84.

[70] *Laos Hearings,* 1969, pp. 481, 483–85; *Thailand Hearings,* 1969, pp. 689–90; Branfman in Adams and McCoy (eds.), *op. cit.,* pp. 231–41.

[71] *Thailand Hearings,* 1969, p. 812. Senator Symington deplored the secrecy surrounding the Thai irregulars in Laos. See *ibid.,* p. 814; and Branfman in Adams and McCoy (eds.), *op. cit.,* pp. 244–5; Godley's testimony, May 9, 1973, *op. cit.*

at new bases built in Thailand for the training of Laotian pilots and Thai irregulars bound for Laos.[72]

This heightened Thai-U.S. military intervention is no longer based on SEATO but is justified repeatedly as a response to R.L.G. "requests" to "safeguard Laotian integrity and neutrality" following North Vietnamese "violations of the agreements." Once it was justified as an effort "to save American and allied lives in South Vietnam which are threatened by the continual infiltration of North Vietnamese troops and supplies along the Ho Chi Minh Trail."[73] Continued U.S. bombing of Laos is still justified on the grounds that the Laotian conflict is part of the one Indochina war.[74] This increasing identification of the Laotian situation with the war in South Vietnam served as the pretext for a major U.S.-South Vietnamese invasion of Laos in early 1971.

To invade Laos had long been a favorite project of several U.S. policy-makers. In 1967, at the height of U.S. bombings over North Vietnam, Ambassador Ellsworth Bunker in Saigon "recommended a thrust into Southern Laos cutting off the Ho Chi Minh Trail so Communist forces to the south would wither away." Washington vetoed the idea then as violating the Geneva accord; as a provocation of China; and as requiring more U.S. divisions. But then General Westmoreland also believed that the United States could "win the war" by invading Cambodia and Laos to destroy Communist sanctuaries.[75] After the invasion of Cambodia in May 1970, several U.S. military operations were launched in Laos. In February 1971 25,000 South Vietnamese soldiers, supported by 9,000 U.S.

[72] Report by J. W. Lowenstein and R. M. Moose, staff member of the Senate Foreign Relations Committee. The report was made public by Senator Symington on May 7, 1972. Also, *The New York Times,* February 13 and May 8, 1972; and Michael Morrow, "At War: Thai Buildup Continues," *American Report* (New York) September 22, 1972, pp. 1 and 5.

[73] President Nixon's message on Laos, March 6, 1970, text in Adams and McCoy (eds.), *op. cit.,* pp. 401–6; State Department spokesman's statement, *The New York Times,* February 27 and April 17 and 18, 1973.

[74] Testimony of Ambassador Godley, May 9, 1973, *op. cit.*

[75] Robert Shaplen, *The Road from War: Vietnam 1965–197* (New York: Harper & Row, 1970), p. 342.

troops and air cover, invaded southern Laos. Another 1,600 Thai troops were flown into Long Chen. This was called a "limited operation" to shorten the war, protect U.S. forces in South Vietnam, and buy time to improve the South Vietnamese Army enough so that U.S. troops could be withdrawn in safety. But the invasion failed: the South Vietnamese retreated hurriedly in March, and the D.R.V. and Viet Cong proved the invasion's ineffectiveness by launching an astonishingly successful offensive in South Vietnam a year later.[76]

The invasion, however, highlighted two important developments. First, the United States was confident from the outset that China would not intervene, and it assured China that its security was not threatened.[77] Second, Premier Souvanna's role as a mere bystander was highlighted. He was not even informed about the invasion and expressed mild displeasure; however, realizing his total dependence on the United States, he again denounced the D.R.V.[78] Laos had clearly become an appendage of Vietnam in U.S. planning.

U.S. manipulation of Premier Souvanna's "neutralist" coalition government has brought Laos into integrative but subordinate relationship with America's interventionist partners, Thailand and South Vietnam. The Thais take an active role in Laotian affairs, including military. South Vietnam invaded Laos with impunity without even bothering to give Souvanna prior notice.

The R.L.G.'s closer relationship with Thailand and South Vietnam has exacerbated its conflictual relations with the Pathet Lao and the D.R.V. The R.L.G. and the Pathet Lao have engaged in fighting ever since 1963, punctuated by occasional rounds of ineffectual talks. In October 1972 they resumed negotiations and on February 21, 1973, reached a

[76] See *The New York Times* for the whole month of February, and March 25, 27, 29, and 30, 1971.

[77] Despite its wordy warnings, China not only remained inactive but also halted its work on the "mystery" road from Yunnan into northern Laos. Chou En-lai's current visit to Hanoi was dismissed by Rogers as designed to comfort the D.R.V. over its setbacks. *The New York Times,* February 15, 19, and March 10 and 1, 1971.

[78] *The New York Times,* February 9 and 13, 1971.

peace agreement providing for immediate ceasefire, joint commissions to deal with political and military situations and a coalition government of National Union. But within two days the agreement was torn up by renewed fighting and U.S. bombing.[79]

Once again political deadlock and military conflict reign supreme over Laos. The Pathet Lao stand, enunciated in the five-point plan of March 6, 1970, insists that (1) the United States must stop its "intervention and aggression"; (2) the United States must stop bombing Pathet Lao areas; (3) there should be general elections; (4) there should be a provisional government during the period between a ceasefire and the elections; and (5) the country must be reunified. However, Souvanna Phouma insists that the D.R.V. must end its "aggression" in Laos first. The two parties can go round and round in circles this way forever.[80]

The R.L.G.'s relations with the D.R.V. have also been purely conflictual since the 1963 break with the Pathet Lao. On June 6, 1963, Souvanna Phouma charged that D.R.V. combat troops had joined the Pathet Lao, and demanded an ICC investigation.[81] Since then he has been perorating that

[79] *The New York Times*, February 22, 23, and 27, and April 17 and 18, 1973.

[80] *Asian Recorder*, 1969, p. 8828; *The New York Times*, January 30, 1971, and January 23, 1972; *Asian Student*, November 25, 1972. Text of the Pathet Lao plan is given in Adams and McCoy (eds.), *op. cit.*, pp. 439–43.

[81] See Souvanna Phouma's notes to Co-Chairmen, June 6, 1963, and June 15, 1964, in *Asian Recorder*, 1963, p. 5442 and 1964, pp. 5815–16, 5994; and the Western Ambassadors' communiqué in Vientiane, June 29, 1964, in *ibid.*, p. 5943. In 1963 the United States charged that 10,000 D.R.V. soldiers were stationed in Laos. Subsequent official testimony placed the number at 6,000 and claimed that the D.R.V. troop level in Laos began to increase in 1964 (see *The New York Times*, January 8 and March 1, 1963; and *Laos Hearings*, 1969, p. 328). Since then the United States has given conflicting estimates of D.R.V. troops in Laos ranging from 48,000 to 67,000, and, in February 1971, 70,000 were estimated to be resisting the invasion of Laos. Critics claim that with 50,000 Pathet Lao troops fighting in Laos, Vietnamese "stiffeners" are not greatly needed, and that in June 1970 there were "at the very most 5,000 North Vietnamese troops engaged in combat in Laos" (the rest being engaged in supply and transport on the Ho

China and the D.R.V. must stop interfering in Laos. In May 1969, after a break of four years, the D.R.V. sent an envoy to Laos to promote cordial relations and to assure Souvanna that D.R.V. forces would be withdrawn once U.S. bombing of Pathet Lao areas ceased. Souvanna has rejected these overtures. He defends U.S. bombing and demands that D.R.V. "aggression" should cease first. The United States finds this line most agreeable and further demands that the D.R.V. withdraw its forces from Laos and "desist from further use of Laos territory for purposes of interfering in the internal affairs of the Republic of Vietnam."[82] Laos has been so inextricably caught up in the Vietnam War that a Laotian settlement long ago became contingent on one in Vietnam.[83] The tragedy is that even after the Vietnam settlement, peace still eludes Laos. Reinforcing the intransigence of the rightwing Laotian military is the U.S. government's ready willingness to bomb Laos "at the request" of Souvanna Phouma.

Finally, the post-1962 alliance of "neutral" Laos with the United States and Thailand has also dangerously intensified conflictual relations between the two traditional rivals, Thailand and the D.R.V. Today, Vietnamese "stiffeners" in the Pathet Lao army and 20,000 Thais in the Armée Clandestine and the Royal Lao Army are fighting each other. Both Thailand and the D.R.V. view each other as direct threats to themselves and their allies. Prior to the escalation of Thai-American intervention in Laos in the 1960s, 1,600 Lao residents of northeast Thailand trained by the D.R.V. and Pathet Lao had avoided direct contact with the ongoing insurgency in northeast Thailand. This no longer appears to be so since 1969 because of Thailand's role in widening the war in Laos.[84] Thailand today professes readiness for friendly rela-

---

Chi Minh Trail). See President Nixon's statement on Laos, March , 1970, and Branfman in Adams and McCoy (eds.), *op. cit.*, pp. 69, 278–80.

[82] Souvanna Phouma's statement, July 25, 1969, and Hanoi's denial of July 27, 1969, reported in *The New York Times*, July 28, 1969. Also *Asian Recorder*, 1969, pp. 9014, 9184.

[83] Girling, *loc. cit.*, p. 380.

[84] Gurtov, *op. cit.*, pp. 17–18; *The New York Times*, May 5 and September 22, 1969; J. L. S. Girling, "Northeast Thailand: Tomor-

tions with the D.R.V. but on the precondition of a divided Vietnam and its own preeminence in Laos. This might not be acceptable to the D.R.V.[85]

CONCLUSION

It is indisputable that the impact of U.S. intervention on Laos itself has been crushingly total and pervasive. Laos' capacities are so minute that it has not been able to deflect the enormous interventionary power of the United States. The R.L.G. is so dependent on the United States' purse strings that the U.S. establishment in Vientiane has become the real government of Laos.[86] Consequently, Laos has no choice of alternatives or diplomatic maneuverability left in conducting foreign relations with its Southeast Asian neighbors. U.S. capacity to make and unmake governments in Laos ensures that whoever wishes to be Premier in Laos must toe the U.S. line. Thus, the once "unacceptable" Souvanna Phouma, who since 1962 has complied with U.S. demands, has enjoyed unparalleled tenure as Premier of Laos. America's hold over Souvanna is so complete that his government is virtually locked in a conflictual relationship with the Pathet Lao and the D.R.V. At the same time, the R.L.G.'s relations with Thailand have become so close that the term "Thai-Laotian integration" is more descriptive than the term "Thai-Laotian alliance." Souvanna has even had to maintain a stable alliance relationship with the South Vietnamese, whom he acutely distrusts.

U.S. intervention has also restricted the options and maneuverability of the Pathet Lao, which has had no choice but to ally itself with the D.R.V., the U.S.S.R.[87] and Communist China as the only powers willing and capable of helping it resist U.S. intervention. However, we must not forget that

row's Vietnam?" *Foreign Affairs*, January 1968 (Vol. XLVI, No 2), p. 396.

[85] *Selected News from Home*, December 8, 1972–January 25 1973, the Royal Embassy of Thailand, Washington, D.C.

[86] See Part III, "America in Laos," in Adams and McCoy (eds.) *op. cit.*, pp. 283–390; and Girling, *loc. cit.*, p. 374.

[87] The U.S.S.R. is a major donor to the Pathet Lao. See "Laos The Underground Men," *Newsweek*, April 9, 1973, pp. 55–57.

the Pathet Lao, though an ally of the D.R.V., is a force in its own right and has genuine nationalist objectives in Laos that predate U.S. involvement and are independent of those of the D.R.V.

Moreover, U.S. intervention has brought Thailand and the D.R.V. into a *de facto* conflict, though no formal state of war exists between them. This is an aggravation of the pre-U.S. traditional relations between those powers. On the other hand, by setting up a separate political unit in South Vietnam, the United States has created a seemingly cordial relationship between Thailand and South Vietnam, unprecedented in their history. But this "alliance" is highly precarious because South Vietnam itself is so unstable that without U.S. intervention it would become a nonentity or, more correctly, a southern part of a unified Vietnam.

What would have happened had the United States not intervened in Indochina at all? To the best of one's judgment, Thailand, Laos, and Vietnam would have emerged as modern states. The process of modernization and consolidation of Thai and Vietnamese societies into nation-states has been going on at least since the turn of the century. Laos was extremely backward, but after World War II Lao nationalism began to develop quickly. Moreover, forces of modernization in this age of technology and ideology can mold a society of several ethnic groups into a modern state faster than ever before, even though the problem of ethnic minorities may remain. The Pathet Lao, the first to embody an alliance between the lowland Lao and the mountain tribal groups, had the necessary ideological zeal and institutional framework to be the catalyst of this process with international aid. But it was never given a chance to do so.

As for Laos' relations with Thailand and Vietnam (presumably unified), they could have resembled the stable relations of Lan Xang's first three centuries of existence. An amiable, cooperative relationship could have arisen, as the formation of the Southeast Asia League in September 1947 attests. Though small and weak, a Laos under Pathet Lao nationalist influence would not have agreed to become a vassal of either Thailand or the D.R.V.[88] If warfare had broken out among them, it could not possibly have been as devastating as that brought on by U.S. intervention simply because their own destructive capacity would have been far more limited.

What would happen if U.S. intervention were withdrawn? The United States admits that without its bombing, the Laotian Army would collapse.[89] The Pathet Lao, with mere D.R.V. "stiffeners," has been able to defeat the Royal Lao Army, which has had U.S. and Thai "stiffeners." Thus, only massive saturation bombing by the United States keeps the Souvanna Phouma government in power. If it is stopped, the Pathet Lao will most likely succeed in unifying the country and forming a government. Its left-wing government would for some time be friendly to the D.R.V. and opposed to Thailand, though not necessarily opposed to the United States. If the United States can reach accommodation with China and the U.S.S.R., it can also do so with a left-wing or Communist government in Laos or Vietnam. However, the United States would have to reinterpret its interests in Laos so that a Pathet Lao victory would not be thought of as a loss of American "prestige," which it will not do so long as it views D.R.V. activity in Laos as "aggression" and "unlawful support to Pathet Lao rebels." Unless a fundamental alteration in U.S. objectives occurs, U.S. intervention in Laos will not end or even decrease.

If, on the other hand, the United States withdraws its intervention and permits Laotian events to take their own course, the left-wing Pathet Lao government is likely to remain in conflict with the current government in Thailand because of the question of ethnic and national loyalty of the Lao people in northeastern Thailand. From its systematically draconian measures, it is evident that the Thai government is unsure of the loyalty of these people and fears Pathet Lao

[88] Even as an ally of the D.R.V., Souphanouvong remained a fiercely patriotic Lao. It is in deference to Lao pride that the D.R.V. advisors usually stay in the background. See Tran Van Dinh in Adams and McCoy (eds.), *op. cit.*, pp. 425–38.

[89] *Laos Hearings*, 1969, p. 511.

infiltration and subversion. To allay these fears a peaceful agreement between the two governments could be worked out; or, failing that, Thailand, with U.S. help, can continue counterinsurgency measures in the northeast. It is doubtful Thailand would intervene unilaterally in Laos to upset a Pathet Lao victory. The pragmatic element in Thai foreign policy would militate against such a rash move. It is not without reason that the Thais have toyed with neutralism whenever they feel U.S. interest in Thailand weakening. A neutral foreign policy would not be against Thai national interests. Like Burma and Nepal, who have coexisted with Communist China, a "nonaligned" Thailand could coexist with China, the D.R.V., and a left-wing Laos. The withdrawal of heavy U.S. military involvement in Thailand could even generate political forces that would demilitarize the Thai government. Like Pridi Phanomyong's government (1946–47), such a Thai government might forge amicable ties with the Pathet Lao and D.R.V. governments.

As for the D.R.V., it has intervened in Laos for two reasons. One is the ideological-military alliance with the Pathet Lao, and the other reason is the D.R.V.'s need of the Ho Chi Minh Trail to reunify Vietnam. If U.S. intervention in Indochina ends, the *raison d'être* for D.R.V. intervention in Laos would cease. But this is a big "if." Although the ceasefire in Vietnam has taken place, the United States has reaffirmed its right to continue to supply unlimited military and economic aid to the Thieu government. This move is hardly likely to prompt Thieu to agree to reunification of Vietnam. If Vietnam remains divided and if the D.R.V. decides to continue the struggle for reunification, Laos will remain a conduit for North Vietnamese *matériel* into South Vietnam. If Vietnam is unified or at least South Vietnam comes under a government in which the P.R.G. has a proportionate role, then there is a strong chance that South and North Vietnam can communicate directly across the border. In that case, the Ho Chi Minh Trail would cease to be a valuable supply route, the D.R.V.'s presence in Laos would be terminated, and the reason for a D.R.V.-Pathet Lao military alliance would cease. The alliance itself might continue on its own momentum for some time, but later the factor of Pathet Lao nationalism and the problems of a common border would create a D.R.V.-Pathet Lao relationship based on practicality and compromise rather than the euphoria of ideology.

Finally, no study of U.S. intervention in Laos can overlook the physical destruction that has resulted from this intervention. The devastation of the war and total dependence on the United States has utterly ruined the Laotian economy.[90] Over 50,000 of Laos' 91,000 square miles have come under heavy U.S. bombing. At least 700,000 to 1,000,000 in a population of less than three million have been displaced. Since the very survival of Laos under the impact of this bombing is now in question, an end to U.S. intervention would at least give Laos a chance to survive and exist, whether in a stable or conflictual relationship with its neighbors.

[90] *The New York Times,* January 24, February 25, and June 17, 1972.

The Soviet Presence in Southeast Asia: Growth and Implications

MELVIN GURTOV

In the past five years a more active diplomacy, increased trade and cultural contacts, and an expanded naval presence in Southeast Asia have established the Soviet Union as a dynamic factor in regional politics. Interpretations of Soviet behavior and its implications for regional security range from the view that Soviet intentions are essentially benign, reflecting the natural evolution of the U.S.S.R.'s global concerns, to the view that there is an evolving strategic design to establish the U.S.S.R. as a major Pacific power. Most observers agree, at any rate, that the increased Soviet presence is "dramatic." But the question remains whether it is "dramatic" only in comparison with previous years, which is undeniable, or because it betokens ambitious objectives and broad expectations for which the Soviet leadership is prepared to undertake new political, financial, or even security commitments.

SOURCES OF INCREASED SOVIET INVOLVEMENT[1]

In Southeast Asia until the 1960s, Soviet interests were largely left for the Chinese to promote. The limited direct role of the Soviet Union was best illustrated by its marginal involvement in the Viet Minh revolution (until the Geneva Conference, when U.S. intervention became a threat), and by Soviet policy in Burma which, despite the Khrushchev-Bulganin state visit of 1955, was not competitive with the

[1] Portions of this and the following section are from the author's article on "Sino-Soviet Relations and Southeast Asia: Recent Developments and Future Possibilities," *Pacific Affairs,* Winter 1970–71 (Vol. XLIII, No. 4), pp. 491–505. Reprinted with permission.

Chinese either in diplomacy or in influence over the Burmese Communist movement.[2] Unfamiliarity with Southeast Asia,[3] as well as preoccupation with ideology, moreover, bred conflicting, mostly inappropriate, models of political development and revolutionary doctrine. This is not surprising, since Moscow was simultaneously attempting to formulate universally relevant strategies for wooing newly independent governments away from "imperialism" and toward socialism, on the one hand, and for assuring the ultimate victory of indigenous Communist parties, on the other. The Soviets—and the Chinese Communists, who followed their lead in third-world doctrine (but not always policy) during the 1950s—often could not reconcile their interest in outbidding the West in state-to-state diplomacy with their leading role in the worldwide revolutionary struggle against "imperialists" and "reactionaries."[4]

The concept of "national democracy" was advanced in Soviet writings in the early 1960s to reconcile these two interests, but it ran afoul of Peking and only marginally (in Indonesia) projected Soviet influence into Southeast Asia. "National democracy" rationalized Moscow's preference for

[2] On Sino-Soviet rivalry in Burma, see Aleksandr Kaznacheev, *Inside a Soviet Embassy: Experiences of a Russian Diplomat in Burma* (Philadelphia: J. B. Lippincott Co., 1962).

[3] This is reflected in the slow development of Soviet scholarship on Southeast Asia. See Peter Berton and Alvin Z. Rubinstein, *Soviet Works on Southeast Asia: A Bibliography of Non-Periodical Literature, 1946–65* (Los Angeles: School of Politics and International Relations, University of Southern California, 1967).

[4] For some views on the evolution of Soviet doctrine between 1947 (when the Cominform was founded) and 1960, see John S. Reshetar, Jr., "The Soviet Union and the Neutralist World," *The Annals,* November 1965 (Vol. CCCLXII), pp. 102–12; Donald S. Zagoria, "Sino-Soviet Friction in Underdeveloped Areas," *Problems of Communism,* March–April 1961 (Vol. X, No. 2), pp. 1–13; Charles B. McLane, *Soviet Strategies in Southeast Asia: An Exploration of Eastern Policy under Lenin and Stalin* (Princeton, N.J.: Princeton University Press, 1966); Fritz Ermarth, "The Soviet Union in the Third World: Purpose in Search of Power," *The Annals,* November 1969 (Vol. CCLXXVI), pp. 31–40; and David Morison, "Africa and Asia: Some Trends in Soviet Thinking," *Mizan,* September–October 1968 (Vol. X, No. 5), pp. 167–84.

dealing with anti-imperialist, anticapitalist governments while ignoring their suppression of Communist parties and their frequently heretical adaptations of socialist economics. It was, so the Chinese charged, an antirevolutionary doctrine, for it seemed to rule out revolutionary violence and the obligation of Communist parties in power to assist those trying to get it. Instead of using nuclear parity with the United States as the basis for more intensive efforts to undermine imperialist strongholds in Southeast Asia and elsewhere, Peking contended, the Soviets were content to bank on peaceful transition to socialism, thus writing off local Communist movements.[5] As Donald S. Zagoria has written,[6] Peking and Moscow were at odds on three specific points concerning revolutionary strategy: the timing of external support and encouragement of liberation movements; the leading force behind them (whether the party, which Peking seemed to prefer, or an alliance of the bourgeoisie and the workers, which Moscow urged); and the prospects for peaceful transition to socialism (with Peking insisting that the transition was possible only in the few cases—e.g., Burma, Cambodia, or Nepal—where bourgeois regimes could be effectively prevented or influenced from strengthening their ties with the imperialist bloc).

Although circumstances, such as those in Laos before the 1962 agreements and in Vietnam during 1964, compelled Khrushchev to depart from a doctrine that meant patience and caution, his policy even in those cases was based on the "general principle [that] he did not want to get involved militarily."[7] The Chinese publicly countered that the Soviet Union needlessly feared a direct confrontation with the United States, was only half-heartedly assisting the Viet-

[5] See, for instance, "The Differences between Comrade Togliatti and Us," *Jen-min jih-pao* (*People's Daily,* Peking), December 31, 1962; and *Kuan-yü kuo-chi kung-ch'an chu-i yün-tung tsung lu-hsien ti chien-i* (*A Proposal Concerning the General Line of the International Communist Movement*), Jen-min ch'u-pan she, Peking, 1963.

[6] Zagoria, *loc. cit.,* pp. 4–7.

[7] Ermarth, *loc. cit,* p. 35.

namese revolution, and, while preaching "united (socialist) action" on Vietnam, was colluding with the Americans to settle the war short of a D.R.V.-NLF victory. Peking's charges were not completely unfounded, since the Soviet leadership (as revealed, for instance, in the Pentagon Papers) probably was prepared to settle for much less in Vietnam than was Hanoi. In broader perspective, however, Sino-Soviet differences on Indochina were important because of the challenge Peking raised to Moscow's authority over the Communist movement in the third world, not because they revealed Peking's propensity to run high risks for the sake of revolutionary allies.

With the start of the American air war against the D.R.V. in February and March 1965, the new Brezhnev-Kosygin leadership mounted a major assistance program, highlighted by air defense equipment, instructors, petroleum, and wheat. Between 1965 and 1970, Soviet and East European aid (military and economic) to the D.R.V. came to about $3.5 billion.[8] Yet, to date, massive aid has not bought Moscow leverage over Vietnamese strategy, any more than it has for China. Indeed, the Vietnam experience probably demonstrated anew to the Soviet leadership the limitations on its influence over revolutionary allies like the North Vietnamese. It may also have taught the Soviets that so-called "local wars," involving large-scale American intervention, could readily occur and could not easily be limited despite nuclear parity, as the Chinese had said. A third possible lesson for the Soviet leadership was that, in the absence of more reliable logistical capabilities, access to (and mobility in) Southeast Asia would remain limited and too dependent on Chinese goodwill. In that circumstance, too, the Soviets might be forced into unwanted commitments to socialist parties or governments if U.S. escalation occurred suddenly and caught Moscow unprepared.

---

[8] See Douglas Pike, "China, North Vietnam, and Ping-Pong Balls," *Asia Quarterly* (Tokyo; in Japanese), July 1971 (Vol. III, No. 3), p. 195. U. S. Secretary of Defense Melvin R. Laird estimated in 1971 that Soviet military aid to the D.R.V. was 65 per cent (about $500 million annually) and Chinese aid 25 per cent of the total. *Los Angeles Times*, September 13, 1971, p. 17.

A similar lesson about the limitations of the ruble's purchasing power may have been learned in Indonesia. The Sukarno government, recipient of the largest Soviet economic credits and military aid of any non-Communist Southeast Asian nation, proved to be a wasting asset for Moscow in the early 1960s. The Soviets found their investments going not to promote socialism, economic development, or support of Soviet foreign policy, but to finance Sukarno's "confrontation" with Malaysia. Nor was Soviet aid sufficient to keep Sukarno from establishing close ties with China. Sukarno's removal from power after the Communist Party of Indonesia (PKI) was crushed in the fall of 1965 may have been a blessing in disguise for Moscow. It opened the way to diplomatic initiatives toward Indonesia's neighbors. Trade agreements were signed with Singapore (April 1966) and Malaysia (March 1967), and diplomatic relations were subsequently established with both countries.

The events in Indonesia were probably also instructive to Soviet leaders in that they showed the unpredictability of identifying with revolutionary movements in Southeast Asia (which tend to find Chinese doctrine much more attractive anyway). Accordingly, during the latter half of the 1960s, Moscow ignored the Thai Communist Party in favor of maintaining political and trade ties with the Royal Thai government, an active supporter of U.S. policies in Indochina. Rather than compete with Peking for the allegiance of the Red and White Flag factions of the Burmese Communist Party, Moscow left the field to China and gave assistance to the military government of Ne Win. The image of a non-revolutionary Soviet Union, interested in promoting peaceful coexistence, was reinforced at Tashkent in January 1966 when Soviet mediation produced agreement between India and Pakistan on a mutual withdrawal of forces in the west.

It is probably no coincidence that at the very time the instruments of Soviet policy in Asia were changing, Soviet writers were reappraising Southeast Asian—and, for that matter, third world—politics.[9] In seeking an explanation for the failure

---

[9] One of the most critical early reappraisals was N. A. Simoniya, "Concerning the Character of Revolutions of National Liberation," *Narody Azii i Afriki,* No. 6, 1966, pp. 3–21. The theme of

of socialism and Soviet influence to take root, Soviet specialists pointed to obstacles such as the lengthy colonial histories of these countries, the greater concern of their new governments for internal development than for relations with the socialist world, their lack of internal cohesion (and need for a vanguard party), and the divorcement of often incompetent military regimes from mass politics.[10]

On the implications of these political conditions for Soviet policy, the key question once again was how the "objective situation" in the new states corresponded with Marxist-Leninist doctrine. Some writers seemed inclined to bend ideology as much as necessary to rationalize Soviet solidarity with politically and economically different countries. Others —the ideological purists—saw no contradiction between the "fundamental tenets of Marxism-Leninism" and the course of political development in the new states. The difference involved much more than ideology, for the ascendancy of the second view signaled acceptance of a leading role for the Soviet Union in stimulating the development of a "socialist consciousness" in states where the working class was unorganized and where proletarian revolutionary leadership could not be expected. Through Soviet bloc aid programs, and especially close working relations with governments ("economic cooperation"), the international socialist system could be linked up with the political systems of countries "on the road to socialism" or interested in "noncapitalist development."[11]

Simoniya's article is that because Soviet writers have exaggerated the role of international conditions in determining the political and economic course of newly independent states, they have often been overoptimistic about these states turning to socialism. The postrevolutionary development of the new states, says Simoniya, might be capitalistic—and in fact most of them have taken the capitalist road. Simoniya adds that in some states that profess adherence to the Soviet model, socialism in practice has diverged sharply from socialism in theory.

[10] For reviews of the literature, see Morison, *loc. cit.;* "The Ebb Tide?" *Mizan,* September–October 1966 (Vol. VIII, No. 5), pp. 189–201; and "Third World Socialisms—A Harder Soviet Look," *Mizan,* July–August 1968 (Vol. X, No. 4), pp. 151–55.

[11] In these latter analyses, Mongolia was frequently cited as the most relevant example of a society that was making the transition

OPPORTUNITIES IN
THE TRIANGULAR COMPETITION

In the wake of Tashkent, the Chinese Cultural Revolution presented Moscow with a major opportunity to erode Chinese influence in Southeast Asia. Dissemination of Maoist propaganda by several Chinese embassies led Soviet commentators to raise the specter of a "yellow peril" to independent governments.[12] "Adventuristic" Chinese policies were said to have undermined the positions of national liberation movements and played into the hands of the imperialists. Peking's emphasis on armed struggle not only, in the Soviet view, disregarded other methods of promoting the worldwide interests of Communism; it also compounded Moscow's difficulties in attempting to erode the American position in Asia.

The chance to cut into American predominance in the region came with the change in administrations in 1968. Reduced U.S. involvement in Vietnam and statements by American leaders about a reduced military presence in and commitments to Southeast Asia after the war indicated a general policy reassessment. On top of these developments came the British announcement of withdrawal from "East of Suez" (primarily meaning Singapore) by 1971. Soviet leaders must have noticed the reaction of several states in the region which were allied with or friendly to the United States: they indicated more serious interest than before in all-Asian economic and political regional associations. From the Soviet perspective, although these countries (such as Thailand and Malaysia) were consistently "pro-imperialist" in their poli-

---

to socialism mainly because the Soviet Union responded positively to Mongolia's requests for aid. See the discussion and review of the literature in "Socialism and the New States: A Stronger Soviet Line," *Mizan*, September–October 1966 (Vol. VIII, No. 5), pp. 202–8.

[12] See the articles by V. Shelepin, "Maoist Intrigues in the Third World," *Novoye Vremya* (Moscow), June 27, 1969; V. Matveyev, "Washington, Peking and Southeast Asia," *Izvestia*, August 31, 1967; Ernst Henry (pseud.), in *Literaturnaya gazeta*, September 27 and October 4, 1967, and January 1, 1968, the last trans. in *Current Digest of the Soviet Press*, January 24, 1968 (Vol. XX, No. 1), pp. 3–7; and V. Kudryavtsev, *Izvestia*, April 13, 1968, trans. *ibid.*, May 1, 1968 (Vol. XX, No. 15), pp. 27–28.

cies, the organizations to which most of them belonged, and which might become more prominent "after Vietnam" (ASPAC and ASEAN),[13] were pledged to eliminating "foreign" bases and were hostile to China. Soviet suspicions of these organizations' independence probably did not diminish, and the Soviet preference for dealing with countries individually probably remained. Nevertheless, to judge from the statements of Soviet leaders during 1969, new prospects were seen for attracting these "bourgeois" states away from the United States at little cost by taking advantage of anxieties in Southeast Asia about American disengagement and the Chinese threat.

At the international meeting in Moscow of Communist and Workers' Parties (June 5–17, 1969), Leonid Brezhnev for the first time spoke of the desirability of "collective security" in Southeast Asia.[14] As the analysis of one authoritative Soviet commentator suggested, Brezhnev was concerned that (1) China's leaders had not abandoned their aim to establish an anti-Soviet third-world bloc, which China is historically, economically, and geographically well situated to attempt; and (2) the C.P.R. was so anxious to discredit Soviet policies in the third world that she was prepared to engage in discussions with the United States to divide up "spheres of influence."[15] "Collective security" was therefore explained as offering So-

[13] These are the Asian and Pacific Council and the Association of Southeast Asian Nations.

[14] For other analyses of the speech, see Peter Howard, " 'A System of Collective Security,' " *Mizan,* July–August 1969 (Vol. XI, No. 4), pp. 199–204; and Hemen Ray, "Soviet Diplomacy in Asia," *Problems of Communism,* March–April 1970 (Vol. XIX, No. 2), pp. 46–49.

[15] V. Shelepin, "Maoist Intrigues in the 'Third World,' " *op. cit.* In his view the Ninth Party Congress in Peking (April 1969) "confirmed that Peking is striving as before to win a dominant position in the 'third world' and to use its people in the global struggle for its own hegemony . . . They [China's leaders] are using all means to achieve this aim: the authority of the Chinese revolution and objective factors which draw the economically backward countries closer; the political immaturity of the peasant masses; and the petit-bourgeois illusions of certain leaders of the national movement."

viet support for the efforts of Southeast Asian nations, individually or collectively, to liquidate their foreign bases and stand ready to "repel any intrigues of the forces of imperialism and expansionism."[16]

Brezhnev made no commitment then or thereafter to the Soviet Union's refraining from supporting leftist revolutionaries (Soviet influence is limited to the Pathet Lao and factions of the Indonesian and Philippines parties), or to forming or joining a regional security organization. The substance of "collective security," as it turned out, depended on what Southeast Asian leaders chose to make of it. And since the response was at best equivocal, the thrust of Soviet activity in the region remained unilateral and bilateral, designed to make credible Moscow's contention that Asian governments can choose a third road besides accommodation to China or participation in the American security system.

ASPECTS OF INCREASED SOVIET INVOLVEMENT

A principal characteristic of Soviet penetration into southern Asia since the late 1960s has been its high visibility. An expanding Soviet navy and merchant fleet have undertaken hydrographic studies and increased trade, gone on "show-the-flag" missions, and been granted access to a number of ports from East Africa to Singapore. A brief enumeration of these activities will give some idea of their geographic as well as functional scope.

Probably as an adjunct of involvement in the Middle East and the Persian Gulf, but also related to increases in maritime activity in the Indian Ocean, the U.S.S.R. has gained

[16] V. Matveyev, in *Izvestia*, May 29, 1969. The full paragraph relevant to Brezhnev's June 7 remark is: "The independent states that have risen on the ruins of colonial empires do not need any guardians. They have the opportunities and means of defending their own interests, including the interests of security. The liquidation of foreign military bases in this part of the globe would provide the prerequisites for creating bases of collective security, and then those very countries which have defended their freedom will, by their joint efforts, strengthen peace and repel any intrigues of the forces of imperialism and expansionism." See also Matveyev's article of August 31, 1967, in *Izvestia*.

access to ports in Aden, Somalia (Mogadishu and Berbera), Yemen (Hodeida), and Mauritius. The announced purposes of such access differ, however. In some cases the Russians are improving harbors and docks; in others they are rebuilding ports or refueling and docking Soviet trawlers.[17] In Southeast Asia, Singapore agreed in 1970 to Soviet use of that island nation's extensive berthing facilities for all types of Soviet vessels. Coupled with access privileges reportedly granted Soviet ships on the east coast of India (Vishakhapatnam) and in the Andaman Islands (Port Blair), the Soviet Navy has thus acquired important stopovers between the Black Sea and Vladivostok.[18] These will provide much-needed (and long-denied) facilities for refueling, repairs, and replenishment of supplies.

In part, this access may relate to modest increases in Soviet trade with southern Asian countries (mainly India, the D.R.V., and Malaysia) and Japan. Trade with Asia is, of course, still only a fraction of total Soviet trade; but it will probably grow and, given the virtual absence of Soviet ships in prior years, probably does require that new port facilities become available to facilitate transporting their own and other countries' goods. The figures below reflect the trade situation through 1971.

But the political and strategic connotations of the trade are also pertinent. On December 25, 1970, the Royal Thai government signed its first trade agreement with the Soviet Union after years of operating on a barter basis. The agreement was preceded by several others concluded by Bangkok with the East European countries. It was followed by another that permits the Soviet national airline, Aeroflot, to land in Bangkok. In the same period, the Soviets were wooing Singapore's Prime Minister Lee Kuan Yew. At the end of an official visit

[17] See the articles by T. B. Millar, "Soviet Policies South and East of Suez," *Foreign Affairs,* October 1970 (Vol. XLIX, No. 1), pp. 70–80, and "The Indian Ocean—A Soviet Sea?" *The New York Times,* November 13, 1970, p. 35; also, *The New York Times,* October 18, 1970, pp. 1, 16.

[18] After the successful end of the Bangladesh struggle for independence, Soviet ships were invited to clear the major port of vessels sunk during the fighting.

SOVIET TRADE WITH SOUTHERN ASIA AND JAPAN*

S.E.A. Trade Partner	Soviet Imports					Soviet Exports				
	'65	'68	'69	'70	'71	'65	'68	'69	'70	'71
Burma	12	—	3	1	2	5	2	2	3	3
India	187	165	199	243	226	194	165	154	122	116
D.R.V.	28	16	15	70	22	67	143	170	166	139
Indonesia	29	17	21	25	10	49	5	3	4	10
Malaysia	101	90	110	111	78	—	—	2	2	2
Singapore	—	2	1	3	4	3	6	6	6	4
Thailand	1	—	—	1	4	2	3	3	3	2
Pakistan	4	10	21	28	35	12	33	36	32	26
Ceylon	17	15	13	12	14	19	11	8	5	8
Japan	160	167	237	311	356	167	352	321	341	377

(in millions of rubles)

*Sources for trade statistics are: *Vneshniaia torgovlia SSR za 1969 god: statisticheskii obzor* (USSR Foreign Trade in 1969: Statistical Handbook, Moscow, IMO, 1970, pp. 12-13; *Yearbook of International Trade Statistics: 1968*, United Nations, New York, 1970, p. 870; *Monthly Bulletin of Statistics*, June 1970, June 1972, United Nations, New York, 1970, 1972, p. 17.

to Moscow, the Prime Minister signed a communiqué that expressed the intention of further expanding trade, scientific, technical, and cultural cooperation.[19] Diplomatic and trade relations with the Philippines also may develop.[20] Improved relations with Thailand, Singapore, and the Philippines would probably not have been possible except for diminished confidence in Bangkok about the U.S. security commitment, concern in Singapore about economic losses due to the declining British presence "East of Suez," and pressure on the Marcos government in Manila to develop more diverse foreign relations. The Soviets have been quick to exploit these opportunities.

The strategic possibilities for the Soviet Union relate to the extraordinary growth of the Soviet Navy's Pacific Fleet in the last few years. The fleet consisted in 1970 of approximately 80 diesel submarines, 25 nuclear submarines, and 86 major surface ships, reflecting not only the overall modernization that has been occurring in the Soviet Navy but also the increased importance assigned the Far East.[21] For a fleet this size—excluding merchant shipping—the need for stopover points between the Mediterranean and Vladivostok is evident, although future increases in nuclear submarines and the phasing out of diesels might decrease that need.

If one keeps in mind the scope of U. S. Seventh Fleet operations, however, the Soviet Pacific Fleet has not really been

[19] Text of the communiqué is in *Pravda,* September 24, 1970.
[20] Trade with the Soviet Union was approved by the Philippine parliament in 1967 but failed to materialize. Early in 1972 President Marcos announced that trading relations would be established with the U.S.S.R. and other Communist countries, including China. President Marcos is on record as favoring diplomatic relations with Moscow but has seemed hesitant to take the plunge despite opposition pressure to adopt new policies toward the Communist world. For background, see "The Soviet Union and the Philippines: Prospects for Improved Relations," *Mizan,* May–June 1968 (Vol. X, No. 3), pp. 96–101. Not long ago, a commentary (Radio Moscow, January 28, 1971) observed that trade and technical ties between Moscow and Manila would greatly benefit the Philippines' economy and would respond to growing Filipino interest in ending their "one-sided orientation" toward the United States.
[21] Figures are from *The New York Times,* November 13, 1970, p. 35.

an imposing presence in Southeast Asia. The first showing of Soviet warships occurred in March 1968, soon after the British announcement of withdrawal from Singapore. Since then, while their number has run as high as 25 ships (including submarines), the reported average is from 6 to 15 annually.[22] Their activities include several show-the-flag visits to ports in the region; participation in a major naval exercise (most of which, however, was not in Asian waters); and probably the usual gamut of intelligence operations, in which case the Seventh Fleet is a likely focal point.[23] Additionally, the Pacific Fleet has been involved in hydrographic work and perhaps also in oceanographic studies being conducted jointly with Indian scientists.[24]

SOVIET OBJECTIVES

How should the expanding Soviet presence in Southeast Asia be interpreted? As already suggested, Soviet access to ports in the Indian Ocean area, and the increased number of Soviet warships seen there, may be necessary because of increasing trade and the need to protect the merchant fleet. As one writer has noted: "Already Russia has the world's sixth largest merchant fleet; and Moscow has announced that it will be increased by 50 per cent by 1975, with a growing proportion of the fleet in the Pacific and Indian Oceans, and with a consequential urge to have oceanic routes and port facilities assured."[25] This "urge" might become stronger in a

[22] *The New York Times*, October 18, 1970, p. 1. A year later, a spokesman for the U. S. Department of the Navy reported: "Russia now continuously maintains an average of approximately ten combatants and auxiliaries in the Indian Ocean area." U. S. House of Representatives, Committee on Foreign Affairs, Subcommittee on National Security Policy and Scientific Developments, *Hearings: The Indian Ocean—Political and Strategic Future*, 92d Congress, 1st Session, July 20–28, 1971, GPO, Washington, D.C., 1971, p. 180.

[23] See Millar, "Soviet Policies South and East of Suez," *loc. cit.*, pp. 72–73.

[24] *Red Star* (Moscow), January 8, 1970, and Tass international service broadcast, January 6, 1971.

[25] George G. Thomson, *Problems of Strategy in the Pacific and Indian Oceans*, National Strategy Information Center, New York, 1970, p. 23.

future conflict in Southeast Asia, should Soviet ships making deliveries to the ports of beleaguered allies have to be convoyed. In Vietnam, Soviet ships bearing military and economic supplies for the D.R.V. did not challenge the U.S. coastal blockade in 1972. In the future, they may not prove so reluctant to risk a confrontation if sufficient naval firepower can be assembled.

It is also plausible to hypothesize that the Soviet naval presence today has a strategic defensive mission. Submarines and trawlers improve Soviet ability to keep track of U. S. Polaris submarines, and generally to assure that the Indian Ocean is not dominated by a hostile power.[26] As one American analyst has argued,[27] U.S. nuclear submarines constantly patrol the Indian Ocean, linked up to a vast communications and servicing network that extends from North-West Cape, Australia, through Diego Garcia to Ethiopia. The Soviet Government, lacking sufficient antisubmarine warfare capability, may need an expanded fleet in the area to monitor American activities and offset U.S. strategic delivery power.

Politically as well as strategically, Soviet naval forces in the Indian Ocean also appear intended to encourage resistance among the region's governments to U.S. gunboat diplomacy. As phrased in one Russian statement:

> [The] Soviet naval presence on the oceans and seas curbs the imperialist warmongers, preventing them from carrying out their policy of blackmail and pressure . . . Soviet warships . . . are defending with honour the interests of their country and its friends, standing guard over the freedom of navigation and merchant shipping. The Indian Ocean, like any other ocean, can and must

---

[26] Visibility of the fleet may also be a function of both national and service pride. "The creation of a modern ocean-going Navy of the U.S.S.R. has put an end once and for all to the domination of the so-called 'Atlantic' powers of the world oceans." *Communist of the Armed Forces*, No. 12, June 1970.

[27] See the statement of Dr. O. M. Smolansky of Lehigh University in U. S. House of Representatives, *Hearings: The Indian Ocean*, pp. 195–96.

be used by all states for promoting international cooperation.[28]

The statement referred to a widespread interest in "the demilitarization of the Indian Ocean," a phrase compatible with the later declaration of nonaligned countries at Lusaka (Zambia) in September 1970[29] and with Secretary Brezhnev's proposal in 1971 for a mutual U.S.-U.S.S.R. naval force limitation in the Indian Ocean and the Mediterranean.[30] Soviet naval power may not yet be able to deter U.S. maneuvering on the high seas, as was demonstrated during the Indo-Pakistani war over Bangladesh,[31] but Soviet leaders can use their naval weakness to bargain with Washington (which Washington has not shown a willingness to do) and impress third world countries that Moscow alone wants to keep cold war confrontations away from the Indian Ocean.

Although U. S. Defense Department officials consistently testify otherwise, the main strategic advantage achieved by the Soviet military presence in South Asia is with respect to China, not the United States. Particularly on the subcontinent, Soviet military and economic aid to India since the mid-sixties has developed into a partnership that could be meaningful in the event of renewed Sino-Indian hostilities. Indian air bases

[28] Captain 1st Rank T. Belashohenko, "U.S. Big Stick Over the Indian Ocean," *Soviet Military Review,* 1969 (No. 12), p. 52.

[29] The Lusaka Declaration called for making the Indian Ocean "a zone of peace." It urged adoption of a statement by all countries agreeing that the area should be free from "great power rivalries and competition . . . , either army, navy or air force bases, . . . [and] nuclear weapons." Text of the declaration is in U. S. House of Representatives, *Hearings: The Indian Ocean,* pp. 202–4.

[30] Brezhnev's proposal was reported in *Washington Post,* June 12, 1971.

[31] According to a classified CIA document obtained by the columnist Jack Anderson, the Soviet Ambassador to India warned that entry of the U. S. Seventh Fleet into the Indian Ocean to interfere in the conflict might bring a Soviet naval response. But President Nixon dispatched a task force headed by the nuclear-powered aircraft carrier *Enterprise* with some 2,000 marines aboard, on the public pretext of assisting American citizens to leave Bangladesh. See Anderson, "Bay of Bengal and Tonkin Gulf," *Washington Post,* January 10, 1972.

and sea lanes might be used by the Soviet forces against China —which perhaps are the kinds of activities Chinese commentators had in mind when they said "gunboat diplomacy" was a Soviet objective in the Indian Ocean.[32]

For the Soviet Union to challenge U.S. naval supremacy in Asia—that is, to be able to exert naval power for political and military advantages, as the United States has done, and thus to neutralize U.S. superiority—would require a substantially greater investment than Moscow is now making or seems interested in making in the Pacific Fleet. Alternatively, Soviet leaders would have to divert resources from two traditionally more important areas of Soviet security concern, Europe and the Middle East. Either course would entail a major shift of Soviet strategic and political priorities. It would also mean new military needs, some of them quite expensive: helicopter carriers equipped for antisubmarine warfare,[33] aircraft carriers, ballistic missile-bearing surface ships, and naval marines trained and equipped for quick movement. Even then, it is unlikely that Washington would sit still, given its present advantages in naval firepower, sea and air bases, mobility, communications, and training.[34]

Beyond all these obstacles are the political complications that would surely arise if the Soviet leadership were to seek military bases in Southeast Asia. The governments that have agreed on trade, diplomatic, and maritime relations with Moscow have become more, not less, sensitive to foreign military

[32] See, for example, *Jen-min jih-pao,* May 13 and June 9, 1969.
[33] The Soviet Union now has two such carriers, the *Leningrad* and the *Moskva,* stationed off Norway and in the Mediterranean.
[34] As reported in the previously cited U. S. House of Representatives hearings on the Indian Ocean, U.S. assets in the area include: the Seventh Fleet and the Middle East Force; regular training exercises in antisubmarine warfare and in coordination with SEATO and CENTO allies; periodic submarine crossings and port visits; communications and logistics for U.S. naval forces from Australia to Ethiopia via Diego Garcia; access to bases in Bahrain and (under a 1966 agreement) the British Indian Ocean Territory; commitments from Britain, Australia, and New Zealand to the defense of Malaysia and Singapore under a 1971 Five-Power Agreement; and major naval and air bases in Thailand, South Vietnam, the Philippines, and Taiwan.

involvement in their territories. Even if the Soviet Union were to reverse its present position and become interested in acquiring naval or air base rights in the Indian Ocean area, it is questionable whether governments close to Moscow, such as New Delhi or Hanoi,[35] not to mention any others, would grant such rights except under great threat from another power. Without the kind of relatively unimpeded access such as the United States presently enjoys in Southeast Asia, Soviet deployments would have to be limited. And without forward air bases to support naval and ground operations, Soviet land and sea forces would be highly vulnerable.

To sum up, Soviet activities in Southeast Asia would seem to have the following purposes:

(1) *Politically and psychologically*, they indicate the reach of Soviet power and political interest to Southeast Asia and an intention to exploit anxieties that may still exist in the region about declining U.S. involvement and Chinese-supported insurgency. The Soviets would hope to encourage the trend among the region's governments toward less direct forms of association with the United States, particularly with regard to U.S. bases. There does not, however, appear to be any Russian interest in taking on security obligations in Southeast Asia; the Indian subcontinent, Japan, and the border with China have much higher priority among Soviet Asian interests.

(2) *Economically*, Soviet activities seem mainly to aim at improving trade prospects, chiefly with Japan, having stopover facilities between the Mediterranean and Vladivostok, and increasing their ability to influence developments in the oil-rich Persian Gulf, an area that is probably not vital to the Soviet economy, but is vital to Western Europe, the United States, and Japan.

(3) *Strategically*, the Soviets pose a potential counterweight

[35] The government of India, for instance, has long been rumored to have reached agreement with Moscow on a Soviet base in Visnakhapatnam. But U.S. officials have reported that the Soviets have no base rights there or anywhere else in the Indian Ocean area. See U. S. House of Representatives, *Hearings: The Indian Ocean*, p. 175.

to U.S. and British naval supremacy in the Indian and Pacific Oceans. They have the means now to increase their surveillance and intelligence-gathering missions and to protect the sea lanes their merchant fleet is developing. They do not seem to believe that their interests in Southeast Asia or their opportunities there justify attempting to acquire bases or significantly expanding the Pacific Fleet to take on strategic offensive missions.

China's Policy
in Southeast Asia

FRANK LANGDON

China's foreign policy has undergone a tremendous change since the Cultural Revolution, not only because China has greatly modified its single-minded confrontation with all the other major powers, but also because it has begun to seek cooperation from other governments without much regard for their revolutionary character. The acceptance of American overtures and welcome to the American President in Peking were undoubtedly stimulated by fear of Soviet attack since 1969, but the abandonment of the long cold war between them and their actual cooperation have strengthened both countries' dealings with the Soviet Union. The enormous gain to China from the new or renewed government-to-government relations, and from its entrance into the United Nations, is pushing its interest in revolution and liberation movements into the background, and it is giving peaceful coexistence with non-Communist regimes a greater emphasis than ever before.

Although world revolution, along Chinese rather than Russian lines, is perhaps still the ultimate goal of China's foreign policy, it is more immediately concerned with its own security and enhancing its own influence on a global scale. The near alliance with the United States which grew out of the Chou-Nixon Communiqué of February 1972 is designed to help China counter its major perceived security threat, the Soviet Union.[1] On the other hand, its diplomatic efforts to lead the

[1] Thomas W. Robinson, "China in 1972: Socio-Economic Progress Amidst Political Uncertainty," *Asian Survey*, January 1973 (Vol. XIII, No. 1), pp. 3–4.

small and medium powers, even if they are not revolutionary, in the global struggle to attain economic as well as political independence of the hegemony of the two Super Powers are directed at achieving a new influence with a broad spectrum of states.[2]

China has abandoned the long-held hope that the United States could be driven from Asia and that China could become the dominant power, secure behind a ring of Communist or friendly neutral border states. It now accepts the more realistic likelihood that even if the U.S. withdrew from Asia, major powers such as the Soviet Union, Japan, and possibly even North Vietnam would continue strongly to influence an area such as Southeast Asia in ways which would be contrary to China's interests. For the time being, China views a U.S. presence in the region as desirable to counter, or balance, Soviet influence as it is the only power with sufficient naval and air capability to do so. As is discussed later, this consideration probably accounts for the Chinese willingness to overlook the American bases in Thailand in discussing better relations with that country. China quarreled in the past with North Vietnam over what it considered to be the only desirable strategy in Vietnam: protracted warfare on the Maoist model in order to defeat fully the United States and drive it out of Asia, and the avoidance of negotiations except to receive capitulation. After the change of Chinese policy it was with real consternation that North Vietnam received Chinese advice to negotiate and compromise with the United States, without even defeating the Thieu government in South Vietnam, in order to bring the war to an end.[3]

China has supported and still supports some anticolonial and liberation movements in the Middle East and Africa with arms and even with personnel, but it has been and is much

[2] "Speech by Chiao Kuan-hua, Chairman of Delegation of People's Republic of China," *Peking Review*, November 19, 1971 (Vol. XIV, No. 47), pp. 5–9; Harry Harding, Jr., "China: The Fragmentation of Power," *Asian Survey*, January 1972 (Vol. XII, No. 1), pp. 7–11.

[3] Douglas Pike, "North Vietnam in 1971," *Asian Survey*, January 1972 (Vol. XII, No. 1), pp. 22–23.

more concerned with such movements in Asia, especially in the states of Southeast Asia. The liberation movements and revolutionary governments which have received the greatest support have been those of Indochina. For the other Southeast Asian countries China has given endorsement and some very limited material backing to Communist or liberation movements which are pro-Chinese. However, it is now reducing such backing and is making an effort to cultivate the governments in power by offers of flood relief, willingness to trade, and exchanges of sports teams and business delegations. For most of the Southeast Asian governments the problem is the extent to which they should respond to these overtures or exercise caution for fear of heightened insurgency or difficulties with their resident Chinese populations.

China pretends to see no inconsistency in advocating both revolution and peaceful coexistence.[4] Its leaders say that liberation movements must obtain popular support and meet the needs of their own countries, and that China does not commit aggression by direct intervention in other countries, as do the two superpowers, the United States and the Soviet Union. In practice, however, China may increase or decrease its support for insurgent groups with regard to such things as training, weapons, sanctuary, hosting exiles, receiving official insurgent missions, propaganda campaigns, and various types of official and unofficial statements of approval. Strong verbal or material backing is seldom given as a result of a government's willingness to recognize China diplomatically.[5] China only openly endorsed Burma as a target for revolution when anti-Chinese riots occurred in 1967. When a government refuses Chinese offers of recognition and aid or adopts hostile policies such as recognition of Nationalist China, opposition to Peking in the United Nations, signing defense treaties with the United States, or giving military bases to the

[4] James Reston, "Official Transcript of the Wide-Ranging Interview with Premier Chou in Peking," *The New York Times,* August 10, 1971, pp. 14–15.
[5] Peter Van Ness, *Revolution and Chinese Foreign Policy: Peking's Support for Wars of National Liberation* (Berkeley: University of California Press, 1971), p. 175.

Americans, China may be quick to back liberation movements against that government.[6] During the Cultural Revolution those Communists or insurgents in other countries who showed devotion to Maoist ideology and methods were given enthusiastic endorsement by Peking in order to further its dispute with Moscow and strengthen its leadership of the Third World. This subservience was apt to be counter-productive to the success of the local movement, as in Thailand and Malaysia where its popular impact was weakened.

It is necessary to explore these types of aid activity to insurgent groups as well as overtures to governments with respect to each of the states of Southeast Asia to explicate fully China's policies toward that region.

Burma has long served as the model of China's policy of friendly coexistence with its smaller non-Communist neighbors. It was one of the first states with which China made a border treaty in 1961. Thereafter, enormous numbers of officials of both countries visited back and forth in what was called a cousinly relationship (Pauk-Phaw).[7] Burma carefully maintained a policy of neutrality in which it avoided military cooperation with other states to prevent provocation of China. China in return sponsored trade with Burma which was especially appreciated as supplying consumers' goods which it could not have obtained elsewhere. An interest-free $84 million loan was also given to Burma in 1961.

The Burmese government, however, practiced a form of neutrality which did not always favor China to the extent that the latter desired. It did not result in official Burmese denunciation of American policy in the Vietnam War, nor in denunciation of any other party. On the contrary, Burma covertly accepted an $88 million military assistance program from the United States.[8] Burma also refused to permit Naga

<hr />

[6] *Ibid.*, p. 176, also pp. 166–86.

[7] Frank N. Trager, "Sino-Burmese Relations: the End of the Pauk-Phaw Era," *Orbis*, Winter 1968 (Vol. XI, No. 4), pp. 1039–45.

[8] Robert A. Holmes, "China-Burma Relations Since the Rift," *Asian Survey*, August 1972 (Vol. XII, No. 8), p. 692.

tribesmen from India to cross its territory for the purpose of guerrilla training in China. This contrasted with the other friendly non-Communist neutral, Cambodia, where Prince Sihanouk was forced to tolerate North Vietnamese army sanctuaries which China supported. On its part, China never gave up covert support of the Communist Party of Burma (White Flag Communists) whose leaders received training and sanctuary in China as did antigovernment rebels among non-Burman ethnic minorities in Burma. During the Cultural Revolution in 1967 the outbreak among the overseas Chinese in Burma instigated by Chinese embassy personnel resulted in anti-Chinese riots despite Prime Minister Ne Win's attempt to calm the antagonized Burmese. After the rioting the Chinese government openly backed the Burmese Communists and verbally encouraged them to overthrow the government.[9] The Burmese armed forces succeeded in driving the Burmese Communists from southern and central Burma, where they were conducting a terrorist campaign, to the north near the China border where some clashes occurred with the Chinese People's Liberation Army.

When Chou En-lai managed to get back control of the Chinese foreign ministry from Cultural Revolution Group extremists in 1968, hostility to the Burmese government declined and Chinese support of people's war in Burma did not reach the level of that then directed toward Vietnam, Thailand, Laos, and Malaysia. In 1969 Ne Win made efforts to achieve a reconciliation, and the following year ambassadors of the two countries returned to their posts. In 1971 Ne Win visited Peking for the first time since 1966;[10] a new trade agreement was approved, and the large unused portion of the interest-free loan cut off in 1967 was made available again. During this period the Chinese media also refrained from hostile verbal attacks on Burma. While the early 1970s saw a significant improvement in Sino-Burmese relations, the Chinese government did not cease all support for antigovern-

---

[9] *Ibid.*, pp. 686–91.

[10] "Chairman Mao Meets Chairman Ne Win and Madame Ne Win," *Peking Review*, August 13, 1971 (Vol. XIV, No. 33), p. 3; "Chairman and Madame Ne Win in Peking," p. 4.

ment forces in Burma. In April 1971 the Burmese Communist "Voice of the People of Burma" began to broadcast with Chinese support.[11] Also, two weeks before Ne Win's visit Chou En-lai was photographed in Peking with the vice-chairman of the Burmese Communist Party, and the *Peking Review* printed the Burmese Party's congratulations on the Chinese Party's fiftieth anniversary which called Ne Win an "imperialist lackey."[12] Thus, by 1971 China had ended its overt hostility to Burma and had returned to its earlier policies of friendly diplomacy, trade, and economic aid. At the same time it has seemed determined to continue at least moral support to Burmese rebels in order to maintain its revolutionary image with the Soviet Union and the Third World and to remind the Burmese government of its ability to make life unpleasant for it. Burma's policy of comparatively strict neutrality has not changed, but it did terminate the American military aid in the interest of reconciliation with China by June 30, 1971. To maintain China's goodwill and its own independence, the Burmese government has also refrained from any participation in regional bodies such as the Association of Southeast Asian Nations (ASEAN) and has felt compelled to tolerate at least covert Chinese encouragement of small-scale subversive and insurgent activities in Burma.

North Vietnam presents a sharp contrast to Burma in being the only Southeast Asian state led by a Communist government and in receiving much direct military assistance from China. Chinese Communist association with Vietnamese Communist leaders goes back to the 1920s, and Chinese assistance was given in the 1940s to Ho Chi Minh, Pham Van Dong, and Vo Nguyen Giap when they were refugees in China. Vietnamese divisions were trained in South China in 1950, and in 1955 China provided a $325 million loan for

[11] Deirdre Mead Ryan, "The Decline of the 'Armed Struggle' Tactic in Chinese Foreign Policy," *Current Scene*, December 1972 (Vol. X, No. 12), p. 4.

[12] Holmes, *loc. cit.*, p. 696; "From Central Committee of Communist Party of Burma (sic)," *Peking Review*, July 23, 1971 (Vol. XIV, No. 30), p. 16.

reconstruction of North Vietnam after the ceasefire with the French. However, despite China's dedication to being the center for world revolution, it has not been wholehearted in its support of its fraternal revolutionary neighbor. Like the Burmese government, the Vietnamese Communist leaders have refused to be subservient to China; they quarreled with Peking over the use of the reconstruction loan and did not follow China's example closely in domestic social change. Relations were relatively cool until the American escalation of the Vietnam War in 1964 despite Vietnamese support of the Chinese in the Sino-Soviet dispute. Fearing an American attack upon itself, China stepped up its aid to Southeast Asian liberation fronts and Communist movements. In 1965 it had as many as 30,000 to 50,000 People's Liberation Army personnel in North Vietnam to repair the bombed out communication lines.[13] The Sino-Soviet dispute, however, led to Chinese delays in transporting Soviet military equipment to Vietnam in 1965, even at the risk to its North Vietnamese comrades and consequently to its own security.[14] However, annual agreements were begun by China and Vietnam providing economic, technical, and military aid, and a new loan agreement was made. Because of the necessity of Soviet support, particularly in planes and missiles after American air attacks, North Vietnam has had to take a neutral position in the Sino-Soviet dispute but has still managed to get help from both sides despite the Chinese refusal to moderate the dispute.

As early as 1963 North Vietnam dropped the emphasis on China's revolutionary model to insist on its own independent policies. Contrary to China's urging it has shown a preference for large-scale engagements with American forces instead of complete reliance on guerrilla warfare, willingness to negotiate, emphasis upon the urban proletariat instead of the peasantry, and its own plans instead of adulation of Mao and

[13] Daniel D. Lovelace, *China and "People's War" in Thailand, 1964–1969* (Berkeley: Center for Chinese Studies, University of California, 1971), p. 79.

[14] Robert O'Neill, *Peking-Hanoi Relations in 1970* (Canberra: Australian National University Press, 1971), p. 2.

the Cultural Revolution.[15] China has shown a greater enthusiasm for the National Liberation Front of South Vietnam and its Provisional Revolutionary Government than it has for the North Vietnamese upon whom the South Vietnamese depend.[16] Despite the necessity of funneling all South Vietnam insurgent aid through North Vietnam, China tries to enhance its influence with the South Vietnam Front and its revolutionary government in competition with North Vietnam. This can be seen in the official visit of the Provisional Revolutionary Government's Foreign Minister, Madame Nguyen Thi Binh, to China in December 1972.[17] China accepts the ambassador of the Provisional Revolutionary Government as the representative of the only legitimate government in South Vietnam. It strongly opposes the Thieu regime in Saigon, and at the Tokyo meeting of the Economic Commission for Asia and the Far East (ECAFE) in April 1973 it called for the Saigon government's expulsion from that body.[18] Insofar as the Provisional Revolutionary Government hopes to have some independence from the North Vietnamese, Chinese recognition and support is valuable to it, and both governments have an interest in mutual support against North Vietnam.[19]

From pursuing a hard line on the Vietnam War, even more intractable than that of North Vietnam, during the Cultural Revolution, China shifted its general policy during the early 1970s. China as well as the Soviet Union became intent on improving relations with the United States, and by 1972 both wanted North Vietnam to negotiate an end to the war. The

[15] John C. Donnell and Melvin Gurtov, "North Vietnam: Left of Moscow, Right of Peking," in Robert A. Scalapino, ed., *The Communist Revolution in Asia* (2nd ed.; Englewood Cliffs, N.J.: Prentice-Hall, Inc., 1969), pp. 174–75.

[16] O'Neill, *op. cit.*, p. 2 ff.

[17] "Chairman Mao Meets Foreign Minister Nguyen Thi Binh," *Peking Review,* January 5, 1973 (Vol. XVI, No. 1), p. 5; joint communiqué, pp. 14–15.

[18] "China Attacks Khmer, Russia at ECAFE," *Japan Times Weekly,* International Edition, April 21, 1973 (Vol. XIII, No. 15), p. 2.

[19] O'Neill, *op. cit.*, p. 11.

basis of the Vietnamese war policy began to disintegrate as it was no longer as feasible to play off the Chinese against the Russians.[20] Despite Chou En-lai's frequent trips to Hanoi to reassure the Vietnamese, the new Chinese foreign policy was a terrible shock to North Vietnam.[21] Peking strongly supported the Paris Agreements of January 7, 1973, which enabled the American forces to withdraw completely from South Vietnam shortly afterward.[22] China also participated in the international conference in February to ratify the agreements. The outcome was the recognition that there were two regimes in South Vietnam: the Saigon government backed by the United States and the Provisional Revolutionary Government backed by China and North Vietnam. There was no victory for either side, and both the North Vietnamese and the United States are prepared to continue to sustain their respective parties in the south. This may be not unwelcome to China as it will check the expansion of North Vietnamese and Soviet influence. Had the North Vietnamese won a free hand for the Provisional Revolutionary Government in the south, they could have dominated it through their military and economic aid. Since North Vietnam itself is heavily dependent for military aid on the Soviet Union, the latter might have strengthened its foothold in the region. The Thieu regime can count on continued American air and naval support, if needed; American bases in nearby Thailand were strengthened, and American power continues to balance that of the other major powers (thus being in accord with China's new policy). This does not bode well for the commitment to revolution, but China is still backing the Provisional Revolutionary Government which may be inclined to look to

[20] Douglas Pike, "North Vietnam in 1971," *Asian Survey*, January 1972 (Vol. XII, No. 1), pp. 22–23.

[21] Douglas Pike, "North Vietnam in the Year 1972," *Asian Survey*, January 1973 (Vol. XIII, No. 1), p. 55.

[22] "Agreement on Ending the War and Restoring Peace in Vietnam," *Department of State Bulletin*, February 12, 1973 (Vol. LXVIII, No. 1755), pp. 169–74; "Chinese Party and State Leaders Warmly Greet the Signing of the Paris Agreement," *Peking Review*, February 2, 1973 (Vol. XVI, No. 5), pp. 3–4.

China for some countervailing influence in the contest among the Communist regimes.

In Laos, China has managed to maintain diplomatic relations with the Royal Laotian government in Vientiane and at the same time give considerable support to the insurgent Lao Patriotic Front under the leadership of the Lao People's Party (Communist). The Indochina war only spread to Laos in 1953 when it was invaded by the Viet Minh who were accompanied by some radical Laotians. The ceasefire with the French in 1954 resulted in no formal division of the country such as ensued in Vietnam, but the Free Laos Front, as it was then called, nevertheless located its regime, termed the "State of Laos" or "Pathet Lao," in the two northern provinces. There it regrouped its own military forces which together with the Vietnamese troops had occupied the mountainous eastern two-thirds of the country, an area which they hold today.[23]

China took part in the 1954 Geneva negotiations and supported the settlement. Viet Minh troops were withdrawn for a time to what is now North Vietnam. Unlike the Vietnam parties, the Free Laos Front managed to participate in a tripartite coalition government in Vientiane together with so-called neutralist elements under Prince Souvanna Phouma, the present Prime Minister, as well as some right-wing elements. When this coalition quickly broke down, warfare was renewed between the two Laotian regimes with much external aid: China, North Vietnam, and the Soviet Union provided aid to the Pathet Lao and the neutralists, while the United States aided the rightists. Again a Geneva conference was convened with the same parties in 1961–62. China again supported the settlement and the resulting coalition which broke down once more. Despite this unprepossessing train of events, China has maintained its diplomatic representation in Vientiane with the Royal Laotian government, but also has con-

[23] Bernard B. Fall, "The Pathet Lao: a 'Liberation' Party," in Robert A. Scalapino, ed., *The Communist Revolution in Asia* (2nd ed.; Englewood Cliffs, N.J.: Prentice-Hall, Inc., 1969), pp. 185–211.

tinued to support the Pathet Lao with material and personnel aid as well as maintaining a consulate in Phong Saly and a mission in Khang Khay in the Pathet Lao area. As China regards the Pathet Lao as a legitimate party in the coalition governments provided for by both the Geneva Agreements, it has kept up its ties with both regimes in Laos while giving strong preference to the Pathet Lao.[24]

Because of its dispute with the Soviet Union, China not only put obstacles in the way of Soviet arms aid deliveries to North Vietnam but also insisted that some Soviet aid to Laos be reduced. It induced North Vietnam to refuse the direct use of airports and roads to the Russian planes and vehicles. The Chinese apparently intended thus to limit Soviet influence and activity in North Vietnam and Laos even if it weakened the common Communist front in the Indochina war. Thus, China further showed its willingness to put its concept of its national interest before that of Communist internationalism. The result of the interdiction of Russian equipment to the Laotian neutralists was a loss of their strength and a further extension of the Pathet Lao's domination of most of the mountainous area through which North Vietnam sent troops and supplies to South Vietnam. North Vietnam also kept its troops in the Pathet Lao area to guard the Ho Chi Minh Trail and to spearhead attacks by Laotian forces against the Royal Laotian army.

Neither China nor North Vietnam has favored attempts to overthrow the Vientiane regime or extend Pathet Lao control over the lowlands in order to avoid stimulating a large-scale American intervention in that area. By at least some superficial honoring of the Geneva Agreements they have imposed a check upon the United States and insured a certain amount of foreign diplomatic and political support to a somewhat neutralist Vientiane regime that tolerates Communist activity in the Lao Patriotic Front area. After the United States escalated the war in 1965, the necessity for maintaining

[24] For the as yet unimplemented third agreement for another coalition in Laos, see "Agreement on Restoring Peace and Achieving National Concord in Laos," *Peking Review*, March 2, 1973 (Vol. XVI, No. 9), pp. 7–9.

the Royal Laotian government in order to facilitate Communist operations in the Lao Front area became even greater. This further explains China's continued good relations with Vientiane. During the Cultural Revolution Chinese propaganda material was distributed in Vientiane which resulted in open ridicule in pro-Nationalist Chinese newspapers. Prime Minister Souvanna Phouma was quick to appease the Chinese by closing down the offending papers. No anti-Chinese outbreaks occurred as in Burma or as threatened in Cambodia to jeopardize relations. Nor were the more responsible Chinese leaders willing to disturb the Royal Laotian regime.

In the Patriotic Front area there was some response to the Cultural Revolution where the local leadership did display some enthusiasm for Maoism.[25] This may have reflected some dissatisfaction in respect to the dominance of the North Vietnamese who were the source of much of the aid coming to the Lao Front and whose military forces dominated the region. To cite an example, the Lao Front disliked North Vietnam's frequent use of Pathet Lao troops for coolie work in transporting supplies to South Vietnam. The Lao Front thus seemed to have an interest in cultivating the Chinese for the sake of countering the North Vietnamese, as do the South Vietnamese Front leaders.

In the current phase of the Indochina war the United States has covertly intervened, as has the North Vietnamese army, by forming local forces of Meo tribesmen which are recruited, trained, and paid by the United States Central Intelligence Agency and supported by "privately" owned bombing planes. These are aided by "volunteers" recruited among ethnic Lao in Thailand and trained and paid by Thailand. China has not provided fighting men but has about 20,000 troops building and guarding the only modern paved road in the Lao Front area.[26] The Americans scrupulously avoid flying bombers near this road, which provides direct

[25] Chae-Jin Lee, *Communist China's Policy Toward Laos: A Case Study, 1954–67* (Lawrence: Center for East Asian Studies, University of Kansas, 1970), pp. 138–40.

[26] Joseph J. Zasloff, "Laos 1972: The War, Politics and Peace Negotiations," *Asian Survey*, January 1973 (Vol. XIII, No. 1), pp. 61–66.

access from China to Laos and potentially to Thailand and beyond, although the road has not yet been carried to the Thai border. It also enables China to give more direct support to the Pathet Lao.

As in South Vietnam and Cambodia, China is heavily committed to a local Communist-led organization which is dominated by North Vietnam. However, it has maintained good diplomatic relations with the non-Communist government and has consistently displayed support for a coalition regime. China's new policy displays less wholehearted support for North Vietnam and puts more emphasis upon checks of its rivals by a balancing of influential outside states and groups within Laos. This is manifested by China's support for new coalition attempts in Laos. Such a regime would be less likely to be dominated by Hanoi and would provide more scope for Chinese influence, as Laos is a corridor to much of Southeast Asia beside South Vietnam. China probably favors a coalition regime in South Vietnam for similar reasons as well.

In comparison to its policy in respect to other Southeast Asian states, China has pursued a rather consistent policy toward Laos since the 1950s—although for somewhat different reasons during different time periods. At first, it backed a coalition government and a balancing of external influences in the country primarily for the sake of the more important struggle in South Vietnam and to prevent the possibility of greater American involvement in this neighboring state. Since the early 1970s it has pursued a comparable policy largely in order to limit North Vietnamese and Soviet influence in the country, to maintain some American involvement, and to project a new image of itself as a pragmatic government which is willing to engage in traditional diplomatic relations and bargaining.

Cambodia, like Burma, is the other small non-Communist neighbor with which China has carried on its policy of peaceful coexistence with considerable success. Unlike Burma, Cambodia followed a policy of pro-Communist neutrality under Prince Sihanouk's Royal Government of National Union. This policy refused cooperation with the anti-Communist military policies of its neighbors but tolerated clandestine activities of the North Vietnamese and the National Liberation Front of South Vietnam. China's first economic aid agreement was made with Cambodia to reward it for the Prince's refusal to accept the protection of the Southeast Asia Treaty Organization (SEATO) sponsored by the United States in 1954 to prevent the spread of Communism in Indochina and Southeast Asia.[27] Unlike Thailand and South Vietnam, Cambodia did not offer military bases to the United States or accept American advisors or military forces, but it did ignore the sanctuaries of the South Vietnamese Front and North Vietnamese government forces in southeastern Cambodia for support of the war in South Vietnam.

This policy succeeded in keeping hostilities out of Cambodia until 1970, despite its important role in the war. The Cambodian Communists who lead what is called the Cambodian People's National Liberation Armed Forces were so weak before the first Geneva Conference that they did not win a separate area of the country, as did the Communists of Vietnam and Laos. When Cambodia attained its independence in 1954, it was all united under Prince Sihanouk. The Cambodian Communists were even more dependent upon their North Vietnamese Communist sponsors than was the Laotian party, and China gave only nominal support to their insurgency (as did North Vietnam), in view of the government's cooperation in Vietnamese military operations in Cambodia.

This policy collapsed when the anti-Communist army commander, Lon Nol, seized control in the Prince's absence in March 1970. China approached him to secure continued toleration of the Vietnamese Communist bases for which Cambodia had been compensated in the past,[28] but the invasion of Cambodia by American and South Vietnamese forces in April ended this arrangement. Even after the Ameri-

[27] Melvin Gurtov, *China and Southeast Asia—The Politics of Survival* (Lexington, Mass.: D. C. Heath & Co., 1971), pp. 167–78.

[28] Harold C. Hinton, *China's Turbulent Quest* (Bloomington: Indiana University Press, 1972), p. 299, Rev. ed.; O'Neill, *op. cit.,* p. 8.

cans and South Vietnamese withdrew about a year later, fighting continued as the North Vietnamese-backed Cambodian Liberation Forces took control of much of the country from government forces. The American forces supported Lon Nol's regime with bombing from the air and supplied military equipment and funds, but the North and South Vietnamese Communists were able to preserve their base in Cambodia. Chinese supplies to Vietnam via the Cambodian coast were stopped, but some Chinese advisors were sent to Cambodia via Laos.[29]

Prince Sihanouk's decision to seek refuge in Peking gave the Chinese government the opportunity to support his government in exile in order to retain some separate influence in Indochina in competition with North Vietnam, which dominated the Communist insurgents. It sponsored an Indochina summit conference in China in April 1973 to which were invited the leaders of the four Communist or liberation movements: Prince Sihanouk, who headed the National United Front of Kampuchea as well as the Royal Cambodian government-in-exile; Prince Souphanouvong, who represented the Lao Patriotic Front; President Nguyen Huu Tho, who headed the Provisional Revolutionary Government of South Vietnam; and Pham Van Dong, Prime Minister of North Vietnam. Chou En-lai gave a banquet where he pledged strong support of China to the four movements which agreed to work together closely.[30]

The personal ties between Sihanouk and Chou were helpful in the current collaboration of the two leaders. During the Cultural Revolution, when Chinese leadership demanded great Maoist orthodoxy from Communists and radical friends abroad, the Cambodian Chinese began radical agitations risking the sort of reaction that occurred in Burma. Fortunately, while Sihanouk took strong measures to control the Chinese and prevent outbreaks in Cambodia, Chou regained control of the Foreign Ministry in 1968 to prevent the sort of hostile policy adopted toward Burma, thus preserving good state-to-

29 *Ibid.*
30 O'Neill, *op. cit.*, pp. 8–9; Hinton, *op. cit.*, p. 198.

state relations.[31] Neither the Cambodian Communists nor the North Vietnamese were as favorable toward Sihanouk as was Chou En-lai, since the Prince had been the one to outlaw the Cambodian Communist leaders and denounce them as puppets of North Vietnam and the South Vietnam Front when he was in power. Nevertheless, they did collaborate with China to permit Sihanouk to secretly visit Cambodia as well as Hanoi in early 1973.[32] While this visit had the effect of legitimating a union between Sihanouk and the Cambodian Communists, in the insurgent areas and in Vietnam as well as in China, it appeared that he would be only the titular ruler of a future Communist-led regime, and hence China was likely to have little influence compared to North Vietnam.[33]

The January 1973 Paris agreement failed to halt the hostilities in Cambodia and Laos, but American pressure has slowly brought the Lon Nol regime to consider negotiation with the Sihanouk-Khieu Samphan group. If Henry Kissinger can induce North Vietnam to agree to halt the fighting in Laos and Cambodia, a tripartite coalition may also eventuate in Cambodia. Kissinger's deputy, the Assistant Secretary of State William Sullivan, has said he believes that China "would rather have four balkanised states in Indochina than an Indochina that was dominated by Hanoi and possibly susceptible to Moscow."[34] As China has given up the hope of excluding the United States, the Soviet Union, and Japan from Southeast Asia and fully understands that North Vietnam is likely to continue jealously to guard its independence from China

[31] Gurtov, *op. cit.*, pp. 118–22.

[32] "Congratulations to Samdech Sihanouk on His Successful Viet Nam Visit," *Peking Review*, February 16, 1973 (Vol. XVI, No. 7), p. 5; John Burns, "Sihanouk Returns Encouraged," *Christian Science Monitor*, April 14, 1973, p. 7; Charlotte Saikowski, "Sihanouk's Stock Rises in Cambodian Impasse," *ibid.*, April 16, 1973, pp. 1, 6.

[33] Denzil Peiris, "And Now, L'État C'est Le Peuple," *Far Eastern Economic Review*, April 16, 1973 (Vol. LXXX, No. 15), pp. 10–11.

[34] Quoted in Edith Lenart, "Sihanouk on the Move," *Far Eastern Economic Review*, February 5, 1973 (Vol. LXXIX, No. 5), pp. 14, 18.

in full accord with China's own doctrine that "nations, big or small, should be equals without distinction," it can maximize its own influence by a peaceful balancing.[35] Coalition regimes seem to promise at least to minimize the strength of its rivals in the area, including North Vietnam, and provide more scope for China to attempt to maximize its own influence through friendly trade and aid. The combining of the Communist and non-Communist elements in the local regimes will enable China to satisfy its desire to support progressive movements without being in conflict with the local government. It is possible that these will be more satisfactory to China than purely Communist regimes would be if they were uncooperative.

China has no diplomatic relations with the five states of maritime Southeast Asia, all of which have Maoist insurgent movements approved by the government in Peking. These governments have tended to be anti-Communist and anti-Chinese and have supported or approved of American intervention in Indochina. Thailand, Malaysia, Indonesia, Singapore, and the Philippines make up the Association of Southeast Asian Nations (ASEAN) which agreed in the Declaration of Kuala Lumpur of November 1971 that Southeast Asia should be a zone of peace, freedom, and neutrality. To be genuinely neutral the members would have to abandon their security arrangements, such as those of Thailand and the Philippines with the United States, and of Malaysia and Singapore with Britain, Australia, and New Zealand. Also, the great powers need to agree to respect the neutral zone. The Soviet Union has countered with the proposal of sponsoring a collective security organization. Since the Chinese leaders have already denounced the proposal as effectively an anti-Chinese alliance, they would refuse to join. It would inevitably become an alliance, like those sponsored by the United States in the past, ranged against China and possibly the

[35] "Down with the Doctrine of Big-Nation Hegemony," *Peking Review*, January 29, 1971 (Vol. XIV, No. 5), pp. 6–7; Harry Harding, Jr., "China: The Fragmentation of Power," *Asian Survey*, January 1972 (Vol. XII, No. 1), p. 10.

United States or other regional nonmembers. Southeast Asia could not become neutral or insulate itself from great power quarrels if it was ranged with one of them against the others.

China has denounced the Soviet proposal as an attempt to revive the China encirclement schemes pioneered by the American Secretary of State John Foster Dulles in the 1950s. China has endorsed the ASEAN proposal in principle, pending more friendly relations. Liao Ch'eng-Chih, a senior advisor to the Chinese foreign ministry, told visiting Japanese newsmen, "China supported the principle of neutrality featuring national independence, democracy, and peace which the Philippines, Indonesia, Malaysia, Singapore, and Thailand have worked out. These countries, however, sometimes say they want to improve relations with China, but at other times they step back, saying they are afraid. We do not fret, rush, or threaten, and we will watch the developments in regard to this situation."[36]

Relations between China and Thailand have been hostile since the early 1950s, but they have been particularly poor since 1964 when American intervention began to escalate in the Indochina war. Thailand has always feared the extension of Chinese influence in Southeast Asia, and has seen Communist movements as a vehicle of such influence.[37] With the establishment of the Communist government in Peking the Thai government became involved in a struggle to prevent the local Thai Chinese associations from favoring Peking against the Chinese Nationalists, and it opposed friendly relations with Peking which might permit extensive Chinese influence in the country. It has also acted as an ally with the United States and invited American air force per-

[36] U. S. Department of Commerce, National Technical Information Service, Foreign Broadcast Information Service (FBIS), *Daily Bulletin* (Asia and the Pacific), March 12, 1973. Hereafter, reference to *Daily Bulletin* will be to FBIS, *Daily Bulletin*, etc.

[37] David A. Wilson, "Thailand, Laos and Cambodia," in Wayne Wilcox, Leo E. Rose, Gavin Boyd, eds., *Asia and the International System* (Cambridge, Mass.: Winthrop Publishers, 1972), pp. 188–89.

sonnel to be stationed in Thailand in the early sixties, and it subsequently supplied forces in South Vietnam.

China was fearful of the American military buildup in Thailand in the mid-1960s, so it openly endorsed the Thai Liberation Movement and the moribund Thai Communist Party[38] by supplying some advisors, weapons, and training to Thai insurgents. North Vietnam was also a principal backer of the insurgents and was in close contact with the Vietnamese refugees who went to Thailand during the war with the French. The Thai Communists showed a gratifying enthusiasm for Maoist ideas and methods during the Cultural Revolution; this pleased the Chinese radicals in Peking, who were engaged in an ideological dispute with the Soviet Union, as it suggested the superiority of Chinese ideas in the Asian Communist movement. However, it was probably counterproductive to the Thai movement which thus appeared more subservient to China. It reduced the importance of the Thai nationalist elements involved as well as raising the old question of the loyalty to China of the ethnic Chinese in Thailand.

Despite the more open Chinese endorsement of Thai revolution in response to the greater Thai involvement in the Indochina war, the increased but moderately sized insurgency has been confined to outlying sections of the country where there are guerrilla strongholds along the lines of the Maoist model. The repeated government campaigns to wipe out the insurgents have not been successful, but, on the other hand, the insurgents have not been able to extend their control beyond some remote villages and rural areas. Nor have they interfered with the American air bases in Thailand which are now a principal source of American firepower being used in Cambodia and Laos. The Thai forces have been withdrawn from South Vietnam, but Thai military advisors pay, train, and recruit ethnic Lao living in Thailand for fighting in Laos as "volunteers."

China has shown, nevertheless, a disposition to improve relations with Thailand in its new policy of the early seven-

[38] Daniel D. Lovelace, *China and "People's War" in Thailand, 1964–1969* (Berkeley: Center for Chinese Studies, University of California, 1971), p. 80.

ties. When Marshall Green went to Bangkok to report on the Kissinger and Nixon talks in Peking, he stated that the Chinese had not since raised the question of the American bases in Thailand as an obstacle to better relations.[39] The Thai, who were initially shocked and startled by the announcement of the Nixon visit to China and what seemed to be a fundamental realignment of the major powers, have begun to show greater independence in their foreign policy and more flexibility toward China. Foreign Minister Thanat Khoman initiated contact with Peking to consider better relations. Progress was interrupted by the dismissal of Thanat and the dissolution of the Thai National Assembly in late 1971, but the military leaders, Prime Minister Kittikachorn and Deputy Prime Minister Praphat Charusathian, then sent a Chinese expert, Dr. Prasitthi Kanachanawat, to China as an advisor to the Thai ping-pong team.[40] He talked to Chou En-lai suggesting that China discontinue its support of the Thai insurgents. Dr. Prasitthi went again with a group of traders invited to the Canton Trade Fair and again talked to Chou. The Chinese leader did not object to the American bases in Thailand, but he did say that China was committed to supporting movements of national liberation. Chou also claimed that China did not interfere in the domestic affairs of other countries. The seeming contradiction may have been meant to imply that China would not undertake direct or large-scale intervention but felt free to continue endorsement and small-scale backing depending on the attitude of the Thai government.

China showed a willingness to increase trade contacts with Thailand, and although Thai laws forbid private trade, the government is willing to permit government-to-government arrangements. Despite the increase of informal trade and cultural contacts between China and Thailand, the hostilities in Indochina continue to be an obstacle to a substantial easing of relations under the present military leadership. The Prime Minister of Thailand continues to accuse China as well as

[39] Saville R. Davis, "Thai Chinese Feelers Starting to Mesh?" *Christian Science Monitor,* May 16, 1973, p. 4.
[40] *Ibid.*

North Vietnam of infiltrating Communist terrorists.[41] The Deputy Prime Minister told newsmen that American air force units "must continue to be based in Thailand until North Vietnamese forces leave Laos and Cambodia and other cease-fire agreements are carried out. We don't lose any national honour, as charged by some persons, by allowing the U. S. Air Force to remain stationed here for regional stability and aid to our own security in these uncertain times. Only when there is real peace in Indochina will there be no more need for an American presence here. At that time we can ask the Americans to leave and then we can proceed with setting up a neutrality zone in Southeast Asia."[42] China too shows its determination to discourage Thai participation in the Indochina war and its still hostile China policy by strong verbal endorsement for the Thai insurgents through its broadcasts of the "Voice of the People of Thailand," and also through its own commentary over the New China News Agency broadcasts.[43]

China's policy toward Malaysia has had a long history of support for insurrection. It endorsed the struggle of the Malayan Races Liberation Army led by the Malayan Communist Party, which was made up mainly of local ethnic Chinese and lasted from 1948 to 1960. When Malaysia was formed with the addition of two British Borneo territories in 1963, China gave strong verbal support to the Indonesian confrontation with Malaysia and contested the legitimacy of the new state. It supported the separate North Kalimantan Unitary State Revolutionary Government claiming Borneo territories, which was made up mainly of ethnic Chinese as well as revived remnants of the Malayan Communist Party and Malayan National Liberation League operating on the Malaysian-Thai border. At this time China hoped to see the success of the Indonesian Communist Party in bringing about a revolution in Indonesia in cooperation with President Sukarno whose anti-

[41] FBIS, *Daily Report* (Asia and the Pacific), March 22, 1973.
[42] *Bangkok Post*, March 4, 1973, p. 3.
[43] FBIS, *Daily Report* (People's Republic of China), August 7, 1972, and March 21, 1973.

colonial and anti-Western policies were directed against Malaysia and toward leading Third World forces. China thus expected to enhance its own influence globally and regionally. It was also committed by its ideology to supporting indigenous liberation and Communist movements such as those in Malaysia, especially when they could be viewed as opposing neocolonial regimes.

Under Prime Minister Rahman, Malaysia was pro-Western and anti-Communist and initially supported American intervention in Indochina. But it gradually modified its anti-China policies as Communist insurgency remained confined to fairly remote areas and was relatively limited in scope. Although some fear continued that closer contact with China might strengthen divisive or subversive pro-China sentiment among the Malaysian Chinese, a contrary view gradually gained ascendance that better relations would discourage the Chinese insurgents and would encourage legitimate domestic Chinese organizations to cooperate with the Malaysian government since it was no longer hostile to China. This is explained elsewhere in this volume in greater detail in the discussion of the overseas Chinese.[44] Neither the communal riots in Malaysia in 1969 nor the temporary expedient of the Five Power Treaty of 1970, to provide added security during British withdrawal, prevented the trend toward a more neutral policy under the new Prime Minister Tun Razak. This nonalignment trend was aided by Malaysia's freedom from alliance ties with the United States and the absence of diplomatic relations with Nationalist China.

In Malaysia, China's new policy overtures of the early 1970s took the form of offers of assistance and trade. In February 1971 it offered $200,000 in flood relief.[45] In addition, a semiofficial Malaysian trade delegation, invited to visit China by a number of Chinese business groups, met Chou En-lai to discuss Malaysian neutralization proposals. Although the Chinese had already purchased some rubber

[44] See R. S. Milne's article, pp. 81–120.
[45] Marvin L. Rogers, "Malaysia and Singapore: 1971 Developments," *Asian Survey*, February 1972 (Vol. XII, No. 2), p. 173.

through Hong Kong and Singapore, an unofficial Chinese trade group returning the Malaysian visit bought 40,000 tons of rubber, as well as palm oil and timber; it also promised future purchases.[46] The governmental Malaysian National Corporation (PERNAS) has now become the sole importer and exporter of Chinese products for Malaysia.

Because of China's ambition to lead the smaller countries in their struggle against the economic exploitation of the big powers, it has strongly supported demands of smaller states to extend national controls over the adjacent seas. It is also interested in exclusive exploitation of its own offshore resources in order to restrict access to them by countries like the United States, the Soviet Union, and Japan, as well as to be in control over navigation in adjacent waters in order to restrict the activities of these states' warships. China has therefore supported strongly the Malaysian and Indonesian claims to the Malacca Straits as inland waters, to the distress of the three big maritime and naval powers whose commercial and military activities would be restricted by their implementation.

Unofficial exchanges of athletic teams and businessmen with China continue. The only official contacts seem to have been the meeting of the Prime Minister with the Chinese ambassador at a reception in Austria during a visit to Europe in September 1972 and the dispatch of Tan Sri Raja Mohar, a special economic advisor of the Prime Minister, to Peking in November. China's offer to set up diplomatic relations has not been accepted, according to Razak, because of hostile propaganda still coming from China.[47] The insurgent Voice of the Malayan Revolution is still permitted to operate from China. Malaysia and Thailand have undertaken joint campaigns against insurgents on their border. In April 1972 Malaysia and Indonesia set up a cabinet level committee to carry on the struggle against Communist guerrillas on the Borneo border. Malaysia has also coordinated its overall policy with that of Indonesia to an increasing extent, and the latter is still fearful, or professes to be fearful, of insurgent activities.

[46] M. G. G. Pillai, "Malaysian Boosting Trade," *Far Eastern Economic Review,* September 30, 1972, pp. 31–32.
[47] FBIS, *Daily Report* (Asia and the Pacific), August 14, 1972.

Malaysia followed Indonesia in walking out of the meeting of the nonaligned states at Guyana in August 1972 in protest against the admission of the Provisional Revolutionary Government of South Vietnam and of the Royal Cambodian Government of Prince Sihanouk, both of which are strongly supported by China.[48]

China now seems quite willing to expand commercial and governmental contacts with Malaysia. Its support for the local insurgencies which it must endorse at least formally for ideological reasons does not seem excessive. Chinese leaders suffer from the need to appease their own radical elements at home and to give lip service to a militant revolutionary image in their quarrel with the Soviet Union and struggle for global leadership. Malaysia may be waiting for Indonesia to move first on restoring diplomatic ties with China, so as not to jeopardize Malaysian-Indonesian relations.

China's initial policy toward Singapore—which, like Malaysia, was regarded as a semicolonial creation—was hostile.[49] China also endorsed the opposition to the government by the indigenous Malayan Communist Party, which in 1968 called for a Maoist armed struggle against the "puppet regimes" of both Singapore and Malaysia in order to establish a "People's Republic of Malaya."[50] This does not seem to have had much effect as Communist activity in Singapore has been comparatively minor, even during the Cultural Revolution.

Under China's new policy of the early seventies it seems prepared to recognize Singapore as a separate and independent country and to initiate better relations with its government and business community. As with the other Southeast Asian countries, trade missions have been exchanged and cultural relations undertaken. The Singapore Chinese Chamber of Commerce sent a mission to China in October 1971 at the

[48] Stephen Chee, "Malaysia and Singapore: Separate Identities, Different Priorities," *Asian Survey*, February 1973 (Vol. XIII, No. 2), p. 157.

[49] Pang Cheng Lian, "Singapore: Optimistic Signs," *Far Eastern Economic Review*, September 30, 1972, p. 32.

[50] Ryan, *loc. cit.*, p. 4.

invitation of China's Council for the Promotion of International Trade. China also offered to have up to ten ships a month stop in Singapore on the way to Europe to pick up shipments at freight rates 40 per cent below those of the Far East Freight Conference which otherwise monopolized shipping rates.[51] Chinese table tennis teams have also come to Singapore. China's willingness to normalize its relations with the government is further suggested by the acceptance of an invitation to the Chinese Ambassador in London to attend Singapore's celebration of its national day.

Singapore's reaction to Chinese overtures has been even more cautious than that of the other Southeast Asian states, for reasons discussed in the paper in this volume on the overseas Chinese.[52] Singapore's majority of citizens of Chinese derivation puts its government in a delicate position in its efforts to follow a multiracial policy domestically and a non-aligned position internationally. The Chinese table tennis team's visit of July 1972 was watched very closely. The Prime Minister's own assessment of local reactions was that he thought Singapore citizens showed identification with Singapore rather than with China. This implied that the government was successful in its efforts to create a national loyalty to Singapore and that it would not be too dangerous to loosen restrictions on contact with China.[53]

Prime Minister Lee Kuan Yew has come forward with resounding support for the continued presence of American bases in Thailand. This seems rather incautious and is a source of annoyance to some, like Thanat Khoman, who would like to see Thailand take a more nonaligned position.[54] The reason for Lee's attitude is probably the fear that any substantial withdrawal of the American presence in the region would

[51] *Straits Times,* November 6, 1971.
[52] See R. S. Milne's article, pp. 81–120.
[53] *Asia Research Bulletin,* August 1972 (Vol. II, No. 3), p. 1095.
[54] Lee Kuan Yew, "Southeast Asia and the New World Power Balance," *The Mirror* (Singapore), April 9, 1973 (Vol. IX, No. 15), p. 6; also, see Lee's views in "Greatest Danger to S.E. Asia—A Loss of Will," *The Mirror* (Singapore), January 29, 1973 (Vol. IX, No. 5), p. 1.

upset the role of the United States in balancing the presences of the Soviet Union, Japan, and China in the area.[55] Lee is also glad to have American bases in Thailand rather than in Singapore, where his own degree of nonalignment would be reduced. Since China is prepared to tolerate American bases to offset the Soviet Union and Japan, provided they are no longer used to carry on hostilities in Indochina, Lee would not necessarily antagonize China any longer by advocating them. China, in fact, is now following a strategy similar to Lee's in entering the balancing game. In addition, Lee is eager to see that local Communist movements remain checked on the other side of Thailand so that they will not easily be able to spread to Singapore.

Foreign Minister Rajaratnam said in Parliament on March 17, 1972, that Singapore must have some form of relations with China sooner or later, but that ASEAN members had agreed that before any member established diplomatic relations with China it would consult and coordinate its action with the others.[56] Singapore will act to enter into diplomatic relations only if Malaysia and Indonesia do so, in order to avoid unnecessarily provoking the fear that Singapore would become some sort of Chinese Communist fifth column in their midst, in view of its predominantly ethnic Chinese population.

The case of Indonesia differs greatly from that of the other countries of maritime Southeast Asia in that it had close and cordial relations with China under President Sukarno until the attempted coup d'état of September 1965, when pro-Communist officers tried to kill the high-ranking anti-Communist army leaders.[57] This led to the destruction of the Indonesian Communist Party, then one of the largest in

[55] Robert O. Tilman, "Malaysia, Singapore and the Philippines," in Wayne Wilcox, Leo E. Rose, Gavin Boyd, eds., *Asia and the International System* (Cambridge, Mass.: Winthrop Publishers, 1972), p. 214.

[56] *Asia Research Bulletin,* April 1972 (Vol. IX, No. 11), p. 788.

[57] Guy J. Pauker, "The Rise and Fall of the Communist Party of Indonesia," in Robert A. Scalapino, ed., *The Communist Revolution in Asia* (2nd ed.; Englewood Cliffs, N.J.: Prentice-Hall, Inc., 1969), pp. 282–84.

the world, and the belief by anti-Communist army leaders who came to control the government that Communist China was behind an attempt to set up a Communist regime in their country. The party chairman, D. N. Aidit, had been in close contact with Chinese leaders and supported the Chinese against the Russians. He also seemed to have adopted a more militant policy of revolution after his visit to China in 1963.[58]

In 1965 Peking gave enthusiastic support to President Sukarno's efforts to oppose the Western powers and "colonialism" in Malaysia, as well as to his plan to set up a separate kind of United Nations for the Third World.[59] After the coup attempt the new strongly anti-Communist army leadership in Indonesia, the liquidation of the Communist Party and of hundreds of thousands of members and sympathizers, and attacks on Chinese residents resulted in a great deterioration in relations with China. In Indonesia the strong racial prejudice against Chinese residents led to innumerable incidents of violence and cruelty against innocent people.[60] The *People's Daily* in Peking even compared Indonesian leaders with Hitler's fascists.[61] Following the coup, in which Peking does not seem to have been directly involved, it did not at first explicitly support or endorse any revolutionary activities against the Indonesian government, and it did not immediately withdraw its diplomats even after attacks upon them. It held on to diplomatic representation and tried to carry on government-to-government relations. At the same time it did not gain any favor with the new government when it implicitly endorsed the Indonesian Communist Party's version of events surrounding the coup.[62]

The Indonesian army finally removed Sukarno in March 1967, and there followed a series of anti-Chinese incidents

[58] *Ibid.*, pp. 289–94.

[59] Sheldon W. Simon, *The Broken Triangle, Peking, Djakarta, and the PKI* (Baltimore: Johns Hopkins Press, 1969).

[60] John Hughes, "China and Indonesia: The Romance That Failed," *Current Scene,* November 4, 1968 (Vol. VI, No. 19), pp. 7–8; Guy J. Pauker, "Indonesia: The Age of Reason?" *Asian Survey,* February 1968 (Vol. VIII, No. 2), p. 142.

[61] Van Ness, *op. cit.,* p. 109; Hughes, *op. cit.,* p. 9.

[62] *Ibid.*, pp. 108–10.

involving official Chinese representatives as well as the overseas Chinese residents.[63] The new leadership also shifted to a
strong pro-Western orientation, and diplomatic ties with China
were finally severed in October. The *Peking Review* then
printed statements by the Indonesian Communist Party's central committee denouncing the earlier peaceful transition policy as revisionism and calling for armed struggle. Only with
this endorsement did the Chinese make the Indonesian government a target for revolution.[64]

Only the pro-Maoist Jusuf Adjitorop, who leads a refugee
group in Peking called the Delegation of the Central Committee of the Indonesian Party, survives from the politburo
of 1965. The Chinese seem to have made no effort to rescue
leaders by helping to spirit them out of Indonesia.[65] They
also seem not to have provided material support to the underground remnants of the party in Indonesia even though it is
committed to armed revolution along Maoist lines.

China's great policy flexibility in 1971 resulted in an invitation to Indonesia to send a team to the Afro-Asian table tennis
tournament. This was welcomed by Indonesia's economic cabinet ministers who hoped for improved trade with China.
However, the suspicions of China by the military leaders apparently prevented acceptance. President Suharto said that
China would have to stop assisting the Kalimantan guerrillas,
to eject the Adjitoropo refugees from China, and to halt radio
propaganda against the government before normal relations
could be renewed.[66]

In August 1972 the Chinese Ambassador to the United
Nations, Huang Hua, attended the Indonesian Ambassador's
reception in New York. The Indonesian Foreign Minister,
Adam Malik, who is more sanguine about contacts with
China, noted that Peking broadcasts were less hostile and that
a table tennis team had again been invited to China.[67] He

[63] Hughes, *op. cit.*, pp. 9–12.

[64] Van Ness, *ibid.*, p. 222.

[65] Pauker, *loc. cit.*, p. 305.

[66] *Asia Research Bulletin*, January 1972 (Vol. I, No. 8), pp.
564–65.

[67] *Asia Research Bulletin*, October 1972 (Vol. II, No. 5), p.
1243.

urged normalization and criticized the military leaders' hesitation in January 1973.

The only obstacle to normalization of relations with China on the part of Indonesia, Malaysia, and Singapore seems to be the hesitation of the strongly anti-Communist Indonesian military leaders who dominate their government's policy. China shows continued willingness to do so, as indicated in the statement of Liao Ch'eng-chih to the Japanese newsmen and the various overtures from Peking. The members of ASEAN would have to consult together before a normalization of relations between the above three states and China, but it is unlikely that the Philippines or Thailand could veto the decision of the others.

The Philippines differs from Indonesia in having had almost no previous contact with Peking, and its Communist movement has been of little importance recently. China has, however, wooed the Philippines to a moderate extent since the Cultural Revolution as it has the other countries of Southeast Asia. As in other Southeast Asian countries China made donations to flood victims in the Philippines in 1970. Trade was encouraged as arrangements were made to ship rice to relieve the shortages from typhoon damage in September.[68]

President Marcos sent his personal and "unofficial" emissary, his brother-in-law Governor Benjamin Romualdez of Leyte, to Peking to talk to Chou En-lai. China was willing to permit direct trade relations, but diplomatic ties could not be had as long as the Philippines maintained them with Taiwan. The President did not go to China himself, for fear of jeopardizing relations with Taipei, but apparently tried to arrange for his wife to go as she did to the Soviet Union.[69] The Chinese Minister of Agriculture, Sha Feng, came to Manila to attend a conference on rice research in April 1972. A Philippine Chamber of Commerce group went to China in 1971, and the ban on all trade with socialist countries was

[68] *Asia Research Bulletin*, April 1971 (Vol. I, No. 6), p. 462.
[69] Bernardino Ronquillo, "The Philippines and China: Will the Lady Be First?" *Far Eastern Economic Review*, March 4, 1972, p. 17.

lifted that year. It was decided that the semigovernmental National Export Trading Corporation would undertake the China trade, a method resembling that used in Malaysia.

It was reported that the chief impetus to the favorable Philippine response to Chinese overtures was President Marcos' fear over the upsurge of Communist activity in his country and, in contrast to Indonesia, the hope that a more flexible policy toward Communist countries would dampen it.[70] In 1967–68, during the Cultural Revolution, the outlawed Philippine Communist Party split into a Moscow-oriented party favoring nonviolent revolution and a Peking-oriented one favoring armed struggle. The defection of Commander Dencio to the New People's Army from the Philippine military with substantial arms has invigorated the Maoist Communists under José María Sisón.[71] The New China News Agency broadcast a report of the Philippine Party's central committee on March 3, 1972, claiming that 90 per cent of its weapons came from the enemy (that is, the Philippine government).[72] The Chinese, therefore, seem to be confining their support to verbal endorsement of the party and the New People's Army.

The Chinese leadership seems much more interested in establishing conventional trade and diplomatic relations with the Philippine government than supporting insurgency. The New China News Agency devotes much more space to private and governmental visitors to China than to the internal Communist movement. Also, in the congratulatory messages to the Chinese Communist Party on the occasion of its fiftieth anniversary published last year, the lack of a message from the Philippine party was conspicuous by its absence, and an article published in the July 21, 1972, issue of the *Peking Review*, entitled "Armed Struggle Roundup," did not mention the Philippines.[73] China's interest seems confirmed by the

[70] *Ibid.*

[71] John H. Adkins, "Philippines 1972: We'll Wait and See," *Asian Survey*, February 1973 (Vol. XIII, No. 2), p. 144; William Pomeroy, "Source Materials on Philippine Revolutionary Movements," *Bulletin of Concerned Asian Scholars*, Summer–Fall, 1971 (Vol. III, No. 3–Vol. III, No. 4), pp. 79–80.

[72] Ryan, *loc. cit.*, p. 7.

[73] *Ibid.*

reports of Filipino journalists who have visited China that top Chinese officials assured them China was not exporting revolution and does not intend to interfere in Philippine internal affairs.[74] At the moment, Chinese support for internal Communist groups seems limited to verbal endorsement of the New People's Army, and this would probably be restricted if the Philippines were willing to cut off diplomatic relations with Taiwan and transfer them to Peking.

The martial law in the Philippines and the present interim governmental regime, which will be in power until the new constitution can be implemented, are said to be needed because of the threat of Communist revolution, but even President Marcos does not think it will be too difficult for the government to cope with it. Martial law is clearly due more to the extensive political, social, and economic unrest in the Philippines, which had reached epic proportions, than to the activities of Communist groups. If anything, the Communist insurgency in the Philippines is probably less critical than it is in most of the other Southeast Asian countries at present. Much of the uprisings and terrorism in the Philippines are due to bandits and the clash with Moslems and tribesmen in Mindanao over the invasion by Christian settlers.

In conclusion it must be said that under the leadership of Prime Minister Chou En-lai, China's policy in Southeast Asia since the Cultural Revolution has become quite similar to that of the United States. China is prepared to go almost to the extent of an alliance in unofficial cooperation with the United States in checking the influence of the Soviet Union, Japan, and, if need be, of North Vietnam as well. At the same time it seems unprepared to give up its verbal commitment to support liberation movements and revolutionary trends, and in some special cases to extend military or political aid to them. One basic restriction on its aid is apparently that it will not send its own military forces abroad, although it is understood that if American ground troops invaded North Vietnam it would be prepared to send Chinese "volunteers"

[74] Ronquillo, *loc. cit.,* p. 17.

(that is, its armies under the pretense that they have volunteered for this duty) as it did in Korea in 1950. Prince Sihanouk says volunteers were offered to him after the American invasion of Cambodia in 1970,[75] but he is prone to exaggeration.

China has given large amounts of assistance in the form of funds, equipment, supplies, instructors, and training only to insurgent movements in Indochina. For the other Southeast Asian countries China gives verbal support to liberation movements or Communist parties, but it is clearly much more interested in establishing government-to-government relations which are a more effective way to influence these countries in ways favorable to China. China is not willing to establish diplomatic relations unless those with the Chinese Nationalists on Taiwan are cut, but it is willing to sponsor cultural and also trade and aid relations which can be quite valuable to other countries. On the part of the Southeast Asian states a number of different factors are impeding a normalization of relations. For Malaysia, which has no diplomatic ties to Taiwan, it is a desire to act in concert with Indonesia, and it professes to fear Peking backing of insurgents. Singapore desires to wait for action by Malaysia and Indonesia. The Philippines is quite reluctant to cut diplomatic ties with Taiwan. The Indonesian military leaders still profess to view China as a major security threat and resent Chinese encouragement of the largely ethnic Chinese insurgency along its own borders with Malaysia. Thailand's military leaders are more willing to meet China halfway but are still blocked by their indirect or unofficial involvement in the Indochina war via American air bases and their volunteers in Laos. Chinese orchestration of its news propaganda and endorsements of its neighbors' insurgencies provides a delicate indicator of its foreign policy in the region as it tries to encourage these countries to modify their policies toward itself and the Vietnam War.

Should the hostilities actually be brought to a halt in Indochina for any length of time or external intervention be greatly

[75] "What Norodom Sihanouk Is Thinking," *Far Eastern Economic Review*, February 12, 1973, pp. 14, 15, 17.

reduced, it seems likely that China will greatly improve its relations with all its Southeast Asian neighbors. Under its present policy it aims at good government-to-government relations and gives mainly moral support to insurgents and revolutionaries, most of whom do not seem capable of success in any of these countries without substantial outside assistance. The United States is unlikely to reduce its influence in the region and may even step up its naval presence. This will be conducive to balancing the other major powers' influence in the region and may enable the present regimes to avoid excessive dependence upon or yielding to any one great power. China now views this situation as favorable to her own interests in the region and seems prepared to play the balancing game in Southeast Asia. The continued presence of the major powers may even help to prevent the local interstate tensions from producing new wars and confrontations if they can refrain from excessive interference in the politics of the local regimes. Despite the complexity of this type of international politics in Southeast Asia, it seems much more likely as an outcome than the formal neutralization scheme put forward by ASEAN members for some kind of withdrawal of the major powers from regional affairs.

Japanese Policy
Toward Southeast Asia

FRANK LANGDON

During the postwar period Japan has pursued five major objectives in her foreign relations: (1) the promotion of her own economic development; (2) the prevention of increased power and influence of nations hostile to Japan (i.e., China and the Soviet Union); (3) the reduction of hostility on the part of both Communist and non-Communist Asian states; (4) the maintenance of economic and security cooperation with a Super Power ally (i.e., the United States); and (5) the achievement of Major Power status and influence. This paper will examine Japan's pursuit of these objectives in its relationships with the states of Southeast Asia. Some attention will also be given at the end of the paper to the influence of emerging trends in international relations on the future course of Japanese policies in Southeast Asia.

Japan's most important goal in Southeast Asia has been the promotion of her own economic development and prosperity through obtaining important raw materials and markets for her manufactures. Indeed, prior to 1965, when Japan's postwar recovery and stability were still in some doubt, the Japanese viewed their other foreign policy objectives chiefly in terms of how they could contribute to economic development. Of all the industrialized states, Japan is the most dependent upon foreign countries for raw materials and fuel.[1] It needs

[1] "Editorial: A Weak Japanese Economy," *Japan Times Weekly, International Edition*, July 8, 1972 (Vol. XII, No. 28), p. 12: "No other country is so vulnerable to developments over which it has no control—whether it be from the standpoint of raw materials, transportation or overseas markets. We have been advised not to

these not only to supply its own people but to manufacture sophisticated exports that can be traded for the resources of other countries.[2]

TABLE 1

Japan's Trade with Southeast and Northeast Asia
(as percentage of total Japanese trade)

Year	Southeast Asia	Northeast Asia
1936	7.8	38.1
1951	9.5	6.4
1961	13.4	2.6
1970	10.2	10.9

NOTE: "Southeast Asia" refers to Thailand, French Indochina, the Malay States, Singapore, Netherlands East Indies, British Borneo and Sarawak, and the Philippines during the prewar era, and to the successor states today.

"Northeast Asia" refers to Taiwan, China, and Korea during the prewar era, and to the successor states today.

SOURCE: Donald C. Hellmann, *Japan in the Postwar East Asian International System* (McLean, Va.: Research Analysis Corp., 1969, RAC-R-46-2, Table 6, p. 29; *Asahi Nenkan 1953*, p. 426; Japan, Gaimu Sho, *Waga Gaiko no Kinkyo* (Tokyo: Okura Sho Insatsu Kyoku, 1971), No. 15, 1971 edition, Appendix 6, pp. 480–81.

In the past, Japan depended upon its Asian neighbors for a major share of its raw materials and markets. This was especially true before the Second World War with respect to China, Korea, and Taiwan in Northeast Asia, and to a lesser extent with respect to the territories of Southeast Asia.[3] However, after the Second World War, Japan found herself

be overwhelmingly dependent upon exports. But as long as we have to import our raw materials, we see no other choice."

[2] Saburo Okita, "Japan in South and Southeast Asia: Trade and Aid," *India, Japan, Australia: Partners in Asia?* (Canberra: Australian National University Press, 1968), p. 132.

[3] Jerome B. Cohen, *Japan's Postwar Economy* (Bloomington: Indiana University Press, 1958), pp. 153–70; G. C. Allen, *Japan's Economic Recovery* (London: Oxford University Press, 1958), p. 164.

unable to obtain many raw materials from China, Korea, and Taiwan. The hostility of newly independent states formerly under Japanese control, ideological differences with the Communist states, and the Korean War all served to restrict Japanese access to markets and resources in Northeast Asia. As Table 1 indicates, more than 38 per cent of Japan's prewar trade was conducted in Northeast Asia, but her postwar trade in this area has never amounted to more than 11 per cent.

It should not come as any surprise, then, that Japan's most important goal in Southeast Asia has been the expansion and development of her trade there. As soon as she regained independence, she set about the task of partially offsetting trade losses in Northeast Asia by increasing trade with Southeast Asia. As the figures in Table 1 indicate, trade with Southeast Asia had not only revived but had considerably increased before Japan ventured into American, Australian, and Canadian markets on a large scale and began to recoup some of her former trade with China and Korea.[4] When the American occupation of Japan ended with the signing of the San Francisco Peace Treaty in 1952, she remained largely cut off from her neighbors, China, Korea, and the Soviet Union, but re-established diplomatic relations with the North and South American and western European states then led in the Cold War by the United States. Most of the Southeast Asian states also signed the American-sponsored San Francisco Peace Treaty, but insisted upon reparations before agreeing to full friendly commercial relations with Japan.[5]

[4] It should be noted that while Japan's postwar trade with Southeast Asia, and more recently with Northeast Asia, has increased, her trade with countries such as the United States, Canada, and Australia has grown even more. During the massive increase in world trade in the 1950s and 1960s, the trade of the technologically advanced countries such as Japan and the United States grew more rapidly than that of the less industrialized ones, which have depended traditionally upon the export of agricultural and other raw materials in their foreign trade. Indeed, Japan even obtains many raw materials from the technologically advanced countries.

[5] Lawrence Olson, *Japan in Postwar Asia* (New York: Praeger Publishers, 1970), pp. 15–32.

In order to promote a restoration of economic relations with the Southeast Asian states, the Japanese managed after prolonged negotiations to arrive at reparations agreements with them in the mid-fifties. The Japanese not only paid off most of these obligations by 1965, but also began to pour large amounts of economic aid into the Southeast Asian countries.[6] As reparations payments decreased in size, the amount of Japanese aid increased, especially after 1965. The reparations payments and economic aid had a crucial effect upon Japanese commercial relations with the Southeast Asian states. They helped enable Japan to sell her manufactures and obtain raw materials in Southeast Asia, despite postwar Southeast Asian fear and resentment of Japan. The reparations were mostly in the form of nonrepayable grants by the Japanese government, but the economic aid was mostly in the form of credits and loans from both government and private sources. These chiefly involved the provision of Japanese technicians, goods, and services for the Southeast Asian countries. Thus, Japanese grants and credits introduced Japanese capital goods into the economically weak Southeast Asian states, which otherwise probably would not have purchased them.[7] This was to Japan's benefit, whatever the outcome of the capital's use in the recipient country.[8] Almost all the non-Communist states of Southeast Asia eagerly sought aid to promote their economic development, prosperity, and stability.[9] Therefore, inasmuch as Japanese economic aid was

[6] Kei Wakaizumi, "Japan and Southeast Asia in the 1970's," *Current History,* Vol. LX, No. 356 (April 1971), pp. 200–6. Robert S. Ozaki, "Japan's Role in Asian Economic Development," *Asian Survey,* Vol. VII, No. 4 (April 1967), pp. 237–44.

[7] Cohen, *op. cit.,* p. 157.

[8] Koji Taira, "Japan's Economic Relations with Asia," *Current History,* Vol. LX, No. 356 (April 1971), p. 230.

[9] It was often sought more eagerly than Japan would give it. Japanese reparations to the Philippines had little lasting effect because Philippine authorities failed to use them for a comprehensive development scheme, and inadequately supervised the use of the capital. Consequently, although Japan was rewarded by the revival of its trade, it has been reluctant in recent years to undertake many of the Philippines' requests for project aid. See J. L. Vellut, "Japa-

regarded as a favor and was requested by the recipient Southeast Asian government, it helped diminish lingering Southeast Asian anti-Japanese sentiment. If the country receiving aid managed to industrialize and raise its standard of living,

TABLE 2

Japan's Trade with Southeast Asia in 1970

(thousands of dollars)

Country	Exports	Imports	Total Trade	Per Cent
Philippines	453,717	533,465	987,182	29.0
Indonesia	103,118	390,061	493,179	14.4
Thailand	449,195	189,598	683,793	18.7
Malaysia	166,465	418,895	585,360	17.1
Singapore	423,034	86,539	509,573	14.9
South Vietnam	146,073	4,554	150,627	4.4
Burma	38,722	12,569	51,291	1.5
	1,780,324	1,635,681	3,416,005	100.0

SOURCE: Japan, Gaimu Sho, *Waga Gaiko no Kinkyo* (Tokyo: Okura Sho Insatsu Kyoku, 1971), No. 15, 1971 edition, Appendix 6, pp. 480–81.

which is the ostensible purpose of economic aid, so much the better. It would become an even better customer of Japan.

Japanese loans also ensured Japan of continued access to Southeast Asian raw materials. Japan relies heavily upon Indonesia, Malaysia, and the Philippines for nickel, copper, chrome, and other minerals. By issuing loans to help Southeast Asians set up mining operations and taking her repayment from the future output of these mines, Japan ensured her continued economic access without courting unpopularity by direct ownership of local operations. Likewise, self-liquidating loans to Southeast Asian logging companies en-

nese Reparations to the Philippines," *Asian Survey*, Vol. III, No. 10 (October 1963), pp. 496–506; Lawrence Olson, "The Politics of Flower Arrangement: Aspects of Japanese-Philippine Relations," *Reports Service*, American Universities Field Staff, East Asian Series, Vol. IX, No. 12 (Japan), December 26, 1961, pp. 4–7.

sured Japan of a future supply of timber, which she imports from Indonesia, Malaysia, and the Philippines.[10]

TABLE 3

Japanese Economic Aid to Southeast Asia
(millions of dollars)

Country	1964–1968		1970	
	Amount	Per Cent	Amount	Per Cent
Philippines	347.8	39.4	505.9	35.3
Indonesia	288.1	32.6	478.1	33.3
Thailand	122.5	14.1	228.0	16.0
Burma	74.2	8.4	*	—
Malaysia	26.8	3.0	66.7	4.6
Laos	9.1	1.0	*	—
Singapore	8.2	0.9	155.7	10.8
South Vietnam	3.5	0.3	*	—
Cambodia	3.0	0.3	*	—
	883.2	100.0	1434.4	100.0

* These are small amounts not broken down by country in the sources mentioned below.

SOURCES: Japan, Ministry of Foreign Affairs, *Highlights of Japan's Foreign Aid*, 1969, inside back cover; Japan, Ministry of Foreign Affairs, *Japan's Economic Cooperation*, 1971, p. 31.

The thesis that Japan's most important goal in Southeast Asia has been the promotion of her own economic development and prosperity is further borne out by the fact that Japanese economic aid has been concentrated in those Southeast Asian countries with which Japan does the most trade. The trade figures in Table 2 indicate that Japan's most important Southeast Asian trading partners are the Philippines,

[10] Olson, *op. cit.*, p. 189; Taira, *loc. cit.*, pp. 225–30, 244; International Institute for Strategic Studies, *Strategic Survey 1971* (London: International Institute for Strategic Studies, 1972), p. 62; Japan External Trade Organization, *Trade and Industry of Japan: Economic Cooperation of Japan*, extra edition, 1970, pp. 23–41.

Indonesia, Thailand, Malaysia, and Singapore. The Philippines, which have the largest export and import totals, is important as both a market for and supplier of raw materials. Indonesia and Malaysia, which show distinctly favorable trade balances, are important sources of raw materials, while Thailand and Singapore, which have unfavorable trade balances, are important markets for Japanese manufactures. These five countries also happen to be the primary recipients of Japanese economic assistance. The figures in Table 3 reveal that Japan poured astonishing amounts of economic aid into these five countries—the amounts given each country in 1970 alone being much larger than the total amounts given over the five-year period 1964–68.[11]

Furthermore, these five states are important to Japan because they straddle the sea routes through which much of Japan's extraregional trade must pass. The Philippines and Indonesia dominate the island areas of Southeast Asia and the trade routes leading to the south and west. Indonesia, Singapore, and Malaysia dominate the straits leading to the Indian Ocean, through which most of Japan's fuel supply comes. Friendly relations promoted by Japanese economic assistance and trade serve to protect these routes and the important commerce that traverses them.[12]

However, the other Southeast Asian states, being located on the mainland and ruled by relatively unstable governments, cannot and do not dominate important trade routes. This, taken together with the fact that these countries do not engage in much trade with Japan (see Table 2), accounts for

[11] This reflects the rapid acceleration of Japan's aid program during the past few years and the fact that grant aid constitutes a fairly small proportion of this program—most Japanese aid takes the form of credits and loans which differ from ordinary commercial transactions only in that their terms are more favorable. See John White, *Japanese Aid* (London: Overseas Development Institute, 1964); Japan, Tsusho Sangyo Sho, Boeki Shinko Kyoky, *Keizai Kyoryoku no Genjo to Mondaiten* (Tokyo: Tsusho Sangyo Chosakai, 1968), and later issues; Japan External Trade Organization, *op. cit.*

[12] Olson, *op. cit.*, pp. 185–96.

the very small amounts of Japanese economic assistance they receive (see Table 3).

Even though the Philippines does the most trade with Japan and receives more Japanese aid than any other Southeast Asian state, Japan probably attaches greater importance to her relations with Indonesia because of its large population, strategic location, and important raw materials.[13] The most important raw material Japan seeks in Southeast Asia is oil. Even though it is only a small part of its enormous total requirements, Japan takes 75 per cent of Indonesia's output. This oil is especially desirable because of its low sulfur content, which reduces pollution. Both the Japanese government and private enterprise are participating in the operation of existing Indonesian oil wells and in prospecting for new ones in offshore areas near Sumatra and Borneo. Japan continued to provide aid to the Sukarno regime after most of the other major powers discontinued it. She also took the initiative in reorganizing a consortium of Indonesia's creditors as soon as Suharto came to power, and provided commodity as well as project aid to try to reduce inflation and economic chaos. At the same time Japan promoted her own commerce and created important economic ties with Indonesia by underwriting (with government yen credits) Indonesian imports of Japanese textiles, fertilizer, electric equipment, chemicals, and spare parts. Japan also obtains freight earnings by carrying much of Indonesia's (and the Philippines') trade with other countries in Japanese ships.

Japanese investment in Southeast Asia has been relatively small, and was at first confined to assuring future supplies of minerals and timber by financing their extraction. Until recently, the Japanese usually processed these raw materials in Japan itself, which did little to promote the local industrialization desired by most Southeast Asian states. Although Japan's government project aid usually consisted of long-term low interest loans for electric power installations, roads, railways,

[13] Kenneth T. Young, "The Involvement in Southeast Asia," *Forecast for Japan: Security in the 1970's,* edited by James William Morley (Princeton, N.J.: Princeton University Press, 1972), pp. 200–2.

and other bases for industrialization, she was hesitant to construct things such as oil refineries, copper refineries, and fertilizer plants in Southeast Asia. It was only in the late 1960s and early 1970s that Japanese firms and joint ventures of Japanese and Southeast Asian businessmen began to process more raw materials locally. The pressure to export "polluting" industries, the search for cheaper labor, and the gigantic surpluses of foreign exchange have compelled Japan to invest more in manufacturing abroad. Also, Southeast Asian criticism of the selfishness of Japan's previous aid policy has forced Japan to plan its commercial operations more carefully so as to coordinate them with Southeast Asian aspirations for development. Both the Philippines government, some of whose development projects have been rendered uneconomical by Japanese export competition, and the Indonesian government have demanded such a coordination of Japanese commercial activity and aid policy in their respective countries.[14]

Thailand, Singapore, and Malaysia are more developed economically and better governed than Indonesia and the Philippines, and have less fear of economic domination. These countries have proven good markets for Japanese consumer goods and for the location of many Japanese manufacturing and assembly plants.[15] Included among these plants, which have been installed by both Japanese corporations and joint ventures involving Japanese and local Chinese businessmen, are home appliance factories, automobile assembly plants, textile mills, and many other medium or small manufacturing concerns. Many involve assembly of items already produced in Japan, so that local profit has been limited. Singapore and Malaysia have taken protective measures to encourage Japanese businesses to do more processing and manufacturing locally. Thailand makes Japanese investment as attractive as possible and is less insistent on a greater degree of local manufacture.

A few large-scale manufacturing enterprises have been sponsored by Japan in Southeast Asia. One is the Malayawata Steel mill in Malaysia, which is 39 per cent Japanese-owned.

[14] *Mainichi Daily News,* March 25, 1972, p. 1.
[15] Olson, *op. cit.,* pp. 196–218.

Another is the Jurong Shipyard, a joint venture involving Ishikawajima-Harima Heavy Industries—which owns 51 per cent of the concern—and the Singapore economic development board. These are long-term efforts which involve a commitment to cooperation and participation in local development, as desired by the Southeast Asian governments.

Elsewhere, Japanese engineers and construction companies have participated in international efforts at flood control and power development on the Mekong River in Laos and Cambodia. Japan has given similar aid to South Vietnam, and has also provided Burma with reparations and economic aid. Generally speaking, however, Japan has not invested significant amounts in any of these four countries, which have often been saddled with unstable regimes and are not favorable climates for free enterprise commercial development. South Vietnam is flooded with Japanese consumer goods, but this is only a tiny fraction of Japan's trade with Southeast Asia.

In conclusion, it should be noted that Japan's quest for Southeast Asian raw materials and markets has been quite successful. She has skillfully used the tools of economic aid and investment to become the leading trader in Southeast Asia, having surpassed the United States and several other major industrial states in the 1950s and 1960s with nearly one-quarter of the total trade.[16] Japan is presently the largest single trader in every country of the region except the Philippines, where she is second only to the United States, and in the states of Singapore and Malaysia, where she is second only to Britain.[17] However, even though Japan has become both the leading trader and the leading provider of economic aid in Southeast Asia, she is not free to dictate any commercial policy she wishes in that region.[18] The governments of South-

[16] Other major traders in Southeast Asia include Britain, France, West Germany, Holland, Australia, New Zealand, and China; however, none of these states even begins to approach the volume of Southeast Asian trade handled by either Japan or the United States.

[17] Donald C. Hellmann, *Japan in the Postwar East Asian International System* (McLean, Va.: Research Analysis Corp., 1969), Table 2, p. 22, and Table 3, p. 24.

[18] Donald R. Sherk, "Foreign Investment in Southeast Asia: A Reconsideration," this volume, pp. 355–81.

east Asia have demanded that Japan begin to coordinate her commercial activities with their national development plans, and several major industrial powers, including the United States, are strongly competing with her for Southeast Asian markets and raw materials. Japan can do much for herself and for Southeast Asia—but only if she takes the interests of her partners and rivals more fully into account.

A second Japanese goal in Southeast Asia has been the prevention of increased influence there of nations hostile to Japan, such as the Soviet Union and China. Japan has sought to achieve this goal by strengthening the political, economic, and social stability of Southeast Asian non-Communist regimes with Japanese economic aid. Although economic change and development can have a destabilizing effect on societies, Japanese officials generally consider that prosperous trade and effective economic aid, to the extent that it can be absorbed, will strengthen incumbent regimes and make revolutionary movements less likely and less effective. A prosperous and growing economy may implement peaceful social change by providing jobs and improving living standards. Japanese officials consider this to be the effect of economic growth in Malaysia, Singapore, and Thailand, which are bulwarks against the spread of the Indochina war.[19]

As a liberal democratic regime, Japan has long depended upon close ideological, technical, trade, and defense relations with other industrialized liberal democratic states.[20] Therefore, since Japan does not have sufficient military power or financial resources to defend and develop the Southeast Asian region by herself, she naturally seeks the cooperation of her fellow liberal democratic powers in preventing the growth of Soviet and Chinese influence in the region. Toward this end, Japan has actively solicited financial support for the Asian Development Bank, an organization designed to strengthen the non-Communist states of Southeast Asia with

[19] Based on interviews in the Japanese Foreign Ministry in 1969.
[20] Japan, Gaimu Sho, *Waga Gaiko no Kinkyo* (Tokyo: Okura Sho Insatsu Kyoku, 1971), No. 14, 1970 edition, part I, pp. 64–65.

development funds drawn from Japan, the United States, Canada, Australia, and other donor nations.[21] The Bank's headquarters are in Manila, in deference to the Southeast Asians it seeks to aid, but its president is a Japanese, in recognition of Japan's role as the chief donor country and her assumption of a leading role in regional economic development.

Japan's first striking initiative as a leader in regional development was to call a Cabinet-level conference on Southeast Asian economic development in April 1966 without consulting the United States.[22] Participants in the Tokyo meeting were Malaysia, Singapore, the Philippines, South Vietnam, Laos, and Thailand (Indonesia and Cambodia sent observers). Japanese Foreign Minister Shiina's purpose in calling the meeting was to encourage positive steps toward Southeast Asian development by the countries of the region themselves. Japanese officials regard agricultural development as a means of, first, supplying food from within the country concerned without depending on loans or using foreign exchange needed for more essential imports and, second, generating capital through exports of foodstuffs and raw materials. Citing the example of Japan's own experience, Shiina emphasized the necessity of agricultural progress as a basis for industrialization. Despite some suspicion by the Southeast Asians that they were being cast in supporting roles as providers of raw materials, Japan succeeded in calling a separate meeting to promote Southeast Asian agricultural development.

In December 1966 the vice-ministers of the appropriate departments of the nine countries listed above met in Tokyo and agreed to long-term low interest loans under an agricultural development fund. Then, in April 1967, a second Cabinet-level conference involving Japan and the Southeast

[21] "We hope for the external industrialized countries to expand Asian aid, especially the United States, Canada, Australia and other advanced countries of the Pacific area" (Japan, Gaimu Sho, Keizai Kyoryuku Kyoku, "Tai Ajia Enjo no Kihon-teki Kangaekata," October 1969, p. 3). See also T. F. M. Adams and Iwao Hoshii, *A Financial History of the New Japan* (Tokyo: Kodansha International, 1972), pp. 463–65.

[22] *Asahi Nenkan 1967*, p. 301.

Asian states resulted in a proposal that the Asian Development Bank handle this agricultural development fund. Later that year, the Japan-United States Joint Economic Committee supported this step. Japan offered to give half of the projected fund of $200 million, and the United States also agreed that some of its contribution to the Bank could go into such a fund. The fund eventually became a reality, the result of an important Japanese initiative and contribution to regional development efforts.[23]

Both Japan and the Southeast Asian states are taking positive steps toward more joint economic development. Since 1966 the Cabinet ministers of the Southeast Asian states and Japan have continued to meet on an annual basis to discuss general regional development efforts. These meetings have been criticized by Peking and Moscow as a kind of economic aggression connected with the Vietnam War. This attitude is not justified by the circumstances, nor was any aggression intended by Japan or the other participants. Indeed, Japan has welcomed North Vietnamese participation in these meetings after the hostilities in Vietnam have ceased. However, even though there was no formal intent to challenge the Communist states, these regional development efforts were certainly intended to strengthen existing non-Communist regimes in Southeast Asia, thus making it easier for the Japanese and more difficult for the Communist powers to influence them.[24]

Japan has supplied Southeast Asia with diplomatic and political, as well as economic, leadership. She has served as both a planner and a mediator for the Southeast Asian states. Japan's participation in the international planning for the Mekong River and her contribution of money and engineers has enabled her to increase her political voice in the affairs of continental Southeast Asia, even though she was unwilling to use her military power there. She joined with Indonesia and Thailand in convening the May 1970 conference on the Cambodian crisis, an unsuccessful attempt by several concerned

[23] S. P. Chopra, "Canada, Japan Help Asia Bank But Only with Strings Attached," *The Vancouver Sun*, June 3, 1969, p. 5.

[24] This policy also leaves Japan more exposed as the United States reduces its military engagement in Asia.

Asian states[25] to mediate in the Indochina war and check its spread. Japan also made two unsuccessful attempts to mediate in the conflict between Malaysia and Sukarno's Indonesia;[26] however, this occurred prior to 1965, when Japan's influence was still rather meager, because she had not yet become a sponsor of regional organization and a large provider of economic aid. Since then, Japan has offered to participate in any arrangements necessary to terminate the Indochina war, to take some part in peace-keeping, and to help with reconstruction. By thus helping to resolve Southeast Asian regional disputes and reduce the possible use of armed force, Japan hopes to weaken potentially hostile forces and ensure her ability to pursue peaceful commerce in the region.

In conclusion, it should be noted that Japanese aid and investment in Southeast Asia has had a definite strategic impact (even though Japan does not formally admit this to be an aid policy objective) in that it has somewhat restricted the growth of Soviet and Chinese influence in the region. Generous rehabilitation and development aid to Indonesia, Malaysia, and Singapore has helped stabilize regimes in those countries which had fought or were fighting Communist, or at least Communist-supported, movements. Japanese embassy officials in Thailand are even said to regard their country's aid to Thailand as a means to "stop Chinese Communism."[27]

Japanese aid and investment in Southeast Asia has also had the subtle but important effect of declaring Japan's commitment to her standing interests in the region. The Japanese-managed Jurong Shipyard in Singapore, which provides repair facilities for ships carrying imports and exports to and from Japan, symbolizes Japan's permanent interest in freedom of shipping through the straits in the area.[28] Recent

[25] Japan, Indonesia, Thailand, New Zealand, Malaysia, Australia, the Philippines, South Vietnam, Laos, Korea, and Singapore.

[26] Young, *loc. cit.*, p. 188.

[27] Olson, *op. cit.*, p. 214.

[28] More than 90 per cent of Japan's fuel oil passes through these waters. The new supertankers are compelled to go through the Sunda or Lombok Straits until the Malacca Straits can be deepened or bypassed by a canal or pipeline through the Isthmus of Kra. The Malacca Straits route is also subject to new claims by

reductions of both British and American commitments in the area have opened the door to increased Chinese and Soviet influence, raising some fears in Japan for the safety of her future commerce. In 1969 some Japanese businessmen even advocated Japanese naval protection of shipping routes through the Malacca Straits and across the Indian Ocean.[29] These advocates were countered by Tetsuya Senga, secretary-general of the defense production committee of the Federation of Economic Organizations, Japan's principal big business organization. Senga said that to escort ships even as far as Malacca was beyond present Japanese military capacity and would only antagonize Southeast Asians.[30] The former chief-of-staff of the Maritime Self-Defense Force concurred in the impracticability of such a move with Japan's present forces. Even the coming Fourth (1972–76) and Fifth (1977–81) Defense Buildup Plans do not contemplate sufficient ships to cope with present Soviet or future Chinese naval attack forces. This being the case, economic aid, investment, and regular trade have necessarily become both a substitute for and a supplement to Japan's military capacity to defend friendly Southeast Asian regimes from powers hostile to Japan.

While Japan has sought to prevent an increase in the power and influence of its major Communist antagonists, it has also taken some important steps to reduce tensions between the Communist and non-Communist states in the region. These steps have sought to reduce the possibility of a war

---

Indonesia, Malaysia, and Singapore that these are internal waters subject to their control, raising the possibility of new user's fees and possible refusal of passage of warships. Ships could go nearer to Australia, but all present alternate routes are longer and involve more time and expense, which is reflected in the cost of oil. Japan is cooperating with Singapore, Malaysia, and Indonesia in a more accurate and detailed charting of the waters in the Straits.

[29] Mainichi Shimbun Sha, *Anzen to Boei Seisan* (Tokyo: Mainichi Shimbun Sha, 1969), pp. 142–44.

[30] U. S. Department of State, American Embassy, Tokyo, *Summaries of Selected Magazines,* October 6–20, 1969, p. 20. A 1969 visit to Singapore by ships of the Japanese Navy had been less than well received.

and to facilitate a possible normalization of East-West economic and political relations. Probably the outstanding example of this policy was Japan's successful attempt to prevent the Asian and Pacific Council (ASPAC) from being turned into an anti-Communist or anti-Chinese organization.[31]

When ASPAC held its first meeting in Seoul, June 1966, the states participating in the Vietnam War insisted on a communiqué denouncing nuclear testing and supporting a United Nations resolution for the unification of North and South Korea; however, Japan and Malaysia managed to prevent any direct criticism of China's nuclear tests. At the second ASPAC meeting in July 1967, Japanese Foreign Minister Miki called for peaceful coexistence with China as a long-term goal and said it would be difficult for Japan to remain in the organization if it served as a meeting-ground for Vietnam War participants and supporters.[32] However, when the 1968 ASPAC meeting rolled around, the anti-Communist members were upset about the imminent Vietnam peace talks in Paris and the planned withdrawal of the last British contingent from Singapore, and talked of forming some sort of military alliance. Foreign Minister Miki met with many delegates before the meeting to lobby against such a development, and in his major address he urged the following basic principles: that the Council not be opposed to any country outside its membership; that its members exchange views even though they differed; that the members not attempt any conclusions or agreements; and that they take flexible and prag-

---

[31] Yoshihisa Kajitani, "Asupakku no Genei to Jittae," *Asahi Janaru,* Vol. XI (June 15, 1969), pp. 21–26. Japanese intellectuals and newspapers have kept up a campaign against Japan's participation in ASPAC (see the following *Asahi Shimbun* editorials: "ASPAC wa Kaisho Shita Ho ga yoi," June 14, 1972, p. 5; "Tai-Chu Shisei Tenkan Saguru," June 13, 1972, evening edition, p. 1; "Nitchu Seijoka o Hyomei e," June 12, 1972, evening edition, p. 1). Other ASPAC members are South Vietnam, South Korea, Thailand, Taiwan, the Philippines, Malaysia, Australia, and New Zealand (Laos sent an observer). Burma, Indonesia, Singapore, and Cambodia refused to join, although an Indonesian representative has attended one meeting as a guest.

[32] Kajitani, *loc. cit.,* p. 26; *Asahi Nenkan 1968,* p. 297.

matic approaches in all their activities. He successfully inserted an agreement in the final communiqué that the members would not try to form a military alliance.[33] However, the communiqué still viewed conditions in mainland China with caution, and expressed sympathy for South Vietnam's struggle for independence. Although ASPAC thereafter avoided taking an explicit anti-Chinese stance, it was not until the 1972 meeting that its members, with Japan in the forefront, began to exhibit a willingness to establish ties with Peking. Japan openly stated her desire to normalize relations with China; South Korea's President Park implied that Communist states might be welcome by calling for the Council's doors to be kept open to nonmembers; Malaysia sent only an ambassador to the meeting out of deference to Peking; and even South Vietnam modified its anti-Chinese stance.[34] While Japan cannot be credited as being the only force in bringing about this new trend,[35] she certainly can be credited with preventing ASPAC from becoming an explicitly anti-Chinese and anti-Communist organization during the late 1960s. In doing so she probably helped avoid an exacerbation of relations between the Communist and non-Communist states of Asia and helped facilitate the present détente between China, her Southeast Asian neighbors, and the United States.

Japan has also promoted her objective of reducing the hostility of her Communist and non-Communist neighbors by (1) keeping her Self-Defense forces small, and (2) confining them to her home islands and refusing to consider intervention anywhere else. Japan's land force (179,000 men) is very small, not only in comparison with China's (2,550,000 men) and the Soviet Union's (2,000,000 men), but even in comparison with Taiwan's (390,000 men) and North and South

---

[33] *Asahi Nenkan 1969,* p. 301.

[34] Elizabeth Pond, "Asian Council in Turnaround Opens Doors to 'Non-members,'" *Christian Science Monitor,* June 17, 1972, p. 2.

[35] Certainly the important mutual steps taken in 1971–72 by the United States and China to improve their relations with each other strongly influenced those ASPAC members who suddenly warmed to China at the 1972 meeting of the Council.

Korea's (360,000 and 560,000 men, respectively).[36] Japan's military spending is also very small compared to that of other states. The countries listed in Table 4 either spend at least a billion dollars a year for military purposes or else have larger

TABLE 4

Comparison of Military Expenditures
(millions of dollars)

Country	Military Expenditure		GNP	%GNP	Military Personnel
	1970	1971	1970	1970	1970
Israel	1,429	1,484	5,400	26.5	75,000[a]
South Vietnam	1,028	564	4,000	25.7	500,000
Egypt	1,262	1,495	6,430	19.6	318,000
Soviet Union	53,900	55,000	312,000	11.0	3,305,000
China	7,600–8,550	8,000–9,000	—	9.5	2,880,000
Taiwan	482	601	8,300	8.8	540,000
United States	76,507	78,743	977,000	7.8	3,066,000
Britain	5,950	6,333	121,000	4.9	373,000
Pakistan	—	714	16,000	4.4	392,000
France	5,982	5,202	148,000	4.0	506,000
South Korea	333	411	8,300	4.0	634,250
Sweden	1,146	1,192	31,200	3.7	23,000[b]
Australia	1,261	—	34,400	3.6	88,280
Netherlands	1,106	1,161	31,300	3.5	116,500
India	1,535	1,656	49,000	3.4	980,000
West Germany	6,188	5,961	185,000	3.3	466,000
Italy	2,599	2,651	93,200	2.8	414,000
Canada	1,931	1,687	78,200	2.5	85,000
Indonesia	272	—	11,600	2.3	319,000
North Korea	—	849	—	—	401,000
North Vietnam	584	—	—	—	492,000
Japan	1,640	1,864	195,000	0.8	259,000

[a] 300,000 when fully mobilized
[b] 750,000 when fully mobilized

SOURCE: International Institute for Strategic Studies, *The Military Balance 1971–1972* (London: International Institute for Strategic Studies, 1971), *passim.*

armed forces than Japan. These countries are listed according to their military expenditures expressed as a percentage of their gross national products (GNP). Japan's military expenditure is extraordinarily small beside that of the major

[36] International Institute for Strategic Studies, *The Military Balance 1971–1972* (London: International Institute for Strategic Studies, 1971).

and middle powers, as well as that of many small states. In terms of absolute amount spent and the size of armed forces, Japan ranks with the middle powers but stands far below other countries whose GNPs are the size of hers. Japan's military equipment is constantly being modernized and improved, but her military spending—even though it increases by about 20 per cent a year—is still modest compared to that of China, France, or Britain.

Furthermore, Japan has consistently refused to use her own armed forces for purposes of intervention anywhere else. This is especially true with regard to Southeast Asia. Japan did permit American use of air and naval bases in Japan for the defense of Taiwan and South Korea, and she even permitted some use of these bases with regard to the conflict in Southeast Asia; however, she refused to even consider defending those countries with her own forces.[37]

Thus, Japan has indeed tried to reduce tensions between the Communist and non-Communist states in the Asian region —particularly those tensions between herself and China. She is cautious to avoid any public identification of potential enemy states for fear of giving offense and increasing hostility toward herself. She succeeded in blunting the anti-Chinese character of ASPAC, a potentially important regional organization, and has taken the lead in trying to improve regional relations with China. Finally, Japan's military policy is purely defensive (and conventional); she deliberately avoids any involvement likely to antagonize either major or minor powers. This essentially defensive policy is firmly grounded in Japan's widespread disillusionment with the imperialism of her prewar leaders. It also guarantees a friendlier reception for Japanese trade and business in Southeast Asia.

[37] Yet, until the Tanaka Cabinet restored friendly relations with China in 1972, China continually accused Japan of a revival of militarism—a charge primarily meant to condemn Japan's role in maintaining American military influence in Asia, but also meant to deter Japan from large-scale rearmament or overseas intervention. For example, when the 1969 Nixon-Sato agreement returning Okinawa to Japan also provided for Japanese participation in the defense of the Ryukyu Islands (which would put Japanese forces closer to Taiwan and China), China took it as evidence that militarism had already revived in Japan.

Japan has pursued her objective of maintaining economic and security cooperation with a Super Power ally or "protector" by nurturing close ties with the United States. Central to this has been a security treaty which loaned bases to the United States in return for protection against any attack upon Japan, especially by the Soviet Union. This treaty was revised once in 1960 to take into account Japan's increased status and influence in the international community and was then extended indefinitely in 1970.[38] The bases were to be used primarily for the protection of Taiwan and South Korea by American forces,[39] but Okinawa, which remained under American administrative control until 1972, was used to support some operations in Vietnam and Southeast Asia. After Okinawa reverted to Japan, it too could only be used for the defense of Taiwan and South Korea.

America's increased participation in the Indochina war created a dilemma for Japan in view of, on the one hand, her goal of minimizing Communist hostility toward herself and, on the other hand, her desire to maintain good relations with the United States, on whom she depended for defense and much of her essential trade.[40] Japan needed to maintain good relations with the Americans, but feared that even limited military cooperation with them might draw her into war.[41] Furthermore, the Vietnam War was extremely unpopular in Japan, as it was elsewhere. The solution for Japan was to give verbal support to America's defense of non-Communist regimes in the region, a goal in which Japan had

[38] George R. Packard, *Protest in Tokyo: The Security Treaty Crisis of 1960* (Princeton, N.J.: Princeton University Press, 1966), Chapter 2; Martin E. Weinstein, *Japan's Postwar Defense Policy, 1947–1968* (New York: Columbia University Press, 1971), pp. 100–3.

[39] U. S. Department of State, *State Department Bulletin*, Vol. LXI, No. 1590 (December 15, 1969), pp. 555–58: Sato-Nixon Communiqué of November 21, 1969, paragraph 4. See also Weinstein, *op. cit.*, p. 63 and pp. 95–100. The 1972 Chou-Nixon Communiqué implies that the Taiwan commitment is no longer necessary.

[40] Packard, *op. cit.*, p. 63.

[41] "Japan Won't Police Asia: Military Role Rejected," *The Vancouver Sun*, July 10, 1970, p. 10.

a stake, but to carefully avoid any direct involvement in the warfare. Diplomatic support was given to American objectives by Japan's Prime Minister, her Foreign Minister, her representative to the United Nations, and her diplomatic personnel elsewhere, even to the extent of qualified approval of the Johnson Administration's continued bombing of North Vietnam. The greatest support was given by the Japanese Prime Minister, who spoke approvingly of American efforts in South Vietnam during two separate trips through Southeast Asia.[42] This occurred in 1967, just before a visit to Washington to press for the return of Okinawa. Japan's verbal support apparently had some effect, as the Americans promised to return Okinawa in a few years and promptly initiated steps toward its reversion to Japan.

On the other hand, Japan made no direct war contribution in the form of men or matériel. Japanese economic aid to Saigon between 1964 and 1970 came to about $9.7 million and was confined to innocuous items such as hospitals and medical assistance.[43] Even though she is the leading donor of aid to Southeast Asia, Japan ranked only sixth among donors to Vietnam behind the United States, West Germany, France, Australia, and Canada. Japan's trade with South Vietnam was comparatively moderate in size: in 1969 her $226.4 million trade with South Vietnam represented only 6.7 per cent of her total Southeast Asian trade, and this dropped off sharply in 1970. Still, large numbers of Japanese consumer goods, such as motorcycles, televisions, radios, and cameras, entered South Vietnam, resulting in charges of profiteering which induced Japanese companies to undertake construction of a hospital, a diesel power plant, and a bridge over the Mekong in 1971 as private business aid.

To sum up, even though Japan wished to maintain good relations with the United States and has given diplomatic support to American policy in Vietnam, she has never modified her noninterventionist stand. For more than twenty years,

[42] The Prime Minister held talks with, among others, Chiang Kai-shek and the leaders of South Vietnam, which critics at home in Japan interpreted as support of America's policies in Asia.

[43] Japan External Trade Organization, *op. cit.*, pp. 71–72.

despite constant American urging, she has refused to use her own forces to defend Taiwan or South Korea, and has been even less eager to do so in Southeast Asia (although some Japanese are concerned about the defense of Indonesia and Malaysia). Rather, Japan has avoided participation in the defense of Southeast Asia herself, only to reap the commercial benefits of American military expenditures in Thailand and Vietnam. Apparently this arrangement satisfies the United States, which has accepted Japan's lukewarm support and has even returned Okinawa, thus placing Okinawan bases under the special restrictions applying to American bases in the rest of Japan and ending their availability for Southeast Asian operations.

Japan's pursuit of her final foreign policy objective in Southeast Asia—the achievement of major power status and influence—has largely depended on her successful pursuit of the other four objectives examined above. Despite her lack of military power, or rather her reluctance to use what power she has, Japan should probably be credited with exercising the influence of a major power in Southeast Asia. Indeed, Japan's noninterventionist military policy has probably enhanced her regional and global influence. Her practice of avoiding military commitments and confining her small, conventional forces to her home islands has not only earned her great moral authority, it has enabled her to return to commercial prominence in Southeast Asia and the rest of the world as well. As long as the Americans dominated much of maritime Asia and were willing to protect Japan and her Southeast Asian neighbors, Japan was free to concentrate on her recovery and development and to carry out her foreign policy chiefly by economic means.[44] Her policy resembled that of the United States in the nineteenth century when it enjoyed the protection of the British Navy and was able to concentrate on its own economic development.

Unlike virtually every other Major Power, Japan has earned her status and influence almost solely on the strength

[44] Denis Warner, "More Japanese Sea Lanes," *Kansas City Star,* August 13, 1971, p. 39.

of her economy and sage diplomacy. She has arrived at Major Power status primarily because of her economic aid program, which was stepped up significantly after 1965 (especially in 1969 and 1970), and her impressive initiative in sponsoring diplomatic conferences to coordinate economic planning on a regional basis. These aid and development programs, inextricably bound up in Japan's trade and foreign investment policies as they were, eventually gained Japan a reputation as both a generous (if shrewd) benefactor and a very wealthy nation.

These regional economic activities enhanced Japan's global status and influence as well as her regional influence. By providing a large amount of economic aid, leading in regional organizations such as ASPAC and the Asia Development Bank, carrying on considerable foreign trade, and growing enormously wealthy, Japan closely resembles world powers such as the United States, Britain, and France, all of whom earned a good part of their international status and influence in the same fashion.[45] Japan has gained entrance into the exclusive "club" of the ten richest non-Communist states, and has become an indispensable member of important international agencies such as the Organization for Economic Cooperation and Development (OECD), the International Monetary Fund (IMF), and the General Agreement on Trade and Tariffs (GATT).

Having thus become a financial and political power with both regional and global influence, Japan now seeks to exercise financial and political leadership on at least a regional level. As an Asian state which has recently industrialized, Japan feels she has both a better understanding of Southeast Asian development problems and a more important stake in regional peace and development than do external industrial powers. Therefore, since 1965 Japan has sought to serve as the leader of the developing states of Southeast Asia.[46] While this desire for regional leadership brings her into competition with China (and to some extent with the United States and the Soviet Union), it may not necessarily lead to sharp antagonism. If Japan's relations with China continue to improve,

---

45 White, *op. cit.*, pp. 9–10.
46 Young, *loc. cit.*, pp. 180–88.

they may simultaneously aid in the development of the regional states. Japan has already indicated she is willing to consider aid to Communist as well as non-Communist states, while China has taken steps to establish better relations with several of the more anti-Communist Southeast Asian states which have participated in the Vietnam War.

Finally, it is necessary to consider the emerging trends in Asian international relations and their possible effect upon the future direction of Japanese policy in Southeast Asia. Japan's real capacity to make Southeast Asian states act according to her wishes is still a moot question—she is still weak militarily, and her economic power tends to be exaggerated by her critics. Furthermore, she finds herself somewhat constrained by her anomalous position as the recently defeated imperialist power in the region, and avoids taking any serious initiative into nations' affairs except where it is apt to be welcomed. Consequently, Japan's policies toward Southeast Asia are seldom clear-cut and are usually phrased in the virtuous and broad terms so fashionable in international politics. Therefore, it is necessary to look at Japan's past actions rather than her statements to find a clue as to how she will respond to emergent trends in the Asian international system.

The two most important trends in Asian international relations are the implementation of the Nixon Doctrine, which calls on America's allies to exercise greater self-reliance, and the new détente between China and the United States.[47] The Nixon Doctrine as applied to Southeast Asia has slowly moved toward the disengagement of American ground combat forces in Vietnam and the strengthening of South Vietnamese armed forces to assume the major role in defending their country. Without abandoning its treaty commitments or its ambition to prevent the spread of Communist penetration in Asia, the present administration apparently hopes that

[47] A third trend of some importance in Asian international relations is the Soviet Union's continuing bid for Indian and Japanese support against China and the United States. See Ray Hemen, "Soviet Diplomacy in Asia," *Problems of Communism,* March–April 1970, p. 46; Masaru Ogawa, "Gromyko's Visit," *Japan Times Weekly,* International Edition, Vol. XII, No. 5, (January 29, 1972), p. 3.

American arms, money, and naval and air striking forces will be sufficient to enable local regimes to protect themselves.

The improvement of American relations with Peking in 1971 and the 1972 visits of President Nixon and Prime Minister Tanaka to China helped to reduce old Cold War tensions, but left Japan in an awkward diplomatic position vis-à-vis her Super Power ally and "protector," the United States. For one thing, the ending or reduction of American containment of China and the beginning of closer American cooperation with the Soviet Union made the need—and possibly the determination—of the United States to defend Japan and other Asian countries less certain. Furthermore, while Mr. Nixon went to considerable lengths to obtain an invitation to visit China, no American President has ever visited Japan, which had thought herself to be America's chief ally in Asia.[48] This sudden improvement of America's relations with China without first consulting Japan as promised, along with the sudden levying of an import surcharge against Japan (and other states) to force her to revalue her currency called into question America's support for Japan.

The result of the above trends is that American intervention to protect Southeast Asian allies or Japan is likely to be a little less automatic. This development will no doubt foster a re-evaluation of Japanese defense policy, and may even result in increased Japanese involvement in Southeast Asian regional security. She has already enunciated a vague but persistent policy of a more "self-reliant defense (jishu hoei)" which aims at making Japan able to protect herself from conventional attack without excessive reliance on the United States. However, as stated before, the size of present Japanese forces and expected increases in the Fourth and Fifth Defense Plans do not provide for sufficient strength to undertake air or naval defense of the area outside Japan's immediate vicinity, nor do they provide ground forces even on the scale

---

[48] President Eisenhower's projected 1960 visit to Japan was prevented by agitation over the Japan-U.S. Security Treaty. Only in 1972 has President Nixon expressed a new interest in visiting Japan, in an effort to repair the damage done to Japanese-American relations in 1971.

of countries like North or South Korea.[49] Given this modest defense buildup and Japan's present policy of nonintervention, there seems little likelihood of her undertaking to protect Southeast Asia.[50] Although the United States has tried to get Japan to assist in the defense of Taiwan and South Korea for over twenty years, she has refused, except for willingness to permit use of American bases in Japan for that purpose. Japan's leaders deny any intention of changing this policy either now or in the near future, when the new, more passive American policy is fully implemented.

Should current trends be disturbed by an attack on South Korea which the United States was reluctant to intervene against, it is unlikely Japan would go to South Korea's defense, either. Japan also considers the defense of Taiwan unnecessary now that relations with China have improved. It seems much less likely that Japan would go to the defense of South Vietnam, Thailand, or Malaysia were they about to fall to a Communist force of some kind. In any event, Japan's ability to do so would be very limited, unless she were assisted by other countries in the region and obtained weapons and even air and naval support from the United States. Even this kind of intervention would probably require a Japanese defense effort comparable to those of France or Britain, both of whom spend at least twice as much as Japan.[51]

Should relations between Japan and the United States deteriorate due to some sort of trade war (as seemed remotely possible in 1971), it is conceivable that American protection of Japan would be even more in doubt. In that event, Japan might rearm on the scale of France or Britain just to insure

[49] Even though Japan's defense expenditures double about every five years, her 180,000-man Land Self-Defense Force has scarcely increased for over fifteen years. Most of the money goes for new equipment.
[50] Prime Minister Sato's speech to the United Nations in *Japan Reports* (Japanese Embassy in Ottawa), Vol. XVII, No. 10 (November 1970), p. 1, and Defense White Paper account on p. 3, same source.
[51] James William Morley, "Forecast with Recommendations," *Forecast for Japan*, p. 227.

herself against conventional attacks.[52] Should Japan ever have cause to fear Chinese, American, or Russian nuclear attack, she might have incentive to acquire nuclear weapons; however, these would be little protection against such adversaries since Japan is vulnerable to even minor nuclear forces. Japanese leaders have been extremely reluctant to even discuss nuclear weapons since they are not a very practicable defense for a nation so small in area as Japan. The persistent discussion abroad and among Japanese opposition groups of nuclearization blandly ignores the many impracticable aspects of such a policy and the Japanese government's opposition to it.

There is a possibility that Japan's commercial and political position in East and Southeast Asia might lead to rivalry with China, but rivalry is an incentive for cooperation as well as hostility. The possibility of Sino-Japanese cooperation is enhanced by Japan's recognition of the Peking government. Furthermore, since the United States and China appear to have agreed to avoid any likelihood of putting the United States-Taiwan Security Treaty into operation, it is unlikely that Japan will be required to consent to American combat use of Japanese bases to defend Taiwan in the future.[53]

Whatever the nature of Japan's relationship with China, it seems highly unlikely that Japan could dominate Southeast Asia as some people fear it will. Given China's regional presence and the extensive Southeast Asian interests of other external powers, Japan would probably not be left free to exploit the region, even if she wished to do so. Barring a drastic change of regime in Japan, which is difficult to envisage in the near future, such a policy is not likely to be attempted. Japan is much more likely to help Southeast Asian countries settle their quarrels and push ahead with economic development, if they can get their own affairs under control.

In conclusion, Japan's policy toward Southeast Asia will probably continue along its present course of regional leader-

[52] John K. Emerson, *Arms, Yen & Power: The Japanese Dilemma* (New York: Dunellen Publishing Co., 1971), pp. 402–3.
[53] Text of Nixon-Chou communiqué, *The Vancouver Sun*, February 28, 1972, p. 10.

ship, intimate commercial relations, development assistance, and military nonintervention for some time. If Japan should become increasingly independent as a Major Power (i.e., should she lose her Super Power ally) and acquire a more independent defense policy, she will probably spell out her commitments in more concrete terms. But even in this event, it does not seem likely that she will seek Southeast Asian military alliances or responsibilities; she does not aspire to take on the American role there. And while political and economic cooperation with the Southeast Asian states is important to Japan, such cooperation is not a *sine qua non* for future Japanese prosperity and security, given her ever-increasing economic ties throughout the rest of the world. Thus, any future Japanese military intervention which was not part of a larger regional effort would probably be rejected as not being worth the indeterminate economic, diplomatic, and domestic costs of such an undertaking.

Foreign Investment in Southeast Asia:
A Reconsideration[1]

DONALD R. SHERK

INTRODUCTION

In the minds of many, private direct investment[2] by a rich industrial nation in a developing, recently independent nation is a form of neocolonialism calling for expropriation and embargoes of future ventures. However historically sympathetic one may be with this view, in the decade of the seventies it is anachronistic and is deserving of a Galbraithian expletive: "conventional wisdom."

In most Asian states, second-generation leaders have come to power with a more pragmatic, less ideological approach to the costs and benefits associated with private foreign investment. A major reason for this re-evaluation has been the emergence in the last decade of new models or descriptions of foreign investment presenting new sets of associated costs and benefits.

It will not serve our purposes here to recount in detail the bill of particulars levied against the pre-World War II types and patterns of foreign investment in Asia. The story has

[1] Part of the data presented in this paper came from a longer monograph on investment in Asia presently under consideration for publication. Thanks are due to Geoff Hainsworth for helpful suggestions.
[2] Direct investment involves actual control of the enterprise through ownership of a sufficient percentage of the firm's total equity. This contrasts with portfolio investment which does not involve control but merely the right to a percentage of the earnings. This paper will be concerned only with direct investment since it is far and away the most important type of private capital going to the developing countries of Asia.

been told elsewhere, often and well.[3] Suffice it to say that foreign investment was accused of warping the colonial economy with the projects involved representing mere "outposts . . . of the developed investing countries"[4] or "foreign enclaves" yielding few, if any, primary or secondary growth stimuli for the local economy.

No specific year can be identified as the time when attitudes toward foreign investment softened in Asia, but generally it was in the early sixties. The major reason for this softening of attitude was the growing recognition that the foreign investment of the sixties seemed qualitatively different from the earlier varieties.

The new models of international investment have, for the most part, emerged from attempts to explain investment in manufacturing activities as contrasted with the more traditional kinds of investment. Prior to World War II most foreign direct investment was of two types: extractive or colonialist. Although the two categories obviously overlap, they are useful in describing early foreign investment experience in Asia.

Colonialist investment, as the term is used here, refers not to the industrial area of investment but rather to the political relationship prevailing at the time of investment. Much of the early investment activity of companies was an outgrowth of nineteenth-century colonial arrangements. Investment in transportation, insurance, trade, and public utilities served to knit the colony into the fabric of the investing country's economy. And these investments were undertaken almost exclusively by the nationals of the mother country. The direct investment of Great Britain in her "empire," of

[3] See Jonathan V. Leven, *The Export Economies: Their Pattern of Development in Historical Perspective* (Cambridge, Mass.: Harvard University Press, 1960); Hla Myint, *The Economies of Developing Countries* (New York: Frederick A. Praeger, 1965); Gunnar Myrdal, *Economic Theory and Under-Developed Regions* (London: University Paperbacks, 1965); Hans W. Singer, "The Distribution of Gains Between Investing and Borrowing Countries," *International Development: Growth and Change* (New York: McGraw-Hill Book Co., 1964).

[4] Singer, *op. cit.*, p. 163.

France in Indochina, of the Netherlands in the East Indies and the United States in the Philippines was, in large part, of this colonialist pattern.[5]

Although both extractive and, to a lesser extent, colonial investments have continued throughout the postwar period, the attentions of the investing and host countries alike have shifted to investment in manufacturing activities. In the case of the United States, foreign investment in the manufacturing sector has grown from 24 per cent of the total direct investment in 1929 to 42 per cent in 1969, and now exceeds petroleum, the second leading category, by nearly $10 billion. Other investing nations have also followed this pattern of growing dominance of investment in manufacturing.

In the developing world in general, and in developing Asia in particular, investment in manufacturing has come to be looked on in a new light.[6] Throughout the sixties the leaders of most Asian nations have become more tolerant of foreign investment in their manufacturing sectors for a number of reasons. First, the mystique of industrialization as the only road to development is still a powerful force throughout the region. Second, for reasons which tend to be more emotional than logical, investment in manufacturing is considered less "exploitative" than investment in extractive industries. As a result investment in manufacturing was frequently solicited at the same time that foreign investment in the extractive field was either prohibited or severely restricted. Third, it was relatively easy to encourage foreign investment in the manu-

[5] For an analysis of how trade patterns were largely governed in the Pacific region by colonial relationships through the Second World War, see Donald Sherk, *United States and the Pacific Trade Basin* (San Francisco: Federal Reserve Bank, 1972).

[6] A number of recent publications could be cited in support of this change in attitude. Three in particular are: International Bank for Reconstruction and Development, *Partners in Development: Report of the Commission on International Development* (New York: Frederick A. Praeger, 1969); United Nations Economic Commission for Asia and the Far East, *Economic Survey of Asia and the Far East, 1970,* Part I: *The Role of Foreign Private Investment in Economic Development and Cooperation in the ECAFE* (Bangkok, 1971); and Asian Development Bank, *Southeast Asia's Economy in the Seventies* (Manila, 1970).

facturing sector through a policy of import substitution. Foreign companies whose products were shut out of the local market because of high tariffs or other trade barriers, were encouraged to engage in local assembly, if not production, to keep their markets, and they frequently did. Finally, and perhaps most importantly, developmental economists and planners also were able to articulate a strong economic case for encouraging foreign investment in manufacturing. The economic case will be presented in detail below (see Host Country Attitudes).

Consequently the sixties marked a marriage of convenience between the investing countries and the host countries of developing Asia with respect to foreign direct investment in manufacturing. In the remainder of this paper, we will examine the foreign investment in developing Asia of the region's two leading investors—the United States and Japan.[7] But, before turning to the details of this investment, some general remarks about the United States and Japanese investment patterns and trends are in order.

WORLDWIDE TRENDS IN U.S. AND JAPANESE DIRECT INVESTMENT

UNITED STATES DIRECT INVESTMENT

The United States is the world's leading direct investor, accounting for approximately 60 per cent of the total stock of foreign direct investment throughout the world. In 1946 the accumulated dollar value of U.S. direct investment abroad was $7.2 billion, an amount which was actually less than that recorded in 1929 ($7.5 billion).[8] The flow of U.S. investment abroad began to accelerate in the late fifties, reaching a total

[7] British investment in Asia, although large, will not be treated in this paper. It tends to be concentrated in India, Pakistan, Ceylon, and Malaysia; was largely of colonial variety; is growing slowly and will soon be exceeded by Japanese investment. Britain's entry into the Common Market may further reduce its interests in the region.

[8] Data on U.S. direct investment presented in this section were obtained from United States Department of Commerce, *Survey of Current Business*, Washington, D.C., various issues.

of $32.8 billion by 1960. The decade of the sixties saw this figure grow by almost two and a half times, exceeding $78 billion by 1970.

In terms of geographical distribution, the postwar period witnessed a concomitant spreading out of U.S. direct investment activity. In both 1929 and 1945, the Western Hemisphere accounted for over 75 per cent of the total value. This figure has dropped constantly over the past two decades and in 1969 reached 46.4 per cent. First Europe and then the rest of the world increased their relative shares. Europe's share of U.S. direct investment increased from 13.9 per cent in 1946 to 30.4 per cent in 1969, and the rest of the world (Asia, Africa and Oceania) increased its share from 8.3 per cent to 23.2 per cent over the same period.

The fanning out from the Western Hemisphere investment in the postwar period was, in part, a result of firms' learning or experience. Investments in Canada and Latin America had been facilitated by familiarity with customs, laws, and language. Experience gained in these regions then convinced businessmen of their ability to operate in more distant areas. Also, as the industrial composition of U.S. direct investment shifted, nearness to the United States became less important. In the prewar period, investments had been mainly the extractive industries, and given the costs of transportation there were strong economic advantages in making such investments in countries close to the United States. Finally, the postwar period saw the dissolution of the colonial systems of earlier years. As a result, the former colonial holdings of the European powers became more open to U.S. direct investment.

The growth of the manufacturing sector in the total U.S. foreign investment position has played an important role in promoting this geographical dispersion. The rapidly growing markets of western Europe together with the tariff policies followed by both the European Common Market and the European Free Trade Area turned Europe into a magnet for U.S. investment. And once U.S. companies found that operating across national borders was relatively easy, they quite naturally enlarged their horizons to include the more distant continents. Revolutions in communication and air transport facilitated this learning experience.

Experienced in operating abroad, more and more U.S. companies began to see themselves as companies of the world, or, in today's terminology, multinational corporations. As such, these companies concerned themselves not just with market shares in the United States but with world market shares, and consequently they endeavored to match the investment thrusts of their competitors. Investments in manufacturing facilities abroad to produce and market final products, which perhaps earlier had been exported from the United States, became incorporated into a global production and distribution strategy of the parent firm. Such a strategy, often referred to as the internationalization of production, enabled manufactured inputs or component parts to be produced in one country, shipped to another country for assembly or further production, and finally sold in a number of other countries. The division of the production process into a series of discrete activities, located throughout the world, according to costs of production, was the logical extension of companies first venturing abroad. It is largely this phenomenon which has led to a considerable expansion of U.S. direct investment in developing Asia.

JAPANESE DIRECT INVESTMENT

It was not until the sixties that Japan began to engage in foreign direct investment to any significant extent. In fact, as of December 1960, the accumulated total of Japanese direct investment abroad was less than $300 million.[9] This is not surprising given the voracious domestic demand for capital to fuel Japan's rapid economic growth, and considering the precarious state of her balance of payments throughout the fifties.

Exchange restrictions (discussed below in more detail) were

[9] Koichi Hamada, "Japanese Investment Abroad," a paper given at the third Pacific Trade and Development Conference held in Sydney, Australia, August 1970. Data compiled by the Bank of Japan is computed on a permission basis. This exceeds the balance of payments data for the same period which records actual flows.

instituted by the Japanese government strictly to control both the amount and kinds of foreign investment allowed. Those foreign investment projects which received approval through the early sixties were designed to secure export markets (e.g., foreign sales agencies) or to obtain vital raw materials (e.g., Alaskan pulp, middle-Eastern petroleum or Australian ore).

By the late sixties, an improved balance of payments, increased protectionism in major Japanese markets, and rising Japanese wages combined considerably to expand Japanese foreign investment. By 1970 the accumulated value of Japanese investment was approximately $3.5 billion and of this amount over $2.1 billion had been registered in just three years, 1968–70. The increased importance of the cost of labor in promoting Japanese foreign investment can be seen by comparing two surveys conducted by the Export-Import Bank of Japan concerning Japanese firms investing abroad.[10] In their 1969 survey, 38 per cent of the new firms going abroad gave as their primary reason the availability of abundant and low-priced labor. A comparable survey made in 1968 showed only 20 per cent of the firms giving this as their primary reason. Conversely, the number listing protectionist or import substitution policies of the host nation as their primary reason had dropped from 47 to 34 per cent over the two years. Most of the "low-wage" investment went to Korea, Taiwan, and Hong Kong, but some has also gone to Thailand and the Philippines.

Another 1968 study of the foreign investment patterns of small enterprises in manufacturing (defined as having capital of less than 100 million yen) underscored this finding.[11] Of 142 investment projects undertaken by these firms, 124 were located in Asia with Taiwan, Korea, and Hong Kong topping the list. And of these same firms the availability of cheap and abundant labor was cited as their chief motive. The firms going abroad in search of low-wage labor appear to be about equally divided between those exporting back to Japan and those shipping to third countries. The anticipation of favor-

[10] *The Oriental Economist,* June 1971.
[11] "Japanese Investment in Southeast Asia," *Fuji Bank Bulletin,* June 1969 (Vol. XX, No. 6), pp. 99–102.

able tariff treatment from the developed few and the developing countries has been an additional motivating factor for such investment.

Projecting Japanese foreign direct investment over the remainder of the decade is a difficult exercise. But enough is known at present to be fairly confident about predicting a range of from $27 to $30 billion. Is this approximately nine- or tenfold increase over the decade realistic? I suggest that it is for several reasons.

To begin with, although there has been considerable liberalization in the exchange controls applied to Japanese foreign investment, they still remain.[12] As recently as September 1970 any proposed foreign investment project exceeding $300,000 had to receive the approval of both the Japanese Ministry of Finance and the Ministry of International Trade and Industry (MITI). Once the project was approved, the company or companies planning the project had then to petition another government agency for the necessary financing. Although this case by case administrative review is often reduced to little more than a formality, it has tended to act as a barrier to overseas investment. And the complete removal of the exchange controls, expected soon, will undoubtedly step up Japan's overseas investment.

Not only will the impending removal of controls accelerate the outflow of Japanese overseas investment in the years to come, the dramatic improvement in the Japanese balance of payments will also add pressure in this direction. Throughout the last half of the sixties Japan's reserves of gold and foreign exchange remained in the $2 to $3.5 billion range, a meager margin of safety given the size of her annual trade; by the end of 1970 her reserves reached $4.4 billion and then in 1971 (the year of the "Nixon shocks") skyrocketed to an amount in the region of $14 billion, and an unofficial estimate in March 1972 placed the value at $16.5 billion.

This rapid buildup of reserves stimulated a chorus of

---

[12] Information on Japanese exchange controls came from Keijiro Tanaka, Representative of the Japanese Ministry of Finance, "Japanese Foreign Investment Growth," a speech given to the American Management Association in New York, March 1971.

voices from abroad (and from some domestic sources) urging the upward revaluation of the yen. In order to reduce pressure for revaluation, the Japanese instituted an eight-point crash program designed to curb the accumulation of reserves, primarily dollars; one point of this program called for a vigorous effort to increase overseas investment.

Under pressure from the United States the Japanese agreed (in December 1971) to upvalue the yen by over 16 per cent. The continued growth in reserves in the first half of 1972 suggests that another change in the value of the yen cannot be ruled out, and with each upward revaluation the momentum for expanded overseas investment will be increased as the yen price of foreign assets is reduced.

What portion of this greatly increased outflow of Japanese direct investment will go to developing Asia is also problematical, but Asia's share of Japan's total overseas investment has been rising (31 per cent in 1969), and an estimate of 25 per cent by 1980 seems conservative. That would mean that between $6 and $7 billion of Japanese investment should be in place in developing Asia in 1980. Such an amount should match, if not surpass, the projected U.S. investment position in the region.

INVESTMENT PROFILES OF JAPAN AND THE UNITED STATES IN DEVELOPING ASIA

Over the last ten years Asia has grown in importance in terms of total U.S. foreign direct investment, yet it remains behind Europe, Canada, and Latin America. As a per cent of total U.S. direct investment, Asia's share has increased from 3.43 per cent in 1959 to 5.08 per cent in 1970, its largest share in the postwar period. The figure, however, includes Japan; excluding Japan, developing Asia's share has risen from 2.49 per cent in 1962 to 3.17 per cent in 1970. Preliminary estimates for 1971 show this percentage as considerably higher, possibly as high as 4 per cent.

The industrial composition of U.S. direct investment in Asia is shown in Table 1. For purposes of comparison other major areas are also included.

It might be noted from the table that Asia and Latin Amer-

TABLE 1
Industrial Composition of
U.S. Direct Investment Abroad—1968*
(percentage distribution)

Region/Country	Total	Manufacturing	Petroleum	Mining/ Smelting	Other
All Areas	100	40.70	29.09	8.29	21.92
Canada	100	43.85	20.98	13.42	21.65
Europe	100	55.59	23.93	.32	20.16
Latin America	100	30.62	28.15	14.73	27.50
Asia	100	37.17	39.63	1.45	21.75
Asia, excluding Japan	100	30.00	40.35	2.46	27.19
Africa	100	14.96	58.62	14.48	11.94
Middle East	100	3.49	91.74	.17	4.60

* Data obtained from *Survey of Current Business,* various issues. In the survey, Asia includes the Far East and the Middle East. I include in Asia only the Far East.

ica have considerably higher manufacturing shares than have, for example, Africa and the Middle East. The similarity between Latin America and Asia, however, is deceptive. In Latin America, three countries, Mexico, Brazil, and Argentina account for nearly 75 per cent of manufacturing investment. These countries have followed development strategies calling for import substitution behind high tariff walls. Most of the U.S. investment directed toward these countries went to maintain domestic markets previously serviced by exports. In Asia, by contrast, a considerable portion of U.S. manufacturing investment has taken place in countries where the local markets are quite small. Here the motive has often been export-related rather than for import substitution. This difference will stand out more clearly when the individual Asian countries are examined.

Asia's share of Japan's direct investment is also growing, but such investment represents a much larger portion of the total than is the case for the United States. The largest proportion was obtained in 1969, when over 31 per cent of Japanese overseas investment went to Asia. Table 2 presents

TABLE 2
Industrial Composition of
Japanese Direct Investment
1951–69 Approval Basis*
(percentage distribution)

Sector	World	Asia†
Agricultural, Forestry, and Fisheries	2.5	6.5
Mining (including petroleum)	33.6	37.5
TOTAL primary	36.1	44.0
Food Stuffs	1.7	4.5
Wood & Pulp	5.0	.9
Textiles	5.3	11.7
Chemicals	1.3	2.5
Metal Products	4.9	5.2
Electrical Machinery	1.9	5.0
Transport Equipment	3.6	2.0
Other Machinery	2.0	1.5
Other Manufactures	1.5	5.2
TOTAL secondary	27.2	38.5
Trade	12.1	1.9
Finance-Insurance	8.7	10.7
Construction	1.2	.3
Other Services	14.7	2.1
TOTAL tertiary	36.7	15.0

* United Nations ECAFE, *op. cit.*, p. 40.

† Asia total will not add to 100 because of the inclusion of branch investment (about 2.5%) in the total.

the industrial composition of Japanese direct investment for the years 1951–69 on a worldwide basis and also for Asia.

Table 3 presents the official investment statistics issued by both Japan and the United States respectively for individual Asian countries on an accumulated basis through 1969. Since the countries do not use the same definition for overseas direct investment, a footnote to the table discusses the difference in treatment.

TABLE 3
Accumulated U.S.
and Japanese Direct Investment
in Asia—1969
(millions of dollars)*

	U.S.	Japan	Total
Ceylon	†	2	—
Taiwan	75‡	60	135
Hong Kong	208	20	228
India	294	17	311
Indonesia	228	192	420
S. Korea	150	15	165
Malaysia	—	36	—
Singapore	177	24	237
Pakistan	87	5	92
Philippines	741	45	786
Thailand	123	78	201
Other	62	114	176
	2,145	604	2,749

* Japanese data were obtained from Japan, Ministry of International Trade and Industry, *Economic Cooperation—Present Status and Problems, 1970*. These data are on an approved basis and exclude reinvested earnings but include long term private loans. U.S. data were obtained from the *Survey of Current Business*, October 1970, and reinvested earnings are computed on a current year transaction basis. (Some individual country figures were provided in unpublished form by the Office of Business Economics, United States Department of Commerce.)

† Included in other
‡ 1968

INDUSTRIAL COMPOSITION

As was shown in Tables 1 and 2, the broad industrial composition of Japanese and United States investment in developing Asia was roughly parallel. For the region as a whole, Japan had 38 per cent of its investment in manufacturing activities and the United States had 30 per cent (37 per cent if Japan is included). The United States had a larger percentage invested in petroleum (40 per cent of total), and Japan had a larger amount invested in minerals and agriculture.

However, within the major categories and in the individual Asian countries a number of important differences can be found. In manufacturing, the Japanese have invested more in the traditional light industries such as textiles, food stuffs and other manufactures. These three categories have accounted for well over half of Japan's investment in manufacturing. The United States, on the other hand, has invested more in the technologically advanced fields of electrical machinery, transportation equipment, and chemicals. Although detailed information on all the Asian countries is not available to bring out these differences, a few countries have published the necessary information.

In Thailand, 43 per cent of Japanese investment is in textiles and apparel as contrasted with 3 per cent for the United States. In Indonesia, of a total Japanese manufacturing investment of $45 million, textiles and light industry account for over 75 per cent, whereas chemicals and heavy industry represent over 50 per cent of U.S. investment in manufacturing. In South Korea, Japan accounts for over 60 per cent of all foreign investment in textiles and apparel, whereas the United States accounts for over 70 per cent of all foreign investment in transportation equipment and over 67 per cent in electrical machinery and equipment.

Admittedly, the data are very spotty for making such a generalization, but the Economic Commission for Asia and the Far East did conclude in reference to developing Asia:

> . . . United States investments (tend) to be large and to be concentrated in oil or mineral development, or technologically advanced fields such as electric/electronic manufacturing and chemicals . . . Japanese investments tend to be smaller and to be directed to lighter industries, such as textiles, and electric/electronic equipment, al-

though Japanese mining and metal manufacturing investments are important in Indonesia and Malaysia.[13]

MODES OF OPERATION

What are the major distinctions in modes of operation of the Japanese and American firms? We can distinguish a few areas in which the firms of the two nations differ, and these will be explored below.

1. *Ownership*

Typically, the Japanese have been more willing to allow local equity participation in their ventures in Asia than have the Americans. A number of explanations have been offered to account for this distinction. One is that the Japanese seem to be better able to deal with minority interests than do the U.S. firms. Another is that the Japanese government has pushed some firms into joint ventures to lower the profile of the Japanese companies in Southeast Asia. Still another is that host Asian countries have been more insistent that local equity be involved in Japanese projects than they have been for American firms. Korea, for example, did not allow Japanese companies to establish wholly owned subsidiaries until recently. Then there is also the fact that the Japanese restrictions on capital outflow from Japan have necessitated utilizing local capital in a number of overseas projects.

Finally, there is the question of the technological level of the investment. As mentioned before, the United States often invests abroad to exploit a particular technique or process. Local participation in management may be seen as incompatible with the need for secrecy. Most of Japan's investment has been in raw materials or in standard manufacturing lines. Here there would seem to be less objection to allowing local participation in management. However, as Japan moves up the line to more sophisticated manufacturing processes, it too may resist local participation more than in the past.

Two countries for which data are available—Thailand and Korea—give contradictory evidence. In Korea, as of October 1970, 79 per cent of U.S. subsidiaries were 100 per cent owned, but only 20 per cent of Japanese subsidiaries were

[13] United Nations ECAFE, *op. cit.*, p. 109.

wholly owned. In Thailand, of foreign firms being established over the ten years 1959–69, Japan accounted for over 70 per cent of all wholly owned foreign firms whereas the United States share was less than 10 per cent. Over the same period Japan accounted for 37 per cent of registered foreign capital and the United States 26 per cent.

Some observers have noted an increased willingness on the part of corporations abroad to "live with" local equity. It is seen as being an asset in recruiting local talent as well as a method to "grease the way" through the bureaucracy. As U.S. firms are forced to compete with a growing Japanese presence, there will be added incentive to allow as much local participation as possible.

2. *Rationale*

Apart from a heavy investment in petroleum exploration and related activities, the major thrust of U.S. investment in Asia in recent years seems to have been motivated by the growth in foreign sourcing or component manufacture and assembly. Countries receiving the most investment in recent years have been those which have sought U.S. investment for export purposes: South Korea, Taiwan, Hong Kong, and Singapore.

Two provisions of the United States Tariff Code have probably increased this flow: Sections 807 and 806.30. Both levy duties on only the value-added component of manufactures and metal processing respectively. For example, if 80 per cent of the value of a final product involves parts imported into the manufacturing or processing country, duty would be levied upon just the 20 per cent portion when it reached the United States. For the developing countries of Asia, Section 807 is the more important. In 1969, of a total of $1.6 billion of imports brought in under this provision (with a duty-free component of $339 million), nearly 22 per cent came from the less developed countries. Of the developing countries, five of the top seven were Asian (Hong Kong, Taiwan, South Korea, Singapore, and the Philippines).[14]

[14] United States Tariff Commission, *Economic Factors Affecting the Use of Items 807.00 and 806.30 of the Tariff Schedule of*

United States investment in Asian manufacturing has increased substantially over the last few years. In 1963, 24 per cent of all U.S. direct investment in developing Asia was in manufacturing; by 1969 this figure had reached nearly 31 per cent, and it appears that it will continue to climb in the years to come. Much of U.S. direct investment in Hong Kong, Singapore, Taiwan, and South Korea is of the foreign sourcing type, where inputs are produced for final assembly elsewhere. Although the small export-oriented economies of Asia have accounted for most of the U.S. foreign sourcing, some is also recorded in Thailand, the Philippines, and Indonesia.

In the case of Japan, raw material acquisition has played a more important role in their Asian investment. Japan, which must import nearly 75 per cent of all its raw materials, has had to continually seek out new sources of supply. In 1968, over $170 million in foreign investments went into natural resources development. In 1969, it was over $314 million, and accounted for half of all foreign investment in that year. During 1951–69, approximately 45 per cent of the total Japanese direct investment in Asia was in the extractive industries.

Japanese manufacturing investment has been of both the import substitution variety and the export-oriented or sourcing variety. Of the latter, it has largely gone to Taiwan, South Korea, and Hong Kong. In fact, Japan's growing stake in South Korea and Taiwan has prompted some observers to comment that the two countries are becoming merely extensions of the Japanese economy.[15]

There are a number of examples of this. Japan applies duty on the value-added component of goods sent to Korea for assembly. Rather than encourage labor immigration, the Japanese companies are going to the labor, and to the labor closest to home. Japan is also considering placing some of its oil refining and metal processing establishments in Korea to reduce pollution of its already highly polluted environment. This "exporting of pollution" is likely to continue.

---

the United States (Washington, D.C.: TC Publication 339, September 1970).

[15] *The Oriental Economist,* March 1971, p. 20.

Most new Japanese investment came to a halt after Taiwan was expelled from the United Nations in October 1971. This result was partly due to threats of China to refuse to permit Japanese companies to trade with it if they invested in Taiwan or South Korea,[16] and also due to the uncertainty of what would become of Taiwan. When Japan re-established diplomatic ties with China on September 29, 1972, Taiwan severed its relations with Japan but took no overt steps against Japan or Japanese businesses in Taiwan. Despite the effort to lessen dependence on Japan by diverting trade to other partners, it is likely to remain very substantial. Toyota Motors, one of the largest automobile manufacturers, intends to continue its joint venture in Taiwan, and even the Japanese Minister of Trade indicated that at least small-scale loans and credits from the Export-Import Bank might be permitted by the government.

3. *Government-Business Relations*

It is often said that the degree of cooperation or collusion between the Japanese firms and the Japanese government is a close, harmonious working relationship. This relationship is sometimes called "Japan, Inc." by foreigners, and is usually contrasted with the relationship between government and business in the United States. On close examination, however, it is difficult to document any qualitative difference in treatment: both countries have risk insurance programs available, assist in financing projects, and supply private firms with economic intelligence concerning markets, laws, customs, and likely difficulties.

4. *Japanese-American Cooperation*

In some fields Japan and the United States have invested in Asia on a joint basis. Some mineral investment projects have been multilateral private ventures as distinguished from

---

[16] The "Four Principles" governing Sino-Japanese trade, which were enunciated by Premier Chou En-lai in the spring of 1970, are: no Japanese firm can expect trade with China which (1) assisted the aggressive regimes on Taiwan and in South Korea; (2) invested in either Taiwan or South Korea; (3) supplied munitions to the United States for use in the Indochina war; and (4) had joint ventures with U.S firms.

joint ventures. Here a multilateral venture refers to three or more participants of different nationalities. Multinational ventures among Japanese, United States, and local interests have taken place in mineral development, banking, and oil exploration. Originally many of these multinational or consortium arrangements involved U.S. participation in the financing of the project because of Japanese balance of payments constraints. But, increasingly, consortium arrangements involve joint management as well. And with the growing concern over the national identity of foreign investment in both host and source countries, this trend is likely to continue.

HOST COUNTRY ATTITUDES

GENERAL RECEPTIVITY

For the Asian region as a whole it is generally accepted that the receptivity toward foreign investment is considerably improved over a decade ago when most foreign investment was branded as a form of neocolonialism. Partly this is a result of the example of success; those countries which have grown the fastest (Taiwan, South Korea, Hong Kong, and Singapore) have deliberately encouraged the inflow of foreign investment. But probably the most important reason has been the absence of a single dominating industrial country investing in the region as has been the case in Latin America. Substantial investment positions in Asia are maintained by Great Britain, the United States, and Japan, and recognizable investment presences are maintained by France, the Netherlands, Germany, and Switzerland—and very importantly, a considerable amount of inter-Asian investment flows have occurred. Hong Kong, Taiwan, and Singapore investors have gone into Malaysia, Thailand, Indonesia, and the Philippines. This diversity of investment sources has had much to do with the development of the view that foreign investment is not a neocolonialist ploy to infringe on the sovereignty of the host country.

The experience of Asia as host for foreign investment suggests that the principle of "countervailing power" is of major importance. In overly simplistic terms, it can be stated that foreign investment dominance by one country is destabilizing and is likely to lead to growing frustrations and hostility, but if the foreign investment position is distributed among a number of countries (more being better than few), it is seen as less of a threat and more of a benefit to the development process. Or, as the former Indonesian Ambassador to the United States has put it:

> It is in our national interest to involve as many countries as possible in the economic development of Indonesia. In this light, neutrality is removed from the impact of economic pressures because these tend to cancel each other out.[17]

Direct investment as distinct from economic aid or portfolio investment is seen to offer a variety of benefits to the developing countries. First, there are the more traditional benefits including contributing to the foreign exchange holdings of the receiving country, stimulating domestic savings and investment, and providing employment opportunities and markets for suppliers. To these benefits have to be added others which, to the present-day development planners, have potentially greater importance for development. These include access to technology; the establishment of contacts with overseas banks, capital markets, factor and product markets; the training of workers in administrative, financial, marketing, and other business techniques; and the development of a class of skilled local managers and entrepreneurs.

With respect to foreign-owned manufacturing projects, they frequently have greater employment impact (especially in urban areas), have more "spillover" effects upon the local

[17] Soedjatmoko, *Asia*, Autumn 1970 (Vol. 19), p. 21. The Ambassador also has pointed out that the diffusion of foreign investment positions is a positive force in reducing "major power antagonisms" in the region and in supporting the "low involvement posture of the external powers in the military and political fields." "The Role of the Major Powers in the East Asian-Pacific Region," a speech given at a conference on "Prospects for Peace, Development, and Security in Asia in the 1970s," May 20–23, 1971, Airlie House, Warrenton, Virginia.

economy (e.g., transfer of skills to other "new" sectors, and demand for local fabricating and material supply), and make available new technologies unobtainable by other means. Given this list of perceived benefits it is little wonder that the kind of overseas firm most coveted by the developing countries of Asia is not the extractive firm, nor the manufacturing firm assembling or producing solely for the local market, but the multinational firm whose local production facilities are integrated into a global production and marketing system.

In general, then, private foreign investment is perceived by most Asian developing countries as playing an important role in the modernization process implied by development. This is less true of investment in nonmanufacturing activities, but even here its contribution is recognized. Yet few if any Asians see this investment as costless, and in country after country attempts are being made, via legislative action and other means, to maximize the associated benefits and minimize the costs.

PERCEIVED COSTS

Any enumeration of the costs associated with foreign investment normally includes noneconomic as well as economic considerations. Below we attempt to sort these issues out and identify the most often-heard complaints. The costs are listed under the headings: economic, sovereignty, and culture.

1. *Economic*

The economic costs of foreign investment are usually described as potential or future costs. They tend to center on how the policies of the foreign corporation may stunt the development of indigenous techniques and skills. For example, although the access to the research and development performed by the parent company is an acknowledged benefit of foreign investment, the complaint is frequently voiced that this access may be bought at the cost of a reduced national R and D capacity. The same fear is voiced over the development of domestic managerial and entrepreneurial skills. Importing such skills in the form of foreign subsidiaries or joint ventures may reduce incentives for developing them in the host country.

With respect to capital flow, it is agreed that capital inflow adds to aggregate savings and investment, but there is concern that the development of a domestic capital market may be inhibited. This concern is increased when the question of foreign banking interests is raised. As is well known, the large multinational corporations like doing business with their traditional banks, and during the postwar period when the multinationals have invested abroad, so have their banks. This is most true for Europe, but it is also happening in the rest of the world. Dominance by foreign banking interests is a real fear in most Asian nations, and therefore, restrictions on such activity is the rule in most countries.

Another fear has to do with the sort of technology utilized by the foreign firm. The complaint is frequently heard that too often the technology used is more appropriate to the factor endowment of the source country than to that of the host country. Production processes are said to be more capital intensive than is warranted, given the labor surpluses in most Asian nations. However, Helen Hughes argues, based on her study of foreign investment in Southeast Asia, that there is little hard evidence supporting this view and that where such evidence exists, it is often the result of excessively protectionstic policies adopted by the host countries themselves, which subsidizes capital intensive techniques.[18]

A final economic cost has to do with the ability of multinational corporations to reduce their subsidiary's tax liability to the host country by arbitrary transfer pricing or adjustments of service fees and the allocation of administrative costs. By pricing components supplied to the subsidiary at excessive levels, the income subject to tax rates in the host country can be reduced. Capable tax administrators can sometimes prevent this, but in developing countries they are in limited supply.

[18] H. Hughes, "An Assessment of Policies Towards Foreign Investment in the Asian-Pacific Region," a paper given at the Third Pacific Trade and Development Conference, Sydney, Australia, August 1970, p. 26.

2. *Sovereignty*

A second category of arguments raised against foreign investment has to do with the threat it poses to a country's independence or sovereignty. More intangible than the economic costs enumerated above, this concern is nonetheless frequently given the greatest weight in the developing countries. Such arguments range from the belief that the presence of foreign subsidiaries interferes with developmental planning in the host country, to the belief that the subsidiary is an operating extension of the foreign policy of the source country's government. Kindleberger, in referring to the perceived political costs of foreign investment, stresses:

> . . . the uneasiness that many people instinctively have when they contemplate the fact that the activities of institutions within their economy and polity are "controlled" from outside the political unit.[19]

And when the perceived threat of foreign control issues from one of the world's Super Powers, such concerns are multiplied.

Although there do not seem to be many documented examples around to support this thesis, enough exist to cause discomfort to host countries. The United States has extended its antitrust policies to subsidiaries of U.S. parent firms abroad. It has prohibited exports from subsidiaries to certain Communist nations and has influenced dividend policies of subsidiaries through its investment control program.

Little more can be said on this issue except that the fear does exist, and probably will continue to color the relations between the host and source country throughout the seventies. It should be added that the perceived threat of foreign control is intensified by ownership policies biased against joint ventures and local participation.[20]

[19] C. P. Kindleberger, *American Investment Abroad* (New Haven, Conn.: Yale University Press, 1969), p. 5.
[20] For an excellent treatment of the perceived costs of foreign investment to the developing host country, see Raymond Vernon, *Sovereignty at Bay, The Multinational Spread of U.S. Enterprises* (New York: Basic Books, 1971), Chapters 5 and 6.

3. *Cultural*

A final category of costs of foreign investment refers to the clash between the cultures of the host and source countries. Most Asians have grown up with the concept of the "Ugly American." What is new to the Asian situation in the seventies is the recognition that Americans have no monopoly on "ugliness." Increasingly, the Japanese are coming in for the same sort of criticisms initially directed at the Americans.

The Japanese businessman is accused of being excessively aggressive, arrogant, and clannish. He is accused of discrimination in his employment practices and of being unconcerned with the development of the local economy. He is supposedly insensitive to local traditions and customs, and is resented for his sexual appetite away from home. These complaints are subsumed under the titles "Ugly Japanese," "Yellow Yankee," and "Economic Animal."

Perhaps resentment of this sort tends to focus on the most recent source of irritation. Americans may not behave differently, but in Asia today they seem to be less criticized for their cultural offenses. One must not fail to consider the possibility that a learning process is at work and that businessmen and officials can learn or be induced to adapt.

INDUCEMENTS AND RESTRICTIONS

The developing countries of Asia have almost all instituted specific inducements to encourage the inflow of foreign investment. Yet there has been little uniformity in policies and the degree of inducement varies widely from country to country.

At the administrative level, a positive measure to encourage foreign investment has been the centralization of the decision-making machinery in an office of foreign investment or a foreign investment board. Most of the countries have such an office, and its existence has tended to reduce administrative delay and costly exploration.

At another level, most Asian countries have adopted a set of investment priorities. Although all industrial areas are usually open to foreign investment (apart from banking), a preferred list of industries typically exists, and investment in such industries makes a firm eligible for a wide range of investment incentives. These are called "pioneer" industries in Malaysia and Singapore, "preferred" industries in the Philippines, and "promotable" industries in Thailand. Such "preferred" or "invited" industries are typically those with the maximum potential linkages to the rest of the economy.

Incentives offered by the host governments for investment in the invited industries primarily apply to taxation status, but other incentives are offered as well. Tax incentives include reduced corporate tax rates, tax holidays ranging up to ten years for all or part of a company's profits, accelerated depreciation, personal income tax exemptions for foreign personnel, and carry-forward of losses. Other incentives used include investment subsidies, concession on import duties paid on inputs, foreign exchange allowances, credit subsidies, and low-cost infrastructure facilities (e.g., cheap power or free land).

Practice in the use of these incentives has enabled the officials in the developing countries to become fairly sophisticated in discriminating in favor of firms advancing priority development goals. For example, tax holidays have been lengthened for firms investing in specific regions of a developing country and thus reducing congestion in the port cities. Firms meeting certain export goals have benefited through reduced tax rates or longer holidays, and in Malaysia firms can increase their tax holiday by using a specific proportion of domestic materials as inputs. This "fine tuning" is likely to increase in the future, and specific incentives will increasingly be linked to exports, to labor policies (including the upgrading of skills), to growth in domestic value-added, and ownership policies.

It is not in the interests of any Asian state to trigger a competitive "war" in the bidding to attract investment. Each incentive offered has a real economic cost associated with it, and care must be taken to avoid diverting all the "economic rent" to the foreign company. To head off such a development, nations of Asia (perhaps through ASEAN and ECAFE) should agree on a host country investment code which would limit the list of allowable incentives. Obviously, the strength of each country's bargaining position with the foreign firm varies greatly. Labor-short Singapore, for example, can afford to be much more selective than can, say, Indonesia. But the direction of the movement is clear, and the typical package of benefits and costs brought by the foreign firm will be required to be increasingly weighted toward the developing country's advantage.

The question of ownership must be seen in this light. Wholly owned foreign firms will continue to be allowed entry into most of the developing Asian nations, but on a very selective basis. The cost to the host country will only be tolerated in those cases where the benefits associated with foreign entry are seen as vital to the development process. This will be true for only a few firms. Put another way, we are suggesting that a foreign firm will find that it will have to offer fewer benefits to the host country if it will tolerate local equity participation.

In general, the role played by foreign investment in spurring the developmental efforts of the Asian nations has clearly been recognized, especially in the last decade. Yet, it is also recognized that more benefits can be squeezed from a given dollar flow of foreign investment and, more importantly, that the development planners in Asia have the experience and knowledge to achieve this through the controls they exercise. A pragmatic cost-benefit, litmus test is likely to be applied to each investment proposal. The investing corporations should be content to live in this world and to become adept at enumerating realistically the costs and benefits of their own projects to the host countries in which they expect to operate.

THE FUTURE

Foreign investment in Asia promises continued expansion throughout the decade of the seventies. There are a number of lines of reasoning supporting this prediction. First, the Asian developing countries will continue to maintain a qualified "open door" policy regarding overseas investment. These nations, however, can be expected to increase the stringency of the tests that each new project must meet. Moreover, the origin and identity of investment projects will become increasingly important considerations in the deliberations of the various investment boards throughout the region.

More important to the prediction of continued investment growth in the region are the conditions in both Japan and the United States, the chief investors in the area. In both countries the economic forces spurring investment in the region will intensify. Japan, faced with a developing labor shortage, a growing concern for the environment, and increased protectionism in its leading markets, will accelerate its outflow of capital rapidly. The recent loosening of investment controls and the upward revaluation of the yen will also contribute to the growth in foreign investment.

United States investment in Asia will also accelerate over the next decade, as the trends for the last several years already indicate. The investment models touched on above all point to greater U.S. investment in Asia, and the approximately 8 per cent dollar devaluation in December 1971 will not materially affect this trend.

Within Asia, and increasingly throughout the world, the United States will see in Japan its chief economic competitor. As the large Japanese corporations led by the giant trading companies move out into the world for production purposes as well as trade, they will trigger defensive investment reactions by U.S. corporations. In the most recent listing by *Fortune* of the 200 largest industrial companies outside of the United States, Japan led the list with 51 companies, Britain having fallen to second place with 46, followed by Germany and France with 26 and 21 respectively. These large Japanese corporations, having acquired the knowledge of operating abroad, an awareness of world market conditions and, most importantly, the financial and technical resources to facilitate foreign investment, are poised for a major expansion in their overseas investment. This will be the most important new dimension in foreign investment during the seventies, and promises to make Asia the scene of the most intense investment activity since the European wave of the late fifties and early sixties.

It is true that there is growing opposition within the United States to allowing U.S. corporations to invest freely abroad.

Of major concern to the American labor movement is the job loss associated with the migration of production facilities. This concern has most recently been manifested in labor's support of the Hartke-Burke trade and investment bill now before Congress which includes provisions for limiting investment outflows. The defeat of this bill, the course of action urged by most economists, should not be interpreted as a clean bill of health for overseas investment. With any major form of international economic interaction, problems will emerge. What must be sought is the proper machinery, both national and international, to address the problems and to seek solutions in a mutually beneficial manner.

Foreign investment will continue as a major force in the world economy, and it is naïve to assume that absence of any control measures would maximize benefits either to host and source country, or to the investing company. We have mentioned the operation of investment boards in host countries. Yet control at the source is also warranted. Both Japan and the United States should create some type of investment institution which would operate to coordinate existing flows of investment, point up potential problem areas, and facilitate the resolution of existing disputes so as to allow the continuance of mutually beneficial private flows of capital throughout Asia.

Canada and the Security of Southeast Asia

LORNE J. KAVIC

The origins of Canadian society, geographical circumstances, historical experiences, and economic determinants
have traditionally combined to limit Canadian interest in
Southeast Asian affairs. Immigration from the area has always
been negligible, and two-way trade and investment flows
have never attained levels of seeming consequence to Canada's
economic health. No Southeast Asian state has ever consti
tuted an actual or potential danger to Canada's territorial
integrity or political sovereignty, nor has Canadian security
ever been directly imperiled by a Major Power striking
through the region. Canadian interest in power-political rivalries affecting Southeast Asia has accordingly reflected a broad
conception of the "national interest," and shifting perceptions of obligations arising from membership in the Empire/
Commonwealth, the League of Nations, the United Nations,
and an interlocking alliance system. Canada's response to
security problems in Southeast Asia has varied with time and
place, encompassing expressions of sympathy and concern,
conciliatory and mediatory diplomacy, and economic and military aid. Successive Canadian governments have consistently
reacted coolly to any suggestion entailing formal military
commitments in the area, but Canadian military personnel
have served there in both combatant and supervisory capacities.

Until the outbreak of the Pacific conflict in December
1941, Southeast Asia appeared to Canadians as a sleepy and
unexciting backwater in the onrushing tide of human affairs.
The colonial pattern of regional government was not re-

pugnant, nor was it perceived as disruptive of the general peace. At successive imperial and colonial conferences prior to World War I, Britain tried to interest Canada in a more active role in imperial defense, but Canadian representatives rebuffed British suggestions, alleging that Canada's transcontinental railway system constituted an important contribution to the security of imperial interests in the Asian-Pacific region. During the war no fighting occurred in the region, precluding the possibility of any Canadian troop deployments in the area in furtherance of Allied strategy. In the period between the two wars Canada showed some interest in the security of Southeast Asia in that it supported Britain's construction of the Singapore naval base which was built between 1921 and 1938 to secure the maritime approaches to India, Malaya and Australia, and which was prompted by the lapse of Britain's alliance with Japan. At the same time the government did not feel sufficiently concerned with the region to make a financial contribution to the building of the base.

World War II witnessed Canada's emergence as a Pacific power prepared to acknowledge the military imperatives of her geographic position and other interests, but it revealed a preference for discharging accepted responsibilities in the North or Central Pacific rather than in more remote areas such as Southeast Asia. Due to the abrupt end of the war against Japan in August 1945, which aborted active participation by Canada's three armed services in the final campaigns against the Japanese home islands,[1] the actual Canadian contribution to the Pacific conflict remained modest—two infantry battalions in the abortive defense of Hong Kong in December 1941, a moderate tri-service role in an assault against an island in the Aleutian chain secretly vacated by the Japanese in August 1943, one Catalina and two Dakota squadrons in Southeast Asia Command, four hundred Army technical personnel in Australia and the adjacent islands, and nearly a hundred Army officers attached to Allied units in Southeast Asia and

[1] For details on the development of these plans, see Colonel C. P. Stacey, *Six Years of War: The Army in Canada, Britain and the Pacific* (Ottawa: Queen's Printer, 1952), pp. 99–104 and 464–67.

the Pacific islands for varying periods of time. Canada had additionally, however, made a material contribution totaling over $146 million to Australia, China, and New Zealand under the provisions of her Mutual Aid program, the assistance to Australia playing an important part in Australian campaigns in New Guinea and New Britain.[2]

Following the capitulation of Japan, Canadians quickly reverted to their traditional preoccupation with domestic and European affairs despite some demands for an early definition of government policies in the Pacific.[3] Prime Minister Mackenzie King claimed in the Commons on December 17, 1945, that "we have much to gain and nothing to lose by not taking too immediate a step in regard to what is most advisable in the intricate situation which exists at the present time in the Pacific."[4] As late as January 1947 the Minister for External Affairs, Louis St. Laurent, could make a major statement on Canada's basic approach to world affairs without once referring to Asia and the Pacific, attesting to the government's continued view of the region as of no direct concern to Canada.[5]

This somewhat detached attitude was, however, progressively eroded as the Canadian people and their elected officials perceived the deterioration of relations between the Soviet bloc and the liberal democracies of the West, and the surge of nationalist feeling in Asia and the Middle East. The traditional primacy of European and North Atlantic affairs continued to dominate thinking at both the official and public levels, but there was an increasing responsiveness to the tur-

[2] Canadian Mutual Aid Board, *Final Report* (Ottawa: King's Printer, 1947).

[3] See C. C. Lingard, "Far Eastern Affairs," *Canadian Historical Review*, December 1945 (Vol. XXVI), pp. 432–37; W. L. Morton, "Canada and Future Policy in the Pacific," *International Journal*, Winter 1945–46 (Vol. I, No. 1), pp. 55–64; and "Canada's Far Eastern Policy," *Pacific Affairs*, September 1946 (Vol. XIX, No. 3), pp. 241–49.

[4] Statement by Prime Minister Mackenzie King in the House of Commons on December 17, 1945.

[5] The speech is reprinted in: Canada, Department of External Affairs, *Statements and Speeches* (Ottawa: King's Printer, 1947), No. 47/2.

bulence sweeping Asia. Major concern remained, as in the past, with East Asian developments, where China's resurgence under militant Communism coupled with Japan's military prostration posed a major headache for U.S. defense planners, typified to some degree by the outbreak and qualified resolution of the Korean War. But substantial interest was also demonstrated in developments in Southeast Asia, the former sleepy colonial backwater rent by disruptive civil, regional, and international rivalries. Canadians by no means viewed the recurring crises in Burma, Malaya, Indonesia, and Indochina as a long-awaited challenge to be eagerly seized upon in accordance with some sort of national mission. But it was clear that, in the prevailing geopolitics, Canada could neither view the area with the former detachment, nor automatically eschew any responsibility in respect of regional security. Close consideration had to be given to the policy dictates and constraints arising out of the country's Pacific relations with the United States, close historical ties with France and the Netherlands, and a belated but sensitive appreciation of the dynamic nature of nationalist forces in the area.

Canadian concern with the stability of Southeast Asia since the conclusion of World War II has not taken the form of membership of any regional security pact or arrangement. Canada was not invited to participate in the negotiations leading to the ANZUS pact and, unlike Britain, felt no regrets at being omitted. The Canadian government declined to respond to "informal British soundings" as the Korean conflict drew to a close about possible participation in the Commonwealth Strategic Reserve planned for the Malayan area, and ultimately established in 1955, and further made it clear that involvement by Canadian naval units in Commonwealth naval exercises held in the general area should in no way be construed as implying any commitment to regional defense. While the Korean conflict was raging, Ottawa did not preclude the possibility of Canada joining a general Pacific security arrangement,[6] but Canada was neither invited nor took

[6] See, for example, statements in the House of Commons by the Minister for External Affairs, Lester B. Pearson, on November 16, 1950, April 19, 1951, and October 23, 1951.

any action to participate in the discussions which culminated in the formation of the Southeast Asian Treaty Organization (SEATO) in 1954.

The posture of successive Canadian governments on Southeast Asian security arrangements has, in part, reflected the fact that the new post-1945 feeling of responsibility in respect to world affairs has coincided with an increasing consciousness of very limited military power; no Cabinet since 1945 has been inclined to overestimate Canada's capabilities and add to the burdens already assumed in the North Atlantic Treaty Organization (NATO), continental defense, and United Nations Charter. The perceived weaknesses of any SEATO-style security pact had been the subject of official comment for several years prior to conception of that treaty, and were enumerated by the Minister for External Affairs, Mr. Pearson, in the Commons on February 11, 1953:

> As I see it, there are three fundamental difficulties which remain . . . in the way of the early realization of a Pacific pact on a multilateral basis. The first difficulty— and it is a basic one—is which Pacific states should be included and which should be left out; the second is how to get the various countries which might participate to agree to team up with other potential members; and finally there is the lack of community of interest and purpose and policy among some of the potential members. Until these problems are solved, and they are certainly not solved yet, a Pacific pact which attempted to be the counterpart of the North Atlantic pact would, I think, inevitably be an artificial creation and might well do more harm than good.

These difficulties were not resolved, in Ottawa's view, by the formation of an organization strongly opposed by such important regional states as India and Indonesia, the views of the former being accorded particular weight during these early postwar years due to its considerable influence among Third World countries. One of the leading papers in the country described SEATO as a "makeshift of the kind that history contemptuously casts aside,"[7] and a political commentator described it as an "outgrowth of the mistaken notion that

[7] *The Globe and Mail* (Toronto), September 11, 1954.

solutions which seemed to have worked in Europe must inevitably succeed elsewhere," and thought that "as such it does not hold very much promise in an area where by far the largest number of states and people distrusts it and views it as a sort of corporate and modified successor to the colonial powers."[8] Canada's nonparticipation in SEATO passed almost without comment in the country's parliament and press,[9] the question having been rendered academic by the government's reluctant acceptance of a role on the International Control Commissions for Laos, Cambodia, and Vietnam persuant to the Geneva Conference on Indochina deliberations.

Although formal military commitments in Southeast Asia have been eschewed to date, other than as may arise from United Nations action, Canada's interest in regional stability has been illustrated with regard to the first and second Indochina wars, which have involved the confusing interaction of Communism and anti-Communism, colonialism and nationalism. It has been displayed in respect to Indonesian nationalist struggles against Dutch colonialism in the East Indies and West New Guinea. It has been manifested in attitudes displayed and actions taken on the question of Indonesia's "confrontation" of Malaysia. It has revealed itself in the form of economic development assistance provided to all countries in the region, save North Vietnam.

The turbulent situation in the Indochina area has posed policy dilemmas for a succession of Canadian governments, given the involvement of valued friends and distant strangers, of formal allies and perceived foes, of cherished ideals and acknowledged expedients. Canadians and their elected representatives manifested almost no interest in the Indochina scene

[8] John Meisel, "Pactomania," *The Canadian Forum*, April 1956 (Vol. 36, No. 423). See also James Eayrs, *Canada in World Affairs: 1955 to 1957* (Toronto: Oxford University Press, 1959), p. 86.

[9] The Vancouver *Province*, a strong advocate of Canadian participation in Pacific mutual security arrangements, was the only major Canadian daily newspaper to adopt a strongly critical position of the government's posture, while Progressive Conservative spokesmen who had previously endorsed Canadian membership in a Pacific pact withheld comment.

until the establishment of the People's Republic of China in October 1949 focused considerable attention upon the Asian scene. Close and friendly ties with France rooted in history and reinforced by membership in NATO ensured more than passing interest in the struggle then raging between French Union forces and the Viet Minh. The Canadian government was fully appreciative of the colonial aspect of the conflict—the nationalist and anticolonial origins of the revolt against French control, and the intransigence of local French authorities toward decolonization. But Canada's historical experience with colonialism predisposed most Canadians to sympathize with the evolutionary, if somewhat suspect, approach of France to accommodating Indochinese nationalism rather than with the violent methods of the Viet Minh, whose "nationalist" claim was badly compromised in Canadian eyes by the increasingly orthodox Communist stamp of the movement.[10] The specter of a Communist triumph in Indochina haunted Ottawa as it did other Western capitals during this period of severe tension in Asia. "If the valiant efforts now being made by France to defend and complete the independence of Indochina were to fail," External Affairs Minister Pearson declared in the House of Commons on February 2, 1951, "the whole of South East Asia . . . might well come under Communist control, and the position of India and Pakistan in that event would in the long run, or in the not so long run, be precarious indeed." An additional concern of the Canadian government was the heavy drain of the conflict on French resources, and especially on France's ability to make the maximum contribution to European and North Atlantic security and cooperative arrangements.

The establishment of Laos, Cambodia, and Vietnam as autonomous states within the French Union in 1949 was welcomed as "a commendable step forward in the attempt to

[10] Even the Cooperative Commonwealth Federation (CCF), which viewed the conflict in essentially colonialist terms and regarded Bao Dai as a "French puppet," dismissed Ho Chi Minh as a "Communist agent." See statements in the House of Commons by Alistair Stewart on March 7, 1950, and by party leader M. J. Caldwell on May 5, 1953.

restore peaceful and stable conditions in Indochina . . .
[which] will provide a means by which the national aspirations of the people of Indochina will be met,"[11] and Canada
belatedly followed the lead of Britain and the United States
in according recognition on December 30, 1952, to the three
states as Associated States of Indochina within the French
Union. Canada was party to a NATO resolution of December
17, 1952, which declared NATO Council agreement that the
campaign being waged by the French Union forces merited
support from NATO members, and made no objections to
French use in Indochina of military equipment supplied under its Mutual Aid program. But a desire to avoid any direct
involvement in a conflict involving a colonial area was reflected in the government's refusal to directly sanction the use
of such equipment, a circumspect position which was not
appreciated in Paris. The dramatic fifty-five-day siege of Dien
Bien Phu, however, was followed with intense interest in
Canada, and strong sympathy for the French Union garrison was manifest at both official and public levels. As the
Prime Minister, Louis St. Laurent, declared in the House of
Commons on May 10, 1954, Canadians "lamented" the fall
of the fortress but "salute with pride and honor the heroic
defenders of the fortress," a sentiment which was echoed by
the leader of the Progressive Conservative Opposition,
George Drew.

Ironically, the fall of Dien Bien Phu was to set in motion
developments which were to involve Canada very directly in
the affairs of Indochina as a member of the International
Control Commissions established at the Geneva conference
on Indochina in 1954. Canada took no part in the talks cul-
minating in the Indochina settlement, but a formal invitation
to participate along with Poland and India on the Commissions designed to supervise the implementation of the ceasefire in Laos, Cambodia, and Vietnam was received by Ottawa
from the Co-Chairmen of the Geneva Conference, Eden of

[11] Statement by the Minister for External Affairs, Lester Pearson, in the House of Commons on February 22, 1950.

Britain, and Molotov of the Soviet Union, on July 21.[12] The invitation came as a complete surprise to the Canadian government, and was not received with particular enthusiasm as it posed extensive problems in terms of personnel, the nature of the task, and the resultant involvement as the "Western" representative on a troika including a nonaligned India and a Communist Poland. After studying the invitation for nearly a week, and with mixed misgivings, some high hopes and a degree of naïveté,[13] the government accepted the invitation out of a professed desire to assist in the establishment of peace and security in Southeast Asia, and so serve the cause of peace everywhere.

The accumulative experience of Canadian observers serving on the Commissions strengthened Ottawa's bias against the Communist Democratic Republic of Vietnam, and as the Viet Cong insurgency steadily mounted in intensity, the government made its position known in unmistakable terms. Formal recognition was extended to the Republic of Vietnam in November 1963,[14] the Viet Cong being dismissed as a creature of the ruling party in Hanoi, whose policy was condemned as "a process of subversion . . . aggression carried on under the guise of a war of national liberation . . .

[12] The selection of Canada as the "Western" member of the troika appears to have originated with Krishna Menon, who broached the matter with Chou En-lai. John Holmes has expressed the view that "the Canadian role in Geneva as an unobtrusive oil can had much to do with our being chosen later for a job on the Control Commissions" ["Geneva 1954," *International Journal,* Summer 1967 (Vol. XXII, No. 3), p. 464].

[13] The appointment of Brigadier Sherwood Lett, a judge, as Canada's first commissioner on the Commission reflected a belief that the role would be semijudicial as suggested, whereas in fact it turned out to be highly political.

[14] Recognition was advanced on the grounds that Saigon was in actual control of the major part of the territory of the state, had undertaken to observe international obligations entered into by its predecessors, had secured the acquiescence of the population, had promised to protect foreign lives and property and to guarantee fundamental freedoms, and had undertaken to maintain cooperation with the Control Commissions. See statement by the Minister for External Affairs, Paul Martin, in the House of Commons on November 14, 1963.

[which] must be identified as such and brought under control . . ."[15] While conceding that South Vietnam had violated the "spirit" of the Geneva agreements by seeking and receiving military assistance from the United States and other countries, Canadian government spokesmen defended the violation as a legitimate response to the North's provocative prior violation of the agreements in promoting subversion in the South aimed at the overthrow of the Saigon administration. Ottawa accepted Washington's version of the Gulf of Tonkin incident, and implicitly sympathized with the determination of the Lyndon Johnson Administration to react vigorously in defense of its interests in the area.

The massive nature of the American military response, however, was viewed with considerable concern by a Canadian population which shared the general international revulsion against the sharp escalation of hostilities, and by Canadian policy-makers who perceived U.S. military policy in the area as threatening a wider conflict rather than affording a credible solution to the security problems of the Republic of Vietnam. The Canadian government added its voice to those advocating a suspension of the air campaign against North Vietnam as a necessary preliminary to deescalation and the commencement of negotiations that would hopefully lead to an equitable settlement which would permit the South Vietnamese people to freely determine their political relationship with the Democratic Republic of Vietnam. An aversion to any overt complicity in the controversial employment of American air power in the war-torn land prompted Ottawa to refuse a request from Washington in early 1965 to sell back some bombs purchased from the United States earlier, to refuse another request in late 1965 to ship practice bombs, some ammunition and spares for de Havilland Buffalo transport aircraft directly to Vietnam, and to dissuade the American government from placing a sizable order for smoke bombs with Canadian firms in early 1967.

---

[15] See speech by Mr. Martin to the Editors of the Foreign Language Press in Toronto on March 26, 1965, in: Canada, Department of External Affairs, *Statements and Speeches* (Ottawa: Queen's Printer, 1965), No. 65/2.

Official sensitivity to the strong feelings of many Canadians on the war was demonstrated by the admission of representatives of the National Liberation Front in 1967 to speak at rallies organized by groups critical of U.S. policies. But official comment remained restrained, in accordance with the perceived limitations of Canadian influence upon American policy in Vietnam, and out of deference to extreme sensitivity in Washington to criticisms and advice from a small neighbor expected to be more understanding of U.S. policies than more distant countries lacking such an intimate relationship.[16] Suggestions that the export of military equipment to the United States be suspended were firmly rejected by the Canadian government on the grounds that such an embargo and the concomitant termination of the Production Sharing Agreement "would be interpreted as a notice of withdrawal on our part from continental defense and even from the collective defense arrangements of the Atlantic alliance."[17]

Since 1968, Ottawa has been noticeably reticent about commenting on developments in Vietnam. The shift of American policy to an essentially defensive and retaliatory strategy based upon South Vietnamese resources backed by American air power and material aid eased public and official concern in Canada about the direction of U.S. policy and, by implication, removed a noticeable irritant upon which the Canadian government felt compelled to comment during the 1965–68 period. Official statements on the subject in recent

[16] The meeting between Prime Minister Pearson and President Johnson at Camp David in 1965, which followed Mr. Pearson's reference to the desirability of a bombing halt in a speech to an American university audience, was reportedly the chilliest on record between leaders of the two countries. Mr. Pearson noticeably declined comment on the war in a speech delivered to another university audience in California in April 1967. Canadian restraint was also partly attributable to fears of economic reprisals. See Mr. Pearson's frank admission to an interviewer in "The Long Happy Life of Lester Pearson," *Maclean's*, July 1967, p. 52.

[17] See Mr. Pearson's reply to representatives from a group of university professors dated March 10, 1967, in: Canada, Department of External Affairs, *Statements and Speeches* (Ottawa: Queen's Printer, 1967), No. 67/8.

years have accordingly been confined to dramatic developments such as the intrusion into Cambodia and Laos by U.S. and South Vietnamese forces in 1970–71, and the major American aerial bombardment of the Hanoi and Haiphong areas in December 1972–January 1973. The invasions of Cambodia and Laos were regretted, but implicitly defended as understandable reactions to long-standing Communist violations of the territories of the two states.[18] No such sympathy was manifested toward President Nixon's use of massive aerial bombardment in late 1972–early 1973 to force Hanoi into a more accommodating approach to the Paris peace talks. Canadian opinion shared the revulsion with which much of the world reacted to this display of crude power diplomacy, and the sense of betrayal of the high hopes for an early ceasefire which Washington had carefully nurtured prior to the U.S. Presidential election. In a move unprecedented in Canadian history, the House of Commons unanimously passed a motion presented by External Affairs Minister Mitchell Sharp on January 5, 1973, calling upon the United States to refrain from resuming the bombing of the Hanoi-Haiphong area and expressing its concern at the continuation of hostilities in Indochina. The motion, approved as the House completed its first sitting day, was the first measure approved by the 29th Parliament.

The apprehension with which Ottawa and many Canadians viewed participation on the International Control Commissions has been borne out by experience. The Commissions performed a valuable service in supervising the exchange of prisoners of war and the movement of refugees from the northern zone controlled by anti-Communist elements. But the presence of the Commissions failed to inhibit, much less deter, an insurgency in South Vietnam from developing into a major conflict engulfing the entire Indochinese area and involving external powers directly and indirectly. It failed to prevent North Vietnamese/Viet Cong violation of Cambodian neutrality, and to influence to any degree the course of

18 See the statements by the Minister for External Affairs, Mitchell Sharp, in the House of Commons on May 1, 1970, and February 1, 1971.

events in Laos, which is sporadically wracked by conflict between Communist, anti-Communist, and neutralist factions aided variously from without. The impotence of the Commissions has sparked periodic discussion in Canada regarding the merits of continued membership, but successive Canadian governments have remained formally "loyal" to a commitment which has entailed a modest, if exceedingly frustrating, effort at enhancing regional stability in a fashion not inimical to Western interests. The experience has made Canadians and their elected representatives less than enthusiastic about participating in the new supervisory body set up to oversee another Vietnam settlement, but the government's decision to provide a small force upon request of the parties immediately concerned, subject to certain conditions, appears to reflect majority opinion in the country, which accepts that Canada has responsibilities which must be discharged, however onerous they may appear.

Successive Canadian governments have also become involved in conflicts in Southeast Asia which did not involve a struggle between Communist and non-Communist parties. As a member of the United Nations Security Council in 1948–49, Canada became quite active in seeking to arrange a settlement between the Dutch colonial authorities and the Indonesian nationalist forces. At this time the government sought to play the role of a mediator rather than an advocate of either side since it was cross-pressured by its desire to prevent a serious alienation between the Western states and the anticolonial forces in Asia, which could lead to diplomatic gains by Communist states in that region of the world. Canadian representatives endeavored with some success to perform a role of impartial mediation through the successive stages of the dispute, including an important contribution to a compromise solution achieved on March 23, 1949, which has been described as "one of the vital turning points in the settlement of the Indonesian problem."[19] It provided the basis for the successful Round Table Conference held in November–

---

[19] Canada, Department of External Affairs, *Canada and the United Nations* (Ottawa: King's Printer, 1949), p. 67.

December 1949 in which the Netherlands and Indonesian leaders reached agreement on a transfer of sovereignty.

Canada was decidedly less sympathetic to Indonesia's subsequent effort to wrest West New Guinea from the Netherlands, and her attempt to destroy the new Malaysian Federation. The Indonesian claim to West New Guinea was considered to be legally tenuous, and the methods employed to advance the claim, which included harassment of Dutch nationals and interests in Indonesia, provoked expressions of deep concern from the Canadian government. Canadian policy on the issue, however, was ultimately grounded in the belief that Dutch retention of the area in the face of adamant Indonesian feelings backed by strong Afro-Asian and Communist bloc support was fruitless—and damaging to the Western image in Afro-Asia. Ottawa thus acquiesced quietly in the decision of the United Nations to transfer West New Guinea to Indonesian control, and provided air transport to the United Nations Temporary Executive Administration (UNTEA) established to effect the transfer.

Indonesia's declared intention to destroy the new Malaysian Federation in late 1963 provoked undisguised alarm in Canada for the security of the fellow Commonwealth state. Creation of the Federation had been welcomed as the best means of ending the colonial status of Singapore and the British Borneo territories, and Djakarta's assertion that it represented a neocolonialist threat to its security was dismissed as a specious rationale designed to camouflage territorial designs and distract domestic attention from the country's desperate economic situation. Increased economic aid and the extension of military equipment aid to Malaysia was supported by spokesmen of all parties in the Commons, and some opinion was expressed which favored suspension of economic aid to Indonesia.[20]

The government remained initially cautious and noncommittal in its public comments on the matter, acknowledging its "regret" at the Indonesian action but suggesting that Brit-

[20] See, for example, statements by W. B. Nesbitt, Gordon Churchill, and Colin Cameron in the House of Commons on November 20, 1964.

ain, Australia, and New Zealand had a more immediate interest in the question.[21] The first indication that military assistance would be provided to Malaysia upon request was revealed by Prime Minister Pearson in the Commons on July 24, 1964, but dispatch of combatant personnel was pointedly ruled out—the assumption being that Malaysia would request defense supplies and perhaps some assistance in training.[22] The government was not prepared, however, to assume either a group commitment, or one indefinite in volume and time, preferring to confine its support to bilateral economic and military aid clearly distinct from the combatant support roles of Britain, Australia, and New Zealand. Following talks with Malaysian authorities and a visit to Malaysia by an eight-member Canadian mission,[23] Kuala Lumpur was offered and accepted grant aid valued at about $4 million and comprising four "Caribou" transport aircraft plus spares, 250 motorcycles for the police, and training facilities in Canada for up to 80 Malaysian military personnel over a two-year period. In addition, Canada agreed to make available increased economic aid and credits to cover the purchase of trainer and transport aircraft.[24] As regards Indonesia, the Canadian government sought to maintain a proper perspective on its

[21] See statements by External Affairs Minister Paul Martin in the House of Commons on November 28 and December 21, 1963, and May 4, 1964. Canada had maintained a similar posture toward the Malayan Emergency in 1948–60.

[22] Speaking in the House of Commons on November 19, 1964, External Affairs Minister Martin emphasized that the government had no intention of sending troops for purposes of combat to any part of Asia, except pursuant to obligations under the United Nations, adding that Australia and New Zealand had a more immediate interest than Canada in Malaysian security.

[23] The mission concluded that Canada could best contribute to Malaysian security in the fields of air transport and training.

[24] Malaysia purchased twenty CL-41G "Tutor" jet trainers in 1967 and nine "Caribous" in 1968–69. The training scheme was extended following expiration of the initial term, and Canada's association with the Royal Malaysian Air Force deepened with the loan of Air Commodore K. R. Greenway to serve as air advisor to the Chief of Staff in 1967–70. His role, however, was restricted to training and organization in accordance with Ottawa's determination to remain noninvolved in operational matters.

actions out of consideration for its size and potential importance, and in recognition that it was suffering from extremist nationalist feeling and the administration of an unstable president. Suspension of economic aid, which consisted only of wheat and flour, was ruled out for the professed reason that "assistance of a nonmilitary kind given by Western countries has not traditionally borne any political motivation."[25] But Indonesia's use of three "Otter" aircraft provided as Colombo Plan aid in 1958–59 in its "confrontation" campaign provoked Ottawa to suspend, on January 20, 1965, the proposed sale of twelve "Otters" initially envisaged for civil use in West Irian.

Canadian interest in the stability of Southeast Asia has been further evidenced in the field of relief and development aid, commencing with a $15 million reconstruction loan extended to the Netherlands East Indies in October 1945[26] and expanding to embrace bilateral and multilateral programs affecting every non-Communist country in Southeast Asia. Since the inception of the Colombo Plan in 1951 as a Commonwealth response to the acute development problems of India, Pakistan, and Ceylon, Canadian bilateral disbursements have totaled approximately $77 million (1951–71)[27] encompassing, in order of emphasis, technical assistance, food, education, natural resources, transportation, and health and social services. Malaysia, designated a "country of concentration" by the Canadian government, has received about one-third of this aid followed by the Republic of Vietnam, Indonesia, Burma, and Thailand with minor aid being provided to Cambodia, Laos, and the Philippines. Canada has also expended or committed $4,320,000 toward the construc-

[25] See statement by the Minister for External Affairs, Paul Martin, in the House of Commons on September 9, 1964.

[26] Canada agreed to make a further $50 million available when the government's lending authority was increased, but the promised funds never materialized due to political and constitutional factors culminating in the emergence of the Republic of Indonesia in December 1949.

[27] Fiscal years ending March 31. Disbursements have consistently represented only 65–75 per cent of allocations due to the competitiveness of other donors for good development projects.

tion of two dams in Laos and Cambodia under the Mekong Development scheme, is a charter member of the Asian Development Bank to which she has subscribed U.S. $25 million and committed an additional $25 million for the special fund, and has been an active member of consultative World Bank groups formed to deal with development problems in Malaysia and Thailand. A number of Canadian voluntary agencies have also become active in Southeast Asia in recent years, and have received important financial support from the Canadian government since 1968.

Stability has by no means been the only consideration affecting the level, type, and distribution of Canadian development aid in Southeast Asia, but foreign aid is an admitted integral part of Canadian foreign policy, the primary objects of which are the prevention of war and the enhancement of world stability, however these may be presented in glossy statements of policy. The premises on which Canadian economic aid to Southeast Asian countries are based are, however tenuous the case may appear on close and critical study, (1) a faster rather than a slower rate of economic growth among less-developed countries (LDCs) is conducive to political stability in the world and an international environment that is less hostile to the interests of Western countries like Canada; and (2) these benefits of aid will be enhanced by supporting economic development in those LDCs that are Canada's allies, or at least are neutral, and by not supporting development in those LDCs that are hostile to the interests of the West.[28]

Anti-Communism was the major stimulus in Canada's postwar aid programs, the Colombo Plan crystallizing "essentially to stop the Red and Yellow Perils."[29] Canadian aid dis-

[28] Grant L. Reuber, "The Trade-Offs Among the Objectives of Canadian Foreign Aid," *International Journal*, Winter 1969–70 (Vol. XXV, No. 1), pp. 136–37.

[29] Keith Spicer, "Clubmanship Upstaged: Canada's Twenty Years in the Colombo Plan," *International Journal*, Winter 1969–70 (Vol. XXV, No. 1), p. 25. Speaking in the House of Commons on his return from the first Colombo Plan conference on February 22, 1950, External Affairs Minister Pearson declared: "If Southeast and South Asia are not to be conquered by Communism, we

bursements in Southeast Asia have accordingly been restricted to non-Communist countries to date, although there are indications that this ideological bias will not cause the Democratic Republic of Vietnam to be excluded from benefiting from Canadian participation in the international relief and reconstruction program that is expected to be undertaken in Indochina following an end of the present conflict. There is growing appreciation in Canada as in other Western countries that relief and development aid, like trade, can help to bridge chasms arising out of historical experience and rooted in contemporary alliance patterns.

The perceived relationship between political instability on the one hand and poverty and stagnant economies on the other has become an important consideration in Canadian thinking on development assistance in recent years, and has thus contributed to Canada's continuing interest in Southeast Asian development needs. It has been reflected in primary attention to countries striving to attain the "takeoff" point of development, and a very secondary concern for the more prosperous Southeast Asian states like Singapore, Thailand, the Philippines, and Malaysia, which are now viewed as having reached the desired plateau. It has been evidenced in the announced intention to shift emphasis away from project assistance, which has been infrastructure-oriented rather than people-oriented, and from too much emphasis upon educational assistance which has not been sufficiently relevant to the immediate needs of the LDCs of Southeast Asia. It has been manifested in the designation of Indonesia as an area of "concentration," Canada joining the Inter-Governmental Group for Indonesia and increasing its allocations for this strategically located and potentially important state from $5.75 million (1970–71) to $18 million (1972–73). It has been a central theme in recent official pronouncements on Canadian aid, the government observing in its 1970 foreign policy review that "widespread poverty remains as one of the principal challenges to the equilibrium of the

---

of the free democratic world . . . must demonstrate that it is we and not the Russians who stand for national liberation and economic and social progress."

world,"[30] and that "by cooperation with the countries of Southeast Asia in their plans for national development it [Canada] can make a worthwhile contribution to the well-being of the peoples and the economic prosperity of the area."[31]

The level of Canadian economic aid provided to Southeast Asia has been very modest in accordance with the region's relatively low priority in Canadian perspectives of Third World needs. The area has received only about 5 per cent of Canada's bilateral Colombo Plan disbursements, which have been largely channeled into India, Pakistan, and Ceylon, whereas the area has bulked far more prominently in the aid programs of other Pacific Rim states like the United States, Japan, Australia, and New Zealand, and even of such European countries as Britain, the Netherlands, and West Germany. Nor has Canadian aid been appreciable in terms of the aid receipts of any Southeast Asian nation, representing in 1950–69 only 8.7 per cent of total Malaysian receipts, 1.7 per cent of Burma's, 0.9 per cent of Thailand's, 0.4 per cent of Cambodia's, 0.3 per cent of Indonesian and South Vietnamese receipts, 0.2 per cent of Laos', and it has been negligible in respect to the economic aid received by the Philippines. It has, nonetheless, been of some importance in terms of local development and has, however modestly, thereby constituted a stabilizing influence in the area of long-term importance.

Canada's involvement in matters relating to peace and stability in Southeast Asia has thus been largely derivative in nature, belated in time, and limited in extent. Successive governments and generations have consistently declined to acknowledge the existence of any vital Canadian interests in the region. But there has always existed a general consciousness, however latent or suppressed, of Canada's ultimate stake in the stability of Southeast Asia. Canada acquired a Pacific

[30] Canada, Department of External Affairs, *Foreign Policy for Canadians: International Development* (Ottawa: Queen's Printer, 1970), p. 8.

[31] Canada, Department of External Affairs, *Foreign Policy for Canadians: The Pacific* (Ottawa: Queen's Printer, 1970), p. 20.

frontier by deliberate action, and thus faced direct exposure to such power-political rivalries affecting the Pacific oceanic mass as arose over Southeast Asian issues. Membership in the British Empire and Commonwealth of Nations, acquired by circumstance and retained by choice, has precluded any detachment regarding threats to imperial possessions and interests, and to Commonwealth states, originating within, or directed through, the region. Canada has identified its Pacific security with the United States since the Washington Conference in 1920–21 and the Imperial Conference of 1921. Involvement with the United States in North American defense arrangements since World War II has associated Canada with the interlocked American alliance system blanketing Southeast Asia, committing her to cooperative action in respect to continental defense in the event of major conflict erupting between the United States, China, and/or the Soviet Union over Vietnam or other Southeast Asian issues. Membership in the League of Nations and the United Nations, voluntarily acquired, has included collective security obligations of an indeterminate nature involving the Southeast Asian colonies of member states as well as sovereign Southeast Asian member states.

The formulation of appropriate policies on general and specific Southeast Asian security issues has posed problems of varying complexity and difficulty for Canadian policy-makers. Support for legitimate nationalist aspirations has had to be weighed against sympathy for the perceived dilemmas of friendly colonial powers. Distinctions have had to be made carefully between struggles waged against colonial authorities by broad-based nationalist movements, and insurgencies against colonial and national governments by ethnic, regional, or special interest groups lacking broad popular support. Care has had to be exercised in examining the merits of competitive national claims of regional states. Responsible statesmanship has required that Canadian governments, in their handling of specific issues, make conscious and considered reference to broader regional and international considerations, and that long-term goals not be sacrificed in favor of short-term expedients. Compulsions to act have had to be judged against existing or potential capabilities, and the determination of priorities in the allocation of resources has necessitated compromises between narrow individual, party, or national urges and predilections, and broader national requirements and international obligations.

The resultant compromises have not been devoid of frustrations for well-meaning Canadians, and for expectant friendly governments with more direct interests in Southeast Asia. Ottawa has been variously subjected to domestic criticism for doing too little or attempting to do too much; for reacting too readily, too passively, or at all; for exercising realpolitik or ignoring it; and for confused goals and confusing priorities. Commonwealth governments involved in Southeast Asia would have wished for a somewhat more positive attitude from Canada on matters of the security of the Malaysian area. The United States expected more overt sympathy and support from Ottawa in regard to her Vietnam problem, as did France during her period of embroilment in Indochina. Indigenous governments have undoubtedly desired greater Canadian responsiveness to their local problems and views than they have received. The spectrum of comment on the merits of Canadian policies, however, suggests the basic dilemma which Canadian governments face in their search for appropriate policies regarding an area which has been characterized by a high degree of instability since 1945.

Given the limitations of Canadian resources and the options with which the policy-maker has had to deal, Canada has made a contribution to stability in Southeast Asia, however modest this may appear in comparative terms. Its diplomacy—which has been sensitive and responsible, if not imaginative and assertive—has aimed at strengthening the forces of conciliation, yet has precluded neither the support of friendly governments faced with aggression nor the condemnation of aggression which others prefer to call "wars of liberation." The absence of Canada from regional security arrangements has scarcely detracted from their deterrent value or operational potential, while it has enabled Canada to retain credibility as a potential "impartial" peace-keeper, and has left her free to provide military assistance to friendly countries subjected to threats, subversion, or attack, or desirous of strengthening their local defense capacity. Canada's development assistance in the area has been modest in terms of local needs, but it has helped to strengthen local economies, will, and capacity to withstand threatening internal problems and external pressures. Modest assistance is unquestionably better than none, and the Canadian contribution to stability in Southeast Asia has been more meaningful than is commonly supposed.

IV
International Security
Arrangements

Canada and the International Commissions in Indochina, 1954–72

PAUL BRIDLE

The second successive generation to be born in war is growing up in Indochina. When this article was completed Henry Kissinger of the United States and Le Duc Tho of North Vietnam had just initialed an agreement on cessation of hostilities in Vietnam, thus opening up the prospect of the whole war coming to an end. At least for a time, this emerging settlement will require international supervision. The last time there was a settlement, more than eighteen years ago, the task of supervision was assigned to the international commissions which were then established in Vietnam, Laos, and Cambodia.

These commissions were not concerned with the origins of the war which had been fought between 1946 and 1954, but unresolved issues replete with passions—fears, suspicions, hatreds, aspirations conservative and revolutionary, scores to be settled, the memory of sacrifices made and the readiness to make more—were the ground on which the commissions walked, the atmosphere in which they moved; these conflicting forces were in turn locked into the wider struggle of the power blocs. One cannot understand the efforts and, in the perspective of the present, the failure of the commissions without reference to these conditions.

TOWARD THE GENEVA CONFERENCE OF 1954

The history of Indochina, reaching back to the origins of Asian civilization, has been marked by conflict both internal and external. Nevertheless, long before the French arrived in the 1850s, Vietnam, Laos, and Cambodia were distinct countries. Vietnam consisted of three kingdoms, Tonkin in the north, Annam in the center, and Cochin-China in the south; however, the Emperor of Annam normally held sway over all three. Nationalism was particularly strong in Vietnam, which over the centuries had forged its identity in the fire of struggle with China.

The net effect of the French presence was divisive. It did little to reduce strife among the sects in Vietnam, and the impetus given to Christianity there increased the complexity of Vietnamese society. Also, French rule was exerted from Saigon in Cochin-China (not from Hué in Annam, the old imperial capital) and extended outward to Annam, Tonkin, Laos, and Cambodia which were all designated French protectorates. Indochina was thus centralized, but Vietnam was segmented. The greatest distortion was that imposed by the colonial yoke. While it offered certain advantages to old-style nations moving willy-nilly into the twentieth century and while there was a real cultural bond between the French and the elite of Indochina, the most striking characteristics of the French presence were political domination and economic exploitation.

Toward the end of the Second World War the Japanese expelled or imprisoned the isolated French and proclaimed the Emperor of Annam, Bao Dai, as the Emperor of a united and independent Vietnam in the "Greater East Asia Co-Prosperity Sphere." At the same time King Sihanouk of Cambodia declared independence of French rule, and under Japanese pressure King Sisavong Vong of northern Laos followed suit.

These adventures into self-rule were soon aborted. The French provisional government in Paris promptly reasserted France's postwar aims in Indochina: France would return, liberalizing its administration and making room for the Indochinese states in the French Union. Bao Dai was now prepared to collaborate with France, presumably in the hope that he would be able to negotiate a gradual move toward eventual unity and independence.

On the contrary, Ho Chi Minh, though prepared to negotiate, was determined to control his country's destiny.

Many nationalist movements, most of them Buddhist or otherwise non-Communist, had grown up in Vietnam during the war. By the end of the war several of them had coalesced to form the League of Annamese Revolutionary Parties, the strongest component of which was the Viet Minh, a front for several smaller groups including the strongly knit and deeply rooted Communist party. The director of all three was Ho Chi Minh, recently returned to Vietnam after thirty years abroad in Paris, Moscow, Canton, and other places in China. Now the leading political figure in Vietnam in opposition to Bao Dai, Ho Chi Minh was both an uncompromising nationalist and an authentic Asian Communist. Yet at this time the radical cast of his movement seems not to have been appreciated in the West. In the period before the Japanese capitulation it was the Viet Minh who "created the first anti-Japanese guerrilla forces in Vietnam, that rescued American fliers shot down in Indochina, that provided intelligence to the allies . . . and that received all the credit for anti-Japanese activities during the war"; and when Ho Chi Minh took over Hanoi following the Japanese surrender, the U.S. flag flew over Viet Minh headquarters and senior U.S. officers appeared at Viet Minh functions.[1]

Nevertheless, even before the war had ended, the United States—along with Britain—was giving signs of going along with the return of France to Indochina. At Potsdam, in July 1945, President Truman tacitly reversed the U.S. Indochina policy which President Roosevelt had previously pursued with passion. At this juncture Indochina was only one of many pressing questions on which the allies had to reach pragmatic agreement. The United States, though still greatly desiring independence for the Asian nations then under colonial rule, seems to have been motivated mainly by the overriding demands of rebuilding Western Europe and promoting collaboration between itself and those European nations. Britain, for its part, had its own colonial problems to sort out and did not want to press the Indochina issue to the point of

[1] Bernard Fall, *The Two Viet-Nams: A Political and Military Analysis* (New York: Frederick A. Praeger, 1963), pp. 63 and 100.

possible rupture with France. The complaisance of the U.S.S.R. is less easy to understand. One well-informed observer[2] explains it as a reflection of "real (Soviet) isolation" from Indochina at this time and of the Soviet hope that the postwar provisional government in France would be taken over by Communists.

In the fortnight following V-J day the Viet Minh, more particularly the Communist party of Vietnam, gave an awesome demonstration of tactical strength. At a "national conference" at the village of Tran Trao the party decided, *inter alia,* "as the people's power, to welcome the Allied Forces coming to disarm the Japanese troops stationed in Indochina."[3] This they did. By the time British (i.e., largely Indian) troops had arrived in the area south of the 16th parallel and Chinese troops were pouring into the north (as agreed at Potsdam), Bao Dai had bloodlessly been forced to abdicate, leaving Ho Chi Minh in power in Hanoi, a Viet Minh-dominated "committee of liberation" had taken control of Saigon without firing a shot, and the Democratic Republic of Vietnam—with a broadly based but Viet Minh-dominated government—had been proclaimed.

Ho Chi Minh's next objective was to win international and, in particular, U.S. support. In this, even though the Communist aspect of the Viet Minh movement was played down, he failed. The die had already been cast. The British facilitated, and the Americans countenanced, a quick return of the French to the south. Here, with some Vietnamese support, they once again set Cochin-China aside as a French enclave. In the north the French proved helpful to Ho Chi Minh, for they soon negotiated withdrawal of the Chinese throughout Indochina. In November 1946, after Ho Chi Minh had tried unsuccessfully to gain his minimum objectives by negotiation, the French found a pretext to open hostilities in the north, and the guerrilla war, which had already erupted fitfully in the south, began in earnest.

The interlude of independence hardly lasted as long in Laos. In September 1945, Prince Petsarath, the Prime Min-

2 Bernard Fall, *op. cit.,* pp. 195–96.
3 *Ibid.,* p. 63.

ister and leader of the Lao Issara (Free Laos) movement, proclaimed the independence of the whole country, including the southern portion then ruled by Prince Boun Oum. When the King opposed this declaration a "provisional people's assembly" set up by the Lao Issara deposed him. The French dispatched a force to restore this untidy situation, and the Lao Issara, fighting from town to town, were forced back across the Mekong. They took refuge in Thailand, where Petsarath and his half brothers, Souvanna Phouma and Souphanouvong, set up a Lao Issara "government-in-exile." By May 1946 the French had re-entered both Vientiane and the royal capital, Luang Prabang; the protectorate had been restored, and the King was again on his throne.

Cambodian self-rule was even more short-lived. The independence faction there, the Khmer Issarak (Free Cambodia) movement, was led by the then Prime Minister, Son Ngoc Thanh. In October 1945 he was arrested and deported to France, and French rule was restored. His followers nevertheless continued to work for Cambodian independence.

The *guerre sale,* as the French correctly called the first Indochina war, was waged mostly in Vietnam. It was a bitter struggle not only in its bloody and destructive guerrilla aspects but also in the tenebrous underworld where imprisonment, interrogation, torture, and assassination were commonplace on both sides. At the military level it was fought by French Union and Viet Minh forces.

The French also tried to outmaneuver the Viet Minh and other resistance movements by working out political solutions with incumbent governments in the three states. By the end of 1949 they had negotiated agreements under which Vietnam was unified and all three states were formally brought into the French Union; however, the French continued to control the national armies and much else besides.

In Vietnam, Bao Dai, ending three years of self-imposed exile, was restored to power by the French. However, many nationalist groups continued to work for full independence and the Viet Minh continued to fight for it. At the same time, it became increasingly clear that they were intent on the creation of a radically different social order, one which—rightly or wrongly—they believed their people needed at this stage of their history. Ho Chi Minh, Pham Van Dong, and Vo Nguyen Giap were seen to be leaders of an Asian revolutionary movement as distinctive as that then led by Mao Tse-tung, Chou En-lai, and Lin Piao in China.

Until 1949 the Viet Minh had been largely on their own. The victory of the Chinese Communists in that year afforded them a powerful ally. At the same time, the United States became increasingly concerned about the spread of Communism in Asia and about the potential role of the new China there; the Soviet Union, for its own reasons, began to pay more attention than it had to Southeast Asia. The war in Indochina thus became increasingly international in character. China and the Soviet Union helped the Viet Minh, and the United States helped the French. In 1950 the United States established a military assistance group in Saigon and, by the spring of 1954, was meeting about three-quarters of the cost of French Union military operations.

The war also spread to Laos and Cambodia. The Lao Issara was dissolved in 1949 but Souphanouvong, doubting French intentions and evidently attracted by Ho Chi Minh's revolutionary approach to Indochinese problems, went over to the Viet Minh. In 1950, with their help, he launched the Pathet Lao (Land of the Lao) movement, and in 1953 the Viet Minh carried the war to Laos, capturing much of Sam Neua province and a small part of Phong Saly province, both in the north; by the spring of 1954 there were also combined Viet Minh/Pathet Lao operations in the south. In Cambodia, King Sihanouk abdicated and, taking over the government, proceeded to work for full independence. The Khmer Issarak, which in 1950 had been absorbed into a united front under Viet Minh auspices, nevertheless continued sporadic resistance activities. Just as the French had always regarded Indochina as one, the Viet Minh were treating the three Indochinese states as one field of action.

When meeting in Berlin in early 1954 the Foreign Ministers of Britain, France, the United States, and the Soviet Union decided to convene a conference on Korea in Geneva in April; they also announced that the problem of restoring peace in Indochina would be discussed at that conference. In the interval events in Indochina moved to a somber climax. In March, the now historic battle began at Dien Bien Phu, a fortified position in North Vietnam adjacent to the Laotian provinces of Sam Neua and Phong Saly. Almost two months later, after France had agreed to grant full independence within the French Union to Vietnam (as it had in 1953 to Laos and Cambodia), Dien Bien Phu fell.

THE GENEVA CONFERENCE OF 1954

The Geneva conference on Indochina commenced the same day. Those attending were Chou En-lai, Eden, Bidault, and Molotov (Foreign Ministers of China, Britain, France, and the Soviet Union respectively) and representatives of the United States, the State of Vietnam, the Democratic Republic of Vietnam (D.R.V.N.), Laos, and Cambodia. As far as the Western side was concerned, the government of the State of Vietnam, headed by Bao Dai, was the legitimate government of that country; the Communist side, on the other hand, recognized the Democratic Republic of Vietnam which Ho Chi Minh had proclaimed in 1946. The representatives of both these rival governments entered and left the conference claiming the whole of Vietnam.

The conference succeeded because, in the last analysis, the world powers involved could see no realistic alternative. France was in no mood to continue the war, especially after Mendés-France came to power, and Britain greatly desired peace in Southeast Asia. On the Communist side, some East-West détente suited the general policy of the Soviet Union, and China, with the Korean problem under control (though unsettled), was determined to achieve a negotiated settlement in the other area of major conflict adjacent to its borders; at this time, also, it was anxious to establish itself as a peaceful nation in the eyes of other Asian states.

The United States was at first suspicious that the Communists were using the conference as a screen to enable them to mount further offensives, and in any case seemed to doubt that a satisfactory settlement was possible. It finally withdrew the leader of its delegation and in the end did not associate itself with the final declaration. Instead, it made a declaration that it would refrain from the threat or the use of force to disturb the settlement; that it would view any renewal of "the aggression" in violation of the agreements with grave concern and as seriously threatening international peace and security; and that it shared the "hope" that the agreement would permit Vietnam, Laos, and Cambodia to·"play their part in full independence and sovereignty in the peaceful community of nations"—also that "it would enable the peoples of that area to determine their own future."[4] Separately, the United States proceeded with the organization of SEATO.

Dien Bien Phu was the beginning of the end for the French in Vietnam; the Viet Minh, if left to themselves, could have exacted much more than they got. Nevertheless their Vietnamese adversary, the State of Vietnam, seems to have suffered a genuine sense of betrayal at the conference; while asserting that it would not use force "to resist the procedures for putting the ceasefire into effect," it expressed objections and reservations.[5] The South Vietnamese must in fact have been acutely aware of the trend of events, for—according to President Eisenhower—"had elections been held as of the time of fighting, possibly 80 per cent of the population would have voted for the Communist Ho Chi Minh as their leader rather than Chief of State Bao Dai."[6]

THE GENEVA AGREEMENTS OF 1954

The settlement was embodied in three bilateral ceasefire agreements, a final declaration which took note of them and embodied general undertakings, and some separate declarations.[7] The settlement placed obligations on the parties to

[4] "Further Documents relating to the discussion of Indo-China at the Geneva Conference, June 16–July 21, 1954" (Cmnd. 9239, London: HMSO, August 1954), pp. 6–7.

[5] *Ibid.*, p. 7.

[6] Bernard Fall, *Viet-Nam Witness, 1953–1966* (New York: Frederick A. Praeger, 1966), p. 76.

[7] These documents, commonly known as "The Geneva Agreement," may be found in the pamphlet cited in footnote 4. The description in the balance of this section is a composite based on the final declaration of the conference, the declarations of Laos,

1e conflict,[8] the members of the conference and the inter-
ational commissions. The responsibilities of the commissions,
nd the problems they encountered, can be understood only
1 relation to the responsibilities of the other two groups, es-
ecially the parties to the conflict. It is also necessary to have
1 mind the nature of the settlement, particularly the time-
pan envisaged for completion.

ENERAL PROVISIONS

A central feature was division of Vietnam into two parts by
demarcation line (and demilitarized zone) at the seven-
eenth parallel. It was asserted that this demarcation line "is
rovisional and should not in any way be interpreted as con-
tituting a political or territorial boundary." It was further
rovided that the Vietnamese people were to enjoy "the
undamental freedoms, guaranteed by democratic institutions
stablished as a result of free general elections by secret bal-
ot" and that general elections would be held in July 1956,
nder the supervision of the international commission; con-
ultations to this end were to be held by "competent repre-
entative authorities of the two zones" beginning in July
955.

In Laos, "pending a political settlement," the Pathet Lao
orces were to move into the provinces of Phong Saly and
am Neua and were to be free to move between these
rovinces in a corridor. The government of Laos (presum-
bly, after the political settlement) was to integrate all
itizens, without discrimination, into the national community.

---

ambodia, and France and the ceasefire agreements for Vietnam,
aos, and Cambodia as printed on pp. 9–42 of that pamphlet.
[8] Until French forces left Vietnam in April 1955, the effective
arties to the ceasefire agreement were the French High Command
nd the D.R.V.N.; thereafter, on a "working basis," the State of
ietnam (soon to be the Republic of Vietnam) and the D.R.V.N.
1 Laos the commission first dealt with "the Franco-Laotian side"
nd the Pathet Lao; then, as the French military (some being
lowed to remain) moved into the background, with the govern-
ent of Laos and the Pathet Lao. In Cambodia, when the agree-
ent had been signed, resistance forces faded into the landscape,
ith the result that the commission dealt exclusively with the gov-
rnment of Cambodia almost from the outset.

General elections, in which all citizens were to participate b
secret ballot, were to take place in the course of 1955. Th
perspective for Cambodia was similar.

The conference expressed its conviction that executio
of the terms of the settlement would permit all three countrie
"to play their part, in full independence and sovereignty, i
the community of nations." Clearly, the authors of th
Geneva agreements were asserting that in about two year
Vietnam, Laos, and Cambodia should be united, independen
countries which would no longer need international com
missions or any other form of international supervision.

OBLIGATIONS

The governments which made the settlement undertoo
to respect "the sovereignty, the unity, the independence, an
the territorial integrity" of Vietnam, Laos, and Cambodia an
to refrain from any interference in their international affair:
They also agreed to consult one another on any questio
which might be referred to them by one of the internationa
commissions "in order to study such measures as may prov
necessary to ensure that the agreements on the cessation o
hostilities in Cambodia, Laos, and Vietnam are respected.

In all three cases the ceasefire agreement stated that re
sponsibility for its execution "shall rest with the parties.
Moreover, joint commissions composed of high-ranking mil
tary officers of the parties were established. These commis
sions were to facilitate such joint actions as proper executio
of the ceasefire, effective disengagement of forces, and with
drawal of foreign forces. In Vietnam their responsibilitie
also extended to regulating the demilitarized zone and watch
ing over the transfer of local administrations following re
groupment of forces into the northern and southern zones.

All prisoners of war and civilian internees were to be re
leased and, as applicable, repatriated. Each party undertoo
to refrain from reprisals or discrimination against person
or organizations for their activities during the hostilitie
and guaranteed their democratic freedom. In Vietnam, dun
ing the three hundred days allowed for regroupment of force:
any civilians who were residing in a district controlled b
one party but who wished to go and live in the zone assigne

to the other were to be permitted and helped to do so by the local authorities.

On the other hand, again in Vietnam, no unauthorized person, civilian or military, was to cross the demarcation line, and the armed forces of each party were to respect the territory under the military control of the other; they were to "commit no act" and to "undertake no operation" against the other party.

Foreign forces were to leave Laos and Cambodia within ninety days, a limited number of French troops being allowed to remain in Laos for training purposes; there was a ban on introduction of fresh troops or arms into either country, except as necessary for effective national defense. France undertook to withdraw its forces from Vietnam "at the request of the governments concerned"; military personnel and arms could be introduced from outside but only in limited numbers and on a strictly controlled rotational basis. Apart from two French bases in Laos, there were to be no foreign military alliances.

The parties also assumed an obligation *vis-à-vis* the international commissions. They agreed that the commanders of their forces would afford full protection and all possible assistance and cooperation to the commissions, and their inspection teams under their command who violated the agreements were suitably punished.

THE INTERNATIONAL COMMISSIONS

The international commissions were set up "for control and supervision of application of the provisions" of the cease-fire agreements. They were to be composed of representatives of Canada, India, and Poland, the Indian representative acting as Chairman.

Each commission was to have inspection teams, some fixed in different parts of the country and some mobile. In Vietnam there were to be fourteen fixed teams, in Laos seven and in Cambodia five. There was no limit on the number of mobile teams;[9] however, their scope was circumscribed. Their

[9] At the peak period the number of mobile teams in Vietnam was eighteen, in Laos five and in Cambodia three. The total number

"zones of action" were to be "the regions bordering the land and sea frontiers" of the country in which they worked, and the demilitarized zone. Beyond these zones of action they could carry out their assigned tasks "by agreement with the commander of the party concerned." Within the zones of action, the agreements said, the teams "shall have the right to move freely and shall receive from the local civil and military authorities all facilities they may require for fulfillment of their tasks"; they were also to "have at their disposal such modern means of transport, observation, and communication as they may require." The teams were empowered not only to observe but also to supervise and investigate. They were to be available to settle disputes. If they could not, or if they considered there had been a violation or a threat of serious violation, they were to inform the commission. They were in any case to report on their work. Unanimity was not required; in the case of a disagreement the conclusion of each member was to be submitted.

When the international commission became aware of a situation that seemed to call for its attention it was to undertake the necessary investigations, "both documentary and on the ground," as soon as possible. It could do this on its own initiative, or at the request of the Joint Commission or one of the parties. In operational matters the commission could take decisions by majority vote except when dealing with "violations, or threats of violations, which might lead to resumption of hostilities." The commissions were made responsible to "the members of the Geneva conference." They were to report if they failed to reach unanimity in regard to a threatened resumption of hostilities (a majority and one or more minority reports being submitted); if one of the parties refused to put a recommendation of the commission into effect; and in all cases where their activities were being hindered. (The commissions subsequently decided to make periodic progress reports and to do this via "The Co Chairmen," i.e., the Foreign Ministers of Britain and the

---

of commission personnel, both operational and support, was never more than 600 to 700 in the whole of Indochina.

Soviet Union, who had been co-chairmen of the Geneva conference.)

THE INVITATION TO SERVE ON THE COMMISSIONS

The conference had at first thought in terms of one commission for all three Indochina countries. The Soviet Union, for the Communist side, proposed a commission like the Neutral Nations Supervisory Commission in Korea (Sweden, Switzerland, Poland, and Czechoslovakia), India and Pakistan being substituted for Sweden and Switzerland; as in Korea, the participants would be regarded as neutrals in the sense that they were noncombatants in the war. The Western countries had several plans but all except the United States eventually rallied behind a British scheme to have the commission manned by the "Colombo powers"—India, Pakistan, Ceylon, Burma, and Indonesia. At this stage Chou En-lai proposed that there be a commission for each country; this was accepted. Bargaining about composition continued intermittently and, shortly before July 20 (the date Mendés-France had fixed for signature of the ceasefire agreements), the idea of three-nation commissions emerged. Then, on July 19, Chou En-lai proposed to Eden that India, Poland, and Canada be invited to serve; this was acceptable to Eden and the other conference members and the agreements were framed accordingly—clearly, too, in the hope that the nominees would accept.

The concept of a tripartite commission composed of one uncommitted country, one Western, and one Communist was a logical evolution from the two original plans, each of which propounded a larger and vaguely neutralist body. The choice of India, the leading proponent of nonalignment and an original choice of most participants, was to be expected. Poland had been on the Soviet Union's original list, and the skill of its diplomatists and the imperturbability of its soldiers were widely recognized. The new element was the introduction of Canada. It would appear that, by the part it had played in helping to bring about an armistice in Korea and more generally by the attitude toward Asian problems adopted by Canadian leaders, Canada had impressed itself on Chou En-lai as a country which truly wished to help bring peace to Asia.[10] At the same time Canada enjoyed the confidence of the West.

There was some reason for the Canadian government to regard the invitation to serve in Indochina as a natural development. Canadians were already serving on UN truce observation commissions in the Middle East and Kashmir, and Canadians at home were paying a good deal of attention to Asia. The creation, after the war, of a string of newly independent countries stretching from Karachi to Manila, and the separate emergence of Communist China, had presented Asia in a new light to Canada, whose substantial interest had previously lain principally in Japan. The Asian part of the Commonwealth, in which India now loomed large in Canadian eyes, had recently been the focus of a Canadian initiative in the launching of the Colombo Plan; and the Colombo Plan countries, which by 1954 included practically all the independent countries of South and Southeast Asia, were about to have their annual consultative meeting in Ottawa. As far as Indochina was concerned, with the war reaching a climax public interest was high; in the six months before Canada was invited to serve on the commissions there were more than fifty exchanges about Indochina in the House of Commons.

Nevertheless Canada's reaction to the invitation was less than enthusiastic. In a personal message to Eden on receipt of it, Canada's Minister of External Affairs, L. B. Pearson, spoke of there being no disposition on the part of the Canadian government to evade the new responsibility "which may, however, turn out to be as onerous as it certainly was unsought."[11] A week later, having consulted other interested governments and having studied the Geneva settlement including the commissions' terms of reference, Canada accepted. An official press release said, *inter alia*, "If, . . . by participating in the work of these Indochinese commissions, Canada can help in establishing . . . security and stability in Southeast Asia we will be serving our country as well as the

[10] It is also said that Krishna Menon had suggested Canada to Chou En-lai, but this is not easy to document.

[11] External Affairs files.

cause of peace . . . While it is a matter of regret that . . . supervision of [the] settlement [is] not directly under the aegis of the United Nations, . . . Canadian participation will be fully in harmony with our responsibilities as a member of the world organization . . . The commissions have a reasonable chance of operating effectively . . . If our expectations unfortunately prove ill-founded and the commissions are frustrated by obstruction . . . no useful purpose would be served by continuing their existence . . . We have no illusions that the task we are undertaking will be either easy or of short duration . . ."[12] At the same time, Pearson sent Nehru a personal message in which he said the Canadian decision to serve had "been determined in no small measure by the knowledge that in this onerous task we will be collaborating with India, with which we enjoy close, friendly relations." He assured Nehru that Canadian representatives would be anxious to cooperate in a constructive way.[13]

THE ESTABLISHMENT OF THE COMMISSIONS

The decision taken, the government set to work to implement it. An advance party[14] was dispatched to Indochina, and a high-level delegation was sent to New Delhi to confer with representatives of India and Poland, which had already agreed to serve. There, and subsequently in Hanoi, Vientiane, and Phnom Penh,[15] the commissions were formed and put

[12] External Affairs press release, July 28, 1954.
[13] External Affairs files.
[14] In the peak year, 1955, the total Canadian contingent in Indochina was 170; by 1971 it had shrunk to 36. By the end of 1972 one Canadian Foreign Service Officer in three had served in Indochina, as had 1,300 armed services personnel.
[15] The agreements specified Vientiane and Phnom Penh as headquarters of the Laos and Cambodia commissions respectively but were silent on the location of the Vietnam commission. Hanoi was finally chosen because there the commission could have easy access to the high commands of the two sides which had been meeting in northern Vietnam while the negotiations were going on in Geneva. The commission intended to move to Saigon in 1955, but it was not until 1958 that the "working relationship" established when the French left was stable enough to make this practicable.

to work. Except to make clear that each commission was to have a Secretary-General, the agreements had been virtually silent on administration. With India taking the lead, the commission countries set up a strong organization in each country. Each national "delegation" was headed by a civilian with the rank of Ambassador. He had two principal advisors, one military and one political, and other staff; the teams were manned by military officers. Each commission had a military committee (in Vietnam, called the operations committee) and a political committee (in Vietnam, called the freedoms committee), the members of which were representatives of the delegations. The Vietnam commission also had a legal committee and an administration committee, and it set up other committees from time to time *ad hoc*.

Each commission was served by an international secretariat headed by a Secretary-General who was the Chairman of the Commission; he was assisted by three Deputy Secretaries-General who were seconded by the delegations and who were in charge of administration, operations, and other matters. The international staffs were manned mainly by the Indians who also looked after commission security and communications both with the teams and with national capitals.

Especially in Vietnam, support functions were many and complex, from provision of supplies and equipment to the processing of hundreds of thousands of petitions. The language problem, involving English, French, Polish, and a local language, was handled pragmatically and, on the whole, effectively. The Indians deserve credit for dealing expeditiously with an enormous volume of official minutes and other documents in English which, after all, is not their first language; many Polish officers spoke English or French but those who did not had to rely on their own interpreters; a bilingual Canadian had a certain advantage, being at ease both in the commission and when dealing with local leaders and officials, most of whom spoke French. The main problem posed by language was the difficulty of being sure one could always rely on the impartiality of local interpreters. A more serious administrative problem was transport, for which the commissions were dependent on the parties; the French, as long as they were present, did their best to provide good service, but the facilities offered by the others was frequently deficient or nonexistent.

At the outset all the commissions were somewhat overtaken by events. When the invitations to serve reached New Delhi, Ottawa, and Warsaw, the agreements were already in effect and the date by which the ceasefire was to be completely in force was just three weeks away. The commissions were installed in Hanoi and Vientiane by that date and in Phnom Penh a little later and at once set to work. However, even though organization proceeded rapidly and personnel arrived steadily and in increasing number from all area capitals, it was about two months before the commissions were fully functioning with establishments at top strength and all teams in place. This hiatus did not create major problems, since the ceasefire was well observed and the Joint Commissions were on the ground to get the disengagement process under way; this process was facilitated by provisional assembly areas into which troops of one side or the other were temporarily moved prior to regroupment.

THE COMMISSION IN VIETNAM

During the very early years the commissions displayed energy, ingenuity, and imagination in pursuit of their goals. For example, for quite a long time it was normal for the Vietnam commission to meet nearly every day, often more than once a day, each agenda presenting several knotty problems which the commission sought to bring nearer to solution. In the first few months there was a genuine spirit of collective endeavor and, even after this spirit had been somewhat fragmented, as long as there was still hope of achieving a settlement or at least of keeping the peace, the commissions were able to use the procedures provided by the agreements as a basis for some useful actions. Thereafter, in terms of their mandate, their activities became increasingly futile, and their morale gradually deteriorated.

In Vietnam the commission's most active period was the first "three hundred days," the time during which regroupment of forces into the northern and southern zones, the

that 15,000 of theirs were still held, and claims and counter-claims went on for years; however, by March 1955 the main job had been done. While many internees were released at the time of the main prisoner-of-war exchange, it soon became clear that others were still in custody. By conducting investigations in prisons in the south the commission was able to obtain the release of some internees, but it could never get into prisons in the north; this whole problem, merged with the larger issue of the rights of all persons known to have been politically hostile during the war, remained one of the commission's chronic preoccupations.

FUNDAMENTAL FREEDOMS

The part of the agreement which required the parties to refrain from discrimination and reprisals on account of activities during the war, and to permit civilians desiring to do so to move from one zone to the other—and to help them to do so—was not among the provisions the international commission was *particularly* enjoined to watch over. Nevertheless, from the outset Canada sought to ensure that the commission would pay as much attention to these matters as to military aspects. As India and Poland proved to be of the same mind, "freedoms" issues took up a great deal of the commission's time throughout its active years. Canada had especially in mind the situation of Catholics in the north but the commission had equally to concern itself with persons in the south whose democratic freedoms were in jeopardy.

REFUGEES

At the time of the ceasefire there were about 600,000 Catholics in the north. Except for a brief period at the end of the war against Japan, they had long lived under the protection of the French and most of them viewed the imminent departure of their protectors with anxiety. As French Union forces in the north began moving into provisional assembly areas, there was an exodus of Catholics to Haiphong and other centers where the French were still in control. Along with a large number of non-Catholics who had worked for the French or who were used to their regime, they wanted to go south, and during the balance of the "three hundred days" more than 850,000 did so; of these more than 500,000 were Catholics. Most of them traveled by ship or by air.

Early in the process the commission received complaints that persons wishing to go south who lived in, or had assembled in, areas under D.R.V.N. control were encountering serious obstacles. From that time until two months after the expiration of the three hundred days (the commission, in the end, extended the time limit), the commission worked very hard on behalf of the would-be refugees. Mobile teams, and on occasion the freedoms committee, were sent time and again to the more important of the affected areas; there, in spite of frequent obstruction on the part of local authorities, they brought a certain reassurance and did their best to gather information for the commission. Its interventions, in turn, were instrumental in bringing about administrative improvements which enabled substantial numbers of evacuees to leave by bus or ship.

The D.R.V.N.'s position was that their facilities were overtaxed, that propaganda created unjustified fears and that the French and the Church were putting pressure on people to leave; they on their part engaged in their own "psychological warfare" and made it difficult for people to leave. A month before the original deadline expired, the position was so unsatisfactory that the Canadian delegation, having argued unsuccessfully that the problem should be reported to the members of the Geneva conference in a way which would invoke their collective consideration, appended its own recommendations to this effect to the commission's third interim report.[17] This was the first time that the commission found itself unable to act unanimously.

Only a few thousand civilians moved from south to north. Others had difficulty in doing so, apparently because they crowded the deadline. It would appear that during the three hundred days many persons who were inclined to go north either hesitated to make a move for fear of being imprisoned

---

[17] "Third Interim Report of the International Commission for Supervision and Control in Vietnam" (Cmnd. 9499, London: HMSO, June 1955), p. 4.

as undesirables or were discouraged from doing so by the Viet Minh who wanted sympathizers in the south.

REPRISALS

Allegations of discrimination or reprisals on account of wartime activity confronted the commission from the beginning. Some of these allegations were against the authorities in the north, particularly with regard to persons said to be wrongfully detained, but the commission was never able to investigate them effectively. It seems probable, too, that there were many cases of this kind about which the commission did not hear either because the authorities in the south lacked information or because people in the north were nervous about approaching the teams.

By far the greatest number of "freedoms" cases of this kind arose in the south. Throughout its eight more or less active years the commission tried systematically, with the help of its legal committee and its mobile teams, to investigate alleged persecution of persons and groups in the south. Sometimes people were killed or injured in clashes between crowds and state forces; more often internees had not been released or people had been sent to prison or otherwise punished subsequent to the Geneva agreement. The authorities' cooperation was unsatisfactory and frequently nonexistent. This was partly because the commission, though it tried very hard to be circumspect, was treading the line between what was subject to the provisions of the Geneva agreement and what was not—between the individual's right to absolution for political "sins" committed during the war and the state's right to punish the individual for crimes or subversive acts committed subsequently. Moreover, since the courts had jurisdiction in these latter cases, it was difficult for the commission to contest cases in which the courts had made findings. In spite of this, the commission not infrequently ruled that certain groups or individuals were being wrongfully imprisoned and demanded their release.

Until 1958 the commission maintained a united front in dealing with this thorny issue. By that time, in the absence of a political settlement, the likelihood of groups or individuals actually committing subversive acts in the south had increased considerably. The result was that occasionally, when it felt the commission was "overstepping the mark," the Canadian delegation registered dissent over a commission decision to cite the Saigon government for noncooperation in "freedoms" cases. On the other hand, in 1959, the Indians and Canadians ruled, with the Poles dissenting, that a new anti-subversion law passed by the South Vietnam government was not in conflict with the Geneva agreement.

SUBVERSION AND INFILTRATION:
ARMS BUILDUP AND MILITARY ALLIANCE

As time went on sabotage and other types of antigovernment activity occurred with increasing frequency in the south. In 1960 and 1961 the commission received frequent complaints about this from the South Vietnam government which alleged that the actions were being directed from the north; overriding Polish objections, the commission instructed its legal committee to consider whether or not any of these actions constituted violations of the Geneva agreement. It also sought, with little success, to use its teams to prevent infiltration across the demilitarized zone or through Laos and, finally, to determine if such infiltration had taken place.

Throughout its active period the commission worked hard in an effort to check on the illegal entry of military personnel or equipment into either part of Vietnam; it was principally for this purpose that the agreement had specified points in both zones at which fixed teams were to be located. The task proved insuperable. There were innumerable entry points both on the land frontiers and on the coasts, and also at airfields which multiplied as time went on. The commission deployed its limited resources as intelligently as possible, creating mobile components for the fixed teams and sending out additional mobile units, but all to little avail. The ways in which inspections could be circumvented or rendered meaningless were as limitless as the ingenuity of the parties.

As time went on, there was a tendency toward majority commission decisions on arms control, either the Canadian or the Polish delegation being in dissent. In the early years the commission made a concerted but unsuccessful effort to tighten its control where it was weakest—on the Chinese border. By the early sixties attention was to a considerable extent focused on the south which was more susceptible to inspection and which, since the departure of the French in 1955, had manifestly depended upon U.S. military support.

At first, with Polish dissent, the commission was cautious about the military situation in the south, dismissing D.R.V.N. claims that South Vietnam was allied with the United States in SEATO, finding insufficient evidence that the United States was establishing bases in South Vietnam and raising no objection to substitution of U.S. military personnel for French in an active training role. However, beginning in December 1961, the commission was consistently denied the right to control and inspect in the south and was at the same time informed by the South Vietnam government that, in the face of "aggression" directed by the north, it had requested the United States to intensify its aid in personnel and material. Meanwhile, the commission received communications from the D.R.V.N. alleging direct military intervention in the south and "ever-increasing import of war materials and introduction of military personnel" there.[18]

The upshot of the commission's work on the related problems of infiltration and arms buildup was its special report to the Co-Chairmen of June 1962. This report, from which the Polish delegation dissented, accepted the conclusion of the legal committee that "armed and unarmed personnel, arms and munitions and other supplies" had been sent from the north to the south "with the object of supporting, organizing, and carrying out hostile activities, including armed attacks, directed against the armed forces and administration . . . in the south," and that these acts constituted violations of the Geneva agreement. The commission also concluded that South Vietnam had violated the Geneva agreement by "receiving increased military aid from the United States . . . in the absence of any established credit in its favour" and that

18 "Special Report to the Co-Chairmen of the Geneva Conference on Indo-China, Saigon, June 2, 1962" (Cmnd. 1755, London: HMSO, June 1962), p. 708.

"the establishment of a U. S. Military Assistance Command in South Vietnam, as well as the introduction of a large number of U.S. military personnel beyond the stated strength of the MAAG amounts to a factual military alliance, which is prohibited under . . . the Geneva Agreement."[19]

THE LAST EIGHT YEARS

Clearly the balloon was going up. Before long the war began again in earnest. Then the United States assumed a combat role, and the war as we have most recently known it was on. The commission remained in being, but in 1965 its teams, already reduced for economic reasons at the request of the Co-Chairmen, were removed altogether from North Vietnam; the D.R.V.N. asked this following the onset of U.S. bombing there. The grounds given were that the D.R.V.N. could no longer assure the teams' safety, but Bernard Fall reports that after the 1962 special report the D.R.V.N. became concerned that the commission had come down on the side of the West.[20] In the late sixties the teams in the south, because of the restrictions on their movements, were reduced to a minimum there as well.

The most significant official act of the commission in recent years was a special report in 1965 when the United States started bombing the north; the report said that the information about this which had reached the commission indicated violations of the Geneva Agreement. The Canadian delegation felt that this report, by concentrating on a limited aspect, might give a distorted picture. It therefore appended a minority statement in which the bombing was placed in the context of recent attacks on positions in the south, and of what the delegation described as "deliberate and persistent pursuit of aggressive but largely covert policies by North Vietnam directed against South Vietnam."[21]

In the years since 1965, as the war continued and mounted

19 *Ibid.*, pp. 7–10.
20 Bernard Fall, *Viet-Nam Witness*, pp. 80–81.
21 "Special Report to the Co-Chairmen of the Geneva Conference on Indo-China, Saigon, 13 February 1965" (Cmnd. 2609, London: HMSO, March 1965), pp. 4–5, 12–15.

in tempo, Canada from time to time sought to have the commission fulfill its traditional function, e.g. investigating and reporting on the situation in the demilitarized zone; but the other members did not agree with this approach. Between 1964 and 1968 the Canadian government, which was publicly putting forward peace proposals of its own, also tried to interest the other governments on the commission in using the commission as a vehicle for "bringing the parties closer together"; to this initiative the others' response was unenthusiastic.

In 1964 and 1965, in the course of official visits to Hanoi, the Canadian commissioner carried to the government there a total of five messages from the U.S. government which, at its request, the Canadian government had agreed to convey; on three occasions he was able also to bring back North Vietnamese reactions. The first two of these messages were designed by the United States to make clear to the D.R.V.N. leadership the nature of U.S. policy in Indochina and the reasons for it, and at the same time to warn the D.R.V.N. of the very serious consequences which would ensue upon its continuing to commit what the United States considered to be aggressive acts against South Vietnam. The third message was an effort to elicit a direct D.R.V.N. response. The fourth, which had already been conveyed through the Chinese in Warsaw, was designed to make clear that U.S. bombing of the north, which had just started, had limited objectives. The fifth was an effort by the United States to interest the D.R.V.N. in "working toward a solution by reciprocal actions on each side."[22] The D.R.V.N.'s reactions were consistently adamant and, on one occasion, angry.

The Canadian government believed that, in allowing its representative to carry these messages and to report reactions, it would reduce the possibilities of misunderstanding, and it regarded this office as consistent with its responsibilities as a member of the international commission. While the role it undertook was delicate in the extreme, particularly in regard to reporting reactions, it is surely difficult to imagine the

[22] Statement by Secretary of State for External Affairs in House of Commons, June 17, 1971.

Canadian government conscientiously refusing to discharge a function which is not uncommon when warring countries wish to communicate. It should also be borne in mind that the Canadian government was not fully informed by the U.S. government of its plans and intentions and that it was understood throughout that Canada did not associate itself with the content of the messages passed.[23]

In 1972, after India entered into diplomatic relations with North Vietnam while retaining consular relations with the south, the South Vietnam government decided that the Indian delegation and the Indian component of the commission secretariat should leave South Vietnam. As a result, the commission transferred its headquarters back to Hanoi. This episode revealed a commission in disarray. The same body which, in 1954–55, had been a force for peace in a war-torn land and which, even as late as 1965, had maintained a dignified common front when the D.R.V.N. had obliged it to withdraw its teams, was now pathetically divided. The Canadian position from the outset of the 1972 dispute was that it was a purely bilateral matter between India and South Vietnam. The manner of its resolution, with India and Poland unilaterally publishing their version of events[24] and Canada responding with a public statement of its view,[25] showed a sad lack of mutual confidence in this matter between Canada and its partners. Particularly as between Canada and India, it was a far cry from the day when each country, out of a common experience, had welcomed the other as a colleague in the commission.

[23] Separately, in 1966, the Canadian government sent Chester Ronning (retired Canadian diplomat and Far Eastern specialist) to Hanoi as a special representative with the rank of Ambassador. Mr. Ronning's mission, which took him twice to North Vietnam, was carried out with the knowledge and approval of the U.S. government and brought an offer of Canada's good offices as a means of initiating direct peace talks. There was no thought of Canadian mediation. The intention was merely to start a dialogue between the contending sides. Although that later happened, this 1966 Canadian effort came to naught.

[24] External Affairs files.

[25] External Affairs press release, October 3, 1972.

THE COMMISSION IN LAOS

Fundamentally, the Laos commission faced a different situation from that with which the Vietnam commission had to deal. Like the latter, it was instrumental at the outset in helping the parties to regroup forces and to release prisoners. The latter soon ceased to be a problem, but in regard to regroupment the Laos commission was faced with a much more intractable situation than the one which faced the Vietnam commission. A dispute over the extent to which the Pathet Lao were to control their regroupment area, the northern provinces of Sam Neua and Phong Saly, underlay the events of the next three years.

The commission was able to expedite the withdrawal of foreign forces, both French and Viet Minh, but in the case of the latter it found that geographical and other complexities made fully effective supervision difficult. In another area of responsibility, that of arms control, the commission made a frank admission of its incapacity to conduct more than routine supervision. It informed the Laotian government that it was not equipped to patrol the long, remote, and mountainous northern and northeastern borders of Laos, and an assertion by the Canadian delegation that any government complaints of arms shipments or troop movements over these borders should nevertheless be investigated got short shrift. In Laos, finally, there was at the outset no deep-rooted hostility between the factions; therefore, while such hostility developed later, it never became as terrible as it is today in Vietnam and, for the commission in Laos, "freedoms" problems were never much more than problems of harassment or discrimination.

During its first phase, between 1954 and 1958, the Laos commission had two main preoccupations: the military situation, which arose out of the confrontation in the two northern provinces, and the political situation, about which it had to be concerned because the agreement stipulated that the Pathet Lao regroupment was to last until there had been a "political settlement." In both these main areas of concern the commission helped materially in bringing about a settlement.

The commission operated at three levels, though handicapped by inadequate transportation and some obstruction: it sent out teams to investigate armed clashes and other incidents, which were frequent during the first two years, and then exhorted or reprimanded one or both of the parties in appropriate terms; it addressed recommendations and resolutions on both military and political issues to the parties; and it arranged and encouraged meetings and negotiations between them. From an early date, the commission took its decisions either unanimously or by majority vote as seemed appropriate. As in all substantive matters covered by the agreement, it was the parties which had to make the decisive effort to reach a settlement, and such an effort was made in 1956–57, when Souvanna Phouma re-emerged as Prime Minister and launched a policy of neutrality for Laos. On this basis he was able, in a series of negotiations with Souphanouvong, the Pathet Lao leader, to make an agreement which ended hostilities and laid the groundwork for reintegration and general elections as foreseen at Geneva.

In 1958, this settlement having been reached, the commission was advised by the Laotian government that its presence was no longer required, and it adjourned *sine die*. Not long afterward, the Pathet Lao having done surprisingly well in partial elections, Souvanna Phouma was forced to leave Laos by right-wing elements and the settlement broke down. By this time Laos was beginning to be important to the North Vietnamese as a route for the movement of personnel and supplies into South Vietnam. The Americans, determined to stop this, backed increasingly reactionary governments. The Pathet Lao returned to the jungle and, with Viet Minh support, engaged government forces. Then, almost miraculously, a small neutralist force led by Captain Kong Le emerged to bring Souvanna Phouma back on the political scene. However, the right wing drove him into an alliance with the Pathet Lao, the war went on and the military situation became as dangerously polarized as it had been in Vietnam in 1954.

The upshot was the conference "for settlement of the Laotian question" which took place in Geneva in 1961–62.[26]

[26] Participants were the countries which had taken part in the 1954 Geneva Conference (Britain, China, France, the Soviet

The United States, though it was at first skeptical, soon took a leading part and, following the Khrushchev-Kennedy meeting in Vienna, worked hard to achieve a settlement partly as an experiment in détente and partly in the hope that it would induce the Soviet Union to curb the use of the Ho Chi Minh Trail.

The conference underwrote a tripartite "government of national union" in Laos and affirmed respect for the "sovereignty, independence, neutrality, unity, and territorial integrity" of that country.[27] It also brought the international commission back with terms of reference which were somewhat less satisfactory than the 1954 agreement, partly because some key provisions were inevitably ambiguous but mainly because each member of the governmental troika theoretically had a veto over commission investigations.[28] (This stemmed more from the government's own rules than from the international agreements.) However, due to Canadian efforts at the conference and strong administrative action by the Indians in Laos, the commission acquired and operated its own small fleet of helicopters and had other means of transport under its own control. The commission's principal achievement in the first two years of its second phase was to provide indirect but energetic support for the formation and continuance of the union government and thus for a neutral Laos.

However, even before overt fighting had broken out again in Vietnam, hostilities were once more opened in Laos. Collusion with the Pathet Lao by a faction of dissident neutralists had led to assassination of their leader, Quinim Pholsena;

Union, the United States, North Vietnam, South Vietnam, Laos, and Cambodia), other states contiguous to Indochina (Burma and Thailand), and the commission countries (Canada, India, and Poland). This conference was different from the 1954 conference in that the United States participated fully and, along with South Vietnam, signed the resulting agreement. This made for direct confrontation between the United States and its friends on the one hand and the principal Communist powers on the other and made closely negotiated terms inevitable.

[27] "International Conference on the Settlement of the Laotian Question, Geneva, May 12, 1961–July 23, 1962" (Cmnd. 1828, London: HMSO, October 1962), pp. 15–18.

[28] *Ibid.*, pp. 19–24.

this, in turn, had once more polarized the Laotian factions. The neutralist forces that were loyal to Souvanna Phouma, at first supported by both the Soviet Union and the United States, lost the support of the Soviet Union and eventually ceased to have a truly independent existence. During this period, at the request of Souvanna Phouma as head of the government and in spite of noncooperation on the part of the Poles, the commission was able to document the presence of Viet Minh in Laos, but, because of a right-wing veto in the tripartite government, it was unable to launch an investigation into the operations of Air America, a U.S. organization which was supporting paramilitary operations in the north.

In recent years, under the impact of the war in Vietnam, fighting in Laos has been more intense, a new element being systematic U.S. bombing of the Ho Chi Minh Trail and other areas. At the same time, while the government of national union has remained in being, there is a *de facto* division of the country, and, under the force of circumstances, Souvanna Phouma's government has become increasingly dependent on the United States. The international commission has been reduced to skeleton strength and, in spite of Canadian efforts to have it conduct investigations, it has had little to do.

THE COMMISSION IN CAMBODIA

In principle, the international commission in Cambodia was called upon to perform much the same services as those in Laos and Vietnam, but the actual demands upon it have not been heavy. Although close supervision of withdrawal of Viet Minh troops was beyond the commission's capacity in 1954, it effectively discharged its other responsibilities during the first year or two of its tenure. Once through the initial phase, it reduced its strength but did not leave, mainly because Prince Sihanouk wanted it to help fend off apprehended encroachments from South Vietnam and Thailand. Canada strongly opposed commission involvement in cases of this kind, arguing that the commission must concern itself with violations or threats of violations by North Vietnam, which was one of the parties to the ceasefire agreement on Cambodia, but that it could not properly concern itself with actions by states which were not parties to that agreement. Canada's partners did not agree, and the commission soon became involved in border disputes involving South Vietnam and Thailand.

When some expatriate Viet Minh moved tentatively back into Cambodia in the late fifties, the commission was able to expose their activities. However, in the late sixties, when the Viet Minh began seriously to establish and then to expand their Cambodian sanctuary, the commission failed to take effective action in spite of Canadian efforts. Toward the end of 1969 it was requested to leave by the Cambodian government, and it adjourned *sine die*. Thus it was not present when a right-wing coup overthrew Sihanouk and forced him into exile and when the war spread to Cambodia in a more intense form than before.

THE COMMISSIONS' DIFFICULTIES: AN APPRECIATION

THE COMMISSIONS' MANDATE

The commissions' difficulties may be considered at three levels—their mandate, its application, and the situation in which they had to operate. It is not sufficiently understood that their mandate was limited in scope and was meant to be limited in time. The parties were responsible for implementing the agreements, the commissions being agents appointed to watch over the process. (The idea that the commissions were to "control" arose partly out of a desire for control and partly out of a natural misconception of the word itself, a poor translation of the French "contrôller," which in this context really means something like "keep on top of.") Nor is it generally remembered that the commissions' mandate was conceived as lasting something like two years, the time envisaged as necessary to complete a settlement in all three countries. It was hardly surprising that the commissions' position became increasingly untenable as the years rolled by and the goals established in 1954, and then in 1962, became more and more blurred and distant.

On the other hand, even within their theoretically limited

frame of reference the commissions' mandate was onerous. The Geneva negotiators should not be unduly blamed for this; a great many thorny issues were crying out for solution, and the negotiators were quite right to try to cover most of them in the agreements. They were equally right to direct the commissions' attention to a few central tasks. At the same time, the commissions were in fact expected to supervise any or all of the provisions of the ceasefire agreements and had to establish their own priorities. In short, except in Cambodia, the commissions had too much to do.

In Vietnam, especially in the first phase, the commission bravely divided its energies among many important tasks; in Laos during the same period, it concentrated on what then seemed essential, i.e. controlling the military situation and promoting a settlement. Either way, something suffered; in Vietnam both subversion and the arms buildup went unchecked too long; in Laos the presence of foreign forces went undetected. Then, too, rightly or wrongly, the commissions were to do more than observe and report; they were actively to inspect and investigate. It was their duty to help the parties settle disputes and their right to exhort them to comply with the agreement and to report them for not doing so. Perhaps they should have set up larger organizations. There was nothing in the agreements to prevent this. On the other hand, partly because the Communist countries always opposed large commissions, they would never have gotten the necessary financing from the Geneva powers. In any case in Indochina bigness pays diminishing returns; its geography conspires against policemen.

The commissions' task was complicated by their assumption of responsibility for political as well as for military matters. This they were entitled, though not specially enjoined, to do. The Vietnam commission might have been wise to leave "freedoms" issues largely to the Vietnamese; yet, had it done so, many thousands would have been added to the rolls of the sufferers. The commission in Laos might have left the political problem alone, but, if it had, there might not have been a settlement.

Particular aspects of the agreements created problems,

partly because of conflicting articles. For example, in the Laos agreement two articles taken together seemed to mean that, pending a political settlement, the two northern provinces were a Pathet Lao sanctuary, whereas another article could be interpreted to mean that the government, and hence its forces, enjoyed full constitutional rights there. This same article was in conflict in another sense with the article about the political settlement, for the latter was undefined and the extent to which the government was obliged to negotiate was therefore unclear.

The parts of the agreements which created most problems for the commissions were those which imposed restrictions on them. The most serious of these were the limitations on the teams' freedom of movement. Except in Laos, beginning in 1962, teams were also inhibited by being made dependent on the parties for transport.

APPLICATION OF THE MANDATE

In the realm of application the chronic problem was lack of cooperation from one or both of the parties. Obstruction was by no means constant but it was all too prevalent. It took many forms, from failure to produce documents to placing obstacles of one sort or another in the way of teams; in its most extreme form it made a mockery of the commissions' presence. There were occasions, too, when a commission—or one of its teams or delegations—was subject to actual harassment, as during the anticommission riot in Saigon in 1955 or when the Pathet Lao destroyed a commission helicopter in Laos in 1963. Generally speaking, the cooperation of the parties was considerably less than the commissions had a right to expect even under their imperfect terms of reference.

A feature of the commissions' operations which has been commonly misunderstood is the method of taking decisions. The areas of work in which unanimity was required were such that decisions on conducting investigations and other operational matters could be taken by majority vote; in the case of decisions which had to be unanimous (such as conclusions or recommendations on certain matters), in the absence of unanimity a majority report and one or more minority reports could be submitted.

What, in the Canadian experience, sometimes hampered the commissions was not the unanimity rule but rather the unanimity principle, which could be carried to ridiculous extremes. The unanimity principle was in itself a good thing; indeed, the Canadian government supported it in the early days of the agreements, both in 1954 and in 1962. It made for a harmonious commission and, in the case of recommendations to the parties, for maximum effect. It was soon apparent, however, that differences of view were so great on some issues that compromise was impossible and that it was necessary to act by means of majority votes or separate reports. In this the role of the Indian delegation was crucial.

The commissions' records are replete with examples of India siding with Canada against Poland—and *vice versa*. However, in the nature of things no action desired by Canada could be taken without Indian support. Even during the commissions' active years this was sometimes a trial because, either out of a desire for unanimity or for some other reason, India might postpone a decision longer than Canada would think desirable. During the last eight years or so, while the war has been raging, this has been an acute issue between India and Canada; India, like Poland, has seen no point in commission action under these circumstances, while Canada has favored it. The result has been commission inaction, contrary to Canada's wishes; the last substantive reports from any of the commissions were written in 1965.

Apart from this, the actual method of reporting to the Co-Chairmen never created any insuperable difficulty. In this realm the real trouble was that reports, whether unanimous or otherwise, seldom had any effect. The Co-Chairmen represented all the other members of the Geneva conference but, in fact, were also guardians of Communist and Western interests respectively. This sometimes meant long disagreement, occasionally never resolved, about publishing a particular report or document; sooner or later (occasionally, all too soon) a government on one side or the other would publish it anyway. This was all part of a propaganda war in which the commissions were inevitably involved.

More fundamentally, the commissions felt the lack of an effective authority to which they could be responsible and to which they could turn for guidance and support. On rare occasions the Co-Chairmen, on receipt of a report, would address a joint reply to the commission or to the parties. On one occasion—when the crisis in Laos was reaching a peak in 1960–61—action by the Co-Chairmen proved decisive and was in fact an extension of the kind of diplomacy which had made the 1954 agreement possible. Most of the time, however, the Co-Chairmen failed to agree and the commissions were left on their own. This was perhaps in the nature of things: if the members of the Geneva conference—or the Co-Chairmen as their agents—had enjoyed a more formal authority than they did, the commission would have been in peril of a veto from the top.

THE REALITIES OF THE SITUATION

In the last analysis it was the realities in Vietnam which defeated all the commissions. Laos and Cambodia, if they could have been left alone, would have settled down much as foreseen in Geneva. It was in Vietnam that the battle lines were really drawn. In China, Communism had captured—and was leading one wing of—what is perhaps the major revolution of this century, the emergence of all the nations of Asia from colonial controls and Western pressures, and in doing so had achieved power throughout the mainland; in Vietnam the Viet Minh were determined to do the same. The United States, generally uneasy about the possible spread of Communist power throughout Southeast Asia and beginning to fill the power vacuum in Vietnam which the defeat of France had created, was equally determined that the Viet Minh should not prevail there.

At Geneva, the United States could find no practicable basis on which the Viet Minh could be opposed directly. The settlement finally worked out there, via a series of intricate and interrelated negotiations, was a compromise which gave the Viet Minh less than they had at first demanded but more than the United States would have liked; at the same time, it gave assurance of a final political settlement as soon as the most immediate problems had been sorted out. Vietnam was to be temporarily divided but within two years was to be reunited by free elections.

Neither the D.R.V.N. nor the State of Vietnam was greatly impressed by this assurance with regard to the future. The ink was hardly dry on the paper in Geneva before the Vietnamese who wanted a united Vietnam under Ho Chi Minh were diligently insuring against failure. Still, they evidently had a certain hope that it might be possible somehow to work matters out via the agreement, and they seem to have been genuinely shaken in 1955 when, with U.S. support, President Ngo Dinh Diem (who replaced Bao Dai) began energetically to build a separate state in the south and when, by his words as well as by his actions, he raised the specter of indefinite partition. Here, as much as in early and deliberate intervention by the north in the south, is the source of today's terrible dilemma.

The 1954 negotiators may perhaps be excused for not foreseeing this prospect or, at least, for ignoring it if they did. Peacemakers must be compromisers and take some calculated risk. At the very least, the Geneva agreements visualized the future of all three countries of Indochina in terms which, at some not too distant date, may be realized. A not insignificant factor may be the Buddhists in Vietnam, the neutralists in Laos, and the followers of Sihanouk in Cambodia, none of whom should be lightly written off. To put it another way, it is the Vietnameseness of Vietnam which is likely in the long run to prevail; perhaps the same, *mutatis mutandis,* could be said of Laos and Cambodia. These are countries with very long histories and with societies at least as different from those of the West as the latter are from Communist societies. In the past one hundred years, and particularly during the past twenty-five years or so, they have been subjected to alien influences of both the Western and Communist variety; they will survive both.

Reflections of this kind, if they existed in the fifties and early sixties, were cold comfort to the peacekeepers on the ground. Formally, the Vietnam commission from time to time drew the Co-Chairmen's attention to the failure of the parties to make headway with reunification, and once—in 1956— the Co-Chairmen addressed messages to all concerned about the need for this and about the corresponding need, until the political objective was achieved, to hold the agreements in respect. On a day-to-day basis the commissions in all three countries, and their teams, simply had to work away as best they could, even though conditions had begun to deteriorate and boredom and frustration were becoming the order of the day. This was not easy for men who had been accustomed in other spheres to meeting high standards of performance; nor was it easy for their governments. Still, in an imperfect world, it was the peacekeepers' modest contribution to the rough-and-ready work the peacemakers had started. Although, in terms of their mandates, the commissions finally failed, it is possible to hope that some of their disinterested actions, whether regulatory or catalytic, may in the long run prove to have been less futile than they now seem. Just as international commissions will be out of place when a settled peace comes to Indochina—or if, on the contrary, the war is resumed— so they can have, and in the past have had, a real value in periods of struggle and adjustment. There certainly have been times when the factions, though contending among them-selves and abusing the commissions, have secretly recognized their temporary usefulness as international "lightning rods."

THE DELEGATIONS: AN APPRECIATION

The Poles not only brought to the Indochina commissions impeccable military and diplomatic credentials. They were also good Communists, particularly well attuned to Soviet international policy. They understood and served the com-missions' objectives but were fully prepared to subordinate them to the needs of their Indochinese ideological partners. Their tactical sense was Machiavellian, in the classical sense of the word. Depending on the situation, they could be in favor of investigations in general; but if necessary, they could equally plausibly oppose investigations on "their side."

When India came to the commissions it was the leading

proponent in the world of nonalignment, of "dynamic neutralism," a sort of pragmatic neutrality which it carried into the commissions and which, except for one brief aberrant period after the Chinese "invasion" of India, it practiced as a member of them. This made the Indians formidable but sometimes difficult partners. They could be very strong in the fight, as in the early days in Vietnam or when promoting and later working to preserve a neutral government in Laos; but, after the unanimous method of conducting business had broken down, their attitude toward one set of problems sometimes seemed to be conditioned by the way in which an opposing set of issues had (or had not) been dealt with, the effort evidently being to strike a long-term balance. For example, in Laos in 1964 the Indians stalled for a long time on investigations into the presence of Viet Minh; this may have been because nothing could be done about Air America and they were loath to have the commission act in a seemingly one-sided manner. However, this sometimes worked against the Poles as much as against the Canadians. The Indians were particularly allergic to what might seem to them to be extreme, prolonged, or even propagandistic initiatives by either of the other delegations.

It was during the period of hostilities which began in the early sixties that Canada found the attitudes of the other two delegations especially trying; they, on their part, probably found the Canadian attitude equally difficult. It is the Canadian government's view that India and Poland consistently refused to allow the commissions to perform their prime responsibilities during those years. India has taken the position that renewal of the war created a situation which the commissions were not intended to deal with; the Polish view would probably be similar.

When India entered into diplomatic relations with North Vietnam in 1972, while retaining only consular relations with the south, it took a step which, strictly speaking, was none of the commission's business. Nevertheless by taking this step India seemed to sense that its supervisory role in Vietnam was coming to an end. In the old commission it was acceptable for Canada and Poland to recognize only one part of

Vietnam, but this was not so in the case of India; as a matter of practical politics India, the only professedly nonaligned country on the commission, was looked to for balance. It would appear that by about 1965 India, while remaining in the commissions and continuing to support the Geneva agreements, had concluded that the residual tasks for the commission which had been in Vietnam since 1954 would be minimal and that it was in the interests of India as an Asian country to recognize the government in Vietnam which it had always considered likely to prevail in the long run and which, ideology aside, may have seemed to it to be more representative of the national aspirations of the people of Vietnam at this stage of their history than any other serious contender. The 1972 recognition would seem simply to have formalized this position.

Canada has tried to act impartially as a member of the commissions. It was always understood that Canada would bring a Western outlook to their discussions just as India and Poland would bring neutralist and Communist outlooks respectively; but it was equally expected that, in judging a particular issue, all three would do their best to be objective. Canadian delegations attached importance to this both in principle and in practice. At the same time, either in pursuit of a legitimate objective or in reaction to a stand taken by one of the other delegations, Canadians could be vigorous protagonists.

It is important, when forming an opinion about the objectivity of Canada in the commission, to have in mind the distinction, necessarily characteristic of the work of all three delegations, between their roles as "advocates" and their role as "judges." It was in the nature of things that Canadians should be alert to the interests of the non-Communist side and ready to defend those interests if necessary. This was neither reprehensible nor, in the long run, unhelpful if matched by impartiality in reaching conclusions and in taking necessary actions regardless of which side was in the dock. In this regard Canadian delegations were seldom, if ever, found wanting. On the other hand, at least from the point of view of the other delegations, Canadians sometimes had a tendency to be overly legalistic or to display missionary zeal in pursuit of goals.

Canadians who are convinced that, in the commissions, Canada was a sort of stooge of the United States should be aware that most of the time the United States was impatient with the commissions—and with Canada as a member of them—and that it frequently made its impatience abundantly clear. Canadians who are concerned about Canada, because of the commissions' weakness, having been forced into a humiliating role as a member of them, might be a little reassured by the knowledge that, by and large, Canadians serving in Indochina have been trusted and respected by people of all political persuasions there; this has helped to create a human bond between that part of the world and ours.

THE CANADIAN ATTITUDE TOWARD THE GENEVA AGREEMENTS AND TOWARD FUTURE PEACEKEEPING IN INDOCHINA

The Canadian government thought well of the Geneva agreements when they were concluded and has always wished to see them implemented. One of the main reasons for Canada continuing its commission membership has been the fact that, even though the United States and South Vietnam did not fully accept the 1954 agreements (though they did accept the 1962 agreement), none of the countries directly concerned has formally repudiated any of the agreements. This has suggested that there might be elements in these earlier approaches—including international supervision in some suitable form—which could be reconstituted as part of a new settlement if one were needed in any one of the three countries.

During the past four years, as the possibility of peace in Indochina has seemed to come within grasp, Canada's Secretary of State for External Affairs has frequently made statements in which he welcomed the prospect of the war ending and reflected on the peacekeeping aspect. The Prime Minister has also spoken about this.[29] It has been made abundantly

[29] For example, at press conferences in Melbourne (Australia), Singapore, and Tokyo, in May 1970, and in statements to the CBC and to the press in October 1972.

clear that the Canadian government has long been dissatisfied with the conditions under which the commissions have had to operate; at the same time the conditions under which Canada would be prepared to serve again have been described.

The Canadian government's basic position over the past four years has been that it would consider constructively any request for Canadian participation in truce supervisory arrangements when in its opinion, based on the lessons of the past and the circumstances of the request, an operation held the promise of success and Canada could play a useful role. In regard to Vietnam,[30] in a statement to the press in December 1972, the Secretary of State for External Affairs said that the government would wish to have assurances that all four parties which had been involved in the fighting in Vietnam would invite Canada to participate and would be bound by the agreement; that there would be a continuing political authority to receive reports from the commission members; that the commission would have the necessary freedom of movement; and that there would be arrangements for a member's withdrawal from the commission.[31] Subsequently, in the House of Commons, the Minister added further precision, saying *inter alia* that Canada would like the commission's proceedings to be normally open to the public and that Canada would wish to have the right to publicize its own position if necessary.[32]

On January 24, 1973, following President Nixon's announcement of agreement on a ceasefire in Vietnam, the Secretary of State for External Affairs made a statement in the House of Commons along the following lines:

[30] The supervisory body set up by the new ceasefire agreement on Vietnam is one which would serve in that country only; presumably, if there are ceasefires in Laos and Cambodia, where the Geneva agreements are still in force, commissions will be expected to serve there also, but the exact nature of such commissions in the future is not yet clear.

[31] External Affairs press release, December 3, 1972.

[32] Statement by Secretary of State for External Affairs in House of Commons, January 5, 1973.

The Government is profoundly relieved at this historic news, and profoundly grateful for it. At long last, it seems, agreement has been reached to stop the fighting in Vietnam. The way to peace will then lie open. All Canadians will welcome this . . .

A first look [at the ceasefire documents] suggests that the conditions and considerations which we communicated to the parties have to some degree contributed to the terms which have been agreed on for the establishment of a new commission . . .

The Government has decided that when the ceasefire documents have been accepted by all four parties, and when all four parties have clearly invited Canada to take part, the government will then confirm that Canada is ready to take part initially . . . Canada will be prepared to serve on this limited basis for an initial period of sixty days. Canada will be prepared, during that period, to do what it can to discharge the obligations which would flow from full membership in the new commission. A full and formal reply to the invitation for full membership, however, will have to await a number of things: first, it will have to await a very thorough study and analysis of all the agreements, and of the full nature of the parties' commitment to the agreements. It will also have to await the lessons of our experience of participation in the initial stages. It is no secret to anyone that we have serious doubts about what we are being asked to undertake . . .

Meanwhile, let there be no misunderstanding about what Canada will be doing in Vietnam. We will not be there to keep the peace ourselves; that is for the parties to the ceasefire. What we can do is observe how the parties are fulfilling their obligations under the ceasefire, and report on this. From time to time, we may be able to help them through mediation. But it is not up to us whether or not there will be peace in Vietnam. If the parties fulfill their obligations, there can be peace; if they do not then nothing Canada or any other country on the commission can do will prevent the ceasefire from being broken . . .

The people of Vietnam have endured beyond measure a tragedy of indescribable proportions. Every

Canadian prays that the ceasefire will lead to a lasting peace. We can do nothing less than seek some means of contributing effectively to such a peace, and to the reconstruction of that suffering region.

Prospects for Regional Security Cooperation in Southeast Asia

T. B. MILLAR

Southeast Asia is a turbulent, heterogeneous area where rival imperialisms, great and small, have clashed for several thousand years. National and subnational groups have fought or maneuvered for fertile land, for water, for temples, for political, economic, religious, or cultural dominion. They have fought mainly among themselves within the peninsula and archipelago, but they have also of course resisted—with varying degrees of success—outsiders, or neighbors assisted by outsiders.

The Southeast Asia with which we are now concerned, and the wider Asia of which it is a part, is in a measure the result of "European" influences exerted during the nineteenth and early twentieth centuries—British, French, Dutch, Portuguese, Russian, North American. They made no single European impact, even if there were elements of a common Western modernism. In each part of Asia, different influences were at work, on widely differing kinds of people, with widely different results. In none did the influences fill a vacuum, but acted on existing cultures, social systems, and political movements. The injection of Western ideas and technology reinforced or gave a diverting push to trends already evident. And in the long run of history the European colonial impact may come to be seen as a relatively temporary and limited gloss on primarily indigenous or more widely universal developments. By the middle of this century, local nationalist pressures, the absorption of Western technology and ideas, and the blow to European rule caused by an *Asian* imperialistic power (Japan) made it possible for most Asian states to reject Western dominance, even though some of them became frightened or covetous of one another, or divided within by rival competitors for power.

In modern times, the states of Southeast Asia have not felt impelled to join together to resist external pressures, whether British, French, Dutch, or Japanese. They were themselves too weak, often too divided, and often more suspicious of one another than of the foreigners who arrived bearing gifts and opportunities as well as arms, alien government and rapacious company accounts. Such cohesion or collaboration as developed did so under the various imperial mantles, and when the mantles fell or were rent apart many of the original divisions remained, although new states came into being as the legacy of common imperial administrations. Even current cooperation—in Indochina, Malaysia-Singapore, Australia-New Zealand (if we may include them in Southeast Asia)—similarly draws much of its impetus and most of its strength from major external quasi-imperial powers.

In looking at Southeast Asia today, therefore, in an attempt to see how far regional security cooperation has come and how much further it might go, we have few precedents and fewer traditions. As to the future, the first questions we must ask are whether such cooperation is desirable and among which states, whether it is needed or sought; against what common danger or sense of danger it would be directed.

There are of course already several arrangements for regional cooperation in the Southeast Asian region, two being specifically concerned with defense or security—SEATO (South East Asia Treaty Organization), and the Five-Power defense arrangement. The members of SEATO are legally the United States, Britain, France, Pakistan,[1] Thailand, the Philippines, Australia, and New Zealand. France and Pakistan have become substantially inactive members, and at the June 1972 Council meeting in Canberra, both were absent. The members of the Five-Power group are Britain, Australia, New Zealand, Malaysia, and Singapore. Three states—the U.K., Australia, and New Zealand—are thus members of both.

[1] After some years of taking a limited part in SEATO, Pakistan formally withdrew in November 1972.

This is not a coincidence. From the beginning of SEATO, each of these three states saw its presence in Malaysia (or, earlier, in Malaya and in Singapore) to be a function of its membership in SEATO.

The Southeast Asia Collective Defense Treaty, which gave rise to SEATO, was signed soon after the 1954 Geneva Conference on Korea and Indochina, and was a direct result of Communist military successes in those two areas. The treaty area did not include Korea or Taiwan, but its terms for countering overt or covert aggression were applicable to South Vietnam, Laos, and Cambodia if those states and the members so wished.

A good deal has been said about the decline of SEATO. People have suggested that it is "dead but doesn't know it," is effete and useless, is the final grin on an already disappeared paper tiger, and so on. These views, I believe, have misunderstood the situation. Mark Twain, seeing his own obituary notice in the newspaper, said that the report of his death had been grossly exaggerated. So it is with SEATO. It is not what it was, but then it probably never was what some people would have liked it to be. For some years the United States was reluctant to have any military planning under SEATO, or any force declarations. The French had only a temporary interest, to protect the changes in Indochina and French economic, political, and cultural investment there. The British were mainly interested in protecting the northern flank of Malaya. In doing so, they (and Australia) believed they were helping to keep secure part of the Treaty Area, and providing a base for rapid deployment if necessary into member or protocol states. Pakistan wanted help against India, which SEATO provided in arms and perhaps psychologically, but not as a military alliance.[2] Australia and New Zealand were prepared to do a great deal for Malaya (not a member) but much less for the Philippines or Thailand, with which they had few links.

There were thus grave weaknesses in SEATO from the beginning. When crises occurred—in Laos in 1961 and in

[2] Other members made this clear to Pakistan, in Manila when the Treaty was signed.

Vietnam in 1964—the coherence of SEATO wilted, and those members that wished to act had to do so as individuals rather than as a collective, the 1962 Dean Rusk-Thanat Khoman statement providing an appropriate rationale.[3] The essential strength of SEATO has always been the American commitment, just as that of NATO has been. The United States entered SEATO to meet a specific threat rather than an area situation—to keep Communist power above the seventeenth parallel and out of Laos, Cambodia, and Thailand. One can make a case for claiming that this objective was substantially maintained for a long time.

Whatever the reasons may have been for the American involvement in the Indochina war, SEATO was the context, and an increasingly important context for the U. S. Administration (as other rationales diminished in credibility) in obtaining acquiescence by Congress and the people in an increasingly costly, prolonged and uncertain conflict. It will continue to provide the context, despite the gloss of the "Nixon doctrine," so long as any commitment remains. Few people, if any, believe that involvement in Indochina will ever return to its previous scale; many people believe that it will disappear altogether within a very few years, under the impact of changed American policies. But it still, as of today, exists. It is part of the near future, and we cannot ignore it.

We cannot ignore it not so much because of South Vietnam, nor even because of Laos and Cambodia which are in almost desperate straits, as because of Thailand. There is no American commitment to Thailand outside of SEATO, but there is a very definite commitment to Thailand under SEATO. And despite the downgrading of SEATO which the Nixon doctrine clearly implies, despite the elimination of force declarations and the end of contingency planning, de-

[3] On March 6, 1962, following a deterioration in the situation in Laos, the Thai Foreign Minister and the U. S. Secretary of State issued a joint declaration in which Mr. Rusk assured Mr. Thanat that in the event of a Communist attack on Thailand, the United States intended to give full effect to its obligations under SEATO and "reaffirmed that this obligation . . . does not depend upon the prior agreement of all other parties to the Treaty, since the Treaty obligation is individual as well as collective."

spite the reduction of American forces in Thailand, I do not
see how the United States could in the next few years unilaterally abrogate its commitment to Thailand, any more than
it could abrogate its commitment to South Korea. And South
Korea is more competent to deal with overt attack than Thailand is with covert. So long as the United States is committed
to SEATO, Australia and New Zealand and possibly the Philippines and Britain are likely also to be involved in varying
degrees, although the Australian Labor Party government
that came into office in December 1972 has been far cooler
to SEATO than its predecessor was. France may keep a nominal attendance in Bangkok, as did Pakistan for so long, the
latter policy being partly perhaps (as the cynics said) to
obtain information for bartering in Peking.

The activities of SEATO today are mostly concerned with
countersubversion.[4] We are unlikely to see American ground
forces defend Thailand or any other part of Southeast Asia.
But much else can be done—in aid of various kinds, logistics,
air support, equipment, training, etc.

Why is Thailand important to the United States? It is important for providing a relatively stable base so long as American forces are or may be involved in Indochina. It is
strategically important as a buffer between a potentially Communist Indochina and a potentially unstable Burma. It is important because of the other major powers which might seek
to replace American power there. It is a friendly ally, and no
friendly ally is lightly discarded. It provides a political entree
into Southeast Asian circles, and a listening post for the whole
region. It contains substantial American investment. But
might not Thailand come to feel that it must make the best
possible terms with China and North Vietnam even if those
terms involve total American withdrawal? May the United
States not feel that, if it can be arranged in Peking or elsewhere, withdrawal from Thailand over a period of two to

---

[4] Detailed information on these activities is of course not made
public, but the SEATO role includes training in countersubversion,
and the collection and pooling of relevant information. In a body
such as SEATO, the security of such information must present
formidable problems.

three years would be a low price to pay for a real delay in renewed Communist military activities? This rather Machiavellian assessment has been imputed in some quarters to Mr. Nixon and Dr. Kissinger.

If Thailand did decide that it wanted relations with Peking of a kind that could only be obtained by a total U.S. withdrawal, then that withdrawal would occur, and SEATO would be dead and buried. We have yet to see evidence that this is what Bangkok wants or needs;[5] or, indeed, that improved relations with China could not be managed within the context of continuing American defense aid. Western Europe and the Soviet Union provide such a precedent or analogy. The favorable change in the Sino-American relationship appears sufficiently well-based and enduring as to suggest that the American presence in Thailand is unlikely to affect it. But let us consider further which is the more important to Mr. Nixon—Peking or Moscow. There is surely no doubt that however romantically attractive the forbidden city may be to the American Marco Polos, or useful in foreign or domestic political ways, it is far less a threat to American interests than is Moscow. There has been no Chinese invasion southward, and the United States decided to withdraw from Vietnam virtually irrespective of Peking's attitude. It is not going to intervene on the ground in Laos and Cambodia, irrespective of Peking's attitude. It would like to see a settlement for the whole of Southeast Asia which would enable it to withdraw to a basically offshore position, but this is not going to happen quickly. In any overhasty withdrawal of that kind, the beneficiaries would be both Peking and Moscow, and the United States would lose present advantages in its global strategic position. Clumsy American diplomacy in the subcontinent has already contributed to an Indo-Soviet security agreement (within a wider treaty), the wording of which is stronger than the comparable paragraphs in ANZUS or SEATO. We can hardly expect that the United States will offer the Russians similar opportunities in a Southeast Asia fearful of in-

[5] The coup d'état in Bangkok produced what appeared at first to be a policy less amenable to changes in foreign policy, but the trend toward finding a regional *modus vivendi* has since resumed.

creased Chinese hegemony. For their part, the Russians would presumably rather have the Americans in Thailand than the Chinese, if that were the alternative.

My first conclusion, therefore, is that SEATO is not a wholly spent force, and will continue for a few years, primarily as a vehicle for American aid to and a reduced presence in Thailand; the prime objective being to counterinsurgency activities in northeast, north, and southern Thailand and at least for a time to provide a base in Thailand for operations in Indochina. When the Philippines Foreign Minister, Mr. Romulo, called at the June 1972 SEATO Council meeting in Canberra for a revitalized, refashioned SEATO, he omitted to mention what a new SEATO would do. Any refashioning can only be within the context of SEATO's operating on a greatly reduced scale and with dwindling political capital.

The second arrangement in being—the Five-Power—is the replacement for the Anglo-Malaysian Defense Agreement, to some of the provisions of which Australia and New Zealand were attached by exchanges of letters, and which was held to apply to Singapore despite the absence of a formal agreement. AMDA came to an end on October 31, 1971, and the Five-Power agreement between the same five states came into being the following day. This is not a formal public treaty; it is an arrangement contained within a communiqué and subsequent exchanges of letters with detailed annexes attached. The operative paragraph of the communiqué merely declares: "in relation to the external defence of Malaysia or Singapore, [the five] Governments would immediately consult together for the purpose of deciding what measures should be taken jointly or separately in relation to such attack or threat."

Strength is given to what is clearly a very loose arrangement by the presence in Malaysia and Singapore of forces from the three external powers, known by the title of ANZUK. ANZUK, a combined force under a single commander, has at present a battalion from each country, up to eight frigates and a submarine, a small section of British Nimrod maritime reconnaissance aircraft, two squadrons of Australian Mirage

III interceptor fighters, and other air components. The five powers have a Joint Consultative Council and an Air Defense Council controlling an integrated air defense system. Australia provided the first ANZUK Commander, and the first commander of the integrated air defense system.

Five-Power came into existence for various reasons: (1) the two local states—Malaysia and Singapore—wanted to go on receiving the military help of their Commonwealth friends; (2) Australia and then New Zealand decided in early 1969 to keep forces in the Malaysian area after the declared British withdrawal from the region by the end of 1971 (as announced by the Wilson Government) and needed a framework for doing so; (3) the 1970 British elections returned to power a Conservative government more willing than its predecessors to maintain forces east of Suez for the purposes of protecting British interests and connections there.

It is worth looking at the declared and possible additional reasons why the five states should be cooperating in this way. One unstated reason is inertia. There was a defense organization in existence, with forces deployed. This began (as a collaborative exercise) in 1950, in a small way, to help with the Malayan Emergency. It was developed into ANZAM, and in 1955 received additional forces from Australia and New Zealand, including two battalions of infantry, which could conceivably be used in a SEATO situation. It was used during Indonesia's small war with Malaysia, known euphemistically as "Confrontation." To dismantle this whole apparatus and leave Malaysia and Singapore to fend for themselves would be difficult because of administrative inertia as well as because of political reactions. Britain's proposed total withdrawal (in 1968) was made more bearable because Australia and New Zealand decided to remain. Britain's reasons—economic costs, changing political priorities, obvious remoteness—did not apply to Australia and New Zealand. As a corollary, the Heath government's decision to keep some forces in the area made the Australian and New Zealand decisions more acceptable to their own electorates.

As is only to be expected, the five states in the agreement have seen different value in it. While certain public pronouncements have been made, they do not accurately state the full position of the governments concerned. My interpretation would be as follows.

Malaysia has an internal security problem, from Communist terrorists in its northern areas near the Thai border, and in eastern Malaysia-Sabah and (especially) Sarawak. It also has a potentially explosive communal situation between its citizens of Malay and of Chinese race. It fears Singapore as a potential focus of loyalty for Malaysian Chinese, as a possible source of Communist infection, or perhaps later as a base or springboard for China or the Soviet Union. It fears the possibility of a revival by some subsequent Indonesian government of claims to the Borneo states. It is concerned that the Philippines may reactivate its claim to Sabah, as a former part of the Sulu Sultanate. The Five-Power arrangement may not help with the communal situation, but it does offer some reassurance over the others.

Singapore probably sees the principal advantage of Five-Power as ensuring the general security and stability of the island and thus confidence for capital investment and economic development. Singapore fears Malay "ultras" in Malaysia, and what they may do in the future, not only to Singapore, but also to Malaysian Chinese or even perhaps Indians, many of whom have relations in Singapore. It sees itself as somewhat of a Chinese nut in a Malay nutcracker (Malaysia and Indonesia). It values the money spent in the island by foreign forces and their dependents. It would be delighted to have its excellent defense facilities—much too large for Singapore's own needs—used by two or more other major powers: by the Americans, by the Russians, by the Japanese, who would act both as a restraint upon each other and as competitors in jingling the Singapore cash registers.

Both Malaysia and Singapore have developed their own ground force capacity. Navies have been slower, for obvious reasons, and air forces slower still. The ANZUK forces have thus helped to provide both states with a capacity for maritime air reconnaissance, naval interception, air observation and interception, air transport (including helicopters), and training for local forces in these expensive activities and their associated facilities.

For the United Kingdom, under its Conservative government, Five-Power enables it to contribute at modest cost to stability in a region in which there is still extensive British investment; it helps with surveillance of the waters of the Indian Ocean, where the Soviet Union now customarily has more naval and associated ships than any other country (except, at times, France). It keeps lines into the only two Asian Commonwealth countries prepared to have as close a relationship as this, with consequent value for information and communications. It encourages Australia and New Zealand to refrain from retreating into "fortress" defense policies and psychologies.

For Australia, the arrangement serves diverse interests. It provides a context for a continuing British presence east of Suez, which is something of a counterweight to Soviet intrusions. It provides opportunities—even imperatives—for Malaysian-Singaporean defense cooperation, without which the relationship might deteriorate into public tension or even conflict. It offers those states an assurance against—or an alternative to—other external pressures or involvements: Soviet, perhaps Japanese, Chinese, or Indonesian. It would not be in Australia's (or Britain's) interest to see any of these powers dominate the vital passages between the Indian and Pacific Oceans. The arrangement also provides Australia with extra links to its closest Asian partners and a bridge to the continent. It brings New Zealand into forms of cooperation with Australia which might not otherwise exist. It offers bases and training facilities within an area of possible operations. But further, one always has to consider the alternatives to a particular course of action. What many Australians tend to forget about Australia's relations with Malaysia and Singapore and the general policy of "forward defense" is that the Australian government does not face a decision whether or not to put forces into Malaysia or Singapore, but whether or not to reduce or remove forces already there. These are very different kinds of decisions.

But the Five-Power arrangement has been the subject of

debate and controversy, and the Australian government's attitude toward it has begun to change since 1971 and 1972. Clumsy diplomacy (on both sides) has exacerbated Australian relations with Malaysia and—in different ways—with Singapore. The strengthening of Australian relations with Indonesia coincided with Malaysian initiatives toward a neutral Southeast Asia.[6] Prior to the Australian federal election in December 1972, the Australian Labor Party Leader (Mr. E. G. Whitlam) and Deputy Leader (Mr. Lance Barnard) advocated a reduction of the Australian forces in Malaysia and Singapore, and after winning the election the new government proceeded to put those reductions into effect. Probably by the end of 1974, there will only be one or two hundred Australian servicemen left in the region, after nearly a quarter of a century of active military presence.

New Zealand has a different viewpoint from either Britain or Australia. It is three thousand miles farther from Southeast Asia than is Australia, and does not feel the hot Asian winds blowing around it. It would like British forces to remain east of Suez; it believes in defense cooperation with Australia; and it wants to contribute to the general security of the area.

The Five-Power agreement or arrangement, therefore, is in a state of transition. It will provide measures of security cooperation between its members for a time, but the Australian withdrawal has substantially attenuated the arrangement, which cannot be adequately shored up by proposals for joint exercises. Five-Power was never envisaged as being permanent. It is hard to see what it will evolve into, or indeed whether it will now evolve into anything at all.

There are several other situations where a measure of regional defense cooperation exists notionally or in fact. Malaysia and Thailand are supposed to be cooperating to elimi-

[6] On June 9, 1972, during a goodwill visit to Indonesia, the Australian Prime Minister (Mr. William McMahon) appeared to raise doubts about Australia's interest in the Five-Power arrangement. He said the agreement "only relates to the obligation to consult," and was not strictly necessary (*The Australian*, June 10, 1972).

nate the Communist terrorists operating across the common border. From time to time, one hears reports that the cooperation is better than it used to be but not as good as it might be. My inquiries lead me to believe that it is virtually non-existent. The Thais feel that it is not their problem; or to the extent that it is, that they cannot do very much about it. They do not want to stir up a hornet's nest. And they never have entirely forgiven the Malaysians over the question of ownership of the border provinces.

There have been many reports of Thai forces operating in Laos, with the tacit assent of the Royal Laotian government, and with the aim of protecting the routes into Thailand. South Vietnamese forces have also operated in Cambodia at different times, with varying degrees of Cambodian enthusiasm.

A recent and quite interesting development has occurred between Indonesia and Australia. Relations between the two countries have become surprisingly cordial, and Australian economic aid has grown rapidly ($A56 million was given in the three years until June 1973). Forms of military cooperation are being considered which would have been deemed impossible only a few years ago, including joint naval exercises. The first practical result was an agreement to exchange information of a defense nature. In June 1972 the then Australian Prime Minister announced a grant of $A69 million in civic aid to Indonesia to take effect from June 1973, and $A20 million in defense aid, over the next three to four years beginning in January 1973. This is in addition to the gift of a squadron of Sabre aircraft, valued at $A10 million. This aid —given or promised—has been noticed, and commented upon with some apprehension, in Papua-New Guinea.

In November 1971, Indonesia, Malaysia, and Singapore agreed to cooperate in ensuring safety of navigation in the Straits of Malacca and the Straits of Singapore. At the same time, Indonesia and Malaysia, while recognizing rights of innocent passage, agreed that both straits were not international waterways; Singapore "took note" of their position.[7] The Malaysian-Indonesian view evoked a strong protest by

[7] *The Straits Times,* November 17, 1971.

the Soviet Union on March 2, 1972, and the United States and Japan have also made it clear that they insist on unrestricted passage.[8]

In these circumstances, what is the significance of the proposal by Malaysia that the Southeast Asian region become a "zone of peace, freedom, and neutrality," free from external interference, with the United States, China, and the Soviet Union as the guarantors? I think one must see this as a kite displayed for domestic viewing, flown to gauge international currents of air, and wearing respectable but as yet transparent colors. The fact that Tun Razak has had the proposal endorsed in principle by the other members of the Association of Southeast Asian Nations (ASEAN)—Singapore, Thailand, the Philippines, and Indonesia—does not indicate any enthusiasm on their part for neutralism.[9] As the Singaporean Foreign Minister was reported as saying, "We all have different approaches to this goal of neutralism." The Thais, despite some feelers of their own toward China (prior to the Thai coup of November 1971) have publicly doubted the likelihood that China will eschew its announced intention of overthrowing non-Communist governments in the region. The Thais are unlikely to discard what remains of the American umbrella, nor are the Filipinos, despite resentment at client status, and regular but largely ritualistic anti-American fulminations. The prospect for a combined Major-Powers guarantee seems extremely remote. However, some movement to reduced dependence and a more balanced relationship with the major powers is possible.[10]

---

[8] *Asian Almanac,* 1972, pp. 5222–24, summarizes this situation. The Argentine, which has a somewhat similar problem over the Magellan Straits, supported Malaysia.

[9] *Asian Almanac,* 1972, pp. 4979–83, gives the text of the declaration and communiqué following the meeting of ASEAN Foreign Ministers in Kuala Lumpur on November 25–27, 1971, plus official comments on the concept.

[10] Agence France Presse reported from Manila on April 20, 1972, that a Filipino Nationalist Party Senator, Salvador Laurel, was told by officials in Peking that China would respect the neutralism of Southeast Asia but that all military links between the countries concerned and the United States must first be annulled.

Some people see ASEAN as a potential security system, or as developing military overtones. There are Americans who would like this to happen, to enable greater and faster U.S. disengagement from the region. There are also Indonesians who seem to see it as desirable, including General Panggabean, Commander-in-Chief of the Indonesian Armed Forces. Foreign Minister Adam Malik has publicly refuted the idea, but some of his officials have privately canvassed it. I think we can accept that the Indonesian government is prepared to allow some ambivalence to appear.

The only other significant proposal for a regional security arrangement in recent times was made by the Soviet Union in June 1969, at the time of the Sino-Soviet confrontation on the Ussuri and Amur rivers, when Mr. Brezhnev raised the possibility of a Soviet-backed regional security system in Asia. It was difficult to find out exactly what he had in mind, and it seems probable that he did not exactly have anything in mind, but was "trailing his coat." While polite noises were made in some of the capitals concerned, the proposal was not taken up. It was rather too obviously anti-Chinese, looked rather too much like a Soviet SEATO, but a SEATO to which the Russians were not prepared to contribute the forces which alone would make it effective but which would simultaneously raise problems of their own.

The proposal was reactivated in March 1972 by Mr. Kosygin and Mr. Brezhnev, following Mr. Nixon's visit to China. Again it was far from clear what they envisaged. The speeches of both leaders were high on principle and low on detail. *Izvestia* on April 7 linked the idea to the Soviet proposal for a European security conference, claiming that the need for collective security in Asia and the Pacific was no less than in Europe. The Soviet Union seems to view its treaty with India as a prototype for similar agreements between itself and Asian countries, and between Asian countries themselves.[11] Its treaty with Iraq, and India's with Bangladesh, lend substance to this. On the other hand, public resistance to Soviet alliance

[11] Radio Peace and Progress, Moscow, on March 15, 1972, urged Asian countries to conclude "corresponding bilateral or regional treaties."

diplomacy has been displayed by Egypt and Yemen. The Brezhnev proposal has not been taken up bilaterally by any Asian government other than India. India in any foreseeable circumstances would be reluctant to enter a wider security system. On April 18, 1972, Mr. Fukuda, then Japanese Foreign Minister, told the Diet budgetary committee that a collective security system in Asia which did not include China was "totally inconceivable." Continuing Sino-Soviet estrangement and the Sino-Japanese rapprochement do not improve the proposal's prospects. The Prime Minister of Malaysia, Tun Razak, said in Parliament on May 18, 1972: "Malaysia has its own neutralization proposals for peace and security in the region, which we regard as more practicable and feasible and which we think the Soviet Union would have no difficulty in accepting."[12] In October 1972 the Soviet government again pressed, through its official publications, for a new Asian security pact.

We can expect that the Soviet leadership will continue to pursue throughout the region, through single or multiple channels, a diplomacy designed to reduce both Chinese and American influence while increasing that of the Soviet Union. It is not interested in regional security for the sake of regional security. It is not in a hurry.[13]

What do Southeast Asians fear, which might force them together? They all (including, I would suspect, North Vietnam) fear China. This might not seem to remote foreigners to be a reasonable fear, but it exists. China dominates the region, psychologically. But it is hard to believe that any of the countries will group together to meet a real or imagined Chinese threat. As they see it, such a grouping might be considered a public provocative act. It would indicate ungener-

[12] On a visit to the Soviet Union in early October 1972, Tun Razak negotiated an agreement for economic and technical cooperation. He also pressed his views on neutralizing Southeast Asia. He indicated that if satisfactory neutralization arrangements were made, foreign bases would have to be phased out.

[13] A good summary of the early development of the Soviet proposal is contained in Marian P. Kirsch, "Soviet Security Objectives in Asia," *International Organization,* Summer 1970 (Vol. XXIV, No. 3), pp. 451–78.

ous and therefore probably counterproductive fears of the giant neighbor. It could never be sufficient on its own to thwart any Chinese aggression, and under the Nixon doctrine it will be increasingly on its own. On the other hand, if China is *not* aggressive, such a grouping would not be needed. Mutual animosities among the Southeast Asian states are in any case, for the most part, more immediate than their fears of China. There are also some politicians (including Thais and Malaysians) who feel that China can be appeased and placated by appropriate ceremonies.

Laos, Cambodia, South Vietnam, and Thailand all fear North Vietnam. Some cooperation is theoretically possible, under U.S. encouragement, but tends to be inadequately coordinated, and subject to the area's traditional tensions. The future of the Indochina states is in any case highly uncertain.

Might ASEAN be widened to include Burma and the Indochina states? When ASEAN proves its worth to its existing members, it may perhaps attract others, but this is very uncertain. After a Ministerial meeting in 1972, a Heads of Government meeting was postponed a year. Might the Asian and Pacific Council (ASPAC) take on a defense role? There is no evidence that its principal members would allow it to do so, and Australia has virtually withdrawn from ASPAC. The Republic of China (Taiwan) and South Vietnam are fragile members, and South Korea is in process of mending fences with the North. The increasing respectability of China and all the implications of the Nixon doctrine are reducing the rationale of ASPAC as an anti-Communist association. Might a narrower grouping such as a revitalized Maphilindo be more likely to succeed? This could suit Indonesia, but for that reason would probably again rouse the fears of the others.

Japan has yet to stir the kinds of fears that set Defense Ministers meeting. It is not an apparent military threat; nor has it encouraged anyone to think that it would support regional defense efforts. It has a strong interest in the stability of the area, and in free access to raw materials, markets, and trade routes, but it has no evident intention of being involved in military conflict on the Asian mainland, except perhaps, in a crisis, in Korea. As a Japanese professor said to me once, "World War II taught Japan that to pursue economic objectives by military means is a very uneconomic thing to do."

I believe that there is room for a far higher degree of co-operation than now exists between the non-Communist Southeast Asian states, Australia, and New Zealand, in military training of various kinds, in defense production and infrastructure, but it seems unlikely that such increased co-operation will occur.[14] External competing pressures are too great, and local initiatives and imperatives insufficiently compulsive.

This is not an optimistic picture, if one's desideratum is a Southeast Asia armed to its collective teeth and working as one. Yet small countries can by vigorous diplomacy and purposeful will stand up to larger ones, or if necessary make accommodations without losing their identity or virility. Superficially, one might believe that a "patchwork quilt" of regional economic, political, and military arrangements is emerging, but the fabric has too many holes and too little real strength of its own. A new multilateral balance is possible under the influence if not the guarantees of the major powers. What seems more likely is that, as in the last thirty years, the new arrangement will not balance, but will stagger under internal tensions and competing unequal pressures from one crisis to the next, yet without erupting into major war.

[14] The Australian Prime Minister, Mr. Whitlam, has strongly advocated regional arrangements in Southeast Asia, but of an economic and not a defense nature. His proposals have run into difficulty, partly because he had hoped to include China, which was not acceptable to Indonesia.

Security Preoccupations and Power Balances After Vietnam

"Security" is a profoundly ambiguous word, especially when one is looking at the relationship between great powers and small in a particular area of tension and conflict. Even in a relatively stable power-balance, a Great Power's concept of its own security needs (for instance the Soviet Union's concept of what political conditions are necessary in Eastern Europe to ensure Soviet security) may be incompatible with the interests of the smaller powers concerned. In such a case "collective security" may be an international equivalent of the "protection" sold by a racketeer to a small businessman: a euphemism for monopoly of threat.

However, despite the difficulties of definition and concept, it is becoming possible, as the United States diminishes its involvement in Vietnam, to see rather more of the shape of future power-rivalries and balances in Asia generally, and to examine the way in which these relationships will affect the search for security and stability in Southeast Asia. The fates of small powers in that region will be determined primarily by larger powers, none of which is actually Southeast Asian, though one state in the area, Indonesia, is substantial enough to be a major element in assessments of future balances.

When the decision-makers of the Powers talk of collective security organizations they generally mean mutual defense arrangements: multilateral treaties, or systems of linked bilateral treaties whose members envisage a threat which is not from one of the treaty partners, but from an outsider. These are not true collective security organizations in the classic sense of the "league against an unknown enemy," an arrangement intended to restrain aggression by any one of its own members. Some contemporary regional organizations may aspire to this function, and in strict theory there is no reason why a regional collective security organization of all Southeast Asian states, and *only* Southeast Asian states, should not evolve in time along the lines of the Organization of American States or the Organization of African Unity. But this appears so distant a prospect that I propose to examine first what seems a closer possibility: the "collective security" system which is really a mutual defense treaty or treaties, based essentially on a commitment of some sort by one of the Great Powers.

Probably, I ought first to justify the implied assumption that arrangements of this sort can be regarded as contributing to security, if only in the sense of diminishing, or at worst smothering, instabilities. The obvious analogy is Europe. Formally since 1955, and informally since 1945, Europe has been organized into two relatively tight military alliances, each based ultimately on the determination and commitment of one of the dominant powers to maintain its own sphere of interest. The two alliances, NATO and the Warsaw Pact, may have looked a little frayed in places from time to time, and both operate to some extent (the Warsaw Pact to much the greater extent) to keep in power regimes which trouble the consciences of liberals. To a substantial degree they represent a sacrifice of freedom to stability. Yet it would be idle to deny that they operate together to provide a security system of sorts, not only by maintaining a balance of power in which each of the coalitions "deters" the other, but also by restraining and managing crises within their own membership. For the evidence of this one has simply to look at the history of the decades since this system first came into formation. The peace has in fact been preserved despite multiple causes for quarrel both between and within the coalitions, and even the apparent likeliest revanchist or irredentist power, Western Germany, has in the course of that time had to modify its earlier national objectives almost past recognition. The only military operations conducted within the European theater for more than a quarter of a century have been suppressions of urban-based insurgencies: East Germany 1953, Hungary 1956, Czechoslovakia 1968, the operations in each case being very short-lived. And by the standards of the rest of the world at the same time, or the standards of the European past, that is a fair degree of security.

Thus it seems reasonable to explore, among other possibilities, the question of whether relationships in Asia have moved or are moving toward a phase in which some such balance of power system might conceivably emerge. On this point we can at least say that the Asian situation has changed profoundly since 1968. Whereas once the only potential candidate for the role of "guarantor" in such a system was the United States, and the only "threat" against which it could have been directed was that from China, it would now seem feasible to think of the prospective diplomacy of Asia as that of "competitive containment," with China as much interested in containing the growth of power or influence by the Soviet Union and/or Japan, as the Soviet Union is of restraining the growth of Chinese influence. The United States has not yet completed its painful protracted withdrawal from Asian commitments, but there can be no doubt that withdrawal is what the electorate wants. Most Americans want this withdrawal to be exempt from any stain of visible American defeat or humiliation, and believe that Mr. Nixon and Dr. Kissinger can secure this condition. But once it is secured, their sense of any remaining American national interest in Vietnam seems likely to be slight.

The increased complexity of the Asian situation makes the emergence of some future arrangements on balance of power lines at least marginally more probable, it may be argued, than it was a few years ago. To justify this statement one must look at the motivations of each of the dominant powers and the degree to which each power is interested in containing or balancing against the others. (Containment may be regarded as merely one of the strategies by which a balance of power policy may be operated, but for the moment the question of what others are available will be disregarded.)

Until 1968–69, it would have seemed unconvincing to argue that the Soviet Union ought logically to find itself with more reasons than the United States to build a system of containment against the expansion of Chinese influence in Asia. Yet since that time it has come to appear rather surprising that this logic was so long concealed. The State Department spokesman who remarked casually that the past twenty years of America's China policy, the years in effect of the "containment" of China, had been "an aberration," has already come to represent an exponent merely of common sense, rather than of radical change of concept. The more, indeed, one reflects upon the period in which the United States elected to regard China as its most dangerous adversary, the more "aberrant," in the true sense, that American view seems, for there is no vital interest of the United States which is or was vulnerable to China in the way several such vital interests are vulnerable to the Soviet Union. (Japan may have been represented as vulnerable by some policy-makers, including Mr. Nixon, in 1954, but the gap between this representation and the reality of power was always very wide.) The American effort at the containment of China was not, by and large, the outcome of hardheaded or imperialistic calculation concerning strategic and economic interests, but the outcome of a chain of events anchored finally to President Truman's moral enthusiasm for a somewhat misconceived notion of collective security, as embodied in the UN. That is, the "containment of China" was largely an accidental by-product of the Korean War. Once the decision had been taken to prevent the seizure of South Korea, and preserve the government in Taiwan, everything else followed, up to the revulsion of feeling after the Tet offensive in 1968, when the real costs of the existing American policy in Asia had to be reckoned up.[1]

But if there was never much real substance of national

[1] The revisionist school of historians of American foreign policy would tend to argue, to the contrary, that American policy in Asia, including this Korean decision, contained a larger element of imperialist activism than of reaction to events. See, for instance, John Gittings' "Touching the Tiger's Buttocks—Western Scholarship and the Cold War in Asia," in *The Study of International Affairs* (London: Oxford University Press, 1972), p. 4.

interest at stake in the American case, there is plenty in the Soviet case, and thus the incentives to operate a containment policy are much stronger, and may prove longer-lasting. Probably it is not even now adequately appreciated in the West how much the Soviet Union seems to feel itself, as an Asian landholder, to be threatened. The Soviet Asian lands are relatively empty of people, and therefore vulnerable, as well as relatively well endowed with industrial raw material resources, and therefore desirable. And the pressure in Asia of people on resources will not slacken during this century. On the contrary, Asia by the end of the century must somehow carry about 55 per cent of the seven thousand million population then expected in the world, so that the future contest for Asian *Lebensraum* seems likely to be more rather than less intense than at present, and to be driven by more urgent forces than elsewhere in the world.

It may be objected that concepts like *Lebensraum* and pressure on resources are crude popular stereotypes about the motivations of foreign policy, and they ought to have no place in an era of advanced technology. But whether this is the case or not, the fact is that crucial decision-makers do appear to be influenced by concepts of this sort, and thus they may have political importance, even if their intellectual substance is rather doubtful. Mr. Brezhnev in his survey of the world after the Nixon visit to China, reflected that two-thirds of Soviet territory is in Asia,[2] and seemed to imply both that he intended to keep it that way, and that he felt it somewhat threatened. Mr. Chou En-lai, in effect, retorted that the Kremlin had picked up where John Foster Dulles left off with regard to the containment of China. That is, both in the Soviet Union and in China there has been a clear and recent indication from the highest policy-making circles that a collective defense system in Asia, anchored in some way to Soviet power and interests, is expected to remain, as Mr. Brezhnev said in 1969, "on the agenda." And of course the change in the Indian attitude between the initial coolness of Mrs. Gandhi's reception of the idea in 1969, and the consider-

[2] *The Times* (London), March 21, 1972, p. 5.

able ardor with which India pursued the Soviet-Indian treaty of August 1971 (after the advent of the Bangladesh crisis and the Kissinger visit to China in July) tends to confirm the impression that the concept has picked up a momentum it seemed initially to lack.

The most theoretically attractive power as a Soviet ally, in terms of "potential" as against "opportunity," is obviously Japan. This is as much for complementarity of economic interests as for political ones. The development of Siberia is a project of immense prospective importance to both, and therefore, by converse, to China. The Tyumin oilfields of West Siberia, which are estimated to hold 45 thousand million gallons of oil, could reduce Japanese dependence on the always-vulnerable Middle East fields which now supply 80 per cent of Japan's imports. An alternative source of supply must become even more attractive in Tokyo as the Arab controllers of these oilfields show an increasing determination and skill at the business of raising prices and extorting more say in the running of the world oil business. The Japanese could provide the funds to improve the existing pipeline from Tyumin to Irkutsk, and lay a new one from Irkutsk to Nakhodka. They could also supply capital to develop the Yakutia coal fields, link the mines with the Trans-Siberian Railway, and so make available a good supply of coking-coal. They could help in the development of the Soviet Far Eastern lumber industry by constructing a new Pacific port.

These projects could be useful and profitable for Japan as well as the Soviet Union, and they would certainly help tilt the military balance further against China, by easing the Russian supply position, which is a major constraint on military action in that theater. The Siberian pipeline would be particularly important in this respect, provided it could be made relatively invulnerable. And there is no doubt that both China and the Soviet Union have contemplated the logistics of military operations in this area: each is keeping a quarter of its armed strength facing the other. Sources privy to American military intelligence have been arguing recently that the whole center of gravity of Soviet military effort has swung over to the Far Eastern front.

Even in the field of maritime interests, the Soviet Union and Japan have seemed to be moving toward policies which are parallel, and which are at odds with those of China. The Chinese government has aligned itself with Latin America and other states of the underdeveloped world in backing a 200-mile-width proposal for the territorial sea. This claim is sharply incompatible with the interests of the major mercantile powers, whether they are old hands in this field like Britain, America, and Japan, or relative newcomers like the Soviet Union. In regard to particular areas, such as the Malacca Straits, the similarity of Soviet and Japanese interests and their variance with the interests of Indonesia and Malaysia have become apparent, as has the ease with which, for the time being, China can align itself with the small powers and assign itself the role of their protector—at least verbally. One can see the way this sort of common interest could develop by constructing not-too-far-out scenarios. For instance, some Malaysian politicians have claimed that the Malacca Straits should really be regarded as a canal, like Suez, with fees charged for passage through it. Russia and Japan would be major users: conceivably they might come to feel their common interests at stake in local decisions, much as Britain and France did over Egyptian and Israeli decisions in 1956. Presumably, in such an instance, the 1956 roles of America and Russia would be open to China, which has already in fact talked of Soviet-Japanese "collusion" in the Straits.[3]

Another instance of the possible future frictions between China and Japan in this field may be seen in the position of the Senkaku Islands. If the 200-mile limit is taken seriously, these islands, and the oil under the sea around them, are part of the territory of Taiwan—which the Japanese have already conceded to be a province of China. But Japan itself may be strongly interested in developing these oilfields, and has made a claim to them as part of the Ryukyus ocean territory. If it ever decided to contest this issue against China it would need an ally, as India did when it decided to contest the issue of

[3] *Far Eastern Economic Review,* March 25, 1972, p. 8.

Bangladesh. And as one crisis produced the Soviet-Indian Treaty, the other could produce a Soviet-Japan Treaty.

Yet despite all the envisageable possibilities of common interests, a substantial doubt must remain whether the Soviet Union can, in the foreseeable future, recruit Japan as the ally it needs in Northeast Asia or interest the cautious Japanese in membership of any collective security or mutual defense system in which the Soviet role would be prominent. The difficulty is that while the *objective* factors might seem conducive to such a development, the *subjective* ones, especially on the Japanese side but probably on both, are not. One might indeed say that neither power has shown much aptitude for being an ally, and the traditions of their past relationship are particularly unfavorable to their developing it *vis-à-vis* each other. The Japanese government has reasons of experience to be coy to Soviet wooing whether on the economic or the diplomatic side, and has not convinced itself as yet that capital sunk in the Siberian ventures would necessarily be well invested. Mr. Gromyko's visit to Tokyo in 1972 (the first meeting at this level since 1967) must undoubtedly be seen as a signal of Russian anxiety to make progress, probably through the negotiation at last of a peace treaty (the Soviet Union was not a party to the treaty of 1951). But the Japanese had until early 1973 been reluctant to accept a treaty without the reversion of the Northern Islands, and the Russians have resisted making this obvious gesture. Perhaps they fear that concession on these territories might appear a precedent for concessions in their border disputes with China. Clearly not much advance toward rapprochement was likely until the Japanese change of position reported in March 1973. Mr. Tanaka is a relatively new hand in foreign policy, as well as a relatively unknown quantity, and might well want to postpone problems of choice between Russia and China, both from the economic and the diplomatic point of view, for as long as is feasible. And Japan has a real talent for procrastination in such matters. But in a way both China and the United States have claims to represent more natural diplomatic friends for Japan than the Soviet Union. Despite the "Nixon shokku," consciousness of the degree of benefit to Japan from the twenty-five years of American protection remains real, at least to most of the policy-makers concerned with defense matters, as does the feeling of a shared civilization with China.

The salience of Japan in the power-political calculations of the Asian future was not likely to be lost for long on the Japanese or the Chinese, though one might argue that it was to a surprising degree lost on—or ignored by—American decision-makers in the initial period of the rapprochement with Peking. An almost deliberate-seeming impression was created in later 1971–early 1972 that the Americans had decided not only to end the "special relationship" with Japan, but also that the Japanese were the sort of allies you needed to beat off with a club before they noticed that your affections had cooled. This was not, of course, how U.S. policy was intended to be presented, but it seems to have been rather how it was experienced. (A Japanese defense analyst commented to the author at the time that he had concluded America would in future "steer a course midway between Japan and China.") The official Washington gloss on policy maintained that, on the contrary, the U.S. intention was to ease out of Asia as gently as possible, with a view to sustaining Japanese orientation to the West at a lower strategic cost. But this soothing version of policy decisions does not seem much to resemble what actually happened between Washington and Tokyo in the late 1971–early 1972 period. There was perhaps a submerged or unspoken resentment under the surface of American attitudes to their Japanese ally, whose security, one might well argue, had cost them two wars in twenty-five years (Korea and Vietnam), wars in which the Japanese themselves had taken no part, and whose economic effects had helped Japan grow rich. There was also perhaps an assumption in Washington that Japan had no real options other than the American alliance: no place to go. But even if it was true that the most *rational* choice for Japan must remain the American alliance, on colder terms, the implied assumption that the most rational option will always be the one chosen does not necessarily follow, especially in the case of Japan. The old slogan "Remember Pearl Harbor" has more than one possible meaning: it ought to carry a freight of memories that rational strategic calculation may give way to the gambler's throw, and that the propensity toward such moves seems somewhat indicated in Japanese diplomatic history.

In any case, Japan in the 1970s seemed to have strategic and political options with much better prospects than the Axis alignment of the thirties. Aside from the cultivation of a continued rapprochement with America, or a new one with Russia or with China, there was the interesting possibility of Japan assuming the classic role of "balancer" in a five-power balance, about equidistant from each of the other powers concerned. Of course, the emergence of a new Pentarchy, somewhat parallel to that of the nineteenth century but on a world rather than a European scale, remained in 1972 a matter of prophecy rather than actual fact, but there were elements in the policy-making of President Nixon and Dr. Kissinger, as well as the actual relationships of power, which seemed to be hurrying it into being.

However, to turn from the possible diplomatic future back to the contemporary world, Japan seemed for subjective reasons an unlikely member of any alliance system which would involve her in undertaking commitments to other powers. Japanese social traditions—political factionalism, conformism, group loyalties, status consciousness, the search for consensus —contribute to a sort of "attentism" and passivity in foreign policy at least for the time being, waiting for something decisive to turn up. The generation gap seems even wider than in most societies, making one dubious about predicting the future. Also Japan derived a sort of advantage by remaining a "threshold" power, not only in terms of nuclear capacity but in terms of what may be called "commitment capacity." All these factors may prove useful assets for the potential balancer in a complex system: they maximize its ambivalences. The balancer has obviously to cultivate a certain isolation from other powers in such a system, and the Japanese have already had some indication that this might pay off well in their case. The hint of Soviet concessions after Japan's involuntary relative isolation from America in 1971–72 was seen by some Japanese analysts as a "windfall gain," indicating future potentialities.

However, the largest single change after 1969 in the prospects for a balance system in Asia was not in the position of Japan, nor even in those of America and Russia. It was in the signals from the then ruling Chinese policy-makers about their future strategies in world politics. (The possibility of a succession crisis for Mao and a new set of Chinese decision-makers sometime in the 1970s had of course always to be borne in mind in assessments of future Chinese policy.) In an earlier study of the subject,[4] I argued that the principal reason why it was difficult to see a balance of power system emerging in Asia was its incompatibility with the ruling Chinese concepts of international politics, as they then appeared. That was written while the Cultural Revolution was still almost in full ferment, and by 1970 it seemed no longer applicable. To the contrary, what was striking about the post-1970 phase of Chinese policy was the degree to which Maoist analysis of the contemporary conflict seemed to impose policy prescriptions closely akin to those which traditional power-political analysis would suggest in the same circumstances. The fervor of revolutionary moralism, which at its height in 1967 seemed unlikely to be satisfied with anything less than demolition of the existing society of states, mutated at surprising speed into something like pragmatic power-calculations. After 1969 Chinese decision-makers found advantageous potentialities in the institutions of the society of states, including international organization (making use of its UN veto over Bangladesh, for instance) and diplomacy (summit diplomacy with Mr. Nixon and Mr. Tanaka; people-to-people diplomacy with ping-pong teams and pandas). There was a clear theoretical rationale for this change in a Maoist text, the essay "On Policy" written in 1941, whose principles for discerning a "rank order" among one's adversaries, and using "temporary allies and indirect allies," were clearly prescribed for the new situation, as its republishing in 1971 indicated. There was as much of bitter historical Chinese

[4] *The Asian Balance of Power: A Comparison with European Precedents* (London: Adelphi Paper, February 1968), p. 12.

experience as of Marxism in this analysis, but that is probably true of "Mao Tse-tung thought" in general. The maxim "Use barbarians to check barbarians," which was a prime strategic guideline of Imperial China, is not dissimilar in essence to a balance policy.

The "rank order" of China's adversaries, as defined by 1971 in Peking, clearly put the Soviet Union first, and seemed otherwise chiefly preoccupied with the military and diplomatic potentialities of Japan. This rank order evolved from the 1968–69 period, which offered, as seen from Peking, four major reasons for downgrading the adversary capabilities of the United States and upgrading those of the Soviet Union. The first of these experiences was the American reaction to the Tet offensive of 1968. Mao had earlier predicted that victory in the war in Vietnam would come from the Americans growing weary of their role, and the aftermath of Tet fulfilled this expectation to a spectacular degree. Then the Nixon doctrine in 1969, whatever its implied expectations about the maintenance of American interests in Asia by other means than those which had proved so painful and expensive in Vietnam, did clearly proclaim considerable American disinvolvement, retirement to the sidelines of the Asian struggle, or at least an opting for the role of "second" rather than combatant.

The other two reasons were provided by the Soviet Union. The Czech invasion and the Brezhnev doctrine in mid-1968 both proclaimed how far the Soviet Union felt itself entitled to go in suppressing heresies in the Communist world. The Chinese felt, obviously, that from a Kremlin-eye view what was sauce for the Czech goose would be sauce for the Chinese gander, if the Russians could turn on enough heat, in a diplomatic and military sense. And then the Amur-Ussuri and Sinkiang frictions of 1969, and various Soviet diplomatic and military signals during that year, seemed to indicate that the Russians were maneuvering for a plausible occasion for a "disarming strike" or even preventive war. Thus by September 1969, from the point of view of Peking, one of its potential adversaries in the triangular balance—the United States

—had shown itself truly a paper tiger (or at any rate a badly wounded one) whereas the other, the Soviet Union, seemed more immediately menacing than ever before. Mr. Chou En-lai made it clear in various interviews with Western journalists and others during 1971–72 that the Chinese program of building air-raid shelters in major cities was begun about this time, in apprehension of a possible Soviet nuclear strike. Unless these apprehensions had been genuine and solid, resources would not have been allocated as they were to this program.

Further, the developments of mid-1969 had been foreshadowed at least since 1965 in the general shape of Soviet policy in South and Southeast Asia. The reinforcement of Soviet aid to North Vietnam in 1965 after the fall of Khrushchev, the Soviet "crisis-managing" role on the Indian subcontinent in the Tashkent Conference of the same year, and the growth of Soviet naval strength and influence in the Indian Ocean area, were all clear portents of the Soviet bid for diplomatic leverage in that part of the world. The increase of Soviet power since then has been steady, and steadily to China's strategic disadvantage. This is true even as it affects third powers. For instance, the relationship between China and India is now much less one of Chinese strategic ascendancy than it was. (China now has an enemy in its rear, the Soviet Union, far more dangerous-seeming than it was in 1962; whereas India has pretty well disposed of the then enemy to its rear, Pakistan.) One can see the degree to which China now regards any increment to the Soviet power base as the most unwelcome of contingencies for itself even in Chinese attitudes to developments remote from Asia. For instance, the Malta settlement, which meant in effect that Britain would stay there as a sort of *locum tenens* for NATO, was welcomed in Peking; it meant that the Soviet Union would not gain that additional base in the Mediterranean, and the Mediterranean is part of the route for Soviet naval power from Black Sea bases round to the Indian Ocean. By the same token, Chinese financial aid went to General Numeiry in the Sudan just after he had suppressed an attempted Communist coup: better a military autocrat than a Moscow oriented Communist party in power in the Red Sea littoral.[5]

These are as clear indications of the current Chinese pre-occupation with power-balancing as was Mr. Nixon's invitation to Peking. As for the American acceptance of (not to say angling for) that invitation, beneath the obvious surface reasons of electoral advantage, there was a much longer-term kind of drive. Revulsion against the costs of the Vietnam War, in terms of the alienation and trauma in America's own society, prompted a desperate search for alternative strategies by which the American national interest in the world might be maintained at a more bearable cost. In balance-of-power terms, this entailed a change in the central configuration of the international system. Both the Korean War and the Vietnam War may be seen, as far as American involvement is concerned, as part of the costs for the United States of an essentially bilateral power balance whose maintenance had proved to require direct American combat of prospective Communist gains: the balance was seen as a "zero-sum game," in which every plus to the other side was a strategic minus to America. No major American ally involved itself as America did in the fighting of these wars. If they were to be regarded as an example of burden-sharing in a collective security system, they would hardly be encouraging.[6] The world of the bilateral balance is a great simplifier of choices, being by definition the world of "one adversary," but it is also a maximizer of burdens, since that adversary has to be resisted everywhere. Because resisting Communist gains in Asia cost the Americans two painful, indecisive wars in twenty years, it created the revulsion in which Senator McGovern,

[5] Even the prospect of unilateral American troop reductions in Europe, adumbrated in the speeches of Senator McGovern as Presidential candidate, was reported by travelers to Peking to be very unwelcome to the Chinese leadership, obviously on the basis that such reductions would reduce the military strength of NATO and thus make extra military resources available for the Russian forces facing China.

[6] One minor American ally, Australia, was relatively heavily involved, both in terms of its domestic politics and in terms of the proportion of its small armed forces deployed in Vietnam. South Korea was a substantial participant in the Vietnam War, as well, of course, as in the Korean War.

as Presidential candidate, could remark candidly that though he did not like Communism, he did not believe America had any great obligation to save the world from it, and that even if substantial powers like Brazil or India became Communist, it would not substantially affect America's interests.[7]

In terms of strategic relationships, this view represented only a slightly further-out position along the road which the Nixon-Kissinger policy had already traveled by late 1972. Both the existing policy and the McGovern proposals were based on an implicit assumption that Communist powers will not, simply by that token, necessarily find themselves with common strategic interests: they do not "add up" into a single adversary. The whole working of a multiple balance is based on the understanding that it may be less burdensome to have several adversaries than a single one: for among several, one can make temporary tactical or indirect allies, as Mao noted, to share the burden of combating the most potent adversary. America, like China, may be said to have reassessed the "rank order" of its potential adversaries, and to have calculated the advantages of "temporary allies and indirect allies" of a differing political complexion.

Professor Wang Gung-wu has described the changes in Chinese policy after 1969 as a "loss of innocence." The same phrase might in a way be applied to America: both powers retreated from their respective brands of international moralism (which in the Chinese case required the support of revolution everywhere, and in the American case the support of "freedom" everywhere) to a more cautious defense of the national interest through diplomatic maneuver and power balancing. This "loss of innocence" in each case was associated with the reassertion of an earlier tradition or doctrine: the Mao essay in the Chinese case, or what one may call the "George Washington tradition" in the American case. Wash-

[7] *Time*, June 26, 1972. Senator McGovern's failure in the 1972 elections does not vitiate this point as an indicator of American attitudes. President Nixon, in fact, managed to convince the electorate that he also was promoting détente and disinvolvement and in a manner less humiliating to American pride than Senator McGovern's proposals would apparently have implied.

ington was of course in many ways an eighteenth-century Englishman who would have imbibed the balance of power concept with his history lessons: the objective of foreign policy as he laid it down for his compatriots was "To secure the blessings of liberty to *ourselves and our posterity,*" that is, to Americans: like Senator McGovern he would have seen no American obligation to fend off distasteful doctrines such as Communism for other countries.

The American President was able by 1972, for the first time probably since Woodrow Wilson's day, to say publicly a kind word about the balance of power concept, and Mr. Nixon did so in a New Year interview. "We must remember that the only time in the history of the world that we have had any extended period of peace is where there has been a balance of power . . . I think it will be a safer world and a better world if we have a strong, healthy United States, Europe, Soviet Union, China, Japan, each balancing the other, not playing one against the other, an even balance." As far as Asia is concerned, of course, one might say that of these five powers, two—China and Japan—have direct, immediate, irreducible, and permanent interests in Asia; one—the Soviet Union—has an enormous territorial stake in Asia and the determination to preserve it. But the two Western elements in the projected world balance, the United States and some putative future "Europe" have more terminable and indirect interests. America will remain a Pacific power, since it has a coastline and a state in that ambience. Yet its commitments could shrink back to Hawaii: their Asian extension dates only from the acquisition of the Philippines, and many Americans would regard the whole imperial adventure in Asia since 1898 as the most disastrous of national wrong turnings. As for Europe, it will affect the Asian situation chiefly indirectly, as an alternative potential adversary for the Soviet Union. Thus for Asia over the long term the important elements in the balance may be China, Japan, the Soviet Union, and India as a threshold Great Power and a Soviet friend, with America and Europe as more remotely concerned bystanders to the drama of the Asian future.

The central tension in this situation would seem to be that

between China and the Soviet Union, and the most important ambiguity that of the future of Japan. The prospects late in 1972 for Japanese future choices appeared still uncertain, but the likelihood of closer economic and diplomatic relations with China showed as the clearest direction of change. Whereas Mr. Nixon's visit to Peking represented, one might say, the proclamation of an already arrived at policy decision, the visit of Mr. Tanaka seemed an actual decision point. The Japanese acceptance of change, as on Taiwan and diplomatic relations, was the more rapid and radical of the two, in some respects. The possible advantages of a rapprochement with the Soviet Union, which might have seemed considerable if the Peking visit had gone badly, could hardly match the moral and perhaps material attractions of easy relations with China, nor did the Soviet bargaining position in the 1972 talks seem to promise much flexibility on the Russian side. The Chinese, on the other hand, seemed to show an impressive degree of enterprise and boldness of thought on future power combinations once the ice had been broken in talks with Japan. Mr. Chou is said to have broached, on the occasion of Mr. Tanaka's first visit, the subject of a possible Chinese alliance with Japan in the event of a Russian attack.

Given this complex, ambiguous framework of dominant-power relationships, what policies or institutions might help the states of Southeast Asia to maintain or improve their respective (and at present inadequate) degrees of security or stability? One hopeful point is that it seems possible that Southeast Asia will show itself less of a field of dominant power rivalry in the foreseeable future than Southern Asia. The rise of India as the most important friend of the Soviet Union, and the fissiparous tendencies of Pakistan seem to provide scope for more sharp strategic changes there. Secondly, it is likely to be one of the objectives of the Southeast Asian states to avoid the excessive predominance of any of the five main powers, as well as excessively sharp contests between any two or more of them. Japan is obviously the best placed to become economically dominant. There is already a considerable degree of restiveness at Japanese economic penetration. The Japanese businessman is not less heavy-

footed in the societies of Thailand or Indonesia than West
erners were before him, and memories of the war and the
Greater East Asia Co-prosperity Sphere are still vivid. A work
ing partnership between Japan and China, if events should
take that quite conceivable turn, would be a formidable development in the eyes of the other peoples of Asia, especially
because the American tendency, whichever party is in power
will be to avoid any Asian commitment which could look
even faintly like "another Vietnam." (The "burnt-child-
dreads-the-fire" aspects of the American experience there may
long outlive the war itself.)

Most of the Southeast Asian states would probably choose,
if they could, to look to the principle of nonalignment, rather
than the strategic choice of a particular ally, as the basis of
their security policies. The most outspoken sponsor of the
nonalignment idea to date has been Malaysia, and it has
tended to use ASEAN as the vehicle for its efforts in this
direction. The other members of that grouping have some
reasons to be hesitant: Indonesia because its need for capital
from America and Japan makes it see some merit in ties with
those countries, Singapore and Thailand because their dependence for security on ANZUK and SEATO respectively
have made them reluctant, at least over the transition period,
to dispense with these organizations. If the concept of nonalignment is to have any substance at all and is not merely a
hopeful euphemism like "peace-loving," it must surely imply
the exclusion of foreign forces and bases from the areas concerned—that is, American and SEATO facilities out of Thailand, British and Australian out of Singapore and Malaysia.

This might prove quite acceptable to the original Western
sponsors of both organizations. As to SEATO, its status as
part of the original and disastrous American commitment to
South Vietnam could make its winding-up welcome in Washington even to those who still feel obliged to defend the
original involvement. ANZUK is of course much more recent and has generated no anguish, but also no particular
conviction. Its main function has been to provide a mechan-
ism to ease the transition period in which Britain has wound
up its commitments "East of Suez" prior to absorbing itself

in its new role as part of "the Europe of the Nine." It might originally have served as a medium through which Australia assumed the role that Britain was abdicating, but successive Australian Prime Ministers[8] have made it clear how limited are the commitments that Australia feels itself willing to take on, hardly extending beyond the least probable contingency, overt external aggression across frontiers. So no great loss would be felt by the outside powers if these two organizations were wound up in the course of some agreed neutralization procedure.

But it is difficult to see what neutralization (as against nonalignment) for this area could mean in terms of obligations by the contemporary Great Powers. In the classic European case, Belgium before World War I, the Great Power guarantee of neutrality meant that Britain was obliged to regard the German breach of the Belgian frontier as a *causus belli*, thus ensuring that Belgium must become the initial battlefield of world war. The relative unpopularity of neutralization schemes in Europe since World War II has in fact proceeded from various such historical demonstrations of what tends to happen to neutral or neutralized small powers

8 Before the advent of the Labour Prime Minister, Mr. Gough Whitlam, his two immediate predecessors, Mr. William McMahon and Mr. John Gorton, though both from the Liberal Party in the governmental coalition which had been in power since 1949, departed quite obviously from some of the assumptions of the earlier policy-makers for that coalition, Sir Robert Menzies and Mr. Harold Holt. They remained strongly oriented to the American alliance and refrained from criticisms of U.S. policy in Vietnam such as were later made by Mr. Whitlam, but they both indicated considerable reserve toward open-ended military commitments in Southeast Asia. Indeed both Mr. Gorton and Mr. McMahon caused some offense in Singapore and Malaysia by the bluntness with which they indicated this reserve, in various speeches and interviews. With the advent of Mr. Whitlam, a more radical reinterpretation of Australian interests in Southeast Asia was initiated, but its details and implications must lie outside the scope of this paper. All that can be said is that the probability of Australia undertaking any open-ended commitment in Southeast Asia was substantially less, in early 1973, than it had been for the previous quarter century.

when the dominant powers are seriously at odds and find their region a convenient pathway or battlefield.

Moreover, even assuming that all the major powers can be successfully excluded from Southeast Asia, at least in terms of their forces and bases, or overt military aggression by any of them (which would be extremely unlikely even without neutralization), the security and stability of the governments of the area would not be very much enhanced. Such a system would be the equivalent of an insurance policy which guaranteed one solely against being struck by a thunderbolt. The more probable threats to the area are those which proceed from frictions between its members, and most particularly those from contests for power *within* the domestic societies concerned. A buildup of the insurgency in Thailand, a revivification of the guerrillas in Malaysia, a working agreement between the various left-revolutionaries in the Philippines, a sharpening of the conflicts between Singapore and Malaysia or Indonesia, Vietnamese pressure on Laos and Cambodia, a revival of the Sabah claim, the failure of the counterinsurgency operation in Borneo, race riots in Malayan cities—these are the likely sources of insecurity for the governments concerned, rather than the Chinese army crossing frontiers. Yet the sense of China as a looming, potentially alarming, shadow above their world is very visible in the diplomacy of the small powers. Even Burma, despite its largely successful relationships and sense of kinship with the Chinese people, showed this kind of diplomatic *frisson* during the Cultural Revolution period. This part of the world has been conspicuously less quick than more distant places to return to diplomatic relations with Peking. There is also for Singapore, Malaysia, and Thailand, particularly, the "Trojan horse" assumption about their own Chinese communities. Diplomatic recognition means Chinese ambassadors and consuls, who may channel an ethnic loyalty toward China which will prove a stronger magnet than the national state. The civilization of China has a tenacious hold on its inheritors, even those whose families have been overseas for several generations.

In view of these psychological factors in the small powers' relations with China, a joint Great Power guarantee of neu-

tralization might prove reassuring, even if it meant sacrifice
of such remaining advantages as are seen in SEATO and
ANZUK, and even though it would not be of much help
in the true intraregional dangers. In fact only the slow-
working processes of economic development and social or
political change can assure stable identities and territorial
definitions to the area, and even they, over the transition
period, may contribute rather to internal and intraregional
conflicts than to peace.